PRIESTESSES

PRIESTESSES

NORMA LORRE GOODRICH

HarperPerennial
A Division of HarperCollinsPublishers

Figures and maps by Michael R. Cap de Ville.

A hardcover edition of this work was originally published in 1989 by Franklin Watts, Inc. It is hereby published by arrangement with Franklin Watts, Inc.

First HarperPerennial edition published 1990.

LIBRARY OF CONGRESS CATALOG CARD NUMBER 89-46501

ISBN 0-06-097316-1

90 91 92 93 94 FG 10 9 8 7 6 5 4 3 2 1

In memory of my English grandmother, Amelia Heath,
and my American grandmother, Maude Collins

To Jana Seely, treasured among former students

ACKNOWLEDGMENTS

Thanks first to my husband, John Hereford Howard, who made delightful, possible, and rewarding my travels to the sites of priestesses in Europe, Africa, Asia, and South America.

My thanks go to fellow scholars from many fields whose interest, encouragement, and real assistance have been so gratefully received: Professor A.R.L. Bell, University Vice-President William Douglas Bookwalter, Professors Muriel Hughes, Stuart J. Inglis, Carl Mosk, Jack Reynolds, and Ralph Ross. Thanks to friends, the historians William Stinson, Bruce Peterson, and Allen Thompson, the cinematographer Gerald Robertson, the artist Michael Cap de Ville, and the music publisher Judith M. Wahnon.

Assistance from most helpful librarians and libraries in Claremont, California, was gratefully received: Denison and Honnold Libraries and staff, and great assistance and encouragement from the librarians Elizabeth Wrigley and Jacqueline Bellows of the Francis Bacon Library here.

Loans of books such as from the following libraries were much appreciated: University of Cincinnati, Cal State at Sacramento, Harvard University, University of Iowa, University of Georgia at Athens, California State Polytechnic University at Pomona, Eastern New Mexico University at Portales, San Diego State University, Southern Illinois University at Carbondale, University of California at Irvine, San Francisco State University, University of California at Los Angeles, Fuller Theological Seminary, Santa Clara University, Sonoma State College, and the Library of Congress.

My gratitude goes also to associates, Harold Schmidt, Kent Oswald, and Roberto Kison.

I wish also to thank former students who have supported me with their deeds and affection over the years: Dr. Geraldine Swain, Captain Carolyn Rogers Ekblaw, the librarians Elizabeth Stockly Galloway, Margaret Helms Bean, and Catherine Stonebraker Kan; and last but not least, Dr. Elizabeth Carr, Catholic Chaplain.

And even now, in the face of philosophies of materialism and of negation so far more powerful than any which Sophocles had to meet, there are yet some minds into which, after all, a doubt may steal, whether we have indeed so fully explained away the beliefs of the world's past, whether we indeed so assuredly define the beliefs of its future, or whether it may not still befit us to track with fresh feet the ancient mazes, to renew the world-old desire, and to set no despairing limit to the knowledge or the hopes of man.

F.W.H. Myers
Essays Classical
(London, 1883)

CONTENTS

Contents

Contents

XIV · THE ROMAN CONQUEST OF GAUL · *324*

Julius Caesar versus the Celts   *324*
Resistance and the High-priestess Velleda   *340*

XV · PRIESTESSES · *361*

ILLUSTRATIONS

PRIESTESSES

INTRODUCTION

IDENTIFICATION

Priestesses thrived in ancient societies in which religion, art, and science were not as yet disjoined. They freely practiced priestcraft in temple communities supporting as many as six thousand priestesses at one site. Such a temple at Ephesus has recently been excavated and exhaustively studied by archaeologists. In ancient Asia Minor, Greece, Africa, and Europe priestesses were venerated, as priests still are today. Women as well as men were then holy persons and leaders in their societies. Their specialties we would say today fell under such varied pursuits as religion, philosophy, prophecy, ethics, writing, dance, temple construction and maintenance, ritual, fund raising, tourism, social work, and medicine.

Ancient priestesses were often born into royal families, and thus were priestesses by birth. They were often queens of the land in Crete, Egypt, and Anatolia. Their ritual enactment of planting and harvest ceremonies ensured fertility and prosperity for all. Thus, in such civilizations the priestess descended directly from her mother, who was High-priestess before her. Similarly, some evidence also suggests that the most august priestess who ever lived, the Delphic Oracle in Greece, bore a child before her final ordeal of installation into that sacred priesthood. As Egypt decayed, priestesses there were limited to dancing in the temple. As the Roman Empire leaned toward collapse, its priestesses disappeared and/or were put to death. In Rome also, priestesses came from the highest aristocracy. But as there were thousands of priestesses in very ancient Asia Minor, it is likely that most were taken from lower social orders and relegated to simple or menial labor. Large temples must have required a huge complement of sweepers and haulers. The pilgrims who thronged there in hordes required care of all sorts.

Our common language handles the priestess problem easily, having already provided us with an unsurprising double vocabulary: priest-priestess, minister-ministress, sorcerer-sorceress,

obstetrician-midwife, preacher-preacheress, prophet-prophe-
tess, clergyman-clergywoman, pastor-pastoress, shepherd-shep-
herdess, parson-parsoness. Though we may never have seen
a preacheress, much less a shepherdess of her flock, our language has already taken note of such eventualities.

More to the point, the English language has also prepared
us for encounters with women in many of the vocations followed by ancient priestesses. Thus, we have professional terms—
priestess names—that may be either masculine or feminine;
unlike Latin, English does not always specify a noun as male
or female. This English list makes no sex differentiation:
chaplain, angel, cleric, celebrant, divine, hierophant, ecclesias-
tic, doctor, healer, theocrat, disciple, missionary, psychic, as-
trologer, predictor, prelate, physician, apostle, teacher, professor, therapist, mathematician, hierarch, pharmaceutist, nurse,
attendant, bishop.

Our language has forgotten, however, that *battle-ax* denotes
not only a vile-tempered woman, but that for countless ages
it identified individual women warriors. These dedicated
priestesses had been trained from infancy to ride horseback,
to fight, and to die gallantly in defense of their homeland and
their temples. The original "women of the battle-ax" were the
now fabled Amazons, a score of whose queens died so very
heroically that even their names, their tombs, their home forts,
and the cities they founded are still recalled and can still be
visited in Turkey and southern Russia. The city of Smyrna,
which is now Ismir in Turkey, was founded by the Amazon
warrior-queen Smyrna.

In the case of the ancient Amazons, a mother church and a
motherland provided a setting in which the warrior-priestesses
were women and/or mothers but also priestesses. The Amazons were warriors, to be sure, and also educators of daughters. The strong tie between mother and daughter in a society
where all the children belonged to all the mothers who were
priestesses seems to characterize the ancient world. Greek men
spoke of preferring to adopt a child from one of the temples
rather than to sire one through marriage.

When courts were convened to define a mother, and to decide whether or not she should be considered a human being

or simply a reproductive organ, this civilization was drawing to a close. At that time, too, priestesses were being phased out, or eliminated.

The societies that venerated priestesses accepted female hierarchies and theocracies because priestesses performed manifold functions in their world. Priestesses acted as celebrants, as calculators of holy days, as counselors and predictors, as astronomers watching the phases of lunation, as warriors, as teachers of their children and mothers of all, as druggists and doctors, as health consultants, and as missionaries and apostles of the Mother Goddesses. They were even represented in sculpture as winged angels on earth.

Throughout the world women are still named for the holiest of ancient priestesses. A "Melissa" is an Asian priestess. A "Delphine" or "Delphina" is a Greek priestess. A "Norma" is an Egyptian mother superior. A "Sibyl" is the highest of Roman priestesses. A "Sylvia" is the priestess who founded Rome. "Iphigenia" was Mycenaean. "Diana" was known worldwide as a moon-priestess. The historical "Velleda," like a "Gertrude," was a Druid priestess who defended Gaul. Isolde was a noble Irish priestess trained in medicine at the time Saint Brigid became the first Bishop of Kildare. The temple of the Vestal Virgins still stands grandly in Rome, and we know their patrician names.

To feast our eyes on the most revered of all the ancient priestesses we must journey to eternal Rome. There, on the ceiling of the Sistine Chapel in the Vatican, Michelangelo painted the Sibyls, who came to Rome from around the Mediterranean basin. The paintings were commissioned by Pope Alexander VI.

With the names of priestesses all around, and with such great memorials of their presence, it should not come as such a surprise that they once existed on earth. The wonder is therefore not that priestesses, even High-priestesses, once tended eternal fires and danced professionally in vast temples. The wonder is that this has already been proven, and long known.

Travelers to Asia Minor have seen at Ephesus six gorgeous representations of Medusa's Head. But it was Sigmund Freud who made the brilliant discovery that Medusa was a priestess.

He understood, he said, her Gorgon Head and terrifying snake coiffure. Priestesses in India today, he pointed out, wear their hair in uncombed, tangled locks.

Doctors and pharmacists know priestesses once practiced medicine, for priestesses were the first to derive aspirin from willow bark sacred to their goddess of childbirth. Anthropologists study priestesses today in the remotest areas of the South Pacific. Writers in Brazil note that there umbilical cords are sacrificed to the priestesses of the Atlantic Ocean.

It is time that ancient priestesses were made the focus of a book. History books of the ancient world rarely or never speak of women theologians or of priestesses. As one of my mentors, F. W. H. Myers, said in the closing words of his *Essays Classical* (London, 1883), there is still much to learn:

> And even now, in the face of philosophies of materialism and of negation so far more powerful than any which Sophocles had to meet, there are yet some minds into which, after all, a doubt may steal, whether we have indeed so fully explained away the beliefs of the world's past, whether we indeed so assuredly define the beliefs of its future, or whether it may not still befit us to track with fresh feet the ancient mazes, to renew the world-old desire, and to set no despairing limit to the knowledge or the hopes of man.

RECOGNITION

If it was not F. W. H. Myers's recognition of the Delphic Oracle that sent this author racing back into the ancient world in a search for priestesses, or if it was not Michelangelo's paintings of priestesses on the ceiling of the Sistine Chapel in the Vatican, then it may have been Martha Graham, called "matriarch of modern dance," who as teacher to the twentieth century and dancer of *Phaedra* and *Circe* inspired this search. In any case, the written evidence of priestesses comes principally from ancient, not modern, historians.

The Asian Greek Herodotus, called the father of history, speaks of them. The Greek historian and moralist Plutarch, who was himself a priest of Delphi and of the Delphic Oracle herself, wrote many pieces concerning them and their works. Procopius, Silius Italicus, and Diodorus Siculus in their histories speak at great length of priestesses and are also eyewitnesses to their lives. Ancient chronologies find the dates of this world from the lists of priestesses at various temple complexes. Julius Caesar, who was High-priest at Rome, fought the Druid priestesses and very carefully omitted to say so; but his *Gallic War* is still evidence of a sort.

Julius Caesar's omissions were remedied by the Roman historian Tacitus. The greatest of ancient geographers, the Greek Strabo, located the renowned shrines of the priestesses in his *Geography*. Three Greek dramatists—Aeschylus, Euripides, and Aristophanes—devoted works to priestesses. Greek poets Hesiod and Pindar celebrated them, as did Roman poets Ovid and Catullus. Great accounts of priestesses and heroes were written by epic poets Homer, Vergil, Statius, and Lucan.

Priestesses were recognized by other eminent scholars of antiquity: Lucian from Asia Minor, the Roman orator Cicero, and the lesser-known Iamblichus, Ammianus Marcellinus, and Dionysius of Halicarnassus. They too saw with Pindar a "priestess throned," heard a paean in praise of Artemis (Diana) sung by women, watched graceful maidens dancing at Delphi. Ovid told of the priestess Manto, daughter of the seer Tiresias. He knew how the Roman Sibyl descended courageously into the netherworld, past the huge guard dog Cerberus, and across the black rivers of Tartarus. Ovid also knew how Zeus had raped the priestesses Callisto and Semele, and retold the story of Iphigenia's sacrifice on the altar. He repeated a prophecy by the Delphic Oracle Themis, and retold the awful revenge of the sorceress Circe, and the murders committed, with malice aforethought, by royal Medea. He further explained that the Greeks looked to one holy family, who were their priests and priestesses by birth: father or mother to daughter or son.

Another stalwart proponent of priestesses was the English scholar George Thomson whose book of 1949, *Studies in Ancient Greek Society*, widened and deepened our knowledge. He found evidence of early matriarchies in ancient India, China, Tibet, Asia Minor, Crete, Africa, Egypt, Greece, and Rome.

By *matriarchy* he meant a society in which the mother heads the family and owns the real property, which she transmits to her heirs. In this system the children belong to her clan, which venerates her and her ancestresses as clan chieftains. Circles of standing stones were everywhere dedicated by the reigning matriarch to her male relatives, of whom her brother took first place after her. The prehistoric Aegean world, Thomson theorized along with Sir Arthur Evans, who had excavated Crete, lived under such a system until about 2700 B.C. We shall soon consider Asian priestesses who lived at around this date.

By historical times, Thomson argued, only traces of an earlier, primitive system remained: Amazons, priestesses, the many goddesses, and their famed temples. The argument was resumed in 1955, and again in 1961 by the English poet and scholar Robert Graves. In his *Greek Myths* he focused upon priestesses in Greece, managing to amass a mountain of evidence in these two volumes. He followed with *The White Goddess* (1961): a *summum* of original thought, backed by evidence indicating that the white-clad goddess worshipped first above all others throughout the prehistoric world continued to be venerated long after that world had tumbled from barbarism to barbarism, headlong into one Dark Age after another.

Meanwhile another English classical scholar, Sir John Forsdyke, in his *Greece Before Homer. Ancient Chronology and Mythology* (London, 1956), had added much more argument and evidence for the existence of priestesses during long centuries in the Aegean world:

> Written records of the Argive temple are not likely to have been older than the eighth century, but the cult of Hera there was of immemorial antiquity, and the succession of priestesses may have gone back to the prehistoric age (p. 37).

Forsdyke also praised (p. 145 ff.) a fifth-century Greek mythographer, Hellanicos of Lesbos, for his canon of priestesses serving the goddess Hera (the Roman Juno), even though Hellanicos listed names, such as Alcyonê and Callisto, without historical or material proof. These former priestesses, Hellanicos thought, had lived three generations before Agamemnon led his fleet to Troy. That city fell while Callisto was High-priestess of Hera in Argos, Greece.

What matters here is that priestesses were listed at all, *and in classical Greece,* which confined women to separate quarters of the house, did not often even allow them out of doors, and did not even consider them fit to sit at a table with their husbands at mealtimes.

Even then, the Greeks complained at having to use women in order to get children for the state, an action which was a man's duty. Greek men ardently hoped that an alternate method could be found.

A study of priestesses, recognized by a few learned persons as having practiced religion in the ancient world, reopens several questions affecting lives today: Why and when did women lose the priesthood? Was there once a society on earth identifiable as a matriarchy? What is the origin of such a hypothesis? What is its history? What is its status, if any, today? Are the ancient priestesses to be considered vestigial? Could there have been priestesses without a preceding period of matriarchal culture? Or are matriarchy and priestess independent phenomena?

In summary, then, we shall recognize a priestess because she is so named, or so placed in a temple, and/or so portrayed in art, history, or in mythology and legend, during her career, and by the services she performs. In art she is also recognizable, and has long been so recognized, by certain religious implements she holds, by the veil about her head, by the horse she rides, by the wings about her shoulders, by her solemnly lovely face, by her priestly attitude in services, and by her adoration during worship.

Her position in the temple varies, of course, but surely one can respect equally the humble and the great. A priestess cleans the altar and washes the implements and the floors. She stands and admonishes the pilgrims to wash themselves, clean their feet, and remain silent. She stands and holds the collection plate. She gives out tokens. The noblest of Roman maidens, called Vestal Virgins, washed the altar once a year. Even the mother of Romulus, a Vestal herself, took the temple vessels to the river and washed them. Or the priestess was High-priestess of the Hittites, of the Egyptians, and Queen of the Empire.

Perhaps she was the archivist, the lecturer, the prophet, the seer, the doctor of medicine, a superb dancer, a sweet singer in the temple, or a performing instrumentalist. The thousands who served Artemis at Ephesus were called "Artemis," and dressed like their deity. The same is true for the priestesses of Hera at Argos and at Samos, and also for the priestesses of Diana near Rome. The High-priestess was usually the daughter of the previous reigning High-priestess. The other priestesses were admitted as babies, as little, nameless girls; for, as in a matriarchy, there were no orphans and no abandoned children. The men in the temple wore dresses, as did the priestesses.

The greatest deity to all of them was the Mother Earth, the Mother of all, named Mâ-Bellona, and Demeter, or Hecate, or Cybele, or Niobe. Her myths abound. When her priestesses were warriors and trained equestriennes, they were called Amazons.

The Great Mother was usually accompanied by lions. She wore a veil too. As Niobe, she wept for her children, as women have always wept for their children, and for the sins of the world. Even carved in stone, like Medusa the Mother, she still weeps all down the side of an Asian mountain. So, certainly, another function of priestesses was to escort the dead, and to weep.

MYTHOLOGY

Based on his studies in classical mythography, Sir John Forsdyke declared in 1956 that most of Greece's history before the Trojan War was derived from mythology, which he defined as "stories of religious origin" (p. 144). Myths differ from legends because the latter contain material specifically verifiable as history, he said, or as geography, we add. Thus, material written about priestesses is largely mythological since it stems from prehistoric religious rites and rituals.

The great English historian Edward Gibbon (1737–1794)

defined prehistoric religion, or "the religion of country folk" (i.e., paganism), as a religion supported by custom, as opposed to Christianity, which he considered a religion supported by argument (*Decline and Fall of the Roman Empire*, Vol. III, Chapter XXVIII).

"But there is the general fact that ritualism precedes mythology," Alfred North Whitehead affirmed in his Lowell Lectures of 1926. He put the replacement of prehistoric religion by an organized, rational religion at around 5000 B.C. But he agreed that myths explain not only the ritual but also the emotion which caused its creation.

A superior contribution to the problem of mythology was made in his *Essay on Man* by Ernst Cassirer in 1944. According to him, no date can be chosen that separates myth from religion. Both deal with a ritual act, an enactment of a rite based upon such strong emotion that its underlying meaning seizes the reader in the unforgettable vise of common experience. The ritual acts are paradigmatic, the theologian Mircéa Eliade also said in a number of wonderful books on religion, acts repeated in static time, and therefore eternally dramatic. Thus, myths and religion both offer everybody solutions and comfort.

As Jung would have it, today's humanity all understand, via the myth, the ancient society where rituals, or sacred dramas, originated. The myth links us to an otherwise lost past when priestesses officiated in rituals. Every aspect of the myth survives: its formulae, its plots, its place descriptions, and its archaic attitudes from a lost world. Thus, the ancient world is recoverable, Jean Seznec said in *The Survival of the Pagan Gods* (1953), its gods having never disappeared "from the memory or imagination of man" (p. 3).

The myths and legends recorded and transmitted by the ancients depended upon the deities the priestesses served, upon the problems they faced, and upon their speculative concerns: motherhood (mothers and daughters), virginity and purity, health and defilement, sacrifice and service, water and forgetfulness, funeral rites and death, earth and fertility, protest and injustice, suffering and sacrilege, and the defense of children. The rituals from which the myths were derived are often the same as those of organized religions: marriage, childbirth and baptism, puberty and initiation, dedication to service, funeral rites, celebrations of the two solstices and equinoxes. The problem-haunted lives of ancient peoples resemble our own: hell vs. paradise, birth and origins, life vs. plague, disease, food vs. drought, sex and fertility, starvation, catastrophes of storm, flood, and earthquake. Above all, men and women alike have always, as Geoffrey Chaucer once demonstrated so clearly, longed primarily for "mastery," for power over the self, over their lives, nature, and the universe.

Historians have always written the story of mankind's past via records, buildings, chronologies, genealogies, wars, monuments, sculpture, art objects, customs, religions, and biographies. By the same token, the cultural and spiritual history of woman can also be at least glimpsed by coaxing priestesses forth from oblivion.

The pattern of denigration set by long, historical precedent is contradicted by our instinctive sense that women, too, once ruled the world spiritually, as they still rule our homes and even our kingdoms. Surely a renewed recognition of women in ancient religions, in their roles as priestesses, is one way to celebrate women everywhere, just as modern psychology and psychoanalysis have also attempted to inspire and console women in our century.

Myths are significant stories of religious content. Unlike legends, which supply geographical details that can be verified, as in the cases of many Amazon priestesses, the myths cling closer to ritual. The more emotionally charged myth gives us startling biographies of famous, ancient women, some of whom were celebrated priestesses, some of whom were deified. The story of Cybele will be a first case in point.

Religion is the profession and practice of religious beliefs by devout members of any society anywhere. Priestesses of whatever rank are therefore also godly persons devoted and dedicated to a life of piety and service. They lived in the ancient world in orders of religious, in small or huge cloistered communities. All were educated for religious duties, and separated by performance and aptitude. Some underwent rites, ordeals, tests, and severe initiations before acceding to consecrated and ordained holinesses. All were bound—servitors, priest-esses, and warriors alike, for all were in religious orders—by holy vows, the breaking of which was punishable by death. They had accepted this burden.

The societies of priestesses were always partially or entirely secret, and priestesses' real names were not to be known and not to be spoken. The purpose of their initiations was *direct contact* with the divine. Their function was principally to main-tain this contact for those who were too weak personally, phys-ically, or intellectually to reach God by their own unaided ef-forts.

The High-priestess herself had successfully endured and undergone the most severe ordeal of sensory deprivation, which we would call brainwashing, that could be devised. She had survived an ordeal, or final period of initiation, lasting thirty or forty days. Her graduation, or up-stepping, succeeded the initiation. This priestess had to demonstrate her overweening desire to participate in God's work. She was tested by isolation techniques, by fasting, deafening noises, potions, threats, signs and signals which she had to read correctly in order to act upon them, by darkness, cold, deep water, red-hot irons, and horrid repetitions, all of which were followed by her final sym-bolic death-to-the-world, rebirth, and resurrection.

Thus, history and legend serve our knowledge, but only myths speak—cryptically perhaps, but deep from the heart of the matter. That heart is ancient religion.

CHRONOLOGY

The Fall of the Empires of the Ancient World
The following chronology was made in order to recall for the reader the historical background of this search for priestesses:

1350 B.C. *The Hittite Empire* included eastern Asia Minor, the Taurus Mountains, the southern coastal cities of Ar-vad and Ugarit opposite Cyprus, the central plateau ex-tending beyond Lake Tuz and perhaps as far north as the Black Sea coast. It also included several centers: Hat-tusas, Carchemish, Alaca Huyak, Kanish, and Mersin.

The Egyptian Empire adjoined it at about the latitude of the southern tip of Cyprus, or somewhat north of the city of Byblos. The centers Byblos, Damascus, Sidon, and Tyre fell within Egyptian rule. To the southeast of the Hittites extended the neighboring territories of the Mitanni; to their southeast, those of the Assyrians and Babylonians.

c. 824 B.C.–c. 640 B.C.   *The Assyrian Empire* then extended from Egypt north to the central plain of Asia Minor, or Anatolia, and south to the Persian Gulf. Greek city-states had by then been founded along the Asian west coast. Phrygia lay to their east. The Cimmerians had settled along the Black Sea coast.

560 B.C.   Phrygia has been replaced by the Kingdom of Lydia. Cappadocia has absorbed the Cimmerians. The *Medo-Babylonian Empire* now extends from Suez to the Persian Gulf, and then across eastwards to India.

500 B.C.   *The Persian Empire* now extends past the city of Kabul to the east, includes all of Asia Minor plus Egypt and Libya, the Aegean coastal centers of Ephesus, Miletus, and Sardis, also parts of Thrace and Macedonia to the north.

323 B.C.   *The Empire of Alexander the Great* is even more vast than was the preceding or Persian Empire. It includes the Oracle of Jupiter Amon to the west of the Nile Valley and Cyrenaica to the southwest, Macedonia to the northwest, plus Egypt, the Syrian coast, Asia Minor, Armenia, Media, Babylonia, Parthia, Aria, Bactria east to the Hindu Kush Mountains and the Indus River valley.

31 B.C.   Augustus Caesar united the *Roman Empire* for a period of peace lasting 200 years. This empire comprised the entire Mediterranean world and eastwards to the Caspian Sea, included Asia Minor, Egypt and North Africa, Spain, Gaul, Britain south of the Antonine Wall, Belgium, the shores of the Black Sea and the Bosporus, the Atlantic coastline of Europe from Gibraltar to the Elbe or Rhine River, with the Danube River and the Caucasus Mountains as a northern frontier. (Germany,

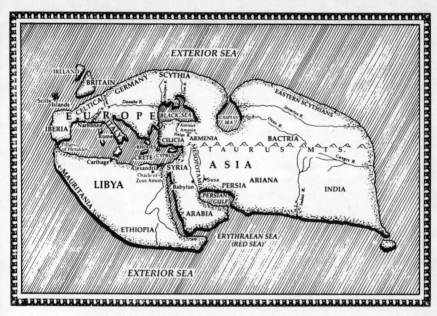

Map 1 Ancient World (From Strabo's *Geographia*)

Northern Scotland, and Ireland remained unconquered.)

GEOGRAPHY

The beauty of the Mediterranean world can hardly be equalled for clear water and gorgeous islands with high mountains never far distant—the Alps, the Pyrenees, and the sacred mountains of the Delphic priestess of earth and the sky god of Greece: Parnassus and Olympus. Even the peninsulas, such as Asia Minor, are surrounded or spined by young, folded mountains, as are northwestern Africa (then called Libya) and the peninsula of Italy. Alluvial plains are abundant there, with deep limestone caverns along their promontories, where the Nymphs had their grottos, shepherds like Polyphemus their sheepcotes, Odysseus his treasure trove, Zeus his nursery and nanny-goat mother. The shores vary from red rock cliffs to swampy or dry coastal plains near where lost rivers plunge down into Tartarus.

The early Greek geographer Hecataeus, who mapped the world around 517 B.C., and the greater Strabo both knew this closed Mediterranean basin as a dangerous land of sudden elevation and subsidence, alternately covered and uncovered by the sea. There earthquakes shook so continuously, once for a period of ten years, that thousands were caught unaware by the explosion of Vesuvius in 79 B.C. Only the Younger Pliny of his family escaped in his fast chariot to write about it in his tremendously moving account. Today Pompeii stands, barren pillars and sunbaked walls, only a mere ten miles of congested, frequently gridlocked traffic from the metropolis of Naples. The explosion of Thera (Santorini) in the eastern Aegean (2000 B.C.–1500 B.C.?) surely shook the world, destroyed Crete and its brilliant Minoan civilization, and deposited ash as far away as Sinai and the Nile Delta. The ensuing tidal waves devastated harbors and fishing fleets across the sea.

The gold temples at Delphi were destroyed by earthquakes four times between about 373 B.C. and the year 279 B.C., when the marauding Gauls, who had been warned not to desecrate that holiest of ancient sites, were driven off in terror by a major quake. In 224 B.C. the ancient island of Rhodes, where Julius Caesar is said to have studied mathematics and drawn up his Julian calendar, took up a collection worldwide to rebuild its harbor and cities.

This Mediterranean-Aegean climate caused successive floods and droughts, however, due to rainy winters followed by dry, hot summers. Then, too, in landlocked areas like these the storms of such short seas presented threats of shipwreck to sailors, sending crashing waves mountain-high even upon the gorgeous resort coasts of Italy and France. Ancient temples for the sea god Poseidon lined these shores, which the grain ships hugged as they relieved the coastal cities from the famine of their recurrent seven lean years. Rome thrived always threatened by empty stocks, always dependent for food upon Carthage and fertile North Africa. Throughout this world the sea goddess of beauty Aphrodite and her priestesses protected mariners. The goddess's husband was the fire god whose forge lay under such volcanic peaks as Chimaera, Aenaria, and Etna. The Sibyl's cavern lay near the caldera called Forum of Vulcan and its flaming fields, while she protected Rome. Gradually and by historical times priests had deposed these priestesses from their coasts and sacred fire mountains, holy hot springs, and dangerous straits.

Ancient history tells of several related phenomena: mass migrations, impoverished and alien immigrants driven from their homelands by overpopulation, high birthrates, over-cultivation of soil, exhaustion of resources, reduction of large territories to deserts, lack of space, food, air, and water. Thus, ancient Greeks turned about and made war on Asia Minor, invading Troy for what they lacked at home, and they overran the Asian coasts after having purposely overpopulated Greece.

This Mediterranean Basin is the world of the priestesses recorded in ancient history, myth, legend, and by artists. It is certainly not the whole ancient world, only what we are accustomed to thinking of as the ancient world. Thus, we have only heard of these priestesses. Our horizons are, undoubtedly, too small.

I

THE HITTITE EMPIRE

"And earlier still were those naked-female figurines in stone—the Venus of Willendorf, etc.—of the period of the Old Stone Age mammoth hunters, circa 30,000 B.C., which, in fact, are the earliest known religious images in the history of the human race."
Joseph Campbell,
"Introduction" to Helen Diner's
Mothers and Amazons (New York, 1965).

HITTITE PRIESTESSES IN PROCESSION

High upon the central plateau of the Republic of Turkey, Asia Minor, unknown to the world of textbooks for centuries, priestesses of the Hittites advance in solemn procession, carved in bas-relief on stone. The stone ruins of the Hittite fortresses, Amazon Gate, Lion Gate, also stand to remind us of a once-great empire. That realm declined and collapsed, as did its archenemy Egypt. Each empire had undermined the other in terrible wars.

The story of the Hittites, or Hatti, now fills chapters in history books and in books of mythology by geographers and other scholars such as Sir William Mitchell Ramsay, John Garstang, Mikhail Rostovtzeff, Kaarle Hirvonen, Gordon Childe, Sir James Frazer, and Edwin O. James.

Travelers know Asia Minor as a peninsula that bridges Asia and Europe, and which also connected Semites and Greeks. On the dry Anatolian plateau, now Turkey, across this land bridge, the religious art and civilization of the East reached Greece. As the Greeks expanded into Asia Minor, a conquest culminating in the empire of Alexander the Great, the religious art and civilization of Greece alternately reached Asia. Anatolia itself could have seen, at the decay of their old Hittite Empire, their religion and culture flower continuously in their satellite kingdoms, such as Phrygia (Troy), Lydia, and Lycia.

The story of those priestesses who solemnly process across their stone memorials recapitulates this history. The myths of these priestesses were transmitted to Greece, adapted, and naturalized, and eventually they were written down by the learned Roman poets Catullus and Ovid.

Central Asia Minor, where the Hittites sculpted their royal priestesses, extends as a plateau 3,000′–5,000′ above sea level. It remains today a land of uncertain rainfall. The legends from such austere highlands tend to be tearful. The long, extremely severe winters of Anatolia succumb to torrid, dry summers, since this plateau is almost entirely ringed by sixteen high mountains. It was therefore a relatively isolated capital. Historians have marvelled over and again at the unshakable equanimity or stubborn tenacity with which such mountaineers for more than two thousand years faced a succession of foreign conquerors. Neither language, religion, nor even placenames were long supplanted. Even the name of nearby Constantinople reverted to the Oriental "Istanbul." Even wealthy Smyrna became "Ismir." And Oriental dynasties gradually replaced the Greek descendants of the heroic, migratory clans that once beseiged Asia Minor and Byzantium.

We must accept this generalization as true, Ramsay urged: all Asia Minor lived by a "homogeneous religion and social organization" (London, 1890, pp. 28–31). They worshipped a Mother Goddess whose original name may have been Niobe. Under many names—Niobe, Cybele, and Artemis—she and her queen-priestesses, warrior-priestesses, and lowly temple servants long reigned over the cultural life of Asia Minor. The cutoff line in the days of the Hittite Empire fell to the east of their administrative centers, near the Halys River. In Hittite territory, which consisted of several confederated states north and south of the Taurus Mountains, the Mother Goddess wore a mural crown for her satellite city states and was paid highest honors.

So whether or not the immigrant Greeks called the Asian

goddess Niobe, Cybele, Artemis, Lato, Leto, or Latona of Delos, they adored her in myth though once she had been worshipped from the Black Sea to Ephesus, where the grandest
of her imposing temples is still today being excavated and restored. The most famous architects, engineers, and artists of
many centuries labored on that temple at Ephesus, which is
still a wonder of the world. Brochures for tourists explain that
the Virgin Mary spent her last years in Ephesus, in view of the
sea.

The fortified city near the modern Boghaz-Keui, in Turkey,
which Ramsay said was once "by far the most extensive ancient
city in Asia Minor," was a "ruling city unaffected by, and earlier than, Greek influence." The circuit of its outer fortifications stretched four or five miles long. From this center the
Hittites administered a confederacy: northwest to Phrygia
(Troy), southwest to the southern or Lycian coast below Ephesus, southeast to the northern slopes of the Taurus Mountains, and northeast past the Halys River and along the Black
Sea coast. For approximately one thousand years, adds Garstang in 1930, they managed to hang on to the Anatolian plateau.

In this ancient domain lie even to this day the vast ruins of
the ancient capital Hattusas, identified by Garstang (Chapter
V) as the chief seat and hub of their empire, c. 2750 B.C. The
ruins of Hattusas are considered the most imposing in Asia
Minor, noted for the sculpted processions, the crumbling
acropolis, and the city's curtain walls, gates, upper and lower
palaces, ramparts, and revetments. The city walls once rose
to heights of 14'. They were 14' thick, buttressed by extra-
mural towers about every hundred feet, and adorned by monstrous sphinxes and lions to ward off enemies from the sanctuaries of the Mother Goddess Niobe, Cybele, Artemis.

Since she was a territorial goddess, the Mother wore a mural
crown. The lion was her symbol. Her chief priestess was sculpted
so, standing or riding on a lion. In her Phrygian temples Niobe/
Cybele was depicted in a chariot drawn by lions. Most scholars
of mythology, notably Theodore Gaster and Sir James Frazer,
have explained that priestesses dressed to resemble the goddess they served, and so are individually indistinguishable from

Figure 1. Hittite King and Daughter

her. While each priestess, observed both Strabo and Herodotus, had a special personal name that was doubtless both sacred and secret and denoted her office, she was also called publicly by the name of the goddess to whom she had dedicated herself, probably for life. Her private name vanished with her at death, or even earlier, when she was symbolically reborn.

A Hittite king and his daughter, the princess dressed as if she were being introduced as a future bride for a sovereign of Egypt, are depicted at Abu Simbel (Fig. 1). She wears a long cape attached to her slender elbows, and the typically high, conical hat of her Hittite people.

A priestess is depicted at Malatia (Garstang, p. 205) as she approaches the Priestess-Queen, the latter a namesake and surrogate Mother Goddess: "Mâ." The priestess here wears a long pleated evening skirt, closely fitted and wrapped around her body like the formal "dress" kilt of ladies in Scotland today. Her hands may be either lowered or raised in worship and reverence. She wears a low, cylindrical hat. Like all Asian

Mother Goddesses the priestesses themselves wear veils that are usually swept off the face. Sculpted in relief on the walls of Carchemish, priestesses in procession are shown holding implements of the sacrifice. Or priestesses are carved in procession as they advance to celebrate the wedding of the Mother Goddess "Mâ" to the Father God known also as "Papa." At spring planting and at harvest this sacred wedding of Sky and Earth was ritually celebrated.

The "Mâ" goddess of Asia Minor, later called Cybele, Niobe, and Artemis, was a nature goddess. As such, she resembled the goddess Ishtar with her lover Tammuz in the Semitic world. In Egypt she was called Astarte. In Asia Minor her first name, after Mâ (Mother), was Cybele. It was she as Cybele who centuries later was brought to Rome at the request of the highest Roman priestess, the Cumaean Sibyl, to save Rome from the Carthaginian conqueror Hannibal, and Rome was saved. Her Asian name Cybele (Kybele) comes from the mountain which was especially sacred to her as its Queen-Bee: Cybele—Mt. Sipylus.

A Sicilian historian, Diodorus Siculus, recounted, before 21 B.C., the famous story of the goddess Cybele (III, 58, p. 271 ff.). Before she was a goddess, claims the myth, the famous Cybele was tested as a baby to see if she could become a holy priestess. From such humble origins rise the great of the world.

THE MYTH OF CYBELE AND ATTIS

In the following very famous myth of Cybele and Attis, we also have an excellent example of a tale of religion, properly and usually termed a "myth," which is also by modern definition a legend.

The book on French mythology by Henri Dontenville (Paris, 1973) makes a distinction clear (author's translation):

> On sait que la différence entre conte et légende consiste en ce que le premier est errant, sans attache au sol, tandis que la seconde prend point d'appui sur des particularités géographiques tres nettes.

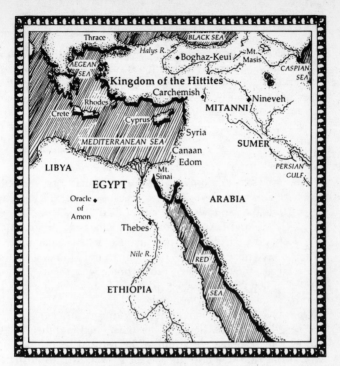

Map 2 Hittite and Egyptian Empires (about 2000–1200 B.C.)

(We know that the difference between tale and legend resides in the fact that the former floats unattached to earth, while the latter stands rooted in very specific geographical localities.)

When he heard that a baby girl was born, the father, who declined to raise her, had her exposed on Mt. Sipylus to die.

But savage leopards (lionesses?) suckled the infant. She did not die. She lived and was adopted by kind shepherdesses. These nurses were so amazed to see a baby girl sucking at the nipples of savage beasts that they took her home. They named her "Cybele" because they had found her on the snow-covered mountain called "Cybelus" (Mt. Sipylus).

As the baby grew into girlhood, she stood out even then among her peers. She possessed outstandingly three attributes: beauty, courage, and intelligence.

Cybele invented the pipe of multiple reeds, cymbals, and the tympanum, all instruments that henceforth accompanied temple dancers.

She became a healer, who cured the illnesses of both animals and children by means of cleanliness and purification rituals.

Everywhere Cybele went, she applied her hands to sick creatures and sick babies, devoting herself to them and to their cure. She loved them in such maternal fashion that she came to be known throughout the land as "Mâ," the Mother from the Mountain.

The story says that once Cybele reached maturity, she fell in love with a handsome youth from that high land. His name was Attis. He is the same who was later called "Papa," or "Our Father." Cybele loved Attis so well that she became pregnant.

It so happened that her parents at that particular time decided to recognize Cybele as their daughter. Thinking that she was a virgin, they took her to their home with them. She went to live in her father's palace, where she was welcomed as the lost, royal daughter of the family.

One day, however, her father the king realized that Cybele was pregnant. In fury he killed her nurses and had their corpses thrown out of doors. In addition, he refused them the necessary burial rites. He also put Cybele's lover Attis to death and had his body thrown out on the earth, to be exposed forever and never buried properly!

Wild with grief for the terrible fate of her nurses, and screaming with anguish at the death of Attis, Cybele rushed madly over Asia.

Letting her long hair fall loosely, like a veil about her head, she wandered through one country after the other, weeping and beating upon her kettledrums.

She still sits weeping upon Mt. Sipylus (Diodorus, III, p. 58).

THE EDUCATION OF A PRIESTESS

This short account, written before 21 B.C. by the Sicilian historian Diodorus Siculus, recalls a series of rituals, or dramatizations, which can be broken into scenes, or parts.

1) Exposure of a female infant,
2) Suckling by animals,
3) Adoption by "nurses,"

4) Naming,
5) Her personal qualities accepted by her community,
6) Proof of her superior talent, in
    a) music, and
    b) dance,
7) Mastery of ritual, i.e., purification,
8) Power over illness,
9) Travels (recognition abroad),
10) Title: High-priestess,
11) Love and pregnancy,
12) Lover reborn as a High-priest, or a king (Ramsay conjectured),
13) Recognition by royalty, i.e., her family,
14) Deaths of her nurses,
15) Death of the High-priest,
16) Mourning of Cybele, frenzied dancing by her priestesses,
17) Permanence of Cybele on Mt. Sipylus (near Smyrna or Ismir, Turkey).

This very ancient myth gives us in synopsis what the sculptures of the Hittites had not managed to give: a biography of a priestess from birth to apotheosis.

We begin Cybele's story, which is the official version as it could have been recited to worshippers in one of her shrines, with the testing ceremony. Myths of heroes usually commence thus, with exposure of the infant in a cradle, perhaps, to be floated away on water. The survival will indicate superiority, i.e., that the royal infant may be worth educating, or may be heaven-sent, or could become a great personage.

Then we have a vote by animals, which are both fierce (unlikely to nurse Cybele) and lordly (probably that beast which is a clan totem, or the king's badge). The other nurses, called "shepherdesses," also represent a symbolic, royal title, as in "The Lord is my shepherd." Here, the ladies (of the court) are "my shepherdesses." The "naming" or baptismal ceremony follows.

Education of the future priestess must be recognized as her due. She "deserves it," is our contemporary thought on the

Figure 2. Cybele (Kybele)

subject of girls. Her achievements immediately following prove her educability. We note, however, the specializations attributed to her: music and dance, both performed superabundantly, especially at ancient temples. We also note that drama originated in ritual at these same temples. Thus, the future priestess's studies have included a course in the memorization and performance of ritual.

Rites of purification were required of all worshippers for two reasons: health or sanitation, and reverence. Nobody approached the services without attempting to become pure in heart, cleanliness also being next to godliness.

The future priestess's fourth study was medicine, which benefits all. Thus, we know that these specialties were practiced by priestesses at Cybele's ancient shrines: music, dance, rites, and medicine.

By Cybele's travels we may understand that her worship involved the entire Hittite Empire, extended into Greece, and eventually spread to Rome itself. That she was High-priestess, whose lover was King and High-priest, seems appropriate. That her lover was her consort appears less certain. Why she became pregnant while unwed, if she bore a child parthenogenetically, or not at all, remains unrevealed.

Comprehensible are the deaths of those who could have testified to her lowly origins, education, tests undergone, love affair, and childbirth. This makes sense if, on the other hand, we recognize their deaths as a series of sacrifices.

It has been long known, of course, that the series of ancient goddesses of Asia followed that earth through its seasons, welcoming the gods of spring with flower parades and great festivals of joy. Cybele's lover probably came to her arms at the vernal equinox; he had curly black hair, one likes to think after reading *Thespis* by Theodore Gaster, and he resembled Aries the Ram. The Persian palace at Persepolis shows stepped entrances for the youthful god of spring.

Similarly, at Halloween he dies before the first snowfall. The Earth mourns him then, as Cybele allows her hair to fall down into long, tangled locks. She is, in other words, the falling leaves and the mourning priestess. At the last she returns to her birthplace on Mt. Sipylus in the Hittite Kingdom of Lydia.

APOTHEOSIS OF A PRIESTESS: THE WEEPING NIOBE

What follows is an interpretational, rather close summary of the Roman poet Ovid's accounts of Arachne and Niobe, (*Metamorphoses*, VI, v. 145 ff.). It was written in Rome before Ovid was exiled by Prince Augustus, 8 A.D.

> Arachne and Niobe lived as children and maidens in Phrygia (or Lydia) near Mt. Sipylus. Arachne was that girl who dared to challenge the (Greek) goddess Athena to a weaving contest. She continued to vaunt her skill even in the goddess's face. She was, as a consequence of her heedless pride, metamorphosed into a spider. Athena squeezed the juice of certain herbs she had got from the Underworld upon Arachne's ears, then on her nose, then on her hair. That turned her almost instantaneously into one black abdomen! So now she spins her spider's web and hangs there on it as it suits her. Everybody knew about

it, from Thebes (in Greece) to Phrygia and Lydia (in Asia Minor).

Niobe probably knew it, too, but never gave the fate of Arachne much thought. Actually she hardly ever paid much attention to wise teachings, cruel punishments, or the workings of the Olympian gods and goddesses.

Niobe had many blessings that she more or less accepted as her due, such as her husband's musical performances, their own ancestry from the gods, their great golden treasure amassed while they were potentates in their own kingdom, and their wonderfully pleasant rules.

One gift in her eyes surpassed all these: the joys of motherhood. Nothing equalled her absolutely overwhelming pride in her children. She lived through them. (She was *The Mother*.)

One day the priestess Manto, who was the daughter of the prophet Tiresias of Thebes, walked through that city. She had fallen into a trance. She spoke words direct from a goddess. She called out a warning to all Theban women: "Go to Leto's temple." Ovid calls her by a Roman form of Lato (Leto): Latona. "Offer up your prayers, to her and her twins. Be sure to bind laurel leaves on your heads beforehand. And prepare to burn frankincense in her honor. Be sure to repeat prayers to the holy virgin Leto, who bore Apollo and Artemis to Zeus. Remember her as daughter of the Titans Phoebe and Coeus."

All who were fortunate enough to hear Manto's words obeyed them.

Beautiful Niobe entered (the temple) also. She was so tall and elegant! She was dressed in a royal cloak of Phrygian make, the gold interwoven with gold. But she was angry. She shook her haughty head. She tossed her hair. She let it fall down and fly about her shoulders like a veil swept off her face.

Drawing herself up to her fullest height she turned about and shouted to the worshippers:

"Are you women crazy? Why are you all binding up your hair with laurel wreaths? For whom? What are these prayers? To whom do you offer these prayers? Has anybody ever seen this supposedly heavenly person called Leto?

"Who is this common woman Leto that you are celebrating at our altars here? Don't forget that I myself am divine! I alone deserve these prayers you are offering up to her. I am the goddess Niobe!

"Do you know who my father was? My father was Tantalus,

King of Lydia! He was in his day the only mortal man found fit to dine with the gods on Olympus! My mother was a sister of the Pleiades. My grandfather is the Titan Atlas who bears the heavenly realm upon his shoulders. My father-in-law and grandfather is great Zeus. When I say Zeus is my husband's father, I celebrate my own glory too.

"This entire country of Thebes, founded by the lineage of Cadmus, now looks up to me as their queen. My husband built these very walls by playing on his lyre. Everybody bows down to us as the reigning monarchs. Look at my palace. Is it not luxurious beyond argument?

"I am as lovely as any goddess (of yours). What matters most is that I am the mother of seven sons and seven daughters. Think how many sons-in-law and daughters-in-law these children of mine will bring me!

"Now that you know the basis of my deservedly high pride, surely you will set me above that Titaness, that daughter-of-a-nobody named Coeus-what's-his-name.

"That Leto was a tramp. (She had been raped by Zeus.) She could barely find a birthing spot. Heaven wouldn't have her. Earth turned her down. The seas themselves refused her a refuge. Finally the small island of Delos agreed to have her: 'I'm just a vagrant isle in the middle of the sea, so come ahead,' it said.

"Her twins were born there. But my births are seven times hers. Naturally, I'm thrilled at that. You had better believe it.

"I have been made a wealthy woman because of all the boys and girls I have brought into this world. The goddess Fortune herself can't trip me up now! If she should take some from me, I've got plenty more. I'm so rich no loss could shake me. Even if I lost three, four of my children, I would still not be reduced to a set of twins, like her. She bore a meager twosome. You might as well say she was barren.

"So leave. Go home. Rip those laurel wreaths off your heads."

Whispering quietly to each other, the women obeyed Niobe. They threw their laurel sprays on the pavement. They broke off their ceremony. They turned their backs to Leto's altar. Under their breath they even so pronounced their goddess Leto's name.

Meanwhile an angered Leto soared to the summit of Mt. Cynthus on the island of Delos where her twins Apollo and Artemis reigned. "Only Hera is greater than me," she told them.

"She is the wife of Zeus. Nobody doubts her majesty. But I too am sacred, powerful, dowered, and famous. And this person questions my status, my altars. You both had better act before my worshippers are all dismissed.

"Can you imagine who threatens me? It is that daughter of Tantalus, who calls herself an aristocrat. She brags her children are more revered than you are. And more than that, she calls me unwomanly because I bore only two infants.

"She has failed to revere the gods. You know her father dared betray their secrets."

"Enough," cried Phoebus Apollo. "No more words that postpone our vengeance." His sister Phoebe-Artemis felt the same wrath. In a flash they soared through the clouds and dropped to earth near the high walls Cadmus had built around his citadel of Thebes.

Niobe's royal husband, King Amphion of Thebes, was busily engaged in teaching his seven sons how to ride, to race, and to drive their chariots around the walls. They had worn the earth down into ruts and sand with their daily practicing. The lads wore fancy riding habits of Tyrian purple, its fuchsia hue making the gold of their horses' harnesses gleam brighter. Proudly they made their mounts arch their necks and raise their hooves smartly above the blowing dust of the track.

The eldest prince, Ismenus, had been named for the Ismenus River near Thebes. He just then came riding by. His charger foamed at the bit. "Alas for me," he cried to his father, but Apollo's arrow had already pierced him through. The prince lurched forward over his horse's neck, slid onto its right shoulder, and plunged headfirst to earth.

The second son, named Sipylus (for his mother's birthplace), then gave his horse its head as he heard the arrow twang and the quiver rattle. It was like a captain who from the bridge sees a storm sweeping across the sea and orders full sails aloft so they can run before the wind. Prince Sipylus urged on his mount, but the arrow that none can either dodge or outrun pierced his throat from behind him, the metal barbs finally protruding from below his chin. The force of it drove him forward until he lost his seat, pitching headfirst down the horse's mane, down the forelegs onto the ground. There his life blood gushed from the wound.

The next brothers, sad Phaedimus and Tantalus, had already completed their riding lessons and had commenced the wrestling lesson with each other. Wet with sweat they grappled until Apollo's arrow transfixed them both, pinning them even closer, chest to chest. Together they cried out in agony and rolled over together on the bare ground, eyes to dying eyes, last breath to last breath together.

The fifth son, Alphenor, watched it all happen. He stood there motionless at first, but recovering, he beat his chest with both fists. Then he rushed to raise his brothers' bodies from the dirt. Thus, like a reverent son, he died, pierced through the thorax by the metal arrow's tip. When they drew out the arrow, they found bits of his lung tissue on the barbed shaft. Alphenor's blood poured into a pool.

The younger brother, who was named Damasichton, died even harder. The first arrow pierced him in the fleshy part of the leg, above the knee, and tore the hamstrings. He was able to reach down to pull it out, even so. As he struggled to pull it through, the second arrow caught him in the throat, the shaft traversing his neck all the way to the feathers on the shaft. A thin jet of blood spurted skywards.

The little boy Ilioneus died last, his arms raised high in prayer. "Save me, all you gods above," he cried, not having yet learned that praying to all the gods at once was actually unnecessary. Apollo pitied him, but he had already aimed and sent that fatal arrow. Fortunately, Ilioneus died more easily. The arrow had punctured his heart.

King Amphion put an end to his grief and to his life also. He drove his dagger into his heart.

The queen heard the news, learned of the grief felt everywhere, and was amazed that this disaster should have struck her family so rapidly. Her amazement turned at once to wrath, that the gods should have misused their power so flagrantly.

Queen Niobe then became unrecognizable. She was no longer the same person who had driven worshippers from Leto's shrine, not the lovely woman who had proudly trod the pavement. No longer envied by her friends, no longer even hated by her enemies, she hastened to throw herself upon the cold bodies—all that was left of her beloved sons. She kissed each one tenderly. Then, raising her sore arms to the skies, she called out to Leto.

"Eat my anguish, you cruel goddess! Devour it! Stuff yourself with my sorrow! Eat your fill of it. I have lost seven sons. I have now died seven deaths with them. Enjoy it. Savor your foul victory, if it is a victory. For even now, wretched woman that I am, I am happier than you. You have killed seven, but I am still the winner over you!"

The next arrow sped forward while Niobe was finishing her taunt. She did not even hear it leave the bow, so daring had her anguish made her.

The seven daughters, all clothed in black, had loosened their hair in token of mourning. They stood around the funeral mound where their brothers lay dead. The oldest girl was struck. She fell over a brother's body from which she was attempting to draw out the arrow. The second daughter dropped as she bent down to caress her mother. A third girl fell as she fled. The fourth fell upon her body. The fifth died as she stood still, shaking. The sixth hid but was slain notwithstanding.

The last and littlest ran to her mother. Niobe threw her arms about her "baby" daughter and enfolded her in her own robe. As she held the small girl she cried:

"Please leave me my littlest child. She is last of all my children. I beg you to spare me this one—just this one."

Before her words had even left her lips, the last child died.

Niobe sat down amid the bodies of her seven sons, her husband, and her seven daughters.

Her sorrowing prayer had turned her lips to silent stone. No hair on her head stirred again. Her face turned white. Her eyes stared from their sockets. Her tongue froze to the roof of her mouth. Her blood ceased to swell her veins. Her neck became rigid. Her arms and feet became incapable of motion. Her abdomen sank flat between her hipbones. Tears streamed ceaselessly down her cheeks and dripped upon her chest. Her image, it is said, was sculpted by her brother Broteas.

Suddenly a circling wind swept her out of there to her native land. There she sits still today, on a mountaintop, and weeps. Her tears flow still, upon the marble (v. 312).

Afterword

Several Greek writers before Ovid had told the story of Niobe in Greece; but, even so, her name was always associated with her native Asian land, and specifically with Mt. Sipylus. Aeschylus, Sophocles, and Homer knew her legend well. She had by their time become a metaphor of grief for all mothers, the world over.

Ramsay climbed many times over the sheer cliffs and narrow rock chasms around Mt. Sipylus where Pausanias said he saw her likeness carved on the north face of a steep cliff. Pausanias had said her eyes still wept in his boyhood there.

Apparently the Asian Mother Goddess Cybele's original name was Niobe. That name comes from India and means "Snowy" or "Snow White." Niobe was the goddess originally called "Mother of Mt. Sipylus," and then "Cybele" for short. The Asian priestesses were venerated as mothers.

Niobe's sculpted figure is carved from a white rock—perhaps marble, as Ovid said, which shows up against the dark cliff even from far away.

If Niobe was both queen and High-priestess, which Garstang and Ramsay have believed, and which seems most likely, then we have read in a myth and two legends the birth, education, life story, and death of that Asian priestess.

II

THE AMAZONS

"... in some cases the names of heroes-gods, as we have them, represent the Greek versions of pre-Hellenic or foreign names. This, I think, is certainly true of some divine names, Hephaestus, Artemis, Aphrodite, etc. .... Therefore Greek etymologies are wasted breath."

> W.R. Halliday.
> Indo-European Folk-tales and Greek Legend
> (The Gray Lectures, 1932). (Cambridge, 1933).

AMAZON PRIESTESSES

Within the kingdoms of the crumbling Hittite Empire were the Amazons, armed troops, or groups of warriors who defended their homelands against foreign invaders. They were so identified by Greek writers in their legendary biographies of the heroes of the Homeric Age.

Two generations after Agamemnon of the Trojan War, migratory peoples continued to deluge Greece and Asia Minor: Heraclids from the lineage of Heracles (Hercules), Dorians, Thessalians, Thracians, Ionians, Aeolians. These "Great Migrations" were still going on around the year 1104 B.C. Adolphe Reinach, one of the most distinguished historians of religion, a scholar also remarkable for his mastery of Oriental/Asian languages, dated the period of defense by the Amazon warriors as extending from about 1400 B.C. to the time of the Trojan War, at c.1200 B.C., and through to the military conquest of Asia by Alexander the Great (356 B.C.–323 B.C.).

The German scholar Bachofen accused the early Greek heroes of being foes of the Amazons, who were real priestesses and women warriors, he charged. Heracles was the worst of all, their greatest enemy. As for the rest of the crew, such as Bellerophon, Dionysus, Pelops, and Achilles, they all not only salted the earth of Asia so that the inhabitants would thereafter die from starvation; they primarily combated women and the Asian social system.

When conquerors destroy the social structure of a civilization, deprive that society of its beliefs, customs, usages, and hierarchy, they effectively extinguish it completely. In Asia the last bright sparks of light were the Asian priestesses who took up arms against foreign conquerors. Those brave women, prepared to die on the spot, were your now fabled Amazons, said he.

Since he was a highly renowned scholar of jurisprudence, greatly honored in Germany, Bachofen then proceeded in hundreds of pages to talk law. Let us speak of Herodotus, he suggested. What does Herodotus say about the legal position of children in Asia? Which two honored historians second him (see his "Lycia," pp. 121–56)? Lycian children belonged to their mothers, you recall. They took their mothers' names. Ask Plutarch how the women stopped the salting of their earth by Poseidon. Read Homer's *Iliad* (pp. 6, 186) and Pindar's *Olympian Odes* (pp. 13, 87 ff.). Then, challenged Bachofen, tell me if you have not seen evidence to confirm my own logical conclusion: Heracles, Dionysus, Perseus, Theseus, and Achilles were *combatants of mother right*. To do that, to obliterate a social order that they detested, they slaughtered the women, especially their priestesses and queens who were then revered in Asia as matriarchs.

George Rawlinson took what was perhaps a less impassioned view, namely, that the Scythians described by Herodotus as "horse-faced women" living in tribes all along the northern and eastern reaches of the ancient world were, in fact, *the same women as the Amazons*.

Now that the Scythian grave mounds in what is now southern Russia have been excavated and their gorgeous golden treasures reported on and photographed by the Metropolitan Museum of Art, New York City, we may at least agree with George Rawlinson that these women were probably (also) Amazons. If so, they may have surpassed both King Tantalus and chief god Zeus as collectors of golden art objects.

Rawlinson wrote that when the Scythians invaded Media, they were commanded by a warrior queen named Zarina (Zarinaea? Czarina?), "a woman of rare beauty, and as brave as she was fair; who won the hearts, when she could not resist the swords, of her adversaries." He told a strangely romantic tale of this lovely Amazon (p. 91):

> Queen Zarina founded the capital city, Roxanacé. The "chief architectural monument" in that city was her tomb. Scythian tombs were enormous mounds of stone covered with earth, containing bodies of rulers encircled by bodies of their beloved horses, gold objects, jewels, and other treasures. [A parallel is the "dragon" (*draco, draconis:* the word is feminine) that guarded her golden hoard in *Beowulf.*]
>
> Zarina's husband was Marmareus (Old Marble Head?), King of the Scythians. She accompanied him into battle. Thus occupied, she was wounded and captured by a warrior named Stryangaeus, son-in-law to the Median sovereign. Turning her charm upon that ruler, Zarina pleaded with him to release her. The king let her go. In a following engagement the prince Stryangaeus himself was captured by King Marmareus, who decided to execute him. But Zarina begged for his life. When she saw that Marmareus would refuse her plea, she killed her husband.
>
> By this time Zarina and Stryangaeus were in love. He visited her court, where he was received most ceremoniously. After he had been royally made welcome, he formally declared his affection. But Zarina refused him, reminding him of his wonderful wife at home, declaring that lady lovelier than herself. She advised her suitor to cool his ardor.
>
> Stryangaeus retired to his quarters. He wrote a letter to Zarina accusing her of murder, and then he committed suicide.

In her doctoral dissertation at Columbia University (1912), Florence Mary Bennett asserted again, evidencing Homer's *Iliad,* that the Amazons were women warriors who fought men warriors. She particularly argued the case of Queen Myrina, whose tomb was constructed on the Plain of Troy, not far from the tombs of Ajax and Achilles. Not only was she the wife of

Figure 3. Amazon

the hero Dardanus and the daughter of Teucer, but cities were named Myrina (one, for example, in Aeolis) in her honor. The Greek epic cycles of c. 750 B.C. rehearsed the stories of other such gallant Amazons. Their tombs were sometimes located in Greece—in Athens, Lesbos, Megara, and Thessaly, according to these early epics. Most epics are legendary, and transmit some history or geography.

Bennett called to her assistance the representations of Amazons in Greek art. Studying vase paintings in particular, she found, first of all, no evidence whatsoever that these women warriors had undergone breast surgery, as is usually alleged. (For centuries scholars had derived the name or word *Amazon* from the Greek, making it mean "without a breast.") Bennett found the Amazons' faces, as depicted by Greek artists, to be calm and lovely, their bodies those of young athletes, their postures on horseback easy and graceful. She noted their short tunics worn as riding habits and their (two) bare breasts. Looking again at the representations of Amazons collected in the National Museum of Athens, Bennett insisted that when mounted they wore, in fact, a short, belted tunic, which she found not only attractive but practical. In many cases the Greek artist had caught the remarkable contrast between the slender girl rider and the strong, sinewy horse she rode.

Bennett was saddened by the depiction of a dead Amazon that she saw in the Museum of Naples, Italy. Clearly dead, the Amazon lay supine, still wearing her distinctive short tunic. Her spear lay under her body. Her lips were open, as if she had died gasping for breath. Her face looked sad, as if her last thought had been painful. Then Bennett noticed a feature specifically stressed by the artist: the one breast visible in the work was the swollen breast of a nursing mother.

Bennett agreed with Rawlinson that the weapons, ivy-leaf shields, battleaxes, and panther-skin capes of the Amazons—such a cape was worn by Queen Penthesilea—also pointed to a Scythian origin. And, in fact, there are still women in Europe with the very long, somewhat narrow faces Herodotus ascribed to the mounted Scythians. One sees such faces today in the Basque country, between Bayonne, France, and Bilbao, Spain. Women there have fairly dark complexions, long faces, heavy brows, and eyes that turn down at the outer corners. They used to be seen frequently after World War II crossing the Pyrenees Mountains on foot, carrying loads of oranges on their backs for the undernourished, tubercular children of war-torn France. They were strong, like the fabled Amazons.

Many of Bennett's findings in this pioneer work are interesting, including her conclusions (pp. 30–76) that:

1. stories of Amazons recall raids from the north into Asia Minor, and that
2. the Amazons were warrior-priestesses, or hierodules who served the Hittite goddess Mâ, or Ma, and specifically fought also as far south as Lydia and Lycia.

Avoiding personalities, the renowned French Orientalist Adolphe Reinach finally addressed the Amazon question historically and theologically, as follows:

1. Until 1870 the Amazons were interpreted as middle voices for some godhead such as Mâ-Cybele. They were as recognizable historically as the Valkyries of German and

Scandinavian myths, mounted women warriors, that is, galloping out of the moon under an overcast sky.

2. The discovery of the Hittites in 1900 changed all that. German, Italian, and English archaeologists pointed out what was plainly evident to all travelers in Turkey: there were Amazons, *women warriors*, sculpted on the ruins of Hittite fortress-cities on the plains of Anatolia. John Garstang went to look, saw, and recognized them as both *priestesses and warriors*. The German scholar Walther Leonhard looked and agreed (Reinach, idem).

3. The lands and affiliated states of the old Hittite Empire coincide with the presence there of Amazons. This includes Phrygia, Lydia, and Lycia:

    a) the ruins of Amasia on the Iris River (south shore, Black Sea);

    b) the valley of the Thermodon and Halys rivers (south shore, Black Sea coast);

    c) the ruins of Themiscyra, the Lykastos River valley, the site of Amisus (perhaps also Mt. Masis, renamed Ararat), the present Mason-Dagh, the present seacoast of Sinope;

    d) Troy and the plains to the west of it, the Bosporus areas east and west;

    e) Contacts were made from Thrace on the west to Colchis in the east, including the Don River in the U.S.S.R., and well into the Caucasus Mountains.

4. The Amazons were celebrated as horsewomen, performing prestigious equestrian feats (very similar to those executed today by her Royal Highness Princess Anne of England). The Hittite princesses often bore names of a horse-goddess: *Hipa* (horse), as in Hippolyte. Such names followed as Lady Godiva of Coventry and Princess Rhiannon of Dyfed (South Wales). The Hittite princesses had charming names that sound almost French: Toudou-Hipa, Poudou-Hipa (Horse Guard), and Goulou-Hipa.

5. The goddesses of the Hittites (and gods) were the same as those of the Amazons: Mâ, Cybele, Atargatis, Artemis, seated and veiled Mother Goddesses, sometimes winged.

6. The animals and totems were also the same. The Amazons were reportedly tamers of wild animals: lions, panthers, deer, bulls, goats, rams, eagles, and falcons.
7. Their priestesses often assumed names of animals, birds, and insects, calling themselves "Bees," "Doves." They brandished double axes nonetheless. Strabo saw six thousand such priestesses at Ephesus, brandishing Cretan axes, added Hecataeus.
8. The Amazon priestesses performed also, dancing like the Scythians, riding bareback in festivals, riding standing on the horse's back, jumping like circus performers from one horse's back to another, leaping across bonfires, shooting arrows while on horseback but aimed at their pursuers. (Such a feat was attributed to Persian cavalry and so called: a "Parthian" shot.)
9. These Amazons were also said to be "man killers" like the Scythian girls, said also to kill strangers routinely.

Reinach does not fail to note the vast numbers of French women equestrians who, he suggested, are modern Amazons. Certainly, he argued, the Trojans migrated from Phrygia at the fall of Troy. And certainly one known Amazon, Queen Cleite (Kleite), founded a colony in Italy. And certainly, the Gauls also migrated into what is now France and were often outranked by their own mounted women warriors.

John Garstang devoted Chapter V of his book *The Hittite Empire* to Amazons whom he saw sculpted at Hattusas. He described them in general terms (p. 86): wide thighs, full breasts, their helmets adorned with feathered crests that floated down their backs, wearing guards over their ears and necks, wearing chain mail over the thorax, their lower bodies clad in short tunics decorated with spirals, their middles encased in either a corset or a wide belt with metal studs. He observed that the short swords they carried in their left hands had curved blades, hilts in crescent shape, and scabbards. They carried axes with curving blades in their right hands. He dated these sculptures in Hattusas at 1378 B.C. Sculpture at the Hittite capital showed, he further noted, a Hittite queen garbed for battle like an

Amazon. They always fought, he said, and according to every tale and recollection of them, they always died.

They fought at Troy, alongside the Trojans, and died there. They died at Themiscyra, on the right bank of the Thermodon River as it flows into the Black Sea. It amazed Garstang that although Greek warriors were always able to wrest the ax from an Amazon's hand before she died, there were other Amazons who came right after her, ready to try again and die as the first one had fallen and died.

Some of these sculptures in Anatolia are eight feet high, and everywhere the women warriors are decked out in finery: curly hair in pigtails, earrings, rosettes, skull caps or conical helmets, cloaks, capes, shoes, robes, togas, embroidery, bracelets, daggers, and one with the outstretched wings of a moon goddess.

One signed her name to her betrothal treaty to King Hattusil, adding her title: High-priestess of Arinna (a goddess). Opposite "Arinna" stood her spouse, the male god of the Hittites, whose name over the centuries varied from Teshab, Hadad, Adad, to Zeus. At the wedding the bride and groom were escorted by pipers playing bagpipes, followed by performers on the trumpet, the guitar, and the plectrum.

All persons reverence Niobe as the Asian Mother of all, added Garstang (p. 176); classical writers reported the same:

1) Pausanias (III, xxii, 4): ". . . stand farther off, you will see a weeping woman bowed with grief. . . ."
2) Homer's *Iliad* (xxiv, 615): "Niobe, turned to stone, upon arid Sipylus broods o'er her sorrows. . . ."
3) Ovid's *Metamorphoses* (VI, v. 310): "Fastened to the rock she weeps, and the marble sheds tears. . . ."

George Thomson included the Amazons among the "Matriarchal Peoples of the Aegean," in which work he endorsed the monumental volumes of Robert Briffault, *The Mothers*, of 1927. Thomson also pointed to the local monuments called "Amazoneia" in Turkey today, and listed the sites of the Amazons (p. 181) in what would become Asian Ionia (Greek territory): Myrine, Mytilene, Elaia, Anaia, Gryneia, Kyme, Pitane, Smyrna, Latoreia near Ephesus, and glorious Ephesus itself.

The ubiquity of the Amazons, Briffault had argued (III, p. 457), proves they were once plentiful, not scarce. Their name, he thought, comes from their own non-Greek language: *emet-chi* = "descended through women." The Greeks, who did not understand this language, spelled it "Amazon," and later thought it meant "without one breast."

Doctors speculate that babies long ago may have been smaller than babies today, with much smaller heads, so childbirth was easier. In any case, Briffault heard or had learned, the Amazons reportedly uttered no cry during childbirth. If a woman cried, her baby was put to death. The Amazons reared no cowards, and no children of cowards. Amazons who died in childbirth were accorded the same funeral rites offered a hero or a priestess in other societies. Robert Graves wrote in his two-volume encyclopedia, *The Greek Myths* (1955), that the Amazon queen Harmonia married Cadmus of Thebes, whose building of that city-state was also recognized in Niobe's story. The early Amazons at some later time lived north of the Black Sea, he knew, along what.is now the Don River, U.S.S.R. From there they emigrated along the Black Sea coast to the Thermodon River and lofty Amazonian Mountains.

According to the traditional ordinances of their Queen Lysippe, men were to do housework, and women were to be warriors. Boys had their arms and legs broken so they could neither fight nor stray. The warrior women's clothes were to be made of leather from wild beasts. Such traditions may be Greek denigration, however.

Lysippe built the city of Themiscyra, where her tribes worshipped Hera's son Ares and the moon goddess Artemis. Her successor queens reigned throughout Asia Minor and Syria, say the Orientalists, building the cities of Ephesus, Smyrna, Cyrene, Myrine, and Sinope. Such centers were named after such Amazon queens as Marpesia, Lampado, Smyrna, and Hippo.

The great temple at Ephesus was founded by these same Amazons and built around the original image of (the Moon) Artemis, which hung upon a sacred beech tree. While Hippo performed the rituals, her priestesses executed the fearsome Sword Dance. (The Sword Dance, eyes front, both hands over the head, slippered feet treading fast between crossed swords, is still performed in the United States and in Scotland today.)

When King Priam was a child, he witnessed the sack of his city Troy by Amazons, during which Queen Marpesia was slain. When her successors—Queens Hippolyte, Antiope, and Melanippe—were slain by the Greek conqueror Theseus of Athens, their axes and sacred regalia were transferred south into Lydia. From those days, the struggles intensified: Queens and High-priestesses Hippolyte, Thetis, Penthesilea, Myrine versus the male Greek conquerors. All the Amazon queens in Phrygia and Lydia died as their three tribes retired south into their major sanctuary at Ephesus.

QUEENS OF THE AMAZONS

The war between the Greeks and the Amazons took place on the south shores of the Black Sea, on the northeastern Anatolian plateau, in Phrygia (the Trojan War of c. 1200 B.C.), in Lydia, in Lycia, and finally as far east as Bactria, modern Afghanistan, around 323 B.C. Among the principal heroes, who led the invasions of Asia, were Telamon, Peleus, Jason, Theseus, Heracles, Perseus, and Bellerophon. They were followed by the Persian Shah Cyrus the Great and the deified Macedonian Emperor, Alexander the Great. The Amazons had also fought Priam at Troy when he was only a boy, and he was an old man at the time of the Trojan War.

Two considerations define this series of attacks and defenses of empires as a series of territorial wars: the attacks are made under the aegis of Greek gods, such as Poseidon and Athena, while the defense shelters under the protection of Asian Mother Goddesses such as Artemis and Aphrodite. Athena was the one goddess who particularly scorned females, except for their surrogate organ, the uterus. Artemis, fiercely virginal, murderous in the defense of her virginity, represented one side of femininity, the Asian point of view. Aphrodite represented the other side of femininity: the joys of physical and spiritual love between man and woman. Homer's hero Odysseus, the favored survivor of the Trojan War, represented the triumph of Athena over Aphrodite.

The Trojans, who were, of course, natives of Asia Minor, dedicated themselves to Aphrodite. Their Prince Paris gave the prized apple to Aphrodite rather than to Hera or to Athena. The other Trojan princes also chose love, except for their sister Cassandra, the priestess, who chose Artemis and lifelong virginity. The chief Trojan survivor of the Trojan War was Prince Aeneas, son of Anchises and Aphrodite herself. Odysseus returned to Ithaca and his wife Penelope, who sat spinning her web—a bad augury for Odysseus, no matter how the myth is rationalized. But the Trojan Aeneas founded Rome. And not only Rome! The Trojans also founded France/Gaul and Britain. Odysseus won the battles, burned the city, survived to rejoin Ithaca, but in the long run the Greeks lost the war. The winners lost and the losers won.

Relying upon Greek myths for a view of the Greeks' prehistory shows a succession of heroic adventures that could be understood as connected sequentially, first of all, and then undertaken cumulatively. Each reinforces and intensifies the other. Adventure number one recruits heroes and a heroine to kill the Calydonian Boar, which has devastated the countryside. Here we have our major heroes introduced, and we are conned into approving what upon reflection impresses us as an ugly story: how Atalanta lost a footrace and her virginity. Thus, she broke her vow of chastity, an act which caused her and her father great sorrow, for it was a breach of good faith.

From the myth of Atalanta we learn two lessons in how a young man can manipulate a young woman by:

1. appealing to her natural sexuality,
2. appealing to her natural desire for riches (which caused Atalanta to lose the footrace, since she stooped to pick up the third gold apple he rolled in front of her).

The myth that illustrates, without preaching, how contemptible women supposedly are, naturally evokes a strong reaction. Obviously Atalanta's fate was death. The golden apples came from the Hesperides, and only a mermaid could eat one and live. Atalanta died in more ways than one.

Adventure number two is the famous story of the Argonauts, retold by a great writer, Apollonius of Rhodes, in *The Argonautica*. Here we begin to understand Atalanta's disgrace. She had been unfaithful to the great goddesses of women: Cybele and Aphrodite. In this second-stage adventure, or war, we might place not only the much more hideous story of Jason and Medea, but also the stories of Theseus and the Amazon Queens, and of Heracles and the Amazon Queen. Their Greek ship Argo was constructed under the sponsorship of the goddess Athena, who was hostile to Asia and especially to Troy.

The ten-year war, Greeks versus Trojans on the northwest point of Asia Minor, is the third great adventure. The Greeks combat under their protecting gods, Poseidon and Athena. The Trojans have, on the other hand, dedicated themselves to their sea-born Aphrodite. The Trojan hero Paris gave the apple to Aphrodite; abducted the most beautiful woman in the world, Helen of Troy, from her Greek husband Menelaus, and was slain at Troy by Philoctetes. The second Trojan prince, Deiphobus, was slain by Menelaus. Another prince, Troilus, along with two other Trojan royals, Memnon and Hector, were all three slain by the greatest of the Greeks, Achilles. Their virgin prophetess Cassandra was raped by Ajax, given as a slave to Agamemnon, and killed in Greece by Agamemnon's wife Clytemnestra. The youngest Trojan princess, Polyxena, was sacrificed on the Greek altar to pacify the ghost of Achilles, who had also slain the young Amazon warrior, Penthesilea.

As for the fates meted out to the heroes—and the heroine—of the Calydonian Hunt, Jason was killed when his ship Argo fell on him. Theseus of Athens was murdered as he wandered, a refugee. Nestor and Peleus lived into old age. And Atalanta was metamorphosed into one of the lions which drew Cybele's chariot. Thus, we see how her weakness, or lack of character, was punished by the Asians.

As for the heroes of *The Argonautica,* aside from Jason, Peleus, and Nestor already mentioned, Prince Meleager, who had led the Calydonian Hunt and who also rowed at the oars on Argo, was killed by his own mother. Heracles was captured by the Amazon Queen Omphale. Achilles's son Neoptolemus was murdered by Orestes at Delphi.

As a result of the Trojan War, Agamemnon was slain by his wife. Achilles was slain by Paris. Patroclus was slain by the Trojan champion Hector. Diomed's wife left him, and he fled to Italy. The King of Salamis, Ajax I, went insane. Ajax II, who had raped Cassandra, was lost at sea. Teucer was banished for not avenging Ajax. Nestor survived all three adventures because he lived the lifetimes of three men, which gives us an idea of chronology here. The Greek Protislaus was the first man killed in battle. Menelaus survived, picked up his errant wife, Helen of Troy, and took her back to Greece. The Trojan women, including the aged Queen Hecuba, were all enslaved and put to work and prostitution in Greece. Troy itself was looted and burned.

The memory of it all has never faded, thanks to beloved Homer. The Trojan Memnon's mother was the Goddess of the Dawn in Egypt. She set up a statue there so her son could be honored after death. Edgar Allan Poe in his day still treasured poor kidnapped Helen in verse six of "To Helen," one of the loveliest lyrics ever written:

> On desperate seas long wont to roam,
>   Thy hyacinth hair, thy classic face,
> Thy Naiad airs have brought me home
>   To the glory that was Greece,
> And the grandeur that was Rome.

Whereas Poe compared Helen to the water-nymph Naias, beloved of Bacchus, others would place her, along with Castor and Pollux, among the gods who undertook these adventures. The Trojan royal hero Troilus is remembered for his betrayal by his beloved and his sad death at the hands of Achilles. Achilles may have been slain by Apollo himself, who had supposedly remained neutral during the Trojan *mêlée*. The Trojan royal prince Glaucus is very well remembered, for he was the father of Rome's first Cumaean Sibyl, for centuries the highest priestess and highest authority in the known world.

The prime hero of Athens was Theseus, who entered the hero's arena with his youthful exploits and his defeat of the

Minotaur in Crete. Before he engaged in the hunt for the Calydonian Boar, he had probably already abandoned his helpful Cretan princess, Ariadne. Although she had lent him the thread which he followed through the Labyrinth, he abandoned her on the Isle of Naxos.

During the voyage of the Argo, Theseus also kidnapped an Amazon queen-priestess named Hippolyte. Some say he also kidnapped another Amazon queen named Antiope, who may or may not have been Hippolyte's sister. Theseus had already kidnapped Helen of Troy when she was only ten years old. His next abduction—after Helen, Ariadne, Hippolyte, and Antiope—was Ariadne's sister Phaedra of Crete. This last bride, or victim, killed Hippolyte's son Hippolytus, or the sea god Poseidon killed him. Rather than let readers suppose Theseus treated his brides to violence, some have preferred to blame Hippolyte. Thus, they repeat Jason's excuse, which was: Princess Medea (Hippolyte) betrayed her city Colchis (Themiscyra) to the Greek hero, and "eloped" with him to Greece.

The final result of the Greek invasions into Asia Minor was the migration of the Amazons to the north shore of the Black Sea. By 800 B.C., says Reinach (p. 305), they had joined Scythian peoples who allowed women more privileges than they ever acquired in Greece, where women enjoyed less and less freedom, in fact, even as the great Classical Age dawned. Some say it died early because of the abuse of Greek women.

The theft of the Amazon's Girdle seems to recall a raiding expedition made by Heracles and Theseus to the Thermodon River valley, where in a pitched battle, Heracles killed a Queen Hippolyte and took from her corpse her golden girdle. Or in the frenzy of the sudden raid upon the Black Sea coast and river, Queens Hippolyte, Antiope, and Melanippe were slain. Accounts seem to equate this adventure with Jason's seizing of the Golden Fleece. The girdle of the Amazon meant more than gold to her, however; it was a sign of her virginity, a belt which she was obliged to wear until she had killed three enemies in war. However that may be, this was not Heracles's last encounter with an Amazon.

A "merry tale" (II, vv. 303–358) of Heracles is told by Ovid in his *Fasti*, or almanac of the Latin year. On a third day after the Ides the Romans paid homage to the mountain god Faunus, whom the Greeks called Pan. Worshippers and celebrants customarily went naked that day because in olden times everybody lived naked in the woods, had no domesticated animals, and drank from their cupped hands. But Faunus in particular avoided clothing because of what happened to him once upon a time.

One day Faunus (Pan) caught a glimpse of a beauty. She wore her hair in long, perfumed ringlets. Her bare bosom shone because of the gold binding on her gown. The person holding the golden parasol over her dainty head was Heracles. The beauty was none other than the renowned Amazon Queen Omphale.

She and her escort passed into a lava and pumice cave on Mt. Tmolus, which is in Lydia. Servants were laying out their supper beside a brook of cool, fresh water there at the entrance.

Before Faunus, as he panted and leered, the queen disrobed. Then she disrobed Heracles and sweetly began to dress him in her own garment. She pulled her Tyrian purple tunic down over his big chest. She tried to hook her golden girdle about his huge girth. He broke her bracelets trying to fasten the clasps. He split her little shoes with his big toes.

Then the queen put on his warrior's clothing, threw his lion's skin over her shoulder, grasped his enormous club, and took up his quiver and arrows.

Clothed thus, Omphale and Heracles sat merrily down to supper. Afterwards they retired to twin beds made up side by side, each in his or her own bed. Tomorrow morning was the celebration for Bacchus who required abstinence.

At midnight Faunus crept into the wet cave, hoping to find all in deep sleep. With outstretched hands he felt his way in utter darkness. On the first bed he came to he ran his fingers over Heracles's lion skin. He jumped back as if he had stepped on a snake barefooted. On the next bed he felt soft fabric that delighted his touch. So he climbed up on that side of the bed.

The next thing he felt were enormously hairy legs. Before he could think what to make of that, he was thrown to the earth by one back stroke of an arm. He fell with a loud thud.

Instantly the queen called for torches. Her chambermaids brought light at once. There groaning on the hard-packed earth lay Faunus in a heap. Heracles burst out laughing. So did Omphale. As for Faunus, he ordered that from this midnight onwards it should be known that he detested clothing, and that his celebrants were henceforth to come to his shrines stark naked.

This "true story" took place, said Ovid, while Romulus and Remus were youths about to found great Rome. Ovid said he wished for a thousand voices and for the soul of Lycian Homer so that he also could celebrate Achilles and the Amazon Penthesilea (II, 119). But alas! Homer also declined to celebrate the brief encounter between Achilles and another Amazon, veteran of several combats, the maiden Penthesilea. Others skirted it briefly: how she met Achilles in battle, how he dragged her by the hair until she fell from her horse, how he fell in love with her dead body, and how he raped her corpse.

The truth of these two Amazon tales, of Omphale and Penthesilea, appears concealed, but may be understood by lifting the veil of censorship: Omphale, like all priestesses of Ma (Mâ), required transvestism of all males allowed in the shrine. In the case of Penthesilea, Achilles felt no love. He raped her corpse to degrade her to the fullest, so nobody could henceforth respect her as a virginal priestess. The Greeks called her unnatural and unwomanly. The enemy warriors then got rid of her body so no autopsy could convict them, throwing her into the Scamander River near Troy.

THE ACCOUNT BY DIODORUS SICULUS
From His *Library of History,* Book II

Diodorus of Sicily discusses the "Scythians, the Amazons of Asia Minor, and the Hyperboreans" of the far north of Europe, the last peoples taken to have resided in Great Britain, says his translator of 1935, C.H. Oldfather, Professor of Ancient History at the University of Nebraska. Specifically Diodorus discusses the Amazons of Asia Minor in two short passages (Book II, pp. 31–37, Book IV, pp. 393–97), briefly describes the Hyperboreans (pp. 37–41), and then goes to a very long account of Medusa as an Amazon Queen in the area of Lake Tritonis (see Map #5) in North Africa, then called Libya. Leaving Medusa for a later chapter, we should now look at Diodorus's corrections made concerning the Amazons of Asia Minor.

Summary of Diodorus 45 and 46, and Commentary Thereof, pp. 31–37

"Now in the country along the Thermodon River, as the account goes," Diodorus commences, taking his facts from Strabo, ruled a queen and her people. This queen was absolute sovereign over her kingdom along the southern shore of the Black Sea. There women waged war just as men do. The sovereign herself, however, surpassed her subjects not only in her "royal authority," but also in her physical strength, and her feats on the battlefield. She conscripted her women warriors, "drilled them" in war games, and conquered her "neighboring peoples." The more people she conquered and annexed, the more expert she became in military exercises. Fortune smiled upon her heroic exploits. Proudly she proclaimed a new title, having herself styled Daughter of War (the god Ares, or Mars).

This Amazon queen surpassed her contemporaries because of her intelligence and also because as a general she had proven her superiority. As was the custom with victorious commanders, she founded her own capital city, Themiscyra, at the mouth of the Thermodon River. In that city just south of the Black Sea coast, she had constructed a royal palace. Her principal occupation, however, was leading her highly trained warriors into battle. She finally conquered over half the coast of the Black Sea, all around its perimeter to the north, at the confluence of the Don River and the Sea of Azov. Her horsewomen thus gained valuable fisheries and subdued an area famous for horse breeding (and Cossacks). This great queen finished her reign heroically, for she died while personally leading a "brilliant" and doubtless successful military maneuver.

Per (matriarchal) tradition, her daughter succeeded her upon the throne of these Amazons. The new queen continued the

traditions established and brought to glory by her mother. She
upheld her laws also, going out every day to train her recruits.
She called up the girls at the earliest possible age, set them on
horseback, and made them practice martial arts to the full extent of their physical ability. For their entertainment and hers
she established superb festivals that went on for days in full
panoply of horse races, parades, and services to the war god
Ares, but especially to their Mother Goddess, the virgin Artemis of Tauris.

One of their last queens, if she was not their last, in fact,
was the warrior Penthesilea. She had been obliged to exile
herself from her home in punishment, some say, for an un-
intentional homicide. During her term of penance she had taken
service with Troy against the Greeks, at the end of the Trojan
War, which had already lasted ten years by that time. The
Trojan champion Hector was killed and dragged four times
around the walls of Troy, before she too fell under a blow
from Achilles.

The honorable death in combat of Queen Penthesilea dealt
such a blow to the remaining Amazons and to their society
that they began very rapidly to die out. Their race was exhausted by so many years of bloodletting. Their queens died
faster than they could give birth to descendants; "consequently in later times, whenever any writers recount their
prowess, men consider the ancient stories about the Amazons
to be fictitious tales" (#46, p. 37), argued Diodorus the Sicilian.

A ROSTER OF AMAZON PRIESTESSES

Name	Fate (when known)	The Accused
1. Alcippe	raped	Poseidon
2. Queen Antiope	abducted	Theseus
3. Arrhippe	raped	King Tmolus
4. Cleite (Kleite)	defeated in bat-tle at Troy, re-moved (like Aeneas) to Italy, founded a new city	

Name	Fate (when known)	The Accused
5. Dioxippe		
6. Eurypyle	slain	Hercules
7. Glauce	died	(a "wife" of Telamon)
8. Hippo		
9. Queen Hippolyte	raped, slain	Theseus
10. Hippothoe	raped, abducted	Poseidon
11. Iphigenia	sacrificed	Agamemnon
12. Queen Lampado	died in battle	
13. Queen Lysippe	died in battle	
14. Queen Marpesia	died in battle	
15. Queen Medusa	beheaded	Perseus
16. Melissa		
17. Queen Myrina	died in battle, buried on the plain of Troy	Priam
18. Queen Omphale	rewarded her slave Hercules	(wife of King Tmolus)
19. Pandaia		
20. Penthesilea	slain in battle, necrophily committed on her corpse	Achilles
21. Queen Thalestris	died in battle, had met Alexander the Great in Bactria, c.329 B.C.	
22. Zerynthia		

THREE AMAZONS

23. Queen Semiramis of Babylon,	who died a natural death, and became a "dove" after death	Medes and Chaldeans
24. Queen Tomyris of the Massagetae	(Scythians east of the Caspian Sea) who warned Cyrus that she would kill him, and who de-	Cyrus the Great

Name	*Fate (when known)*	*The Accused*
	feated him and drowned him head-down in a vat of blood (a death continued into King Arthur's day in Britain)	
25. Princess Rodogune (Rhodogune) of Parthia,	who survived a poisoned cup to wed her true love	Queen Cleopatra of Syria (the evil mother-in-law)

THE SYRIAN GODDESS

> "In every age man has had so lively a sense of his superiority over the other sex that any writer has always been sure to please him who fortified him in this view. Several Greek poets have essayed this task."
>
> Paul Decharme
> Euripide et l'esprit de son théâtre (Paris, 1905).

THE EYEWITNESS

An eyewitness account of Hieropolis, the Temple, and the Syrian Goddess as divinity worshipped in the second century was written in Greek prose by Lucian (Lucianus). This famous, ancient author of some eighty works is called *Samosatensis* because he was born in Samsat, or Samosata, Syria. He was well known in the second century as writer, critic, satirist, and lecturer far and wide in his world: from Asia Minor, Egypt, and Syria, to Italy and Gaul.

Most famous in the ancient world for its brilliant Phoenician civilization in such coastal cities as Tyre, Byblos, and Sidon, the Syria of Lucian descended from both the ancient Hittite and Egyptian empires, which often met in war around Damascus in Syria. It extended to Iraq, Jordan, and Israel. Samosata itself lay in northeastern Syria. Lucian was born, then, not far from the upper Euphrates River, which he mentions familiarly, and about fifty miles northeast of Carchemish. The temple of the Syrian goddess, which he describes, stood at the famous "Holy City," Hieropolis, presumably about twenty miles west of the Euphrates, and fifty miles north and east of Antioch.

De Dea Syria (Concerning the Syrian Goddess) is ascribed to Lucian. Eyewitness accounts of worship in any temple, much less in an ancient temple, seem to be extremely rare; they are therefore very precious. *De Dea Syria* is indeed rare and precious. It is even more than that, priceless, because it is the work of a well-known, much-esteemed author who was, in addition, a native of the area he describes, and someone who could not be mistaken about what he saw and heard. Not only was he analyzing his own homeland and its religious practices, but he was also doing so at the very outset of Christianity, very near the place on the road to Damascus where Paul became converted.

Lucian speaks from two points of view here, as an initiate himself into several ancient religions of the world, but also as an informed but objective spectator. Not only does he marvel at what he saw, but he also tells a story that struck him as extremely memorable. He does not preach, nor does he tell us why he felt that this story had to be told.

Without Lucian's text, which is believable as all eyewitness testimony is believable, we should have no idea of what went on in ancient temples. This work alone presents priestesses at work.

TOURISTS AT HIEROPOLIS
(THE HOLY CITY)

Nobody today would know the location of Hieropolis, this ancient Syrian city, whose temple was dedicated to the worship of the even more ancient Hittite Mother Goddess, were it not for a foreign tourist, speaking no Oriental languages, who told us in her diary that she passed through the ruins of what had been the famous holy city of Hieropolis. She was on her way from northern Israel, the Holy Land, via Antioch, to Constantinople, she wrote.

That kind and thoughtful lady was a French nun. Like so many of her contemporaries, such as the heroes from King

Arthur's courts in Scotland, known to us as Perceval and Gal-
ahad (Saint Samson), this wealthy and cultured French lady
nun wrote in Latin a book called her itinerary. As *Ethérie,
journal d'un voyage* (Etheria, Journal of a Travel) it was recently
re-edited in Paris (1971) by Hélène Pétré. She took her trip,
or made her pilgrimage, around the year 400, starting from
western Europe, and traveling all the way to Egypt, Jerusalem,
Jericho, Bethlehem, Nazareth, the Holy Sepulcher, to Mount
Nebo, and thence from the Holy Lands of the Old and New
Testaments to northern Syria. Thence, she took the long voyage to Constantinople where the British-born Empress Helena
Augusta, a great-grandmother of King Arthur, had encouraged her son to build a city named Constantinople after him.

Archaeologists of today have read *Ethérie* and have located
the site of Hieropolis at the ruins of modern Membij, says
Garstang (p. 303), "on a route from Aleppo to the junction of
the Sojur and Euphrates Rivers, now some fourteen miles distant." What Lucian saw and described minutely can still be
made out today at that spot, adds Garstang, who was another
scholar/tourist there.

Lucian's Account

The temple at Hieropolis came architecturally and spiritually
from earlier holy sanctuaries in Egypt. The Egyptians first
understood the gods and revered the gods, to whom they built
grandiose temples. In Syria at the city of Tyre, we have a temple to a very ancient hero whom the Greeks also worship under the name of "Heracles."

Hieropolis, however, is dedicated to our own ancient Mother
Goddess called "Hera." I am told, however that the real name
of this goddess is Europa, who was carried off to Crete, from
Tyre, by the so-called Greek god Zeus. The Phoenicians know
her story too, of course, but say Europa is not the name of the
goddess worshipped at Hieropolis. Perhaps she was the goddess Aphrodite, who was worshipped at Byblos. But probably
she is the goddess (Niobe) who weeps for the death of her
lover Attis, or Adonis. At Byblos, however, the dead god whom
they mourn is Osiris from Egypt whose head floats there from
across the sea every year. I saw it. They point also to a river

that flows red every year, from the blood of the slain Attis, but I ran that tale down and learned that the redness of the water was caused by blowing red sand upriver.

The temple at Hieropolis is the richest in the world. It is also the most holy, the most awesome, and worshipped every day by the greatest number of pilgrims. The treasures there are truly amazing. The gods speak. Their statues break out in sweat. The statues also move. Not only I, but many people too, have heard a great shout from within the temple, even when it was closed. I heard so many fables there, however, and so many stories told me by absolutely barbaric persons, as well as others that resembled Greek myths, that I have to discredit many of them. But I'll narrate a few.

This temple dated back to the great flood that once covered the earth, just as the Greeks also teach. Here at Hieropolis the earth split open then and formed a horrible chasm. Now there is some truth to that tradition because I saw the chasm, which today is no longer very deep. People there told me that twice every year the water rises until seawater reaches the temple. The fact of the matter is, however, that priests and worshippers from Arabia, from Syria, and from the lands to the east of the Euphrates (the Fertile Crescent) carry water to the temple. They pour it out there and it flows down into this deep chasm in the earth. They do this in memory of that Great Flood.

Another learned scholar told me that the name of the Syrian Mother Goddess was Rhea, who deprived Attis of his manhood. He therefore became a priest, which is a man dressed in women's clothes, as she ordered. This priest named Attis founded the shrine of the Mother Goddess at Hieropolis. You can see that she is the Mother or Moon Goddess. Firstly, she is drawn in her chariot by two lions, which symbolize Earth. She holds a drum in her hand. She wears a tower for her cities on her head. Her priests also castrate themselves in imitation of this sacrifice first made by Attis. Other versions concerning this castration seem to me to be more credible, I must say.

The temple at Hieropolis stood on a hill, but in the center of the city. It was surrounded by walls, one ancient and one modern. The entrance was on the north side where there were those two *phalli* supposedly erected by Dionysus. Twice each year a man climbs up on one of these pillars and sits there praying to the gods for the prosperity of Syria. A second explanation also given me there contradicts the first: that they climb up on the pillar in memory of the flood that swept over the earth and the salvation of those only who climbed the mountain. But I don't believe either one. I think otherwise. I hypothesize that they climb up there to worship Dionysus because the man or priest who climbs replaces the puppet that usually sits astride this huge pudenda. The fellow climbs up just the way a man climbs up the trunk of a palm tree, by means of a small chain. Then once atop, he uses the chain to haul up the gifts worshippers offer him, and also to pull up the supplies for his nest on top. When devout pilgrims shout out their names and offer gifts, they hear the pillar priest intone prayers for them. This surely is the most frequented shrine in the world. People come from all over.

As I said, the entrance to the temple is from the north, but like all such sanctuaries, the temple itself (or the high altar) lies to the east. Like temples in Ionia, the one at Hieropolis also stands on a platform. You go up by means of a wooden ascent ramp (?). Then you come to golden doors and the great hall itself. The whole interior space is solid gold, brilliant to the eye, blazing with light beams. Even the ceiling is made of gold.

Then at the same time you are aware of a heavenly perfume. The fragrance comes over you suddenly, the sort of perfume said to come from sweet Arabia. Up the steep climb it wafts you, lifts you to the shrine's inner hallway. You may believe it: this perfume stays in the folds of your garments, on your body, never entirely vanishes from your skin or your hair.

The inner sanctum, to your surprise, stands open, which is to say, it has no doors at all, and now the climb is no longer steep but gradual. There is another innermost sanctum within this, but reserved for priests alone, and even then, for only the head priests, who are entrusted with the organization of the sanctuary and the enactment of its rituals.

In the vast chamber stand statues of the divinities: the God-

Figure 4. Atargatis, the Syrian Goddess

dess Hera (but the Mother herself is there called Atargatis) and her Priest-King Zeus (but he is there called "Servant of Hadad," which is in the Syrian tongue spelled "Abd-Hadad"). Their two statues have been gilded with gold. She is attended by two lions, and he, by two bulls. The priest's statue is definitely Zeus, however. It is a recognizable iconography, copied by Greek artists over the centuries: same shaped head, same clothing, same seat on a bull-throne. I could not be mistaken here.

That is not the case for Hera. Her image seems a composite of traits and attributes of many other familiar goddesses. As I examine her statue, I see resemblances to Athena, Aphrodite, Selene (the Moon), Rhea, certainly to Artemis, also to Nemesis, and even to the Three Fates. For example, she holds Cybele's scepter in one hand, but her other hand holds the distaff of Arachne spinning her fatal spider's web. On her head she wears a towered crown for the many cities over which she presides as supreme deity. She is not naked, however, like a Greek goddess, but entirely robed and richly girdled like an Asian sovereign (see Fig. 4).

Magnificent jewels are set upon the gold of her statue. They glint and glow against the gold: they are emerald green, or dark like garnets, or flash red fire. Sardinians brought her onyx. Indians, Egyptians, Ethiopians, Medes, Armenians, and Babylonians brought her gifts of emeralds and orange hyacinths.

One thing about her is truly the most wonderful. Let me try to be clear about it. On her head she has a bright light. But it is not exactly fire. But it catches your eye as if it were ablaze. But it really is a gorgeous fire ruby called "lychnis," because it gives off light rays. Even in the blackest night her lychnis exudes red lights all across the dark sanctuary just as if there were thousands of individual candles all lighted. As soon as day breaks, then the red light dims until it appears to be only a bright flame.

There is a second marvel about her statue, which is true, but perhaps is not particularly believable unless you have actually been there and experienced it personally. First of all, you enter walking and you tend to keep walking until you are right up to the statue. Then you look up at her face. What a shock! She is looking down, straight at you. So you walk away after a while. When you turn around, however, from no matter what angle or distance, and look at her again, there she is looking straight into your eyes. If you try passing by her, in front of her, you find that her eyes follow you. It was not only I who experienced this. Others also fell under this spell, this powerful influence of the Mother Goddess. She holds you under her gaze.

A third image crowned with a golden pigeon stands between the two gods. The worshippers take the bird down to the water when they fetch their oblations for the chasm. This ritual is performed twice yearly. The "bird" symbolizes the deity herself, as does the white dove. They have neither sun nor moon goddess per se represented inside the temple since the two can be plainly seen out of doors, they explain. They do have a statue of Apollo as he was, robed and bearded. They sharply criticize the Greek representation of him. The priests carry the statue of the Priest-King on their shoulders. They also have a statue of Atlas.

Outside the temple stand many images of lesser gods, but the statue of Semiramis catches your eye. (She was the Babylonian Queen of the Amazons, who was not slain in combat but who died a natural death. After her death she became a priestess called "dove.") The reason is that she directs you with her outstretched right hand to look toward the statue of Hera in the inner sanctum.

While she reigned as Queen of Syria, Semiramis ordered her subjects to pay her divine honors. After she became diseased and was nearing death, she repented and withdrew her royal command.

The report that a lake adjoined this temple is correct, and there was still water in its center, enough in any case so that the raising of the sacred temple fish continued there. Curiously, some of the largest of these fish had learned to recognize their names and actually came to the shores when called. Some of these tame creatures had been ornamented with gold. One fish had a temple design upon one of its fins. This is a fact. I saw this particular pet fish with my own eyes.

The actual depth of this lake must be great, something like one hundred twenty feet deep. Of course, I didn't walk into it or have any way to measure it exactly. A stone altar rises above the water in the middle of the lake. Some people said they saw it moving in the water, and that it must float there unattached to the lake bed. My idea is that the altar is fixed or affixed to a column that they must have planted upright underneath it. The services before this altar occur daily. The altar itself is beautifully adorned with bright ribbons. Fragrant spices are burned on it, their perfume wafted on the breeze to the onlookers. Then persons wearing gold crowns swim out to the altar and there perform their ritual.

Other returns-to-the-waters take place there also. Great assemblies congregate on the shores of the lake. The first deity to be carried down into the waters is Hera herself. She must not allow her Priest-King Zeus to glimpse the sacred fish before she does. Were that to happen, all present would die, all at once. Then they bring down Zeus. He wants to see his fish before she can stop him. She bars his way. She stands up for her people. She confronts him and forbids him to approach her fish. She begs him to stop. She pleads with him. She has then returned to her birth in water, to herself a goddess born like Atargatis/Aphrodite in the sea. (This ritual combat is performed, like a pageant.)

Their most prestigious ceremony, which attracts the greatest
number of pilgrims, takes place on the shore of the nearby
Euphrates River. This is mere hearsay on my part, however,
for I never went there to see it actually performed. What I did
witness personally was the solemn return of the worshipper to
Hieropolis. Each person carried a jug of water from the river
called "sea." The jugs have remained sealed, however, all this
time. They were sealed with wax at the river.

The worshippers are met upon their return into the temple
precinct by Alectryo the Cock. Each person presents his jug to
the cock, along with a little money gift, of course, and the cock
pecks away at the waxen seal, pulls the string, and unseals the
water jug. Then each worshipper in turn enters the temple
and pours the water down into the chasm we talked about
earlier. That ends the performance of this rite.

They have an especially great fireworks celebration called
Bonfire, which inaugurates the first day of spring. This occasion calls for a great ceremony of sacrifice on their parts. First,
they cut down pine trees in honor of Attis, to whom the pine
is sacred. They set up the trees in the temple precinct and
then drive in their major sacrificial offerings: goats, sheep, and
cattle. Each beast must then be hung alive, as decoration, in
the branches of the pine. They complete its adornment by tying
live birds to the smaller branches. To trim the trees still further, they add ornaments of gold and silver. Then they carry
their replicas of deities in procession around this huge court-
yard. Suddenly they apply torches to the base of each pine. In
a flash all is ablaze. To ensure births, lush crops, and a wet
growing season, people have come from all over Syria, carrying to this fire their own effigies of their household gods. This
is their most important festival, shared equally by all. Persons
who have lost a family member in the last thirty days are, of
course, forbidden to participate. Only after this period of un-
cleanliness may they shave their heads and complete rites of
purification before attending a service there.

You might care to know what happens to a worshipper when
he arrives at Hieropolis. What he does first is shave his head
and his eyebrows. Then he sacrifices a sheep. There is some
divergence of opinion there as to which are the sacred animals

aside from goats, sheep, and kine, and whether or not the pig is sacred and worthy of sacrifice as a burnt offering. After the candidate has offered his sheep to the deity, he carves it, eats it, and puts on his head the animal's head and also its feet. Then he prays, guaranteeing that he will continue such offerings. There he purchases garlands to adorn the bald heads of his group of processants. Everybody has already bathed himself and flushed out his body with draughts of cold water. While he is so engaged at the temple, and however long that period may be, he must sleep on the bare ground.

Professional welcomers speaking the language and conversant with the customs of the various parts of the known world make it their business to greet individual worshippers, to band them together, and to instruct them in the rites, manners, expenses, and customs of Hieropolis. Certain persons prefer, for example, throwing their sacrificial offerings down from the temple platform so that they die in this way. Some even offer their children, whom they have tied up in bags. They declare these are not children of theirs, but calves. Every participant purchases a (souvenir) tattoo, either on his hands or on his neck. You can always tell a Syrian by these distinctive marks on his body.

At Hieropolis, as in certain areas of Greece, young persons are not allowed to wed until they have journeyed here and offered their hair to the deities. Youths also offer their first facial hair. Maidens, whose hair has been sacred since birth, have their locks cut, placed in precious or other caskets, and inscribed with their names. A maiden becomes a wife when she loses her virginity and cuts her hair.

When I was a youth, I journeyed there and offered my own hair at the temple. I saw the casket still there, with my name on it, this time too.

THE RITUAL

Note to the Reader

Ritual will mean here the story of Queen Stratonice as it was incorporated by Lucian into his account. He is repeating an-

P R I E S T E S S E S

other story he heard at Hieropolis. He puts her story in the middle of his eyewitness text or investigative reporting of what he did, saw, heard, and learned at that shrine when it was still a Mecca in the ancient world for thousands upon thousands of avid worshippers.

The hero of the story, whose name the translator Strong latinizes into "Combabus," is a well-known character in Sumerian religion, noted the later translators, Attridge and Oden. This "Kombabos," as they spell his name, was none other than the gigantic Sumerian "Humbaba," guardian of the Mother Goddess's cedar forest. The Goddess may be called Ishtar, or Rhea, or Astarte, or Atargatis; her lover is nonetheless recognizable as the same castrated Attis, or Adonis, or Combabus. He is to die.

What Lucian has given us, Attridge and Oden argue very convincingly, is a history of the various temples erected at this same site of Hieropolis. After one temple has been destroyed, by flood or by foreign conquest, another is constructed:

1. Destruction by flood. Temple rebuilt by Deucalion the Scythian (?), as evidenced by the "chasm," pouring of water, swimmers, and pet fish.
2. Destruction in war. Temple reconsecrated by the "dove," Queen Semiramis of Babylon, dedicated to her mother, Derceto the Mermaid, to whom fish are sacred.
3. Destruction by war. Temple reconsecrated by the Lydian Attis for the Mother Goddess Rhea, who had him castrate himself and put on women's clothes (shades of the Amazon Queen Omphale and Hercules!). The Mother Goddess is here renamed Rhea, but (like Niobe) she is drawn by lions, she beats a drum, and she wears a mural, towered crown.
4. Destruction by war. Temple reconsecrated by Queen Stratonice and her would-be lover Combabus.

The Story of Queen Stratonice

Queen Stratonice was the wife of the King of North Syria. Her stepson fell ill because he was in love with her. His physician found out the cause of the illness. He diagnosed it from several

. 62 .

symptoms: loss of appetite, acute embarrassment, depression, and listlessness. The disease was an unconfessed love that caused the afflicted youth also to suffer from poor vision, a high-pitched voice, unnaturally pale skin, and fits of tears.

The physician tested him by measuring his heartbeat. It rose only when his stepmother approached his bed. "He is madly in love," concluded the doctor, "or insane because of love." The patient's father begged the doctor to cure his son, at whatever cost, by whatever methods.

"It's not his fault," the father cried. "Show your worth. Never mind whose wife she is."

"But what if she's your wife?" the doctor inquired.

"What's the loss of a wife compared to the loss of a son?" the father replied unhesitatingly.

"He's languishing for your wife," the doctor replied.

So the king handed over his wife to his son, and also his crown forthwith, and departed. He went down the Euphrates River, where he founded another kingdom and named it for himself.

Queen Stratonice had already set about her own project, however, which was to build the Mother Goddess Hera a splendid temple at Hieropolis. Hera had warned her in a dream to do this. When the queen subsequently suffered a serious illness from which she eventually recovered, she came to her senses and asked the king to pay for Hera's temple. He had agreed. He gave her the huge sums required, and a regiment with which to build it.

The king had also instructed Combabus about his plans for this project. The young man was to escort the queen, protect her, perform the usual sacrifices required of a sovereign, act as commander-in-chief, in short, and as honorable ruler of the city. The youth protested, alleging his lack of years and experience, his fear of jealousy, and his uncertainty. The king consented to compromise only to this degree, that he would allow Combabus only a delay of seven days during which to settle his affairs and prepare himself.

Upon leaving his father's presence, the youth sank into even greater despair. He felt impending disaster about to crush him beyond reparation. He could see only one solution: he emasculated himself. He laid his pudenda in a golden casket, and embalmed it in the customary way. Then he entrusted the sealed coffer to the king, telling him only that it contained his most precious possession. The king affixed his own seal to it and had it itemized and stored by his treasurers.

Three years later the temple at Hieropolis, terminus of the journey made by Stratonice and Combabus, had been erected. Meanwhile she had fallen madly in love with him. People attributed her wild passion to the Goddess herself, whose command the queen had so blithely ignored in the early years of her reign, and which she ignored until she became ill enough to listen to divine ordinance. The harder she tried to hide her desire, the more she loved him.

Finally Stratonice decided to reveal her love to him in such a way as to safeguard her dignity. One evening she purposely intoxicated herself with wine, whipped up her courage, and rushed into his chamber. There she fell on her knees before him, threw her arms about him, and told him, "I love you, Combabus."

With a hiss of absolute repulsion, Combabus looked down at her in utter disgust. "Get away from me," he cried. "You're drunk."

The queen replied in kind, with threats of what she would do to him. That frightened him, for he believed her. Therefore he told her the whole story. He also showed her proof of it.

Queen Stratonice's passion then turned to affection. All the rest of her life she cherished her priests, who like Combabus had sacrificed their sexual organ to the Mother Goddess.

The priests at Hieropolis had followed his example and emasculated themselves upon taking her service. Therefore they were called "Galli." This name derives from the Gallus River in the northern kingdom of Phrygia whence all eunuch priests of Cybele took their name.

Conclusions

The story of Stratonice would originally have been enacted as a ritual performance in the temple of Hieropolis. Priests and priestesses doubtless shared the roles. The players were probably supported by music and assisted by means of appropriate sound effects like wind, waves, offstage voices, wailing women, hymns, moans of pain, and gasping sounds. The worshippers probably also saw real blood and too-real surgery. At the end of this harrowing experience all must have gazed upwards, enraptured as the mortal Queen Stratonice became, by extraordinary visual effects, the real golden goddess of Asia Minor, enthroned. Everybody would have been proud to recognize her symbols of majesty, surrounded by the aura of her revered motherhood. Every springtime she welcomed the rebirth of the earth and held her beloved lover/son in her arms.

EPHESUS

Ephesus disappeared, despite the fact that it was often placed first among the Wonders of the World, and then reappeared. Her priestesses reappeared with her.

Ephesus has to be called "she" in deference to her own native scholars, who are citizens of the Republic of Turkey. They say that the name *Ephesus* (or "Ephesos," in Greek) was originally the name of the Amazon warrior priestess who founded the city near her rich seaport and breezy valley.

The temple of Ephesus disappeared without a trace except for many chips of precious porphyry marble strewn over miles. Even pack animals balked at having to cross it. The landscape also changed so radically from erosion that the city of Ephesus is no longer on the coast of the Aegean Sea. Now it has no harbor at all. And the city was once, ages ago, flooded purposely with sewage by a conqueror to make the inhabitants move to a new residential site, which is the present Ephesus. Then, too, other conquerors hauled off the columns of Ephesus to build Hagia Sophia in Constantinople. Others set up their furnaces on the very stairs of the Artemis temple so they could burn the marble—marble that had been sculpted by the greatest artists of Greece—in order to extract lime, which is used to strengthen cement.

Passages in books about Ephesus had survived, however. Most important of these was the only ancient treatise on architecture; it was preserved and handed down from the Roman architect Vitruvius: *De Architectura Libri Decem* (Ten Books Concerning Architecture), dated about 40 B.C. His contemporary Strabo had also left a detailed description of the Artemis temple and its situation.

Ephesian priestesses were represented seated on chairs (or thrones), wearing boots with turned-up toes (Hittite), with faces like Sphinx (sphinxes), as if "watching combat" (p. 5). There were certainly "warrior priestesses" (Lethaby: p. 13 and Note #17). Friezes of combat, Heracles, Theseus, and the Trojan War dominated the final Artemis temples. Objects from Ephesus may be viewed today in the British Museum: lions and bulls as door guardians, the Mother Goddess as patroness of all wild animals, watchful and fearsome Gorgons leaning down once from the parapets, Magi from Persia (Iran) advancing with gifts, and lovely, winged Victories about to launch into flight. This temple at Ephesus, concluded Lethaby, must have been intended to celebrate the nativity of Artemis.

"In 1863," said the pioneer archaeologist John Turtle Wood, who was to ship his finds to London, "I decided to undertake excavations all about the valley adjoining the town of Ephesus in the hope of finding the remains of the Great Temple of Ephesus that Pliny and so many other ancient writers talked about and visited. Nobody had seen it since Rome, or since Vitruvius and Strabo measured it. Supposedly it had been buried under rubble and alluvial deposits over the centuries. There was then, above ground, not one trace of it. The area is so large that the task looked hopeless. Many people assured me absolutely," he said, "that this fabulous Temple of Ephesus had never existed."

For six heartbreaking years Wood found nothing but rubble. He sank pits from September to May each year. He suffered from winter rains, flood, exposure, illnesses, and near-fatal accidents during which Mrs. Wood stayed by his side, fed him, accompanied him on foot, and nursed him. When he could not dismount to climb down into the unshored pits, she went bravely down to report what had been uncovered in each.

The site had lain undisturbed for about eighteen centuries, Wood figured. Then in 1869 he jubilantly reported to the Pasha of Smyrna (Ismir) and to the trustees of the British Museum, who had funded him year by year, that he had found the outer wall, which had enclosed the various minor temples as well as the once huge, massive, towering Ionian Temple of Ephesus. That Great Temple of Ephesus, even so, lay a full half mile away, inside this outer wall, he was sadly to discover.

In April, 1869, Wood and his wife survived seven earth-

Figure 5. Artemis

quakes. The mice that year stole all his drawings and papers to eat and to make their nests. It rained so hard that all his pits caved in, and there were many injuries, for the ruins lay beneath sand that over the centuries had silted up the Ephesus valley and harbor. The perennial storks moved back as soon as each column was excavated, and built their nests on top of them. The railway tracks were cut by a flash flood. It was a season of disasters.

All these years Mr. and Mrs. Wood dreamed day and night of finding the cult statue of Artemis—the large statue that stood inside the innermost sanctum (see Fig. 5).

A Turkish official came calling on them one day, Wood remembered. Wood told the official (p. 175) "that this church was dedicated to the worship of a female, whose statue forty or fifty feet high was set up inside it. 'Ah,' said the Mudir, as if a new light had broken in upon him, 'they were *Protestants.*' I did my best to undeceive him. . . ."

In the season of 1871–72 Wood found fragments of a frieze that depicted Heracles struggling with an Amazon warrior and taking her girdle. In 1873 he finally found the temple platform (foundation). That year the aurora borealis was seen one night. The people in nearby Ephesus beat drums, shot off guns to drive away the monster in the sky, killed a cow by accident, and then settled down to eat it. The year was very lovely. Wood never tired of the gorgeous scenery there at the temple site—camel caravans against softly colored mountains. He measured the steps of the vast platform: 18″ of rise, 19″ of tread. There was an eclipse of the moon one night at about seven. Wood found the tympanum, which had an angle of 17 degrees. He painstakingly unearthed superbly carved lions' heads. He officially finished the excavation on December 31, 1873.

Using the measurements recorded by both Vitruvius and Pliny, Wood eventually measured the site:

Platform = 418′1″ × 239′4½″, 14 steps up to the peristyle;
Temple = 163′9½″ × 342′6½″, with two rounds of columns about the *cella* (70′ wide), 100 columns of the peristyle (36 of which were sculpted, reported Pliny; 27 of which were gifts of kings); each column 6½′ in diameter at the base, 55′8¾″ in height.

The frieze again depicted the major subjects: Artemis with Heracles and Theseus, but especially the Amazons. The high altar had been made by Phidias and Praxiteles, greatest of Greek sculptors.

The Great Temple followed the Ionic Order, Ephesus being in those days one of the twelve Ionic cities, or Greek cities of western Asia Minor.

The towering cult statue of Artemis stood in the inner sanctum, as Wood imagined. Strangely enough, art historians do not agree about what the statue represented. The most popular literary and traditional view is that the Asian Artemis was represented as a nursing mother with many breasts. According to that interpretation of her statues, she must have been called "many-breasted," or "multae mammae."

David George Hogarth, reporting for the British Museum in 1908, put it in none too genteel a fashion, as follows:

> The whole front of the figure from throat to waist is covered with pendant dugs, and the arms are extended from the elbow.

In other words, he suffered from poor vision and also from inexperience, being unable to differentiate a woman's breast from a dog's nipple.

Joscelyn Godwin of Colgate University in his book *Mystery Religions in the Ancient World* (London and New York, 1981) reported:

> Whether the curious appendages are in fact meant as breasts, justifying her epithet 'Diana multimamma,' or whether they have some other meaning, even the best scholars cannot decide. Are they grapes, eggs or the offerings . . . ? (p. 158)

In his essay "Ancient Ephesus" of March, 1987, Alexander Eliot wrote firmly:

> She stands stiff as a tree, encased in a sarcophagus of stony garments covered with carved animals . . . , plus a huge pectorial burden: an apron of dates that are often mistaken for breasts (p. 107).

The rounded objects that decorated the person of the Goddess Artemis may have been fruits, since breasts do not grow up to a woman's throat. And there is no need to think of Artemis as Diana, who later in Rome, because of the defeated Amazons, became fiercely virginal. As goddess of childbirth Artemis supervised and medicated mortal women, although she herself had forsworn both maternity and marriage.

The fruits that may so beautifully have adorned her person seem more probably the apples of the Other World, the golden fruits of the Hesperides, more appropriately figuring upon her gold or ivory-and-gold cult statue. If they were not gold, then they were crimson fruits. In Greece, to the Ionian Greeks who built that Wonder of the World to house her, the sacred fruit of Artemis-Hera was always the pomegranate *(Punica granatum)*. The objects originally represented on her chest, and mistaken for breasts, may have been pomegranates, which contain a several-celled, reddish berry. J. C. Cooper's *Encyclopedia of Symbols* lists the various cultures that associate the pomegranate with blessedness, fertility, plenty, springtime, and immortality.

Hogarth listed the attributes of Artemis herself as she was adored at Ephesus:

1. Birds (hawks, eagles, and other birds of prey, as among the Hittites),
2. Bees ("well-known connection"), i.e., priestesses,
3. Cicadas (or the devouring locusts, which a fertility goddess would have to appease); the goddess wore a cicada brooch,
4. Fly (probably also feared because of disease); she wore a fly pendant,
5. Snake (venomous, as seen by the triangular head, and therefore the asp),
6. Mammals (lions, and sacrificial goats, calves, rams, and bulls),
7. The Labrys, or double-ax of the Amazon warrior-priestesses, as in the Hittite Empire, Lydia, Crete,
8. The Crescent Moon (always a symbol of a goddess),
9. The *Cista Mystica* (a covered basket or *cista,* box, or casket containing the sacred utensils for the ritual, called "mystica," which designated these rituals or rites as secret),
10. *Astragali* (objects like bobbins joined together), playthings, says Hogarth, but they more probably were used like dice because the famous group of statuary made by Polycletus is called Astragalizontes, The Dice-Players. (Ancient personages are often represented or told about in myth as gaming, or throwing dice for their souls against Fate or Death. Such games and gaming were represented in Egyptian art.)

The famous cult statue of Artemis was not an ancient but an archaic work. The likeness, Pliny said some two thousand years ago, had been carved neither of stone nor of gold and ivory, like objects corresponding to this description but found elsewhere. The original statue contained a stone (meteorite?)

Figure 6. Priestess of Artemis

fallen from heaven, worn by Artemis inside her particularly
lofty, towered crown. Vitruvius and Pliny, who as Roman
tourists were independent viewers, agreed that the venerated
statue had been carved from cedar wood. Today's archaeologists also think the statue stood open to the sky. The *naos* of
the Artemis temple, then, would have been unroofed. Lethaby
calculated its doorway, facing the cult statue, was 14′ 9″ wide,
protected by a very large screen, probably cast of metal.

The Ephesus Gorgons who guarded Artemis, unlike Christian angels, were furnished with four large wings. Thus, they
recalled mainland Greece's other winged Artemises, whose large
wings grow from a beautiful woman's shoulder blades. The
winged figure of Artemis still signifies *victory* to the awed viewer
of today. Her military escort of flying, death-dealing Gorgons

sweeps ahead of her, very much like those at the most sacred temple of the ancient world: the shrine of the Delphic Oracle.

The "Victories" of Artemis closely resembled the Winged Victory of Samothrace, a statue so awesome that viewers come from around the world to stand beneath her golden beauty in the Louvre Museum of Paris. The French curators fortunately thought to stand their Winged Victory of Samothrace at the top of a pale gold staircase, where she seems about to take flight, wings spread over the viewer, soaring like her ancestresses from Asia Minor and Ephesus.

Artemis herself, as Diana, and her priestesses after her, preserved their maidenhood perpetually. In the Amazon tradition, they were horsewomen, mistresses of the fleet four-footed creatures, especially protective of the large beasts: the bear, boar, hound, goat, and deer. Thus, Artemis is often represented as standing between two stags, which were thought to be the wisest and the oldest of all creatures and were therefore emblems of the Druids. In her temple at Ephesus music delighted the worshippers; priestesses danced to the sounds of the lyre and the flute. Their chorus leader was the Highpriestess herself. Artemis then symbolized silver, calm, peaceful moonlight. As patroness of temperance, purity, and youth, she ushered in the springtime and made the flowers bloom in the bright grass.

Several myths of Artemis relate tales of her and of her sixty Nymphs from the ocean, her twenty Nymphs from the rivers, and her "children," who at age nine entered her temples for education as virgin priestesses.

One story tells how the goddess noticed the pregnancy of the priestess Callisto, who had been raped by Zeus. Callisto would have been hunted to death by the hounds of Artemis if Zeus had not lifted her and her son Arktos into the skies as the constellation Arcturus. Artemis was cruel upon occasion. For example, she loved to bathe in forest pools where unseen by human eyes she could listen to her creatures move about in the woods. One day when she had disrobed and was bathing alone in such a glade, she saw that young Actaeon, instead of respecting her privacy, was watching her. He had thought the goddess (priestess) unable to see him. He made a fatal mistake. She would never have allowed him, or any other bold youth, to brag that the goddess Artemis had shown him her nude body. Instantly she changed Actaeon into a stag. His own hounds chased him, brought him to bay, and tore him into pieces.

Tityus also, wrote Pindar in his "Pythian Ode IV," was "hunted down by the swift dart" of the goddess, which she shot from her invincible quiver. It was her warning to men that they should aim only at whatever loves they were worthy of attaining.

Sometimes the arrows she shot were merciful, as in the case of Corônis in Pindar's "Pythian Ode III." The young woman had unfortunately conceived a child out of wedlock. Rather than allow her to bring this ill-begotten child to term, Artemis struck Corônis down with a golden arrow. The young woman descended to the palace of Hades, God of the Underworld.

Another story of the wrath of Artemis tells how she and Orion went hunting together because she wanted to see if his boasts about killing monsters were true. The two of them were pursued by a gigantic Scorpion. Orion duelled with him, but in vain. Finding that neither valor nor steel enabled him to kill the monster, Orion broke off combat, leaped into the sea, and swam east toward Delos.

All the ancients knew the tragic story of Artemis when she went by the name of Diana, or Selene. This priestess called goddess looked down on earth one night to see the beautiful youth Endymion, who pastured his sheep on the slopes of Mt. Latmos, which rises in Caria, just south of Ephesus. Endymion had fallen asleep. The virginal goddess was moved by his great beauty. She stepped down to him, kissed him, and watched him sleep. Night after night she slipped down the skies to his side. After a few nights of this vigil she grew so pale and thin that finally she failed to take up her station in the dark sky. Seeing what she had done, Zeus offered Endymion a fair choice: death in whatever fashion he chose, or everlasting sleep coupled with everlasting youth. Endymion chose the latter. This is how and why Artemis began caring for flocks of sheep, protecting the young lambs from marauding beasts, and overseeing the breeding and lambing so that Endymion's wealth would increase without his superintendence.

In Italy Diana's unfortunate, doomed lover was the nameless *Rex Nemorensis,* King of the Wood. Always with drawn sword in hand, haggard and worn, this consort was allowed only a short lifetime. His successor had only to catch him asleep or unready. Mythology pictures him as an older man, a Celt with a drooping moustache. Wearing a wreath of oak leaves, which as not only a Druid symbol but also a camouflage in the forest, he warily peers out of a thicket. His wild, anxious face bespeaks a troubled sleep. His tenure is at most seven years. As he slew his predecessor, his successor will at any minute strike him dead—probably in the dark of the moon.

The woodland lake of Nemi—a "mirror of Diana" that attracted worshippers in the earliest days, even before the founding of Rome—lay deep in a volcanic crater among the Alban Hills. Some believed Artemis herself had built a sanctuary there. Others chose to think it had been built by Hippolytus, Orestes, or Orestes's sister, Electra.

In any case, these savage practices show how debased the worship of Artemis became as it spread into western Europe. One was very far, indeed, in Diana's shrine there at Ariccia, from the solemn, white splendor of classical Ephesus.

IV

EGYPT

"It seems probable that the Pyramids, which have already borne inanimate witness to the existence of their creators for nearly five thousand years, will survive for hundreds of thousands of years to come. . . . More than half of Egyptiac history is a gigantic epilogue."
Arnold J. Toynbee
A Study of History, Vol, I, p. 30 (New York and London, 1947).

PRIESTESSES, ERSTWHILE

Contemporary historians John Grahame Clarke and Stuart Piggott set the decline of Egypt as commencing around 1400 B.C., the destruction of Homer's Troy in the decade 1240–1230 B.C., and the collapse of the early Greek or Mycenaean centers of power (also as a result of the Trojan War) at around 1200. Sir Flinders Petrie, one of the most celebrated of Egyptologists, continued this question of chronology in his *History of Egypt* (Vol. III, p. 390): "Egypt had led the civilisation of the Mediterranean for all its youth of five thousand years and more. We must be grateful to it. . . ." Taking another giant step backwards we follow Petrie to the Egyptians themselves, who commence their own history with seven Divine Dynasties. Four rulers of Divine Dynasty I are mythological, and they are identical with the earliest Greek recollections of their past:

Divine Dynasty I (Seven Gods)
1) *Hephaistos* = Ptah   9000 years
2) *Helios*   = Ra   992 or 1000 years
   Sōs   = Shu   700 years

3) *Kronos*   = Geb   500 or 501 years
   Osiris   = Asar   433 or 450 years
4) *Typhon*   = Set (Seth)   359 or 350 years
   Horos   = Har   300 years

In Divine Dynasty II, which reigned for 1196 or 1570 years, and which was also prehistoric, we find again at least four names familiar in both Asia and Greece:

1) *Ares*   = Anhur
2) *Herakles* = Anpu
3) *Amon*   = Amen
4) *Zeus*   = Amen (Amon, Ammon) Ra

Petrie concluded that ten kings were said by the Egyptians to have ruled near Abydos before the establishment of the historical monarchy. The First Dynasty, according to Manetho's listing, consisted of eight historical rulers (c. 4777–4514 B.C.).

As far back as one can peer into prehistoric Egypt, one sees over and again evidence of a male solar worship as symbolized by the Eye of Heaven. In this ancient system of adoration the sun is customarily masculine, and is represented as an eagle in the sky, as a tawny lion on earth, as a wheel revolving across the zenith, as a deadly, golden scorpion, and as the black-armed, whirling swastika.

We begin to understand the opposite feminine pole: Mâ = Cybele = Atargatis = Artemis resting *upon* lions, *drawn by* lions, represented by doves and pigeons and other slow-flying victims of the lordly eagle. The bird of prey descends, having first stationed himself against the blinding Eye of Heaven. The solar worship of Egypt resembles similar cults in Phoenicia, Babylon, Plato's Atlantis, Mexico, Peru, and among the North American Indians. The chief Greek gods are clearly male sun gods: Uranus, Zeus, Helios, Apollo.

As for the Nile Valley, says G. Maspero in his *History of Egypt* (Vol. I, p. 178):

> Women did not hold equal rank with men in the temples of
> male deities; they there formed a kind of harem whence the
> god took his mystic spouses, his concubines, his maidservants,

the female musicians and dancing women whose duty it was to divert him and enliven his feasts.

Maspero sets the record straight by explaining that since in the Egyptian temples of such goddesses as Hathor, Pakhît, and Nît, priestesses "held the chief rank" (p. 178), they were so named: *hierodules* of one of these particular goddesses. *Hierodules* is Greek for priestesses, or holy servitors. He notes (p. 179) that in the city of Sais, by which time the chief priest had become a male, "women of the highest rank, and even queens themselves took the title of prophetess of Nît." In that city from the days of the Ancient Empire "the priestess of the goddess was of equal, if not superior, rank to the priest."

A description of a High-priestess of Isis—and such a priestess will be named Ast or Isis in the Twentieth Dynasty—comes from Lucius Apuleius, who was initiated as her priest. During his initiation the candidate Lucius saw the goddess, as impersonated by her priestess. He recounts her beauty in *The Golden Ass* (my summary):

> First I bathed in the sea seven times, as Pythagoras taught us. Then I called upon the goddess, naming her Demeter, Aphrodite, Artemis, Persephone, Isis, and Queen of Heaven.
>
> Her hair was long and heavy. A chaplet of flowers crowned her head, over which shone a full moon supported by vipers and sheafs of wheat. Her robe was multicolored: white, yellow and red. From left shoulder to right hip she was draped in a sash of gleaming black, tasselled, pleated, embroidered with silver stars and red-gold moons. In one hand she held a gold rattle; in the other, a golden bowl. Along its handle an asp hissed, ready to strike. She wore sandals of victorious palm fronds. Perfume from her body floated over me.
>
> "I am Mother Nature," she said, "queen of the living and the dead, world, heavens, seas, and underworld. Every people know me by their own name: Artemis, Aphrodite, Persephone, Demeter, Hecate, Mâ-Bellona. But in Egypt I am Queen Isis."

With her encouragement Lucius Apuleius confidently approached the end of his ordeals of initiation and undertook her priesthood.

Petrie gives specific examples of how this system of priestess and priest operated. His first example comes from Dynasty

XX (1161–1156 B.C.), during the reign of Ramessu VI, whose daughter was named Ast for the Goddess Isis. As illustrated by this stele of the High-priestess, found at Koptos, the Princess Ast, or Isis, was declared to be daughter to King Ramessu VI, who was then living, and to his Queen Nubkhesdeb, who was deceased. The princess was married, says the stele, to the High-priest of the god Amen. Her new title was "Divine Wife of Amen" and "Adoress of the God." The sacred asp, or viper, was worn by the princess as a symbol of her sovereignty. Usually, as here, the snake's head protrudes just above her forehead. It is called, again in Greek, the uraeus. This wedding of a royal princess transfers *de facto* the royal power to the priestly line, for, as Petrie explains, this wedding became a tradition because

> When the daughter, who wore the uraeus and was heiress of the kingdom, was married to the high priest, the priestly line became the rightful rulers (Petrie, Vol. III, p. 175).

From this stele Petrie was able to date the birth of the Princess Ast at 1176 B.C., and her marriage between 1160 and 1156 B.C., when her father died. She married Amenhotep, then aged thirty or forty. From this stele and the *cartouches* carved on the graves in the Valley of the Kings, Petrie was able to pinpoint the very years when the High-priests seized power as rulers of Egypt. There was a sad corollary: the "increase of priestly rule was accompanied by the decay of administration," which may be a rule of history (Petrie, p. 180). From the date of this wedding the High-priest controlled all revenues and assets of the kingdom, tax collection, treasures, treasuries, granaries, or all foodstuffs, and supreme command of the military.

Priestesses reenter the scene from the Ethiopian Dominion of Upper Egypt (c. 700 B.C.). There a royal daughter is named "priestess of Mut and Hathor," presumably at Karnak. She is praised in poetry as "a sweet of love, the prophetess of Hathor," and as "a sweet of love unto the king," her father. A representation of king and queen during a harvest festival at Karnak shows her shooting arrows, as a priestess of the deity. This King Taharqa's sister-queens were also High-priestesses (667–

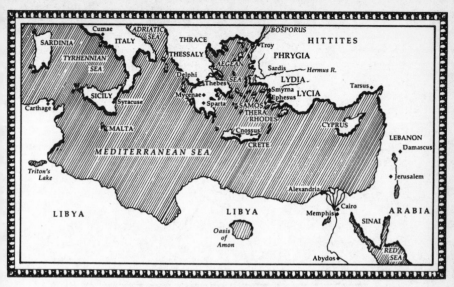

Map 3 Mediterranean Sea

560 B.C.), one in Ethiopia, and one in Egypt. The prominence of women during the century of Ethiopian domination of Egypt indicates, says Petrie (III, p. 308), its "general character."

The Ethiopians at about 625 B.C. had followed a matriarchal system for at least the last eight generations of queens, whereby the succession to their crowns was "rigidly in the female line" (p. 309) from this early history to a queen called "mistress of Kush."[1] Each of these queens was also a king's sister, so that, as Petrie concludes, "sister marriage" was their custom. An Ethiopian queen was also High-priestess at Napata, on the bend of the Nile before it reaches the Third Cataract, and there was another such Nubian High-priestess at Thebes. The queen on the Upper Nile was recorded on the stele of King Tanutamen as "mistress of Nubia," while the other queen at Thebes ruled Lower Egypt from that city and was called "mistress of Egypt." This Theban queen, High-priestess of Amen, dominated her realm and erected a series of chapels in honor of the High-priestesses. The Theban princess re-

---

[1] Kush (Cush) would be another name for Nubia, a region of Ethiopia on the Upper Nile, at the great bend of the River, between the Third and Fourth Cataracts, and to their north and east.

Figure 7. Dancers in the Temple

mained childless by the royal command of Psamtek (Dynasty XXVI) so that the succession would be continually renewed from queen-mothers of the north.

The sarcophagus of Queen Neitagert, who ruled as High-priestess of Thebes (c. 610–594 B.C.), is in the Cairo Museum. She was adopted at age fifteen, says her stele of red granite, which clarified her legal position as ruler. It also lists her personal possessions and vast wealth both in central Egypt and on the Nile delta, and also gives the amounts tithed by her many temples. She herself was daughter of a High-priestess, a "divine adoress," and also "born of the great royal wife" (p. 337).

Less than seventy years later the Persian Shah Cambyses, having had himself declared Lord of Asia, descended personally into Egypt with his army and Greek auxiliaries. The Persians and Greeks defeated the Egyptians after having slaughtered royal children, filled bowls with their blood mixed with wine and water, and offered it as drink to their Greek auxiliaries.

Dame Margaret A. Murray found that before the priestesses disappeared altogether from Egypt, four professions had been open to women: the priesthood, midwifery, mourning, and dancing (*Egypt,* p. 104). The royal priestesses, she said, entered this first profession when still young children. They began by learning sacred songs and dances (see Fig. 7).

The midwives too were honored, being in the sacred tradition of Mother Goddesses. Little apprentice-mourners are depicted raising their arms and shrieking along with the older women mourners.

The dancers began their training so early that they are depicted nude, and some are clearly being trained as acrobats.

The largest number of women were household servants, of course, or slaves.

SINGERS AND DANCERS IN THE TEMPLE

Reflecting upon religion in Egypt, Dame Margaret Murray in her book *The God of the Witches* (London and New York, 1931) concluded that decay had set in very early:

> Early priesthoods appear to have been largely composed of women; as the religion changed, men gradually took over the practice of the ritual. That is clear in Egypt, where the early inscriptions mention many priesthoods of women; in the later inscriptions women are only singers in the temple (p. 65).

Thirty-five years after Dame Murray, Arnold J. Toynbee agreed that while Egyptian civilization lasted for four thousand years, the last two thousand years demonstrated "not so much a living organism as an organism dead but unburied" (p. 30).

The popular religion centered about deified Pharaohs and the celebration of the dead King Osiris. In this ritual that occurred yearly in Egypt the dead Osiris was carried on a boat during his journey west, going into the sunset, actually into a cliff which led him via secret passageways into the Underworld. Thereafter, as the constellation Orion, the dead king passed nightly overhead, below the ecliptic. As new sprouts of grain he returned to life at the yearly Nile River flood.

One great feature of the popular religion inside Egypt, then, concerned this deified king. Throughout his book *Kingship and the Gods* (Chicago and London, 1948) Henri Frankfort spoke of this phenomenon: the deified king served to reestablish the natural order between mankind or earth and the kindly restorative powers of the universe. Were priestesses present at any of these deification ceremonies? The answer is yes.

The most famous deification ceremony performed in Egypt was that of the living king of Macedon, Alexander the Great (356–323 B.C.). After having reduced Syria to submission by conquering Tyre and Gaza, Alexander entered Egypt in 332 B.C. He declared himself ready to become a god during his lifetime. Two historians recorded the details. Priestesses were present. The deification occurred under the aegis of the sun god Ra, which was the official state religion. The Egyptians offered no resistance to Alexander. Priests rather than priestesses, however, were the ones who upon that momentous occasion declared the Macedonian conqueror a "native son."

No High-priestess officiated, or was present, during this ceremony, which was recorded by both Strabo and Diodorus Siculus. High-priestesses and prophetesses seem both to have disappeared from Egyptian temples between the wedding date of Princess Ast (1160–1156 B.C.) and the deification of Alexander the Great. Persons who blame Christianity or Islam for the banning of priestesses may not have a provable case.

Dame Margaret Murray's conclusion appears to be perfectly correct: by the time Alexander the Great stopped long enough in Egypt, before he could have himself accepted by Egyptian priests, priestesses served only as singers and dancers in the temple. In earlier days priestesses in oracles and in temples remained their chief source of income and a major tourist attraction.

One of the most renowned of all ancient oracles lay in Egypt, west of the Nile River, at a large oasis called—for its major source of prophetic utterance—the Oracle of Zeus Amon. This Libyan oasis, said Strabo, lies three hundred miles (470 km.) by land from Alexandria or Memphis, and more or less due west of those cities. Other travelers disembarking on the Mediterranean seacoast must go ninety miles (144 km.) due south to reach this Oasis of Siwah. Alexander determined to be deified there.

How can it be, Strabo wondered, that this far away from the

Nile Delta one finds seashells and large bodies of water in such a terrible desert? One sees waterspouts, geysers, wrecks of oceangoing ships along the route. How can it be? Ask the natives how the ships got there, and they say the vessels were vomited up out of the sand. Then when one looks around at the temples which surround this oasis in the middle of nowhere, one sees dolphins sporting on the columns. In a desert? The ancient geographers I use as my sources, concluded Strabo, say that there used to be a salt-water ocean here, where now it is endless sand dunes as far as the eye can see. The reason may be that the breakthroughs of the Inland Sea at Gibraltar and of the Black Sea at the Propontis lowered the level of the Mediterranean and uncovered what are now the sand dunes along Libya at the promontory of Cyrenaica.

The temple of Zeus Amon was built by the Egyptian King Danaüs, who fathered fifty famous daughters. In this country there is a large, triple-walled fortress enclosing king's palace, court of women, quarters for children and relatives, guardrooms and barracks, and in the center the sacred spring of Zeus Amon and his innermost sanctum.

Under large shade trees nearby stands the larger shrine to the god and a marvel. This is a very strange occurrence, a spring that varies in temperature according to the hours of the day, growing warmer as the night grows colder, growing colder as the daytime heat increases. The god's statue inside this second temple was carried in his boat on the priests' shoulders. When asked for an oracle, the god nodded his head or gave his answer in such a way that the priests, without any will of their own, lurched and bobbed accordingly. The worshipper by this procedure received a clear answer to his question. There were eighty priests in attendance.

A mass of girls and women process after the priests who bear the god's image. They walk along singing old, familiar hymns of praise to the god as they advance. This is the usual ceremony.

The priests led Alexander into this temple. An old man who had charge of prophecy addressed the conqueror. The priests lifted up the god in the boat, and he answered. Alexander asked these questions:

1. Am I to be called legitimate son of Egypt (i.e., heir to the throne)?
2. Shall I rule the whole earth?
3. Have I caught all my father's murderers and punished them all?

The answers were as follows:

1. Yes, you shall henceforth be my own son.
2. Yes, the god has granted you sovereignty over the entire world.
3. Yes, you have punished them all. Your father Philip of Macedon will be forever and ever invincible, as he was in life.

Alexander was so pleased to hear these assurances that he endowed the oracle very richly, and returned to Egypt and his plans for Alexandria.

Alexander the Great thus made peace with the priests at the Oracle of Zeus Amon. Like that god, the Macedonian emperor thereafter also wore splendid horns on his head.

Priestesses in Egypt often wore the horns of a cow in token of their reverence for the horned, or crescent, moon.

The gods and priests in Egypt and for centuries afterwards, even in northern Europe, wore bulls' horns, rams' horns, stags' horns, and the horns of oxen.

V

CRETE

"In my mind, Knossos and Zeus's birthplace join up with the myths of the Cretan palaces and their rulers: Minos, Ariadne, the Labyrinth, and that monstrous offspring of a bull and a woman, the Minotaur."

> Robin Lane
> "Into the Labyrinth,"
> *Departures* (May/June, 1988).

". . . the great antiquity of this (Minotaur) myth is astonishing but . . . there are many instances proving that historical reminiscences in mythical form lived and were preserved through centuries."

> Martin P. Nilsson
> *The Mycenaean Origins of Greek Mythology*
> (Berkeley, 1932).

MOON PRIESTESSES

The moon appealed to primitive peoples, it seems, more than it has ever appealed in historical times, except perhaps for the twentieth century. The theologian Mircéa Eliade put it this way:

> It is really only in Egypt, Asia and in primitive Europe that what we call sun-worship ever attained sufficient popularity to become at any time, as in Egypt, for instance, really dominant (*Patterns*, pp. 124–43).

The sun rises to great prominence. When history is on the march, we understand the appeal of commanders, heroes, conquests, kings, emperors, and armies. Curiously, the sun fails to offer the same old attractions to contemporaries. Now in the twentieth century we are devoted to the moon, to space travel, and we are repelled by the mystique of sovereignty. Eliade says the source of this mystique was the "patriarchy of the Indo-Europeans who came down from the north," bringing with them their adoration of Apollo, the Egyptian and Greek Helios. The Indo-Europeans and Apollo killed the dragons and suppressed "the matriarchal regime" of the Mediterranean peoples.

Neolithic Europe worshipped a Mother Goddess, as did Libya and Syria. Her white navel stone, or omphalos, can be seen at Delphi today. In Crete especially the moon was revered in the form of a triple goddess, mistress of air, earth, and sea.

A Libyan (African) population had migrated across the two hundred miles separating Egypt from Crete. Leaving the western delta of the Nile River, they brought with them the worship of their special Mother Goddess, Neith. The rich art of Crete, as it was first excavated and tabulated by Evans, shows many traces of those indigenous Libyan settlers: a distinctive hairstyle and attire, collared hunting dogs like the greyhounds of the modern Berbers, vessels with carved bulls fore and aft, fish ensigns, *tholoi* or beehive tombs, the cow that leads safely through the dread passage to the underworld, cloaked figures, the men wearing the *penistasche* or Libyan sheath. In front of their ears, both men and women wore long ringlets separated from the rest of their hair, long side locks that sometimes reached down to the waist. Their goddess, Neith, "Great One of the Bow," was figured by a bow, or a double bow, which was characteristically Libyan. As double bow, the design replicated the Libyan sheath of the men. The Libyan tribes were called "Nine Bows." Their art also featured the pet household snake they brought from the African mainland to serve as an "averter" of earthquakes.

After decades of study and excavation at Cnossus (Knossos), ancient capital of Crete and site of its labyrinthine palace, Evans concluded that Cretan culture represented an engrafting of this old Nilotic people, magnificently skilled in arts and crafts, upon the indigenous Cretans. The elegance of the women's dress has caused these resultant Minoans to be called the "Parisians" of the ancient world. The women wore long dresses with flounced skirts, tight waists fitted to the figure, puffed sleeves, dainty shoes, complicated coiffures of curled ringlets, and golden jewelry. The bull vaults of their athletes, who literally grabbed bulls by the horns and vaulted over the charging animals, are still a wonder of elegant performance and daring. The bodies of their athletes are quite distinctive: they are tall and lithe, with slender, flat bodies, very broad shoulders, long arms, tiny waists (certainly about 20″ or less), and muscular thighs. Athletes wore red-and-green costumes.

The celebrated paleographer, John Chadwick, who with Michael Ventris deciphered the Cretan linear scripts, theorized that the Mycenaean or earliest Greeks from the mainland of Greece conquered Crete around 1450 B.C., give or take fifty years. By 1300 B.C. the Mycenaean cities were in full development. Their myth of having to pay a human tribute of youths and maidens to Crete, and of sending Theseus, the father of Athens, to defeat the son of King Minos duplicates such a conquest. The mystery of how Crete fell and why this sea kingdom should so suddenly have collapsed, as did the supremacy of Our Lady of the Labyrinth called "Mistress" or Potnia, has never been solved.

Knowledge concerning Crete has been acquired bit by bit, largely by means of long and patient archaeology. John Chadwick protested this means: "The difficulty of interpreting the dumb finds of archaeologists is nowhere greater than in the field of religion," he asserted.[1]

The evidence of tablets deciphered by Chadwick and Ventris (1956) does prove that there were priestesses in Crete as well as in Mycenaean Greece:

"slaves of the priestess"—p. 124;

"a priestess of the Winds at Knossos"—p. 128;

"at Pylos (Greece) . . . (frequent references to) the priestess"—p. 128;

"a priestess . . . in the service of Potnia (Mistress, Our Lady)"—p. 128.

[1] *The Mycenaean World.* Chapter VI ("Religion"), p. 84.

Potnia (Chadwick, 1967) was not the Greek vegetation goddess Demeter, but the goddess of "Knossos," called "Our Lady of the Labyrinth" (p. 125).

Aside from Potnia, mythology does at least provide a king's list of *Dramatis Personae* for Minoan Crete (Gayley, pp. 488, 523):

			Generation
Zeus = Europa (Hellotis)			
Minos I	Sarpedon	Rhadamanthus	#1
Lycastus	Helios = Perseïs		#2
Minos II = Pasiphaë	Circe Aetes = Hecate		#3
	Medea		#4
Crateus Phaedra	Ariadne (ante 1400 B.C.)*		#5
(m. Theseus)	(m. Theseus)		
Atreus = Aërope			#6
Clytemnestra = Agamemnon	Menelaus = Helen of Troy		#7

Whereas a queen priestess and the cult of a Mother Goddess ruled in the first generation under Europa, called Hellotis or "willow" from that medicinal shrub and tree sacred to the Mother practicing medicine and specializing in the woman's ordeal of childbirth, only subsidiary and vestigial traces of the priesthood of women survived during the Trojan War six generations later.

Under Potnia and other early priestesses of the moon, even the calendar was lunar: seven (or a multiple of seven) full moons to the king's death, twenty-eight days to the month (named for the moon), three hundred sixty-four days to the year. The moon goddesses and priestesses were usually triple, according to what was perceived as three distinct phases of the moon: crescent, full, and gibbous. (Actually the moon in each month orbits, always eastwards, through six phases: first quarter, full, third quarter, crescent, new, and crescent. The full moon is considered fourteen days old. If the ancients arrived at their figure of twenty-eight days because it is a multiple of seven, or because by observing the stars as reference they arrived at the month of twenty-eight days, they calculated incorrectly. The moon actually requires twenty-nine and one-half days in which to complete its orbit around the earth, which has itself moved about the sun during that period of time. Our own calendar does not follow the twenty-seven-and-a-half- or twenty-eight-day month, which is star-based, or sidereal, but the synodic or line-of-earth-and-sun month of twenty-nine-and-one-half days. The first calendar was calculated from three phases, however, which were later altered to four phases by Babylonian astronomers.)

The full moon represented the goddess on earth, and the first woman. She was called Queen of the Night, as in Mozart's opera *The Magic Flute*. The moon represented the beauty and magic of women. According to F. M. Cornford, the classical scholar and translator of Plato, the moon also was symbolic of prophecy, time, destiny, and the Three Fates. Thus, in most ancient times lunar deities were triune: Erinnyes, Moirai, Gorgons, Nemesis, Norns, Walkyries (who also have their opera), and Roman Parcae.

Both Robert Briffault and Marina Warner noted how the Virgin Mary, Star of the Sea, was closely related to the earlier Cretan and classical goddesses of the moon. Warner says:

> The moon has been the most constant attribute of female divinities in the western world, and was taken over by the Virgin Mary because of ancient beliefs about its functions and role, which Christianity inherited.

The parallels found by students of mythology between lunar worship in Crete and all over the world are not only striking but startling: ancient Greece (Hecate and Medea), ancient Germany (Harek), ancient China (#2 of the 12 emblems of the Empress), Egypt (Min), Europe (Oestia or Easter, goddess of spring), Scandinavia (Freyja), Teutonic (the Triple goddesses again: Holda, Harke, and Harfa), American Indian ("the wrinkled, old Nokomis nursed the little Hiawatha"), as among the Hottentots, Buddhists, Hindus, Celts, but most particularly among the Maya of Central America. To them also the White Rabbit, which sits in the arms of the crescent moon, is sacred to the moon goddess Ixchel. Like Clytemnestra and Penelope, Ixchel spins and weaves, or holds the rabbit in her lap. Worldwide, it would seem, the Easter Rabbit lays or brings the Easter Egg. "Lady Rabbit" is the name of the Maya queen.

That frightening representation in Mayan art as shown and explained recently in *The Blood of Kings* stands in complete contrast, however, to the loving word picture painted by Lucius Apuleius about 155 A.D. He had traveled widely in the Mediterranean basin, studying mythology. In his *Metamorphoses* he describes a full moon rising from the sea.

It is a magical hour as the Moon Goddess herself slowly rises out of the waves. She is the only true sovereign of all people everywhere, a majestic and a powerful ruler, he says. She shines as she rises, casting her beneficent spell over all creatures alike, savage or gentled, over all inanimate nature as well. All she surveys are given a new lease on life. As she rises and sets, the moon orders the circadian rhythms of all life forms, of all bodies on earth, or in the heavens, or under the deep waters of the sea.

The Goddess is known, Apuleius says, as governess of the rising sap in the trees, as bringer of rain in times of drought, as regulator of flood waters, as the moist and pallid "star," and as queen of the stormy waves, *Regina Undarum.*

Why has it been, considering this ancient prominence, asked Havelock Ellis (Cambridge, 1929), that when three thousand women are recorded in early Christianity they had by that time become only followers? The answer can hardly be physical, he replies, since men show "no relative superiority of brain-mass," with perhaps some slight superiority being "on the women's side," and when the nervous system appears to be about the same in either sex. It is well known that women fought like men, from Australia to Europe, to Africa, and to Asia. They are often the same size as men. As primitive carriers they were stronger than men. They domesticated animals, and were primitive architects, agriculturists, industrialists, potters, brewers, and doctors.

To primitive woman the moon was always the "measurer" *(mensis)* of recurring cycles, absent only three days each month, and reborn as a new crescent on the fourth day. Thus, artists show the moon priestesses of Crete near the commonly understood symbols of the moon: the spiral, the pearl, the hibernating but resurrected bear, the snail which draws in its horns, the frog croaking to announce rain, plants which die down and lie dormant until spring, the serpent which guards the

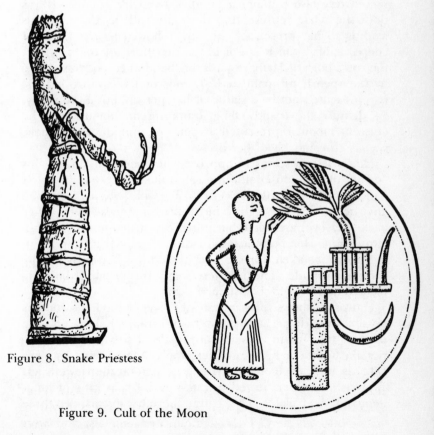

Figure 8. Snake Priestess

Figure 9. Cult of the Moon

Fountain of Youth, and the other one which must be looked
for because he stole the plant of immortality. The young Cretan moon goddess, in commemoration, holds a poisonous snake
in each hand (see Fig. 8).

The worship of the moon at a characteristically small shrine
in Crete shows a priestess with a raised hand, her five fingers
touching the five palmate leaves closest to her. The five here
probably symbolizes the Goddess, as does the open hand. This
seems also to be a portal shrine with one high, open, and sacral gateway; such shrines are described frequently by Evans
for Mycenaean and Cretan Pillar and Tree Cults.[2] Here the
sacred tree also contains a number symbolism (5 - 7 - 4), as
does the pillar representing the deity with its three portals
leading to her presence. They are followed by the "horn of
consecration," which is not the curled horn of the ram, but
the cow's horn of Hathor or Isis, or the Mother Goddess. Thus,
by the open hand, palmate leaf, and cow's horn the Goddess
is represented not by a statue of her person, but aniconically.
As divinity she is indwelling, omnipresent, ubiquitous. The
crescent moon, represented as perhaps four days after new,
speaks affirmatively of her presence.

Her priestess seems to approach her personal shrine, this
"pillar" of her household, in a calm, meditative way. Her left
hand remains effortlessly close to her side. She is not going
anywhere, with her right hand folded in repose behind her
back. Her eyes are open, but unseeing, turned inward in contemplation. Her body leans forward slightly from the waist.
Her torso is naked, for the Cretan Goddess herself is usually
completely nude. The priestess wears the usual, elaborately
pleated and draped, bell-shaped skirt.

Figure 10 shows three priestesses as elaborately gowned as
possible, wearing what appear to be wrapped skirts or wide
pajamas that fall in tiers and are made of stiff brocaded fabrics like taffeta or heavy, gnarled wools. Again their torsos are
bare, as are their feet. Two young women on the viewer's left
approach an older, seated priestess. They bear gifts of long-
stemmed water plants. The central figure has just handed three

[2] See Sir Arthur Evans. "The Mycenaean Tree and Pillar Cult," *Journal of Hellenic
Studies*, XXI, 1901, pp. 99–204.

Figure 10. Cult Scene with Priestesses

florets to the older woman, who is resting comfortably on the ground under a tree heavy with fruit. The third priestess holds in her raised left hand the instruments of the ritual, and in her right hand two stems of another water lily in bud. Ripe figs on small leafy branches decorate the scene on the left.

The central object is the sacred *labrys* or double ax of Minoan Crete. This symbol remains unclear in its meaning, but since at the center of the scene it catches the eye and holds the viewer's attention, it may be an aniconic representation of the absent Mother Goddess herself. Probably the three tubular florets without exerted stigma or stamens are lotus buds that denote the virginity of the priestesses themselves, potentiality undeflowered, in other words. The long stem of the sacred lotus reaches far down into the earth and through the water, like an umbilical cord. The scene actually depicts five priestesses in all: three mature women as central actresses, one small child picking fruit, and an old wizened woman in the central background. Above them all shine the full-rayed sun of summer and the moon in her last quarter. They are separated from earth and the elegant priestesses by a wavy band of cloud.

Figure 11, "Dance of Priestesses at a Sacred Tree," as depicted on a gold ring, is described by George D. Thomson in his book, *Studies in Ancient Greek Society* (Chapter VII, pp. 252–53). Although the gold ring was found at Mycenae, it closely resembles a Minoan cult scene. Thomson notes that the tall priestess on the left is bending over the altar "in an attitude of lamentation, while another is dancing. . . ." To their left is a tree "which a male acolyte is bending down" so the priestesses can pluck the fruit. The costumes of the three figures are drawn very tight around extremely small or wasp waists; the outfits are extremely elaborate in workmanship and ornament. The acolyte must be an accomplished athlete to be able to rotate his waist and torso in a quarter circle. The three figures seem to stand on the smooth top of a wall or a raised surface made of small stones laid end to end. The arc of a moon looms above the elegant coiffure of the dancing priestess.

Figure 12, "Descent of the Goddess," has been described by both Thomson and Evans as three priestesses dancing in a field of lilies, that flower being especially sacred to the Moon Goddess Britomartis of Crete. The lily blooming in branches, as here, denotes virginity and like the more popular lotus connotes the purity and sweetness of spring. It later came to symbolize the Virgin Mary and Sainte Jeanne d'Arc. The priestess to the right of the descending goddess seems to be holding precious small objects, perhaps castanets. The two on the right hail the goddess as she drops down toward their upraised arms.

These nameless women give some idea of Minoan ritual and point the way toward other Minoan women, or women connected to Crete, and openly named in myths: Europa, Pasi-

Figure 11. Dance of Priestesses. Sacred Tree

Figure 12. Descent of the Goddess

phaë, Ariadne, Phaedra, Circe, Medea, and Helen of Troy.
They were doubtless all queens and High-priestesses.

Europa was abducted by King Minos. Medea was reportedly
as wicked as a princess could be, and Helen of Troy is harshly
castigated by twentieth-century historians.

Both the Cretan princesses, Ariadne and Phaedra, were in
hell also, the first having been done to death by Artemis even
though she had not lost her virginity to Theseus, according to
one of several accounts of her possible guilt. Phaedra had been
sent down for being the evil stepmother *par excellence* of Hippolytus. Eriphyle was doomed because she had sold her husband for gold.

In his *A Study of History* Arnold J. Toynbee affixed a note:
"The Monstrous Regiment of Women."[3] Women's work, he
wrote, has caused over the ages the great wars and catastrophes of history. The first case in point is that of the Trojan
Prince Paris who eloped with Menelaus's wife, Helen of Troy,
he said. Women are "undisguisedly . . . mischief-makers." We
see their malevolence as they goad men into fratricidal strife.
Rather than resorting to brute force, women use persistence,
vindictiveness, implacability, cunning, and treachery. Women
are not heroines. They are villainesses. We know about histor-

[3] See the Abridgement by D. C. Somervell of Volumes VII-X (New York and London,
1957), pp. 142–43.

ical women and their grim adventures: Goneril, Regan, Lady
Macbeth, Brunhild, and "Fredegund."

None of the above is absolutely documented as historical, he
might have admitted, except Queen Frédégonde, sixth Queen
of the Franks. Goneril, Regan, and Lady Macbeth are largely
products of Shakespeare's imagination. Brunhild committed
no crime, but was much victimized by her conqueror, somewhat like the ancient Atalanta, a loser in struggles against rapists, i.e., male warriors.

Like the other women who were born into the dynasty of
King Minos of Crete, Helen of Troy was probably also a Moon
Goddess. She was probably glad to go to Troy where women
were not despised, inferred Euripides in *The Trojan Women*.

THE SACRED MARRIAGE CEREMONY

The "notorious regiment of monstrous women" had fortunately been studied by a renowned, classical scholar from the
University of Lund, southern Sweden, in 1925. Martin Nilsson's book on religion in Minoan Crete and Mycenaean Greece
throws considerable light on the mysterious acts and unre-
corded fates of our major criminals, if criminals they were:
Ariadne and her sister Phaedra, both abducted by Theseus
(though they are accused of begging him to kidnap and rape
them).

Ariadne's manufactured scenario accords with that of her
younger relative Medea. She too was said to have betrayed her
religion and her home to elope with their invader, Jason. If
so, why did she later kill their children and to save her life
escape from Corinth? As John Chadwick warned, "plausibility" must be a final criterion against which these old, familiar,
human stories are judged. It seems the only women who kill
their children do so in extreme anguish, when they are fixated
upon the mistaken idea that they are saving the little ones from
a worse fate.

The Mother Goddess known in Asia Minor as Artemis, he
argued, was of Minoan origin. In those more distant times she

was an older and a ruder Artemis found in that wilderness of rugged peaks, deep forests, huge caves, and wet meadows. Her priestesses were wild women from the woods, half naked, savage, and orgiastic. We should not judge them as we would judge a civilized woman. Priestesses were accompanied by wild beasts which they had domesticated, stags, perhaps dolphins and even lionesses, and certainly goats. In those days Artemis, called Eileithyia, faithfully attended women in childbirth.

Ariadne was the same—a partially savage goddess whose yearly cult on Naxos (where the Greeks said Theseus had abandoned her without raping her) was that rare ceremony for a princess: a vegetation myth telling how the goddess died yearly and descended from her sacred tree into the underworld. In the original Minoan ritual Ariadne hanged herself from a tree. This was the salient feature of her worship.

Helen of Troy, who had two temples dedicated to her at Sparta, and who was there worshipped as a divine being, probably did flee to Rhodes at the death of Menelaus. She too is said to have hanged herself from a plane tree. Dolls are to this day hung on trees in her memory. In her case the dolls commemorated her death. A Greek sculpture shows her body with the fillets still dangling from her wrists as per the hanging ritual. Zeus punished Hera in the identical way by hanging her from fillets tied to her wrists. Not only was Helen's a family of tragic women. The Greek world they inhabited regularly turned women's lives into tragedy. There are no happy women in Greek literature.

Neither Calypso, with whom Odysseus lived for seven years and had three children, nor Circe, whom he persuaded to stop changing men into pigs, acted badly towards the Greek survivor of the Trojan War. In fact, Calypso let him continue his journey, helped him build his ship, and instructed him concerning the dangers he would encounter and the ritual he must perform in the Underworld. Books continue to tell it otherwise, that Odysseus was "detained" for seven years until he tired of sexual relations with a particular woman. Circe purified Odysseus, as she had done for both Jason and Medea. And yet her island sanctuary of Ogygia, a navel of the sea, was

surrounded by *alder* trees, or was a *Champs Elysées,* therefore
an abode of the dead. Alders always surrounded ancient burial temples.

These goddesses represented two of the innumerable the-
ophanies of the Mother Goddess, concluded Mircéa Eliade in
Patterns (1958). That was Odysseus's real purpose. Each priestess lived at a holy center, an *omphalos,* either of the earth, which
was Delphi, or of the sea. There grew the Tree of Life, which
reinvigorated the worshippers. There also were one or several
holy springs where the worshipper could undergo therapy in
order to obtain from the priestess either youth, health, immortality, knowledge, wisdom, or burial.

Ancient art represents the scene: a priestess beside the navel
stone, under a sacred tree, beside the spring and a vine. The
vine and naked priestess represented knowledge. As the Sibyl
told Panurge in Rabelais's *Fifth Book:* "Drink." The Sibyl's cos-
mological emblems identify her: stone axes, the sun, *always the
moon,* a throne, an altar, a sacred tree. At the sacred center,
and nowhere else, is found regeneration.

Thus encouraged by the plausibility of the arguments presented by great scholars, who were able to rise above sexuality
alone as the major moving force in the world, we arrive now
at a stumbling block. This involves the queer case of Queen
Pasiphaë, whose story most people find repugnant. This queen
of Crete, who has gone down in history as having had sexual
relations with a bull to whom she bore the Minotaur, a monster that was half bull and half man, was actually the mother
of Zeus Amon, whose Oracle was in Egypt.

Evans saw Pasiphaë as the Great Mother in person while she
reigned as Queen of Minoan Crete, and wife of King Minos
II. As child, as consort, as matron, the High-priestess was
dressed to resemble the Mother. She wore doves on her head
and a tiara. She wore on her shoulder a sacral knot made of
fabric, like the rosette or knot of tartan worn today by a clans-
woman of Scotland, the two falls below the knot dropping forward over the torso if the woman is a chieftainess or wife of a
chieftain, but falling over her back if she is not noble. She
wore the usual patterned and bell-shaped skirt. Rising from
earth she often wielded the double ax. Sometimes also she held

an anchor, which indicated her protection of mariners, like the medieval Madonna, Mistress of the Sea.

As Great Mother, Pasiphaë was also wreathed with snakes to show herself as Lady of the Underworld. She sacrificed the sacred *white* bull to the Lord of the Double Axes. This was a red libation.

The bulls entered the arena in a ring at what Evans called a "flying gallop," but the actual sacrifice occurred, said he (after having excavated and studied the drainage), on the floor of the Royal Villa. The earthshaker delights in bulls, said Homer (*Iliad*, XX). Earthquakes result, it was conjectured, by a huge bull roaring under the earth. He tosses his mighty head and bellows as if a gnat had stung him on the muzzle. The stucco reliefs of bull-grappling may be seen painted in the Middle Palace at Knossos. The bull gallops in, head held high as at a Spanish or Mexican *corrida*. A dark-skinned male athlete in a loincloth vaults over the animal's head. Women votaries process. They are fair skinned and also naked except for a loincloth. Their hair streams down like beads on a string. A girl athlete watches for her chance and then reaches for the bull's horns and somersaults, landing on her feet behind the bull. Then another athlete grasps one horn and vaults from right to left over his forequarters. Pliny said that at some time an athlete, seizing one horn and the muzzle, would vault and break the bull's neck.

As far as your Minotaur is concerned, concluded Persson, this creature reputedly half man and half beast "is to be considered simply as the priest-king, Minos—this is not a proper name, but a title like that of Pharaoh in Egypt—enveloped in the ritual cult dress, the bull's hide, and officiating at the sacrifice in honor of the beast" (p. 98).

The moon is Queen Pasiphaë, who wore horns on her head also, but pointing down, not up. She was the lady god, whose name "Pasiphaë" means "All-Shining," "Shining-for-All." She too was naked and also therefore "Visible to All."

The French archaeologist Charles Picard saw it somewhat differently. Pasiphaë's bull would represent Uranus, God of Heaven. Her horns would symbolize the crescent moon as Isis, Heavenly Cow. Her veil would be the clouds. The Libyans and the Pharaoh Mykerinos, too, had their royal daughters buried in gilded, wooden cows·for the goddess Hathor. Lights and incense were burned before these coffins in the royal city of Sais because the sacred kine preserved the bodies after death. So Pasiphaë was doubtless at some time after death also entombed inside a cow.

No such explanations will be accepted, the great psychologist Ernest Jones (1949) would have said. Scholars will still say Queen Pasiphaë had intercourse with a bull. They will still say that such a monster, half bull and half man, was born from this Minoan queen. As Jones explained it, *"One of the world's commonest beliefs is universally held.* Sexual intercourse takes place between mortals and others, such as supernatural beings" (p. 58).

The Minotaur has always been, for those immersed in folklore and hung up on old wives' tales, not a man but a supernatural creature, part man and part bull.

Authorities in comparative religion and mythology, such scholars as Mircéa Eliade, Theodore Gaster, and Sir James Frazer took a wider view of this story of king, queen, and Minotaur. What the story amounts to, they agreed, was a ritual: the rite of the Sacred Marriage. It was performed in highest style all over the ancient world whenever a general reinvigoration was required. The bridegroom's role was enacted by the king-priest whose bride was the queen-priestess.

This ceremonial wedding restored fertility to the land and the sea, and to animals and people. In Greek it is generally termed *hieros gamos,* and the consummation of the marriage, in Latin, is *connubium.* The bull and cow, the former to be sacrificed and used as a general feast offered to all comers, were easily understood symbols of fertility.

Gaster says this *connubium* and ritual marriage enacted like a modern pageant, dramatized parade, or carnival, were purely economic measures designed to galvanize or "re-vitalize the community resources." The mysteries were danced out as the chorus chanted. The dancers meanwhile circled about the royal couple. The chorus sang as acrobats whirled on a checkerboard floor of black-and-white squares. The actual coronation took place, Cretan coins suggest, within the maze, which was usually designed as a hollow square, with one entrance only, facing the east.

Saintyves in Paris before 1908 had read of such rites as described by missionaries in the field. Tribes who considered themselves descended from a totem animal, such as a bull, considered these beasts avatars of Zeus. The families enclosed themselves, each separately killing the animal at a set time, and eating it. The rite was communion, the most ancient of sacrifices. It exorcised sterility by absorbing into the bodies of the community the totem's magical powers. Brides were fed the animal's testicles. Children born later were considered reincarnations of the totem (King Arthur = the bear). Ovid understood it this way: the Egyptian cow was a woman first, then a cow, and finally a goddess. Perceval presented the iconography of the descending dove.

Zeus pursued Nemesis during a sacred marriage ceremony. She fled from him. When he drew close, she turned herself into a goose. As Mother Goose she laid the awaited egg. Her fifteen temples stood near Lake Moeris, just at an entrance to the Underworld. Geese were sacrificed by the worshippers there. On their way out, some enterprising person probably sold the others a book called *Tales of the Mother Goose*, which is truly an ancient book.

Sir James Frazer thought that the legend of the sacred wedding reflected a union of sun and moon, and that it was enacted as a solemn rite by the king and queen of Cnossus. They wore the mask of bull and cow respectively.

· VI ·

THE GODDESS HERA

*"Also the old female goddesses, dating from matriarchal times,
were naturally concerned with women's affairs."*
Gilbert Murray
Note to his translation of
Eumenides by Aeschylus (Oxford, 1925).

THE GODDESS

The worship of the goddess Hera, her temples, and her
priestesses are associated with the very ancient city-states of
the Mycenaean civilization, which later became Greece. This
Aegean civilization is called "Mycenaean" from the ruins and
artifacts excavated first by Heinrich Schliemann in 1876 (see
Map #4). The fortress found there, with its famous Lion Gate,
Treasury of Atreus, and other tombs, demonstrated to the world
the reality behind not only the ancient epics such as Homer's
Iliad but also the much later Greek dramas such as the *Oresteia*
of Aeschylus.

The people of Mycenae itself were Achaean relatives of the
Greeks, who rose in power and dominions around 1600 B.C.
as Minoan Crete declined or fell. By 1400 B.C. the palace of
Minos at Cnossus had collapsed and the Mycenaeans had even
occupied islands to their northwest: Zacynthus and Ithaca of
Homer's hero Odysseus. The Treasury and tomb of Atreus
would have been built by 1300, in which year there was an
earthquake at Troy, and would have been devastated a hundred
years later. When the Mycenaean cities fell, other invasions by
Dorians and Aeolians swept over the Aegean world. Because
of Schliemann's original archaeological breakthroughs at My-

· VI ·

THE GODDESS HERA

*"Also the old female goddesses, dating from matriarchal times,
were naturally concerned with women's affairs."*
Gilbert Murray
Note to his translation of
Eumenides by Aeschylus (Oxford, 1925).

THE GODDESS

The worship of the goddess Hera, her temples, and her priestesses are associated with the very ancient city-states of the Mycenaean civilization, which later became Greece. This Aegean civilization is called "Mycenaean" from the ruins and artifacts excavated first by Heinrich Schliemann in 1876 (see Map #4). The fortress found there, with its famous Lion Gate, Treasury of Atreus, and other tombs, demonstrated to the world the reality behind not only the ancient epics such as Homer's *Iliad* but also the much later Greek dramas such as the *Oresteia* of Aeschylus.

The people of Mycenae itself were Achaean relatives of the Greeks, who rose in power and dominions around 1600 B.C. as Minoan Crete declined or fell. By 1400 B.C. the palace of Minos at Cnossus had collapsed and the Mycenaeans had even occupied islands to their northwest: Zacynthus and Ithaca of Homer's hero Odysseus. The Treasury and tomb of Atreus would have been built by 1300, in which year there was an earthquake at Troy, and would have been devastated a hundred years later. When the Mycenaean cities fell, other invasions by Dorians and Aeolians swept over the Aegean world. Because of Schliemann's original archaeological breakthroughs at My-

Map 4 Mycenaean Greece

cenae and at Troy, we may now believe the evidence in Homer and other epic poets. Luce says in his preface: "My aim has been rather to present a sustained argument for the antiquity and reliability of the epic tradition."

Luce found in 1975 valid information concerning the Mycenaean world, as it was before 1000 B.C., in Homer, who lived two hundred years later. By Homer's day, adds Luce, the alphabet had been introduced from the Middle East.

According to Martin Nilsson (1927), the chief Mycenaean city centers were these:

1. The Mycenaean fortress at Mycenae,
2. The Acropolis at Athens,
3. The Palace at Tiryns and temple to the goddess Hera,
4. The Heraion at Argos, palace and temple to the goddess Hera.

The goddess Hera belongs to Ionian-Greek sites (Argolis, Euboea, and the island of Samos); in the epic traditions she invariably champions the Argives of the city Argos. The individual "states" or "kingdoms" of the Aegean and Mycenaean world at its apex are as follows: Argos, Olympia, Corinth and Megara on the Isthmus, Delphi in Phocis, Thebes in Boeotia, and Athens in Attica. These city-states are, of course, much younger than the cities of Asia Minor: Miletus, Ephesus, and Smyrna. They are also younger than Crete and Rhodes.

Ignatius Donnelly in 1882 had already argued his case, that Greek mythology may have been Mycenaean or Minoan, but had originally been Atlantean. Each early center had its myth central to that fortress; for instance, Mycenae's was that of Agamemnon, who dated from the prime of that site. Tiryns had both Heracles and Bellerophon. Argos had the Danaïds, those fifty daughters who murdered their husbands, crimes which went unpunished, theorized Nilsson, because the girls must have escaped. Or one may object that they were priestesses protecting their office, and their deeds were therefore legally sanctioned by their devotion to a goddess such as Hera. Sparta (in Laconia) presented its own tales of rape: The olden worship of Helen enters the picture here, Nilsson conceded. There occurred the rape of Persephone, who was stolen away by Hades to be his Queen of the Underworld.

Hera's temples have been found, and her priestesses, from whose priesthoods ancient events were dated and recorded, were listed by the ancient Greek historian Hellanicus.

Before commencing a biographical sketch of the goddess Hera, however, one should rehearse the received opinion about her, what are called the "accepted ideas." The French novelist Gustave Flaubert amused himself immensely by collecting ideas accepted generally by everybody. He thus established everybody's definition of *woman:*

> A woman is of the other sex, one of Adam's ribs. Not "little woman," but "Madam," or "my better half".

The writers of the various encyclopedias currently considered the authorities on every subject generally agree as to Hera herself. They tell us what we may think about her:

> Hera is a most ancient goddess. Her worship predated the conquest of Greece by the Greeks. They transformed her into the wife of Zeus, where originally she had reigned supreme. She had been and she remained the queen of heaven. She also re-

mained the goddess of women, their support and protectress in childbirth.

Hera was said by the Greeks to have been the daughter of Cronus and Rhea, the wife and sister of Zeus, the mother of Hebe, Ares, and Hephaestus.

Zeus became King of Olympus, and husband of Hera. He frequently abused and punished her. She was even tortured by her husband Zeus.

Hera was always represented in art as youthful, majestic, regally and fully clothed, crowned with a crescent moon, carrying a sceptre, associated with her attributes: the peacock, the pomegranate, and the cow.

The Romans adopted her under the name Juno (from "Dione," or "goddess").

Hera was patron of Tiryns, Argos, and Samos, which made her Athena's rival.

The constant quarrelling between Hera and Zeus remains a subject of (low) comedy.

This body of received opinion, like Flaubert's objection to the commonly perceived definition of *woman*, has been corrected by the Oxford English Dictionary and by the works of many classical scholars, such as those by Lewis Farnell on Greek religion (London, 1912). Several corrections in our perception of Hera present an entirely new view of what her biography might be:

1. Hera's quarrels with Zeus illustrate a conflict between her cult and that instituted later by a male-dominated religion. In pre-Hellenic days Hera had no consort. Her cult could not be suppressed, no matter how hard the Greeks tried to suppress it. The "marriage" idea was a *pis-aller*, an awkward compromise.
2. Hera's cult and that of Aphrodite were paired at Sparta.
3. Hera figured prominently in a great pageant, or ceremony, involving a shield. The processants were armed. (At this Heraia the priestesses were Amazons?)
4. Hera reigned at a major temple on the Isle of Samos, renowned for its famous authors, sculptors, engravers, and the engineer who first bridged the Bosporus. Samos was colonized by the Ionians c. 1100–1000 B.C.

5. Hera's major temple, the Heraion, was six miles north of Argos. Her city stood on the south side of the Argive Plain, three miles from the sea, and at the base of another Mycenaean Acropolis called "Larissa." Argos is so situated by Homer's *Iliad*.

6. Homer, Hesiod, Pindar, Hyginus, Plutarch, Pausanias, and Hellanicus, among others, all mention the importance of the worship of this goddess Hera.

7. Since it is generally believed that a High-priestess of Hera was also called a "Hera," then many of the episodes attributed to a goddess were most likely undergone and/ or enacted by a mortal woman; after all, her "matrons" wore horns in her honor. Her festival of *Matronalia* was celebrated at Rome on March 1.

8. Hera is the only "Minoan" goddess whose sanctuaries are known. Thus, she remains truly the "vivific" goddess, as Iamblichus termed her, and the former "Lady, Splendor of Heaven."

Pindar referred to Hera as seated "on her golden throne," as at home in Argos, as the goddess who made marriages perfect, as the "white-armed" foe of the "unflinching" sun god Apollo. Hesiod added Typhon to her other children, but that dragon was perhaps the Python slain at Delphi by Apollo when he took over the priestesses' ancient sanctuary. Pausanias declared Hera to be not only a maid at the same time she was both wife and mother, but also the "Delayer of Old Age," and a goddess of an entire people. In fact, her clay figurines have been widely found, from Babylon, it is said, all the way west to Italy.

Gayley describes the most famous statue of Hera. It stood, said Pausanias (pp. 2, 17, 4), between Argos and Mycenae, and had been made by Polyclitus. It was of gold and ivory. The famous sculptor represented her seated and enthroned in magnificence. Her crown represented the Graces and the Hours. She held a pomegranate in one hand and a scepter surmounted by a cuckoo, symbol of spring (or March), in her other hand.

The cuckoo refers to her rape by Zeus, for he raped his

sister Hera, or a priestess of Hera, as the first of his many, many victims. Hera was said to have been "raped by a cuckoo," or by Zeus as a cuckoo.

Aside from the Hera of Argos, her other famous statues are a torso from Ephesus, now in Vienna; a full-length Hera holding her long staff, now in Rome; a bronze statuette in the Cabinet of Coins and Antiquities, Vienna; the Farnese bust in the National Museum of Naples; the Ludovisi bust in the Ludovisi Villa in Rome; and a Pompeian wall painting of her marriage to Zeus.

Her priestesses were named and recorded by the historian Hellanicus, who was only recently rescued from oblivion by German scholars. Hellanicus was long dismissed because his works exist only in fragments. One of his works in three volumes was called *The Priestesses of Hera in Argos*. Since no records of Mycenaean history were kept, early historians used priestesses as their reference, as in the statement "the forty-eighth year of the priestess-ship of Chrysis at Argos."[1] Fragments of the second book actually refer to mythical times ("the third generation before the Trojan War, when Alcyone was in her twenty-sixth year as priestess in Argos," Pearson, p. 226). A historian, concluded Pearson,

> adopted this system of dating events presumably because the list of Argive priestesses went back much further than any other list of officials, doubtful though its historical value might be for early times (p. 227).

Judging from the fragments of Hellanicus found so far, Pearson concluded that his three books treated mythological times in volume one, mythical and historical in volume two, and the history of the Peloponnesian War in volume three (p. 231).

Sir John Forsdyke's *Greece before Homer* (1956) explained that the first historians of Greece worked despite "no notion of an era and little sense of time" altogether (p. 36). There was no list of government officers in Sparta before 755 B.C., and none from Athens before 683 B.C. Records of Hera's Argive temple are not much earlier, says Forsdyke, "but the cult of Hera there was of immemorial antiquity, and the succession of priestesses

[1] See Lionel Pearson's *Early Ionian Historians* (Oxford, 1939; Westport, 1975), p. 225.

may have gone back to the prehistoric age" (p. 37). Plutarch also had studied an inscription "which dated mythical achievements in music and poetry by the years of Argive priestesses" (p. 50). Hellanicus dated, he adds, a migration of settlers from Italy to Sicily "in the twenty-sixth year" of an Argive priestess of Hera named "Alcyonê, three generations before the Trojan War, and the Fall of Troy in a certain year of a priestess Callisto" (p. 145).

HERA HERSELF

> According to some, the name *Hera* means Splendor of Heaven, according to others, the Lady. Some think it approves her goddess of earth; others, goddess of the air; still others, for reasons by no means final, say that it signifies Protectress, and applies to Juno (Hera) in her original function of moon-goddess, the chosen guardian of women, their aid in times of distress.
>
> Professor Charles Mills Gayley.
> *The Classic Myths in English Literature and in Art*
> (New York, 1911).

The myths claim Hera was born far out in the west, beyond the confines of the Mycenaean world, even beyond the Adriatic or Cronian Sea named for her father. Daughter of Cronus and Rhea, Hera was born in the already fabled (African) Garden of the Hesperides. Hera and Niobe were their star princesses. Hera was married to Zeus, where the apple tree grows, in that Atlantic Garden.

Zeus rose to the position of supreme patriarch, punisher, wielder of lightning and thunderbolts. He roared out of the storm center surrounded by concentric whirling winds, rain, and shafts of daylight. He existed everywhere as *Zeus Pater, Dyaus Pitar,* Jupiter.

Earthly kings, sun gods all, drew their temporal power of life and death over family and kingdom from Zeus. For the Romans he exemplified the earthly *pater familias* who also could dispatch wives, sisters, and daughters into slavery/prostitution.

As the Wolf-God *Zeus Lykaios,* he and his illegitimate son, *Apollo Lykaios,* accepted human sacrifice as their due.

Zeus also performed the *hieros gamos,* where he played the role of the Great Creator of new life, Taurus the Bull.

A major opponent of Zeus, another rebellious Titan, was his consort Hera, Queen of Olympus. She and her priestesses never ceased opposing him. Every time one appeared to have desisted, she was only catching her breath. For example, when the seer Tiresias proclaimed that a woman's pleasure in intercourse was ten times greater than her husband's, a Hera wrathfully blinded him. All Zeus could do to annul that punishment was to grant Tiresias the gift of prophecy, and a lifetime of nine generations.

When Zeus at one time declared Troy most honored, Hera retorted he spoke only for himself (*Iliad,* IV):

> Then Hera, the majestic, with large eyes,
> Rejoined: "The cities most beloved by me
> Are three,—Mycenae, with her spacious streets,
> Argos, and Sparta."

What wrong had angered Hera against Troy, if not that Paris had abducted her priestess Helen from Sparta?

When Hera really angered Zeus, he suspended her in midair, or her priestess, by fillets tied to her wrists. Then he increased her pain by hanging weights on her feet. He still threatened to flog her with a cat-o'-nine-tails. When her son Hephaestus came to his mother's rescue, he was seized by Zeus, who hurled him through the heavens. Hephaestus, even so, comforted his mother again (*Iliad,* I):

> "Mother, be patient and submit, although
> In sadness, lest these eyes behold thee yet
> Beaten with stripes, and though I hold thee dear
> And grieve for thee, I cannot bring thee help. . . ."

Zeus asked Hera if she remembered his passion and her punishment (*Iliad,* XV):

> "When thou didst swing suspended, and I tied
> Two anvils to thy feet, and bound a chain
> Of gold that none could break around thy wrists?
> Then didst thou hang in air amid the clouds,
> And all the gods of high Olympus saw
> With pity. . . ."

Hera's son Hephaestus is the fire god, the name deriving from the Egyptian *pha,* and the Egyptian smith Ptah. Supernatural spirits, priests, headmen, and sorcerers are usually blacksmiths involved in furnaces and metallurgy, which simple people customarily fear and dread. Through her control of air and fire, Hera was able to hasten the sun during the daytime, even obliging him to set before his accustomed time in order to shroud her folk in darkness. They had been in the midst of a losing battle.

Zeus said he could hardly ever control Hera by mere words alone. Usually her craft prevailed over his might. As moon goddess, ward of Poseidon, she also ruled the sea, for which reason the white horses of the sea were her favorites. The inverted horseshoe is a sign of Hera's protection.

Because it symbolized death and resurrection, the color red (like the red pomegranate) was sacred to her. She ordered the illegitimate sons of Zeus seized, torn up, and boiled like red meat. She especially hated Zeus's son Dionysus because he continually incited women to take drugs and then participate in wild orgies. She hated Heracles more than any other so-called hero for his rapes and killings of Amazon warriors. To protect Dionysus, Zeus had him raised secretly in a dark cave. Hera said Zeus had caused Dionysus to become effeminate, and so she drove him insane. Hera watched over her Amazon priestesses, whom she forbade to drink wine, to use any intoxicants, or to participate in Dionysian rites. She hated Dionysus when he wore girl's clothing, as Heracles wore when he was with Queen Omphale. Hera also hated Zeus for having torn off her dress before he began to rape her. She abhorred naked, lewd women.

The foes of Hera were Zeus, first of all, because of his many crimes of rape. Next her foes were these two illegitimate sons of Zeus: Heracles and Dionysus, the first hateful to her, and the second one simply loathsome. Rather than allow her priestesses to bear more illegitimate children after having been raped by Zeus, Hera went so far as to kill them. For this reason, she killed Semele of Thebes. She always championed the Amazons and the Corinthian Queen Medea particularly. Her wars placed her on the side of her own race, the Titans, versus

Zeus. Aside from her wars against Heracles because he defeated women, and her repulsion of Dionysus because of his attempt to hook women on intoxicants, she hated Paris of Troy because he had awarded the apple to Aphrodite, caused the Trojan War, abandoned his own true wife, and abducted Helen of Troy.

On the positive side Hera benefitted women actively, for which reason she was called the Protectress. Zeus, Heracles, and Dionysus could only rarely escape her vigilance. In order to dignify women she established the Heraean Games for women at Argos. The final ceremonies were called "The Shield." The women victors were escorted by shield bearers carrying the prizes. The later Olympic Games were patterned after Hera's original athletic contests for women. The two highest champions were accorded Zodiacal honors.

Hera's greatest service to women was her oracles, one of which was at Delphi. There the Castalian Spring was guarded by her African son Pytho. As great goddess, Hera and her priestesses were considered triune, triple sovereigns over three elements: earth, air, and sea. They supervised a woman's life: virginity, marriage, old age. In the vegetable kingdom, which resembles death, they controlled germination, blossom, and decay; seedtime, fruiting, harvest. They drew up the calendar from the moon's three phases; for the persons who study mathematics and decree the times of day, workdays, night, and holidays are those who rule the world. Thus, understanding this law of the universe, Hera's young acolytes were set to work learning to calculate. Hera and her priestesses also calculated conception, pregnancy, and the time of birth. Hera herself often appeared in her three ages of woman, as maiden, as nymph, and as crone.

Hera's favorite plant was the willow, which eased the long agony of childbirth when the mother lay upon withes. The goddess Flora informed Hera concerning another, very special flower, Ovid wrote (*Fasti*, V, 231 ff.). Flora was the world's authority on flowers, which, being goddess of summer, she superintended.

The goddess Hera had confided in Flora that she was incensed because Zeus kept getting children outside wedlock, having neglected the usual services of a wife. Thus, he had in his own self become both the husband and the wife of the household. Hera therefore desired to remain chaste but bear a child by herself, without having recourse to Zeus.

"I will try all drugs or any drug," she claimed. "I will search the oceans and Tartarus in order to find such a plant. Can you assist me? You look knowledgeable." For some time Flora hesitated, for fear of Zeus.

"There is only one such plant," she admitted finally. "It grows now in my own garden. But I found it in a field near your own city of Olenos in Achaia. The mere touch of this blossom has fertilized a cow. I know because I tried it."

No sooner had Flora touched Hera with the flower than Hera conceived. Her warlike son Ares was born to the west of the Propontis, where dwell very warlike Thracians. In gratitude to Flora, Ares gave her a special place in the Roman Forum, the city of Romulus. In Rome, Ares was called "Mars," the red planet also being named in honor of Hera because she preferred the color red.

Once at dinner Hera ate a salad of wild lettuce plants. As a result she found herself pregnant with her daughter Hebe. Angered when Zeus bore Athena, she ate another special plant and bore her son Hephaestus as her revenge.

Three Roman writers objected to this last version. Vergil, Ovid, and Pliny believed that the west wind of spring, Favonicus by name, fathered Hephaestus. (In Finland they say that Voinamoinen was fathered by the east wind. The Algonquins claim the same for Hiawatha.) The Romans never tired of asking what plant or plants had made Hera pregnant. All they could conclude was that she ate one of two very powerful and therapeutic plants: either the pomegranate or the apple, often confused for each other. In Rome, barren women prayed to Hera, when she was called Juno Lucina, for "an enchanted apple."

As for Hera herself, decided Saintyves in his book on Virgin Mothers, her union with Zeus, if union there was, was barren despite traditions which claim otherwise. Hera probably bore no children at all, the French scholar decided, for which reason she was hailed as the Virgin Goddess: *Hera Parthenia*. She inspired respect, not passion. She protected all women equally, irrespective of age, condition, or situation. The Greeks called her *Kourotrophe* because she was especially eager to educate girl children, whom she endowed with gifts as they progressed in their studies. Her temples were always near rivers where her priestesses performed the most ancient rituals involving water and earth. At each site legions of girl acolytes served or prepared to serve the goddess and her priestesses. Hera attended these girls on their wedding days. On the following day the bride offered her wedding veil at one of Hera's shrines. When she assisted at a birthing, Hera's priestess was called "Ilythya."

Pausanias visited the Heraeum (Heraion), Hera's most famous temple, five miles, he said, from Argos (*Description of Greece*, II):

> Her temple stood on the left-hand side of the road, beside a spring called Eleutherus that was used by the priestesses for rituals of purification and other secret services. The temple itself had been erected at the foot of Mt. Euboia, named Acraea for one of the daughters of the River Asterion. His three daughters had served Hera as her nursemaids. Mt. Acraea was visible from the temple, in front of which was a large plaza named for the second daughter. The river flowed down below before diving into a chasm whence it could not be seen to emerge. Along the riverbanks grew a special herb they called "asterion." They decorated the goddess's altar with its garlands and used it to make crowns for her (statue).
>
> (Commentary by Saintyves: Was this herb the lily of the valley [*Convallaria majalis*]?)
>
> Entering the great hall of the temple, you see on her throne the statue of Hera seated. It is overwhelming in its grandeur, all gold and ivory, one of the masterpieces of Polyclitus. The goddess wears a crown of Hours and Graces. She holds a pomegranate in one hand. Why is that? I'll have to pass that mystery by in silence.
>
> On the summit of the mountain near where this temple is built, you notice the foundations of a much older temple and a few ruins that escaped destruction by fire. This earlier temple burned (423 B.C.) through the fault of a priestess named Chrysis (Chryseis).

This priestess of Hera named Chrysis fell asleep while serving in the temple. She did not notice the fire catching on some
very dry crowns that were too close to it.

The spring called Eleutherus was named for Hera "Ilythia"
or "Eilythia," as she was called when performing her functions
during the delivery of a baby. After having presided at the birth,
which she directed, she had the mother bathed and purified in
these gentle waters.

Every year Hera herself bathed in the spring at Nauplion
(south of Tiryns, close to the Gulf of Argolis) in order to regain
her virginity.

(Commentary cont.: churches in Greece today are dedicated
to saints whose names are the same as Hera's fountain:
"Eleutherus." These saints now perform rites and chant litur-
gies for pregnant women.)

Probably barren women went long ago to Hera's temple near
Mycenae, prayed, made offerings, bathed in the Eleutherus
Spring, and made garlands from the fragrant lilies of the val-
ley that grew along the riverbanks.

The nodding, bell-shaped flowers of the lily of the valley,
with their fluted, almost closed cups, resemble the lotus blossoms offered as symbols of fertility to the Minoan goddess in
Crete.

Hera's other Mycenaean-age temples were at Cos, Eleusis,
Olympia, Plataea, Samos, Sparta, and Corinth.

Figure 13. Zeus and Hera

THE RAPES BY ZEUS

It is time now to consider some of the rapes by Zeus, which, when considered as a group, seem to be less stories of rape than the conquest of ancient matriarchy. Over the centuries the so-called rapes have either not been considered a fit subject for conversation, or they were blamed first upon Hera as an unsympathetic wife, secondly, upon each victim because she must have invited rape by the immodesty of her dress, or by her frantic desire to become pregnant. Rapists are still being so excused.

Most of the persons Zeus raped were identified as "nymphs," which means mature women. The most famous rapes by Zeus need to be listed, examined, compared, and numbered if anything is to be learned from them. How many such rapes could there have been? Who are the victims? Have the victims something in common besides womanhood, beauty, and youth? Were they all exalted, foreign, and highly aristocratic like the goddess Hera herself? Were old women also raped?

Of the myths listed below, number 19 is obviously much older than all the rest, and the only one which shows any harmony between Zeus and women. This last rape, at least, led to marriage.

1. Calyce, a nymph named "Rosebud." Her son was the lovely sleeper Endymion, whose fifty daughters were borne to him by the moon priestess Selene. Endymion slept forever so he would not have to see himself grow old.

2. Lamia is another name for the Libyan goddess Neith. Lamia was once called the "lovely" daughter of Belus, before she was raped by Zeus. He gave her as a consolation present the ability to pluck out and replace her eyeballs.

   Hera would have killed all Lamia's children, who were monsters, but she let Scylla live. Which Scylla this was— the one who became a rock between Italy and Sicily, or the Minoan princess metamorphosed into a bird— is not recorded. Probably it was the latter, the Scylla who lived to become a priestess of Hera, i.e., her "bird."

Lamia herself turned into a hideous, masked Gorgon-like monster after her rapes. Her "foreign" worship was stamped out by the Greeks. Zeus became thereafter the only king on Olympus.

3. The mountain Nymphs were enjoyed so routinely by Zeus that they are called his "concubines." Hera punished the one named Echo for having distracted her from Zeus's sexual activities among them. Echo's punishment was the loss of her voice. Hera's conduct is routinely explained as "jealousy" on her part that her husband, with Echo's assistance, philandered successfully and so widely.

4. Rhea, the mother of Zeus, was raped by her own son because she feared his voracious sexuality and therefore refused to allow him to marry Hera. They quarreled so fiercely that in defense of her honor Rhea turned herself into a great serpent. Zeus continued the war, constantly threatening to rape her. He turned himself into a male serpent and wrapped himself about her in a seven-fold knot that she could not escape. There is no record of progeny resulting from Zeus's rape of his own mother.

5. Themis, the Oracle and Calendar Goddess at Delphi, was raped by Zeus, to whom she bore the Three Fates, who, forever after, were declared subject to Zeus. These priestesses no longer helped to establish the Seasons, or in ordering festivals.

6. Mnemosyne (Memory) was raped by Zeus, to whom she bore mountain Nymphs and the Nine Muses: History, Tragedy, Comedy, Flute, Dance, Epic Poetry, Lyric Poetry, Astronomy, and Dramatic Performance. The Muses were all women whose spheres were brought thus under their father's jurisdiction.

7. Eurynome, the far wanderer, Earth's Moon, was herself raped by Zeus to prove that if she fell to his sexual appetite, then all marriageable girls belonged sexually to him first. She bore the Three Graces, but they shunned Zeus and haunted the mountains, following Artemis and her throngs of virginal priestesses.

8. Styx ("Abhorrèd Styx, the flood of deadly hate") was raped by Zeus, to whom she bore Persephone, say some mythographers who wish to excuse the rape of Persephone by King Hades of Tartarus. Styx was the one underworld river by which all the gods swore: "By Styx, etc. . . ."

9. Maia (Maja, Majesta) was a daughter of the Titan Atlas. She was raped by Zeus, to whom she bore Hermes (Mercury). She became a star in the constellation of the Pleiades, by the setting of which harvest time was measured.

10. Leto (Latona, Lato) was another daughter of Titans, and her delivery of Apollo and Artemis was very difficult. Her island shrine was Delos, where the heavenly twins were born.

11. Danaë was the daughter of King Acrisius of Argos. Her name means "dark of the moon." Her father traced his ancestry back to Poseidon, as did Hera herself. The girl Danaë was very lovely, but an oracle had foreseen that she would bear a deadly son who would slay his own grandfather. Therefore Danaë was enclosed forever in a dark underground prison. Zeus turned himself into a shower of gold, however, and raped her in her cell. The son born of this union was Perseus.

King Acrisius, in great distress at this unfortunate birth, enclosed both Danaë and her child in a wooden chest, in which he set them adrift. They floated on the waters of the Aegean Sea until they reached the islet of Seriphus where a fisherman pulled the chest ashore. He took Danaë and her son to the welcoming king of the place, who consented at first to shelter them. Her son Perseus managed to grow up. He attacked Atlas in his far western kingdom.

Italian myths say even Danaë survived. She brought settlers into the west, where she founded the colony that grew into the city of Ardea. Under the reign of their King Turnus, Aeneas conquered them and attached them to future Rome.

12. Alcmena, whose name means "strong" or "full moon,"

was the daughter of King Electryon of Mycenae and the wife of Amphitryon. Zeus raped her when he disguised himself as her husband. The son of Zeus was Heracles. His twin, or half-brother, was Iphicles. In the case of twins, said Robert Graves, the first (Heracles) would wed a princess at the spring celebration of the equinox while the other would wed one at the fall equinox. In each case, the princess would be given a "moon" name, like Alcmene (Alcmena).

13. Leda's story was so popular that Arachne wove it into her web. Leda, the Lady, was the wife of King Tyndareus of Sparta. She was pursued along the Eurotas River by Zeus who, disguised as a swan, raped her there. Her four children were Helen, Clytemnestra, Castor, and Pollux. The last two were male twins. The first daughter, as child of Zeus, was always considered immortal. Of the twins, Pollux alone was generally thought to have been son of Zeus, and therefore immortal.

14. Nemesis was said to have laid the original egg, which Leda only nurtured and delivered. To escape Zeus, Nemesis had changed herself into a high-flying wild goose, but Zeus as a swan raped her in Greece.

15. Io, whose name means "moon," was the daughter of King Inachus, first King of Argos. Inachus was himself a son of the Titans Poseidon and Tethys, who had nursed the goddess Hera. She followed Zeus one day when he had just raped Io. When he saw Hera coming, he changed Io into a heifer, in which form she was later deified in Egypt as an incarnation of Isis. The Ionian Sea, across which Io swam on her way to Egypt, was named for her. Io was the mother of Libya, and she was also an ancestress of Crete, Thebes, Mycenae, and Arcadia.

16. Semele, whose name means "moon," was the daughter of King Cadmus, founder of Thebes. Her grandmother was the goddess Hera by her son Ares. Semele angered Hera by accepting her seduction and rape by Zeus. Hera therefore advised her to ask her lover to dare show himself to her in full panoply. Semele requested this before Zeus could stop her. Since he had sworn "by Styx"

to grant her request, he descended into her chamber as the Sun and burned her to death. Thus, she saw him as he really was, and died.

17. Aegina was a daughter of the River (god) Asopus of Boeotia, and sister of Evadne and Euboea. Zeus carried her away, and this crime was actually witnessed by King Sisyphus of Corinth. He reported what he had seen and was for his indiscretion condemned to Tartarus, from which he was apprehended while attempting to escape. His sentence was changed to life imprisonment (Ovid, *Metamorphoses*, VII, 172 ff.).

   When Hera heard about it, she sent a plague which wiped out everybody on the island of Aegina in the Saronic Gulf.

   King Aeacus of Aegina tells of the horrors of this disease which left nothing alive on Aegina. The island was repopulated by a race of ants called "Myrmidons." They fought very conscientiously for Achilles in the Trojan War.

   For his piety King Aeacus was appointed after death to be judge in Tartarus, presiding there beside Minos and Rhadamanthus of Minoan Crete.

18. Antiope, whose name comes from "Moon," was a daughter of King Nycteus of Thebes. She became a priestess, or Maenad of Dionysus, whom Hera detested. Once while Antiope was drugged and dancing wildly, she was raped by Zeus. He had disguised himself as a goat so he could join the other amorous satyrs from the woodlands who spent their lives chasing Nymphs and raping them.

   Antiope bore two sons as a consequence of her rape by Zeus: Amphion and Zethus. The babies were condemned to die from exposure on Mt. Cithaeron, but were rescued by shepherds among whom they grew to manhood. Neither knew his divine and royal parentage.

   King Lycus of Thebes and his wicked queen condemned Antiope to be dragged to her death behind a bull. Antiope was able to send a cry for help to her sons, who had been ordered to execute their mother. They rescued Antiope, killed King Lycus, and tied his Queen Dirce by her hair to a bull, which dragged her to her death.

After King Amphion was crowned in Thebes, he showed such superb mastery as a musician that the huge stone blocks he had ordered for the walls of Thebes raised themselves up without any human hand and settled musically into places along his fortification.

King Amphion died tragically through the fault of his Queen Niobe. All his House perished with him.

19. Europa, whose name means "full moon," was the daughter of King Agenor of Phoenicia. She was abducted by Zeus, who was disguised as a white bull. He carried her from the Asian coast across the sea to Crete. They founded the Minoan Dynasty from the sons of Europa: Minos, Sarpedon, and Rhadamanthus.

Her statue or a fresco of this scene, Europa and Taurus, graced the *Porticus Europae* at Rome, and was one of the famous art works of antiquity.

The story of Europa points convincingly to the religious ritual of the *hieros gamos,* this economic measure of a sacred marriage, as enacted by persons wearing bull and cow costumes, and named "Taurus" and "Bossie" (from the Latin *bos* = cow). Eliminating Europa's story with regret that it offers no theory as to how she dared to ride over the sea on a bull's back, we are left with eighteen other "war" myths: Zeus versus Hera, man versus woman.

The god Zeus seems to emerge as winner of these conflicts only six times out of eighteen, leaving Hera victorious twelve times out of eighteen. It could therefore be assumed *a priori* that these myths are most ancient, indeed, and that some recall history and a matriarchy from some prehistoric age before the fall of woman. This fall must have narrowly followed the ousting of priestesses from temples dedicated to educating and caring for women, particularly in their young, most dangerous, years.

The story of the rape of Themis (number 5 above) is so filled with tragic repercussions for every human being that one is horrified reading how Zeus overcame this second priestess and prophetess of Earth at Delphi.

Read first what the Priestess of Apollo at Delphi says in the opening verses to Aeschylus's tragedy *The Eumenides.* The second oracular priestess at Delphi was Themis. She was the older sister of the third priestess Phoebe. Both were gods of the Titans whom Zeus defeated in war. Zeus intended genocide. He intended mass slaughter, to wipe out their entire race, to program and create a new race subject to male gods only.

For this reason Zeus chained the son of Themis on a mountain crag, to eternal torture there on the Scythian "margin of the earth" (*Prometheus Bound,* v. 1). Furthermore, Zeus made Hera's son Hephaestus the Blacksmith hammer the spikes that staked him out there, stripped naked, to that rock. Prometheus still defiantly proclaimed his contempt for Zeus, who knew only one punishment: torture eternally, such as he had ordained for King Tantalus also. "My mother Themis," says Prometheus, "warned me Zeus would defeat us by cunning, and she was right. I am sorry for the dragon Typhon (Python) too," he added, "for he met his death."

The Chorus of Ocean Nymphs decide never to abandon Prometheus, however. These priestesses courageously stand beside him and weep at the fate that befell him because he had brought fire to mankind. Zeus also punished him severely because the benefactor Prometheus had brought the art of writing to mankind. As Prometheus says, "Writing is memory, the mother of all arts" (v. 425). So long as people commit their history to writing, so long will Themis, Prometheus, and Zeus in their war for control of mankind be remembered, if only as prehistoric myth, before history became an academic discipline several thousand years later.

By the rape of Themis and the destruction of her son Prometheus, Zeus forbade future women to learn mathematics and draw up the calendar. At this signal victory Zeus also took control of life and death for all mankind, as indicated by his domination of the Three Fates.

The second victory of Zeus rings another death knell for women from that prehistoric dark age to this. When he raped Memory (Mnemosyne), he took charge of the arts and sciences. When he raped and killed Danaë, he was begetting the future hero Perseus, who would pursue the Titan King Atlas to his mountain beside the Garden, Hera's birthplace.

When Zeus deceived her husband and raped Alcmene, he was begetting the greatest of the Greek warriors Heracles. Again, he had begotten a hero, who concluded the war against the Titans and incidentally wiped out the Amazons from their old homes in Asia Minor.

The story of Zeus, Leda, and the swan, often more discerningly told as the rape of Love (Aphrodite) by the swan (Death), strikes another fatal blow to the heart of woman, even to the hearts of educated, modern young women, who often confess to their teachers that they too live in terrible fear, because they are still legally unequal.

The House of Atreus and Pelops fathered heroes like Agamemnon and Menelaus; the latter married the daughter of Zeus by Leda (whose husband Tyndareus was also bypassed): Helen of Troy. Her sister Clytemnestra married Agamemnon. The curse of Atreus fell upon his descendants: Agamemnon, Clytemnestra, Orestes, Iphigenia, Electra, Aegisthus, Theseus, and Hippolytus, as it had fallen earlier upon Prometheus and upon Tantalus, the father of Pelops. In myth, another older name for Leda is Arachne.

The dying gasp of this tragic family of Atreus occurs in the trial for first-degree murder brought by the plaintiffs, who were priestesses, against the defendant Orestes. The judgment handed down by that judge remains to be reappealed today in a higher court.

The sixth victory of Zeus was won over Nemesis, a daughter of Night.

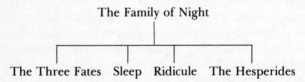

The Family of Night

The Three Fates   Sleep   Ridicule   The Hesperides

Nemesis, who represented vengeance and justifiable anger, existed to punish all persons proud and offensive to others, plus all criminals who had broken a law of their community. Therefore, when Zeus raped Nemesis, he took the law into his own hands, deciding henceforward what was and what it was not legal to do. His first acts were to condemn both Tantalus and Prometheus, among others, to eternal torture in full view of mankind. As Prometheus declared, Zeus was too inexperienced to think of a more suitable punishment.

These myths recording the rapes by Zeus, which we have listed, seem to demonstrate that even in prehistoric times the Mother Goddess Hera of these Mycenaean Greeks won twelve out of eighteen cases against Zeus. In the first case of Calyce, it seems clear that the child of rape Endymion was offered up as a sacrifice to his father Zeus by his mother, the moon priestess Selene. This states clearly that the Mother Goddess will punish a man who commits rape. He will live to lose his child.

Similarly, in the case of Lamia who cried so hard at her rape by Zeus that her eyeballs fell out of her head, the goddess Hera ordered the sacrifice of her children too.

In the case of Echo, who aided and abetted Zeus in his rapes, her punishment for not having spoken out and warned Hera was the loss of her voice, and also, which is worse, the loss of her mind. Echo could only, after an interval, repeat faintly whatever sound was made or uttered elsewhere. Hera's sentence was condign.

Zeus's forcible rape of his mother was so unspeakable that it has been discussed since the early twentieth century in countless works by Dr. Sigmund Freud and subsequent psychoanalysts. They have treated as illness the Oedipus Complex in men and the Jocasta Complex in women.

Although Zeus raped Memory also, he failed to catch their progeny because the Three Graces fled to the protection of Artemis in the deep forests where they were able to remain virginal. Where there was no accommodation in the case of the guilty Echo, Memory's children knew and remembered their origin; they fled to the wilderness. Artemis, as the old Latin Diana, had a very secret shrine at the Lake of Nemi in Italy, where a warrior king stood guard over her priestesses.

The grief of the Mother Goddess at the rape of Persephone by King Hades of Tartarus, a rape originally blamed on Zeus when he forced the River Styx of Tartarus, brought in its wake a continual punishment to every human being ever to live in the northern hemisphere: the end of summer and the onset of winter. Every fall, when the weeping Persephone has to descend into hell, her mother *De-meter* also weeps inconsolably for six long months, letting the sun warm the lands below the equator. Not until it crosses the equator again on April 23, or at the spring equinox, does Demeter's grief diminish. Then she welcomes summer and the return of her darling daughter.

Hera let Maia escape by becoming part of a constellation. Just so, Ariadne had escaped to form the Northern Crown. Leto was severely punished by being unable to find any place on earth for her lying-in. Only Delos took her. And even then, she almost died in childbirth. Hera probably saved her because the twin to the accursed Apollo was Artemis herself.

Hera killed Semele in a shower of gold because the priestess had broken her vow of chastity.

She sent a plague to destroy every inhabitant of the island of Aegina, where only ants were let survive.

The story of Antiope leads to the destruction of Thebes, the death of King Amphion and of all his children, and the tragic monument on Mt. Sipylus in Asia Minor, which portrays the weeping Niobe.

The story of Io, daughter of Inachus, resembles that of Antiope, but refers us to the destruction of Argos and the House of Danaüs, recalling again the fabulous rescue of Andromeda in Libya by Perseus, and the forty-nine deaths of the princes of Argolis by the hands of the forty-nine remaining granddaughters of King Belus of Egypt.

In *Prometheus Bound* Io tells her own sad story to the chained Titan, how her dream that she would be raped by Zeus perseverated, how her father so feared the consequences of her virginity that he threw her out of the house, how she was changed into a wandering cow running over land, sea, and mountains, forever haunted by Zeus and pursued. The Chorus of Ocean Nymphs hear her story and pray to be delivered from rape by Zeus. Prometheus promises them Zeus "will be humbled" (v. 834). They ask if he will be "overthrown" (v. 858). Prometheus replies later:

"I won't take fright and kneel down like a woman . . ."
(v. 940),

and later:

> "One thing is certain, one thing,
> I will not, I will not die" (v. 986),

and at the end:

> "My sufferings are unjust"
> (v. 1018).

VII

PRIESTESSES OF THE DEAD

"This rule of law in the city—of law created by the whole body of citizens—is one of the most characteristic features in the public life of Greece."

> Mikhail Ivanovich Rostovtzeff
> *History of the Ancient World, Vol. I (Oxford, 1927).*

THE FURIES

According to the well-traveled, classical scholar J. V. Luce, the Greek Underworld lay near the west coastline of Greece, approximately fifty-five miles north of the island of Ithaca to which Odysseus eventually returned after the Trojan War. Pausanias had identified this area as Thesprotia in ancient Epirus. The oracle of the dead was situated there, on a rocky bluff to the north side, says Luce, where the Cocytus River flowed into the larger River Acheron of hell. Before it joins the Cocytus, the Acheron emerges from deep gorges, passes the oracle at the confluence, and flows into the sea at Port Splantza. The oracle was on the north side of this confluence, or Y; the dread Acherusian Lake and its feeder stream are now a marsh. These once-phosphorescent waters, adjacent to Rivers of Flame and Lamentation, still unite wildly at this rocky pinnacle, as Luce describes it, and thunder down toward Corfu and Ithaca in the Ionian Sea.

Sailors and scores of scholars have traced the voyage of Odysseus, as they have that of Jason, in the thought that each account recorded one continuous voyage by one individual leader, which is perhaps the case. But, as here, the names of the priestesses with whom Odysseus cohabited for several years, like the names of their islands and shrines, to say nothing of their directions, could be located, and have been located, just about anywhere: Aegean or Ionian Seas, Mediterranean Sea, Atlantic Ocean.

Circe and Calypso, who were certainly among the priestesses of the dead, i.e., of the Underworld, tell Odysseus to watch out for Scylla and Charybdis at the Straits of Messina, Sicily (or at the entrance to the Black Sea), and to navigate carefully, well out past Circe's Cape (Cape Circeio), which is found today on the west coast of Italy. Like the voyages of Heracles, that of Odysseus could even have taken him out into the Atlantic Ocean, past the Pillars of Heracles. Odysseus was also forewarned about the Cyclops under Mt. Aetna, also in Sicily.

Samuel Butler, who offered "proof" in 1897 that the noble girl Nausicaa was the real author of Homer's *Odyssey*, listed nine or ten famous women in that marvelous poem, including Nausicaa and her mother, Queen Arëte. Among them he also placed the priestess Calypso, daughter of either Poseidon or Atlas, but in any case from the race of the Titans. Her name means "Hidden," he noted, and she was a "master mind," if there ever was one. The priestess Circe too, he said, was no lackey and not inferior to Odysseus, not with a royal name like hers: "Falcon." The women in Homer, he observed, always know better, a fact which must have seemed very odd, indeed, to the classical Greeks who despised women utterly. In the *Odyssey*, and this is an argument by which he reasoned the author was a woman, the women even come to the rescue of heroes. In the works of Homer, Andromeda of Libya saves Perseus, for example, and not the other way around.

It does Butler's case little good, however, if one lists again and identifies the other fourteen women who are eternally suffering thirst and hunger—along with the silent, male, and equally damaged souls of Agamemnon, Achilles, and Ajax— in the dark, muddy pit of the Underworld. In hell Odysseus also saw his own mother Anticlea, who had borne him unwillingly, as the result of having been raped. She pleaded so urgently with her son that he gave her a drink of blood.

The injured Princess Tyro of Tyre was there; she had lost her virginity to a river god. Antiope was there, who had been raped by Zeus. Heracles's mother Alcmena, raped by Zeus, was suffering there. The poor mother of Oedipus, the Jocasta who hanged herself after her son slept with her, was there. Chloris was there, an unfortunate mother of eleven sons slain by Heracles. Leda, raped by Zeus, was there. Iphimedeia, raped by Poseidon, was there. Ariadne, perhaps raped by Theseus but branded a traitor anyway, was there also.

A sea priestess of Aphrodite, whose name was Maera, was there, still changed into a dog. She too had been mistreated on earth.

Ariadne's younger sister Phaedra from Minoan Crete, raped and perhaps wed by Theseus, was there. Odysseus also saw the victim Procris, whose husband mistook her for a wild animal in the forest and killed her by accident. Clymene, raped by the sun god Helios, was there.

The last agonized, murdered woman was the famous Eriphyle, whose case was also remembered by the Roman historian Suetonius. There actually occurred, he recorded, three terrible and absolutely unpardonable crimes in the ancient world:

1. Eriphyle betrayed her husband and was killed by her own son, *Alcmaeon;*
2. The Roman Emperor *Nero* Claudius Caesar killed his own mother, the Empress Agrippina II; and
3. *Orestes* of Argos killed his own mother in retaliation for her murder of his father Agamemnon, murdered in retaliation for his sacrificing their daughter Iphigenia, younger sister of Orestes.

The abuse of women and the satires on women in the classical Greek plays of Euripides alone, said the French classical scholar Paul Decharme (Paris, 1906), are shocking to us today. In the seventeen plays which survive from this great spokesman for classical Greece, men married perforce, as a patriotic obligation. They used prostitutes, of whom there was a great supply, for their pleasure. Jason, for one, lamented the situation. Men preferred to buy children from a temple so they could thereafter "live free in free homes, unvexed by women folk" (*Hippolytus*, v. 618 ff.).

The only way for a man to live happily is for him to marry a nitwit, a cipher, say the plays. The faults of women must be punished rigorously. Their husbands must not pity them but lay on the lash, remembering that one man is worth over one thousand women. What are their faults?

1. curiosity
2. love of adornment
3. gossip, slander
4. indiscretion
5. cunning, artfulness, finesse
6. deceit, revenge
7. opposition (strong/weak, shy/bold, fearful/aggressive, etc.)
8. dissimulation, secrecy
9. insanity where "love" is concerned
10. licentiousness, immorality
11. friendliness with slaves, servants, and lower-class persons
12. poor heredity
13. impossible to be guarded securely

The husband must constantly remain alert so he can punish his wife severely at any slight challenge to his absolute power in all things, always. He must never forgive any lapse on her part. He must feel free to divorce her at any moment (unless, of course, she has a returnable dowry). He must keep in mind that women are inferior, and that their inferiority must never be excused and never pardoned.

The role model of a perfect Greek wife remained, continued Decharme, Hector's widow Andromache of *The Trojan Women*. She allowed the Greeks to take her baby son from her arms and throw him headfirst down the cliff to dash out his brains. What she said to her son was: "Go, die, my best beloved. . . ." She was just as resigned thereafter to becoming the concubine of the Greek hero Neoptolemus, to whom she fell by lot.

The truth of the matter is, concluded Decharme, that the Greeks condemned all women. They sacrificed all their women and girls to the selfishness of men. Then, worst of all, *they voted all women inferior to men by law.*

Women in Greece had no equal rights before the law, and therefore virtually no recourse. It would also appear from this grim, hateful picture of what was supposed to be the flowering of Greece that the goddess Hera must very early in the Mycenaean Age have lost her war against Zeus. The sun gods Zeus and Helios/Apollo triumphed henceforth unopposed by her. The priestesses left over elsewhere must still be guarding their remote seascapes, or surviving "hidden," like Circe and Calypso, in outlying waters.

Barely anyone else of authority remained who possessed the will and the daring to oppose Zeus's coterie and offer some defense of Greek women, except the aged crones revered by the Greeks as priestesses of the dead. In their Egyptian temple of Zeus Amon we noted such women walking in the procession, singing holy psalms, dancing pretty dances, and, if never whipped by a Greek husband, ignorant of the fate that awaited them. But powerful, old advocates still kept sharp eyes open. They were the oldest women, the Greek hags of death: the Erinnyes, whom the Romans called "The Furies." Macbeth was to meet them on that "blasted heath" in ancient Scotland.

Rarely seen singly, the Furies were usually a trio of toothless, ugly, old crones with hanks of grizzled hair framing their wrinkled, splotched skins. They were the last avenging deities. They hung on to life just for that purpose: to avenge wrongs. Some Greeks called them avenging "spirits." Others said they were "demons" born in some other race and from some other blood. Others knew they could pursue a criminal like an infuriating fiend, stinging like bees, and biting like horseflies. They swarmed about as do bees (priestesses) when looking for a new hive. They were also called the "Dire Women," for their determination never to abandon pursuit was "dire." When enraged, they were consumed with anger lodged deep inside their hearts. Gaunt, dessicated, skeletal, all loose skin over loose bones, the Furies were implacable. Their names were Tisiphone, Alecto, and Megaera. They were so old they wanted nothing and feared nobody.

Zeus, Apollo, and their toady Athena once attempted to hoodwink the Furies, and change their names from "Erinnyes" to "Eumenides," from "Furies" to "Sweet Girls." That didn't work, but it was a good try. It made a very good story, either way. And calling them "Sweethearts" was safer than to risk an anger that had never been assuaged except with fresh blood. One had good reason to look over the shoulder, for the Furies could fly like rapacious birds of prey. Their hair, some said, was live snakes. They liked being hideous.

As goddesses of the dead, the Furies supervised several domestic crimes: murder of a family member, disobedience (or worse) to one's parents, and inhospitality to travelers and guests. They asked the accused whether he was guilty. If he pleaded innocent, he was asked to swear: "If I say I am innocent and if I am truly guilty, I hope to die." For this oath, many persons died when confronted, eye to eye, by the Three Furies. Their belief that the worst crime a person can commit is murder within his own family *and clan* (or tribe) indicates the extreme antiquity of these death goddesses.

Many violent deaths which befell Greek heroes come to mind, like those of Theseus, who fell off a cliff; Heracles, who was burned alive; Oenomanus, who killed himself in a chariot accident; Diomedes, who was eaten by mustangs; Tantalus, who drowned; and Capaneus, who was electrocuted.

The Furies scourged Orestes the very instant he killed his mother, and he was sick afterwards for several days. They were ready to organize his funeral and sorry to see him recover. Like all priestesses of the dead they would have gone down into the Underworld with him, just to see him safely occupied and his hands full of mud forever afterwards.

The shrines of these priestesses were surrounded by stands of funereal trees: the alder (first of the chieftain trees), the black poplar sacred to Demeter, and the yew. Their priestesses were the Triple Hecate of the Crossways, the three phases of

the Moon, or green, ripe, and harvested grain. Their goddesses' names were Demeter, Persephone, and Hecate, who
was dog-headed.

Both Medea and Circe are priestesses of Hecate. The former's prayers, journey for herbs, and restoration of youth by
cancelling forty years of a lifetime are told in great detail by
Ovid (*Metamorphoses*, VII). Persephone, Queen of the Underworld for six months each year, was their chief goddess, said
Ovid. He told her story, " 'Death' and Persephone," (*Metamorphoses*, V). Ovid also moved her story from Greece to Sicily.

Hades and Persephone

Persephone (Proserpina) belonged, as their descendant, to the
Great Gods of Olympus. She was daughter of Demeter (Ceres)
by her brother Zeus (Jupiter), and she became wife of her uncle Hades (Pluto), who was also brother of both Demeter and
Zeus. Her name Persephone means "bringer of death," and she
was called for that reason the "Dread" Persephone; *"at mihi Persephone nigram denuntiat horam,"* said the Romans with a shudder: ". . . but Persephone gives me notice of the black hour of
my death." According to their own Italic ancestors, the Romans
believed that Hades (Pluto) was the son of their native god Saturn, another name for Cronus. To them, Saturn's day was sacred because he had been the oldest Latin King of Latium, god
of agriculture and donor of all civilization throughout their
western Mediterranean shores.

The story commences in Sicily which is a great, triangular
green island lying over a Typhon named Hades, who stirred
under there, loaded down as he was with fields, mountains, and
cities. Often he had his jet-black chargers hitched to his shiny,
black chariot so he could take a drive in the upper world to see
if it was at all stable.

One day Aphrodite and her son of love Eros noticed him.
Hoping to cast the Underworld also under the charms of Love,
Aphrodite suggested that Eros fire his passionate arrow into
the heart of Hades. The Underworld made up about one-third
of the world, so its conquest was desirable. Eros fired his arrow.
It pierced "Death" to the heart.

It was spring then. The noonday sun sent golden beams
through a canopy of leafy boughs. On bright lawns starred with
flowers, Persephone was playing with her girl friends. As they

ran about the meadows she stooped to fill a basket with the blossoms she liked best, white lilies and purple violets.

Hot with desire, Hades came upon her there and, quick as a wink, took her as his bride. Then she began to cry for her friends and her mother. She looked down and saw that her dress was torn. She let all her flowers strew the grass. Her virginity was lost. She cried bitterly as Hades called his chargers by name and sprang upon his chariot. The rapist drove them breakneck through chasms and rock passes where from bottomless pits the sulphur of the volcano Aetna bubbled and spouted. Always down and deeper down he drove.

The Mother had a priestess named Cyane there beside a purifying spring. She stood up out of the water and cried to Hades: "Lord of the Underworld! You shall not pass by me. Halt! You cannot become our Mother's son this way, by right of might."

Hades whipped his sable horses and drove at top speed past her outstretched arms. The priestess watched him go and sank below the waters of her spring, where her hair turned slowly green as if fanned, and waved in the currents.

Meanwhile Demeter searched high and low for her sweet daughter from when Aurora brushed the first pink wash of dawn across the eastern sky to when Hesperus followed the red sunset down the western sea. When darkness rose from earth, she lit her torches at Aetna's fires and patrolled valley and meadow up and down, there and abroad, over foreign lands and across distant seas, calling always, "Persephone." At last, she turned back to Sicily where she had seen her last that fatal noon hour.

One day she bent down to listen to Cyane's spring, but the priestess could only utter water noises, no speech. Seeing the goddess mirrored in the pool, Cyane thought of a way to help. She tossed Persephone's sash up from the depths. The mother knew at once it was her own child's garment.

As soon as she saw it floating up the current, she burst into sobs of grief, tore her hair in anguish, and beat her breasts. Then she stood up in rage and wasted all the land. She smashed the plows with her bare hands. She blighted crops with her hot breath. She sterilized the soil so nothing would grow. She let the sun burn up the seedlings. She let the rain flatten the hay. She called crows to eat the seed. She sowed weeds and nettles in the crops. She turned it into a Waste Land.

Even in her mad grief Demeter then heard the voice of the

priestess Arethusa pleading with her. Arethusa from her holy
spring begged her to cease her destruction, pleaded for the
innocent lands that had no part in the rape of Persephone, and
prayed for rain. Then Arethusa told the Mother how she herself had come from Greece under the seas to Sicily. On the
shores of the River Styx as it flowed through the infernal regions, she had seen Persephone alive. The young Persephone
was standing there terrified, crying for her mother. But she
looked well otherwise, and she was dressed in full regalia, and
crowned like a great queen.

Demeter hesitated not a second longer. In rage she flew to
Olympus in her chariot and thrust her furious finger in front
of Zeus's nose. "Our child, who was lost, is found. Give me back
my child. I can forgive the rape, but I warn you, I want my
daughter back."

"Calm down," Zeus said. "She is all right. All he gave her was
the gift of love. He is the King of Tartarus. He has to stay
below and rule those realms.

"Let's see. She can rise up to heaven, if you wish. *But I have
no power to break the law of The Fates.*

"The Fates decree that no one who has eaten the apple of
Hell can return ever again to a full life on earth."

The young girl Persephone, The Fates knew, had taken refuge in hell's walled garden. She had already walked there among
its trees. She had also rashly picked one luscious, yellow
pomegranate. She had, as she strolled along, peeled off its yel-
lowed skin, and swallowed seven of its bright red pulpy seeds.
The Fates had been so informed by a boy.

When Queen Persephone heard she had been betrayed by a
boy, one of her own evil subjects, she cast her curse upon him.
Before her eyes he turned into the feathered owl that hoots at
night, that swoops on silent wings upon weak prey, as when a
boy it did to her. Thus, the owl is doomed and alone, funereal,
deadly, harbinger from the Kingdom of Death.

Zeus heard of all that too. How could he resolve the crisis
and show an evenhanded *justice* to his brother, his sister, and
his daughter?

He turned to the cycle of time and rearranged the calendar
to give equal time to Hades and to Demeter: six months of

Persephone's presence with her dark spouse, followed by six
months of summer with her otherwise intransigent Mother.

On earth, as in art, Persephone usually holds a bouquet of
flowers in memory of those she lost: sheaves of wheat, the red
poppies of sleep and death, and Artemis's pomegranates, the
fruit of the Underworld.

Any eating of fruit, even a bite from an apple in the Netherworld, remains a crime punishable by eternal death. It appears so around the world, in one literature after another,
whether oral or written.

Women in the Greek world celebrated such Mystery Reli-
gions, which were for women primarily. They also worshipped
Demeter and Persephone in three or so major festivals, the
Eleusinia in February and September, and the Thesmophoria.
Their Mysteries were kept so secret by worshipper and priest-
ess alike that little is known of them to this day.

PRIESTESSES AS PROSECUTING ATTORNEYS

Architecture and law have both been suggested as the crowning achievements of Greece, the first a perishable and the second a flawed jewel perhaps, while literature as a third possibility now emerges as a contender, or rather, has failed ever
to submerge. Among the seven classics of Greek theater dealing with the trial of Orestes, the three parts of the *Oresteia* by
Aeschylus stand unforgotten and unforgettable. This trilogy is
a monumental work of art.

The defendant Orestes, long since, has confessed openly to
the premeditated murder of his mother Clytemnestra. His
sentence would normally have been suicide, exile for at least
three years, and the biting off of a finger. Years have passed.
He is still alive and in Mycenaean Greece. He has not been
exiled. He still confesses that he committed this murder intentionally and with premeditation. He stands before the society
of his age, to whom he presents an open lack of remorse or
contrition.

The contemporaries of Orestes are stumped. They openly confess their confusion. Orestes has broken a commandment: Thou shalt not kill, especially a member of your own family, clan, or tribe. Orestes pleads in his own defense. Everybody is stumped.

In other words, there is no justice in a land where the law is flawed. Orestes and his contemporaries live in a world where one sees clearly that a murderer can move from court to court. Years go by. The problem is not solved.

Nothing in the *Oresteia* is uplifting. Orestes is no hero who, like Oedipus through no fault of his own, falls from some position of honor to sudden, irrevocable disgrace. Neither Orestes nor anybody else is uplifted.

There exists at the end of the *Oresteia* a makeshift, contrived ending, but no solution. So the problem of Orestes, who still confesses he murdered his mother with malice aforethought, and *is therefore not guilty*, remains with us.

It is not possible to put it more plainly: Orestes's appeal was a sham. Critics say in vain how splendid it all was. Others cry how wonderful to read in Aeschylus about the first recorded jury of twelve good men and true.

Many people read history in order to sharpen their wits about present problems. Drama, which is by nature confrontational, offers us a good workout here for our wits. This workout increases in difficulty and complexity in proportion to the intelligence of the dramatist. Aeschylus must therefore be the world's most perceptive dramatist, because he has set before intelligent readers a problem that succeeding dramatists and librettists down the ages have also tried to solve. Thus, the problem inherent in the trial of Orestes—Orestes versus Mycenaean Greece—must still be relevant.

Aeschylus may have found the key to the collapse of Mycenaean Greece. Recalling the list of ancient civilizations, each greater than the last as it too rose only to collapse, one has to wonder why these civilizations rose but especially why they collapsed. Mycenaean Greece vanished after a glorious history of a hundred years. It vanished faster even than Minoan Crete. What it left was this tragic story of the Trojan War, as told by Homer. To the glory of that civilization, it also left the dramatists Aeschylus, Sophocles, and Euripides some thousand years later, in the fifth century, to attack and attempt to solve the personal problems of the Trojan War. Orestes versus Mycenaean Greece represents that confrontation of an individual versus war and its aftermath.

Orestes, from the House of Atreus, is portrayed in seven masterpieces of the classical theater in Greece. He has therefore been said to be the most popular hero in Mycenaean Greece. If Aeschylus set forth the problem, Euripides died before solving it. He was rewriting his second attempt to understand how it all started, his second *Iphigenia* play, when death overtook him. That play was first performed in 405 B.C., about a year later. It had been completed by his son.

Aeschylus had completed his "trio of plays" by 458 B.C., says Lionel Casson in his Introduction to the *Oresteia* (San Francisco, 1966). That new translation by Michael Townsend of the trilogy, *Agamemnon, The Choephorae* (Libation Bearers), and *The Eumenides,* is a marvel of the translator's art. The third play, *The Eumenides,* is the new name for the Furies. After all the trees have been shaken, the trial ended and Orestes vindicated, the old religion of Greece has been toppled. The old priestesses, long called the Furies, have been declawed, disarmed, and reoriented. Now they even have new names. Instead of revengeful, hideous, old Furies, they are henceforth to be called "Sweet Old Girls," the Eumenides.

Besides the olden Furies, there are other priestesses in the trilogy of Aeschylus: a shocked priestess at Delphi, and even the High-priestess Iphigenia herself. Like angry spotted leopards the three priestesses called Furies came to court in person to press charges against the matricidal hero Orestes. They exited as tamed, tabby cats, if one can believe it. The Oracle, or priestess at Delphi, had already proven herself both incompetent and impotent. The Furies identify themselves:

> We here are Night's primeval daughters; in
> Our land beneath the earth we are called Furies.

The last play spells out their defeat as the new replacing the old (religion); the male god has defeated the priestesses. It was the war of Zeus versus The Fates. It was the eagle (Zeus) eating a pregnant rabbit (Artemis). It was war because of Helen of Troy, a "woman . . . not content / With one husband. . . ." The men at war were vultures rowing the thousand ships of Agamemnon like scavengers in air. But watch out for Agamemnon's wife, Clytemnestra, whose brain is as good as his, and do not readily accept that the Trojan War was commenced by and for a woman.

Agamemnon

The Greeks held Agamemnon as the greatest man of his time. In the general anxiety of wartime, because his fleet could not sail for Troy and because he had to make it sail, he blamed the failure of wind upon Artemis. He therefore sacrificed his younger daughter, Iphigenia, whose throat he cut on an altar so ships could sail on the sea of her blood. It was not a pretty, pitiful young girl he slaughtered. She did not plead with her beloved father not to kill her, once his cherished holy daughter. In her saffron robes Iphigenia was the equivalent of a gagged, nanny goat to Agamemnon.

The death of the future priestess Iphigenia was perceived at home, in the general anxiety, while the men cried war "from the depths of their souls," as a wrong done to a child. The delay in sailing was perceived as a punishment from Artemis upon the Greeks.

As he lay dying, a terrible thought occurred to Euripides in all this tangle of women, children, and war: *What if Iphigenia was to be a priestess?* What of those saffron robes she wore? Why had Agamemnon chosen his younger daughter, and not the older girl, Electra? Was not the very youth of Iphigenia more apt to turn public opinion against Agamemnon? And furthermore, if he did not hesitate to sacrifice a girl, even were she not yet a priestess, before the patroness of all women, Artemis herself, had Agamemnon after all those years of marriage, during which he fathered the son Orestes and his two sisters, Electra and Iphigenia, no knowledge at all of his wife's character? Surely she had lashed out verbally, like a man, many times before she pleaded with her husband not to kill Iphigenia. But he had done so intentionally. He had tricked Clytemnestra into bringing her younger daughter to the Greek camp. The pretext was Iphigenia's engagement announcement to Achilles. The real purpose was to sacrifice her on the altar.

Who ran the country while the men fought at Troy? Who was the planner not for evil, but for the general welfare? It was the wife Clytemnestra. She set up the system of heliographs that kept the home folks apprised of the Greek victory, as it turned out. She issued them the solemn warning: war is war, but there are limits in warfare. Death to the Trojan warriors is acceptable because they entered the conflict for the purpose of death.

But let there be no outrage committed on the part of victorious Greeks, warned Clytemnestra. Let the temples of the gods of Troy be respected. Let there be, on the parts of the Greeks, if victorious, no desecration, no plunder of Troy, no lusting for its wealth, no theft of its treasures, no offense to its gods, and no further evil whatsoever. These Greeks at war in Troy are all men of wealth, she points out to whoever is listening, which is the Chorus of Argive Elders. What justice is there in that, that wealthy men fight a war for Helen of Troy, a woman supposedly stolen when everybody knows she went lightly and of her own accord? Let's balance this male view with a women's view, cried Clytemnestra:

> That is the story; the authority
> Is me, a woman.

I hope it will turn out well, and I don't much care how. "Spoken like a man," say the Argive Elders. "But the black Furies," they add, "may capsize Fortune." The Greeks have rotted at Troy for ten long years of frigid winters, torrid summers. They have been infested with lice. The black Furies have trounced them. This Helen of Troy must herself have been *a priestess of hell* raised in a home, like a lioness cub that when grown ate the family and its sheep. How can Agamemnon plead justice?

This is what I did, announced Agamemnon: I destroyed Troy, slaughtered every living man, woman, and child. I burned the city so that only a pall of smoke, visible for miles, remains to mark the site. Why? All because of a woman, the lion—I,

Agamemnon—ate the blood of the Trojan princes. Odysseus alone survives. He is my loyal friend.

Clytemnestra also survived, as full of wounds as a fisherman's net. She had no tears left, she said. She had wept them dry for grief over her lost daughter Iphigenia.

With my husband returning, said Clytemnestra to her household, my heart is lightened. Here comes my husband Agamemnon. He is our guard dog, the pillar of our house, dry land to sailors lost at sea, a welcome spring to thirsty travelers:

> I want this entrance carpeted with purple
> At once. . . .

Agamemnon objected. Stop rolling on the ground, he told Clytemnestra. Be yourself. All right, if I must walk on your royal purple carpet. Please stop fighting with me. I have a foreign girl here. She is the pride of Troy. Treat her well. His "foreign girl" was the renowned High-priestess of Troy, the prophetess Cassandra. We are very rich, Clytemnestra told her. We treat our slaves well. Come in, slave.

The Trojan prophetess Cassandra halted at the threshold, for she had second sight. She saw the coming catastrophe. It is not a wealthy house, she knew. It is the lair of murderers, past and future, the House of Atreus versus the House of Thyestes.

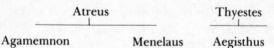

	Atreus		Thyestes
Agamemnon		Menelaus	Aegisthus

Crimes:

1. The wife of Atreus seduced Thyestes.
2. Atreus killed the two children of Thyestes and fed them at supper to their father.
3. Aegisthus and Clytemnestra, who are lovers, are about to slay Agamemnon.

Agamemnon's home is nothing but a slaughterhouse, saw Cassandra. There was blood everywhere. As she stands before the door, Cassandra knows the future. She sees Clytemnestra entice Agamemnon into his bath, throw a net over him, and stab him to death with multiple knife thrusts.

The priestess Cassandra then loudly prophesies *that the Furies, priestesses of death,* are descending upon them all. As they came, they sang a song of guilt. Guilt begets guilt, they sang, just as one crime leads to the next, and the next: murder, revenge, adultery, sacrifice, destruction of Troy, abduction of its women, slaughter of children. I know the evil deeds of these people, Cassandra says. Am I not right? Are these not evil people?

"Who is this murdering woman?" Cassandra asked. "She is the iron lady, the two-legged lioness, the killer Clytemnestra. She will kill me too."

Preparing for her own death, Cassandra laid down her scepter, removed the "prophetic bands" (v. 1208) from her neck, and whatever other prophetic garb from Troy she still wore on her person. "I ought at this moment to be conducting services in Troy," she said to herself, "instead of laying my head upon the chopping board and descending to my mistress, Persephone."

"Her death gives added relish to my joy," said Clytemnestra. She has ended her swan song. The Chorus of Argive Elders blame it all on Helen of Troy, but Clytemnestra refuses to believe it. It was not Helen, she says. It was the "Evil Genius" of this family. They died here because of the evil spirit of the House of Atreus. As for Agamemnon, he killed my darling daughter. She was such a tender little seedling of a flower.

"Where is Orestes?" cries the Chorus of Argive Elders, as the first play of the trilogy, *Agamemnon*, ends.

The Choephoroe, or Libation Bearers

The tomb of Agamemnon is visited by Orestes, who has returned to his country as the result of his father's murder. Orestes explains that what happened between his parents resembles the age-old war between the eagle (sun) and the serpent (earth). Orestes went to Apollo's oracle to ask for an explanation. There Apollo informed him that in order to still the pleas of Agamemnon, whose life is hell in the Underworld, Orestes

Figure 14. Three-faced Hecate

must murder both guilty parties, Clytemnestra and Aegisthus. Otherwise, the Furies will pursue him until they drive him mad.

The Chorus of Slave Women approve Orestes when, pretending to be a foreigner speaking in the dialect of Delphi, he tricks Aegisthus and kills him. When Clytemnestra rushes in and sees the corpse of her co-regent, she asks for an ax to defend herself against her son.

After Orestes has killed his mother, he reviles her body and taunts her corpse, hastening her to Death for her sins and her crime. To him she is the real snake or even a lamprey eel. Her touch to him was poisonous. "She did it, didn't she?" he cries over and again as he lists her wrongs, which he has just righted. There are Gorgons here, he says. Two of them! Look! These dead are no longer rulers. They both lie dead. They were never human. They were dragons, both of them.

At this point the Furies attack him. He sees them and feels their rage. These are the Gorgons. They wear black cloaks. Their hair is snakes, which coil and uncoil, hissing and seething before his eyes. "Putrid gore" drips from their eye sockets. "They are pursuing me," he cries. "I must go away from here, to Delphi."

The Chorus of Slave Women agree, for now they have witnessed murder in the third generation.

The Eumenides

I. Before Apollo's Temple. Delphi.

The aged Delphic priestess introduces herself and her prede-
cessors, all Oracles at Delphi, from Earth to her daughter
Themis to her daughter Phoebe to her daughter and so on,
until Apollo conquered Delphi and installed himself there as
god. The oracular priestess prays for guidance, honors the gods
of Greece, and mounts upon the oracular throne in the Temple of Apollo.

She returns outside, horrified. She describes the awful sight
she saw within the sanctuary. It frightened her so much that
she dropped to the floor. There in the temple, where garlands
hung so beautifully, a bloody man, holding a drawn sword, lay
across the sacred navel stone that marked Delphi as the oracular
center of the earth.

The strange man lay in an attitude of supplication. He had
wreathed an olive branch with strands of wool. Before him lay
sleeping a horde of hideous, old hags. At first sight the priestess mistook them for Gorgons. Then she tried to recall them
from bas-reliefs on the temples. They wore no wings. They
appeared to be black women. They were old and hideous. They
snored. Their nostrils were large and flared. Nauseating matter ran from their eyes. Their clothes were foreign and quite
unsuited to a house of worship. In fact, they were altogether
outside civilized society. Were they foreigners from some unknown land? If so, that land which spawned them must regret
having done so.

The ousted priestess deferred to her master Apollo.

II. Apollo's Inner Sanctum. Delphi.

Here Apollo comforts Orestes, vilifies the Furies as merely old
hags, foul as the mud they rose from. He also warns him that
the hags will pursue him over Europe until he reaches safety
in Athens. There he is to hang tight to the cult statue of Zeus's
daughter Athena, she who was born without recourse on the
part of Zeus to a mother. Orestes is to depend on Apollo, who
ordered him to kill his mother.

Meanwhile Clytemnestra's ghost awakens the Furies, calls

them to order, and urges them to take her part again. Each Fury spits out a curse upon Orestes, the last ones more violently than the first. The Eleventh points her finger at the defilement by blood of Apollo's navel stone. The Twelfth can hardly believe the god would harbor a murderer. The Thirteenth is shocked that Apollo has spurned the law; defied the olden, established Fates; and honored a human criminal in their place. The Fourteenth predicts that Apollo cannot save Orestes now, for others will succeed to the task if the Furies fail. After he has ordered them out of his temple, one shouts at him, "This sorry situation is not partially due to your error. It is entirely so." She adds that in their land matricides are driven out of their homes, that when a grown man murders his mother, then that man must be pursued until justice is served.

III. The Temple of Athena in Athens: The Last Trial of Orestes

The trial begins again in greater earnest, Orestes pleading his case before the altar of the goddess Athena, and the Furies representing the old state religion that not only finds him guilty, but also considers his crime to be without extenuating circumstances. The god of the Furies is Hades, who even from hell sees what occurs on earth. The Furies present themselves to Athena when she enters the courtroom, which indicates that the court is in session. "We are the daughters of Night," they say, "and are called Furies in our own land under the world."

"The accused could have killed his mother because he was afraid of her," says Athena.

"How can that happen?" they ask. "Who could be frightened of his own mother?"

Orestes urges, "Apollo did half the crime. He persuaded me to kill her."

The Furies conclude, "If this man continues to go unpunished, and if the crime of matricide is henceforth allowed by law, then the world we know will disappear into a new order of society. Think how many parents will fear for their lives at the hands of their own offspring. The only rule we could admire eschews both anarchy and tyranny."

Apollo insists: "This man worships me. I have purified him of this blood. I am a witness here that I caused him to kill his mother."

Athena then allowed the prosecution to interrogate Orestes. They question him (questions and answers summarized):

Question: Did you kill your mother?   (v. 583)
Orestes: Yes.
Question: How?
Orestes: I pulled out my sword and cut her throat.
Question: Who instigated it?
Orestes: Apollo.
Question: He persuaded you?
Orestes: Yes. I do not regret having done it.
Question: Why not?
Orestes: She committed two crimes.
Question: What two crimes?
Orestes: She killed her husband (#1) and my father (#2).
Furies: He was not her blood relative.
Orestes: Am I?
Furies: Yes. You are of your mother's blood. You are a murderer.
Apollo: Careful. I was ordered by Zeus to instruct this man.
Furies: Unbelievable. Zeus did that?
Apollo: Agamemnon was a great commander. He was not supposed to be slain by a woman.
Furies: That's good, to allege Zeus. Everybody knows he killed his own father.
Apollo: A mother is only a nurse to a fetus and then to the child. Its parent is the father. Athena is a case in point. She was born of Zeus alone. She had no nurse, no mother. That's the truth.
Furies: Now hear my truth. Either we win this verdict or we will bear down hard on all of you in this country.
Athena: The vote is a tie, so I cast my vote in favor of Orestes. Orestes, you win and are acquitted of all crime.

The Furies call upon their Mother Night to witness what has happened. The modern gods, they say, have trampled down the olden laws of the land. They have dishonored the priestesses of the dead, who now will poison their earth. Justice itself has been scorned. She too will send disease abroad, blight the crops, make the animals sterile, and disseminate hostility and resentment among people.

The goddess Athena requests the Furies to accept her offer of a comfortable abode in that kingdom, plus the respect and veneration they deserve from the Athenians. She also asks them to abandon their priesthood as avengers from hell and become the "Eumenides" instead of the "Furies." They agree and so change their names to "The Kind Persons."

In *The Golden Bough* (Vol. I), as Sir James Frazer studied the myths concerning "The King of the Wood," he came upon two alternate versions of what happened after the trial of Orestes. In the first, after Orestes murdered a king in the Crimea, he and his sister Electra fled to Italy. They brought with them the sacred image of Artemis, which they had concealed in a bundle of sticks. Orestes founded in Aricia, Italy, the worship of Diana (Artemis) there in the wood of Nemi. The second version explains how Orestes managed to purify himself at a temple of Artemis at Troezen, Greece, and so freed himself from the charge of matricide. Before the temple stood a sacred stone where nine Elders performed upon Orestes the disculpation ritual; they used water from the Horse's Fount. At a nearby building at this precinct the descendants of these Elders dined together on specified days. At the spot where their ancestors had cleaned their utensils used in the purification, a laurel tree grew up.

REPERCUSSIONS

In his translation of the *Eumenides* (1925) the Greek scholar Gilbert Murray explained the natural, Greek law of the blood feud: the "doer must suffer." According to the justice understood by Earth, by the first Oracle Themis at Delphi, and according to The Fates and the Fate *(Moira)* ordained as each person's "portion," seeds germinate, fruits ripen, the seasons revolve, the sun shines or rain falls, but blood demands blood. Pride goeth before a fall. Sin requires the punishment of the sinner. This is Nature's way.

The interpretation of justice can be made, if individuals are unsure, by their Elders. If they fail to give a clear and therefore true verdict, the plaintiff may appeal to the Delphic Oracle. That priestess is the highest in the land.

In the rarest of cases—when the individual is unsure, the Elders fail, and the Oracle declares herself disqualified, which was Orestes's situation—the case goes on appeal to the *Erinnyes*. Thus, the Furies represent the ultimate judge, for they guard the law, pursue the transgressor, and personify the victim. Aeschylus faithfully, then, represented Clytemnestra's ghost risen from hell like a hound on the scent of her murderer. The ghost of the mother reawakened the Furies, as Aeschylus dramatized it for us. Orestes's Fate *(Moira)* had already been apportioned him at birth. *Moira* could never be altered.

Behind all justice, as ranged hierarchically, extended the Underworld of the dead, at home there forever. When crimes polluted Earth itself, she notified the community that they were all guilty. In cases of murder unpunished, then the guilt fell equally, by fire, flood, quake, drought, and disease, on all persons alive in the upper world. There was no way to sidestep responsibility for one's brother. Everyone was his brother's keeper. Thus, Jean-Paul Sartre, who also wrote an Orestes tragedy *(Les Mouches,* Paris, 1943), declared with conviction; *"Nous sommes tous des assassins."*

The *Oresteia* ends in peace, said Gilbert Murray. The Eumenides are to be escorted to the sacred hill in Athens where the first temple was built by the virginal Amazons.

The Furies, said Robert Graves (in his *Greek Myths,* 1955, Vol. II, pp. 72–73; Vol. I, p. 288 *et passim)*, were a "hereditary priesthood" from the Clan of the Hesychids. They were born from Night and from the blood of Uranus when Cronos castrated him. They scorned Apollo's excuse that a mother was nothing more than the furrow into which the seed of Orestes had been cast. Both Orestes, he says, and Heracles bit off a finger as admission of guilt. The Furies, whom Pausanias called "august matrons," and not hags, dwelled in the deep pit of Erebus whence they soared, god-headed and bat-winged, to pursue Orestes. They never ceased the chase. They saw him killed finally by Artemis, who had exacted his death to pay for the death of (her priestess) Iphigenia. Thus, the Orestes myth referred originally to the ritual death of the King of the Wood, whose throat was slit by an obsidian knife.

George Thomson (1965) in his discussion of "Man's Lot in Life" (p. 341) says the unwritten laws under which the case of Orestes first fell were not primitive but "found only in the higher stages of tribalism":

> . . . murder within the kin—the most terrible sin that a tribesman can commit. Consequently, when we find the Erinyes described as "curses" and imagined as snakes, we can see in them . . . a particular aspect of those same matriarchal ancestresses whose malediction upheld the inviolability of tribal custom (p. 342).

The curse of the Erinnyes followed each generation, causing the extinction of the families of both Orestes and Oedipus. Thus, the sins of the fathers were visited upon their children.

The book *Mothers and Amazons* (1965) by Helen Diner (Eckstein) explains the case of Orestes by matriarchal law, by which Clytemnestra murdered a stranger, who was her husband and hence not a member of her own clan. But Orestes committed the only unforgivable sin when he killed his mother, a clan member closest of all to him by blood. Athena broke the tie of the hung jury because she believed that she should cast her ballot in favor of Orestes for personal reasons:

> For I did not have a mother who bore me;
> No, all my heart praises the male,
> May Orestes win over your tied vote (p. 36).

"This acquittal proclaims the downfall of the matriarchy and the victory of the Olympian over the chthonical world." The Leader of the Erinnyes utters a last curse: "Woe . . . woe. . . ."

In Boston, 1968, Philip Eliot Slater published a book on *The Glory of Hera: Greek Mythology and the Greek Family*, which could be required reading for all prospective parents. In this book he traced the war between the sexes in Greece from Hera versus Zeus, husband versus wife, to Orestes versus Clytemnestra (mother versus son). Obviously, the marriage "bond was the weakest point in the Greek family" (p. 164). But when matricide becomes a theme of constant preoccupation in a society, as it did in the dramas featuring Orestes, then the family has already collapsed. What society can continue?

> Rejection and derogation of women mean rejection and derogation of domesticity—of home and family life, and hence of the process of rearing children (p. 7).

Slater went back to the late Margaret Mead's *Male and Female* (New York, 1955). In this work, as in her lectures at Columbia University, the celebrated anthropologist discovered that

> to the extent that either sex is disadvantaged, the whole culture is poorer, and the sex that, superficially, inherits the earth, inherits only a very partial legacy (pp. 272–273).

Mead had not finished her discoveries. She pursued these findings to their logical development, suggesting that in a society like the ancient Greek world, where there occurred a total dominance of women by males, there probably followed an end to

> great periods of civilized creativity when philosophies fail, arts decline, and religions lose their vigor. . . . (p. 280).

Greek women were treated with contempt. Their goddess Athena became boyish. Their Hera became vindictive and persecutory. The battle of the sexes had turned there to outright war. Slater's conclusion, for persons observing American society today, is realistic: I am arguing here that the one (American culture of today) springs directly from the other (ancient Greek culture)—that the motivational basis of our own society is simply an advanced stage of the same disease that dominated Greek life (p. 453).

THE PRIESTESS IPHIGENIA

Euripides returns at the last days of his life to Iphigenia, whom he had pictured at Aulis. There the Greek fleet of her father languished while awaiting a favorable sea crossing. Tricked by Odysseus, the poor mother Clytemnestra escorted her younger daughter Iphigenia to her betrothal, she thought. It was rather to her death, which the girl accepted at her father's hands, as he severed her jugular vein.

Then, at the end of his life, Euripides thought better of it. Realizing that the sacrifice of Iphigenia awakened "in the breasts of the ancients the same abhorrence that it does in ours," said Gayley (p. 316), Euripides wrote, or commenced writing, an alternate version: Iphigenia was a priestess.

Whereas some had seen Orestes and Electra escaping with a sacred icon into Aricia, Italy, where they founded a temple to Artemis (Diana), Euripides saw Orestes wandering up north of the Black Sea into the savage lands of the Taurians. Thus, he had Orestes search out another sister with whom to plot the theft of a sacred religious object, and steal away with it and the resurrected Iphigenia to Greece. There they too would found a temple. But there was a problem: Iphigenia was dead.

Therefore in his last drama Euripides shows us what *really* happened among the Greeks at Aulis. At the last minute, after two burly men had hoisted the half-naked Iphigenia up on the altar, which is how Greek artists portrayed the scene, and while her heavily bearded father facing her had already raised the terrible sharp knife aloft, the Asian Mother goddess Artemis substituted a hind for Iphigenia. She then spirited the fainting girl, all the way up a thousand or so miles into the Crimea, where the Scythians dwelled. So doing, Euripides absolved the Mycenaean Greeks of child sacrifice, and involved the Ionian Greeks and Artemis. Even better, he withdrew sympathy from a butchered Iphigenia. Had it not been so poor, it would have been a wonderful solution.

As everyone knew, the native Taurians, Amazons, priestesses *et al.* of what is now the southern U.S.S.R. were totally un-Greek, ergo, savages. They practiced human sacrifice all the time. All strangers they slaughtered routinely, Iphigenia as their High-priestess officiating, if not personally doing the killing.

Specious reasoning aside, it seems appropriate to adopt the alternate tradition, that Iphigenia was a priestess from the word go. Since she was a priestess in a world of men-at-war, she was ideally suited for sacrifice in the first place because the more elevated the victim, the more powerful the pull on the gods to grant her father favorable winds and calm seas for the crossing from Aulis to the Troad.

Everybody else but a schoolteacher, everyone else whose natural sympathy lies not especially with young girls, has admired Euripides and his *Iphigenia in Tauris* (414–412 B.C.). In his evenhanded Preface, Gilbert Murray (1915) spoke about a male victim brought to the point of death upon a Greek altar, touched upon the throat, and let go. That was the Greek rite, he said. Iphigenia had been laid upon the altar of Artemis Tauropolos. The story follows properly: Orestes and Iphigenia. Such stories, Euripides' last play among them, are at best merely "conjectural restorations" of what may have been "early history" (p. vi).

It was not the Greeks, as Murray saw it, who demanded the death of Iphigenia in the first place. It was Artemis. It was also the Asian Mother goddess who intervened in the nick of time, to save the sacrificial offering. This same Artemis put Iphigenia safely down as priestess, although in the savage land of the Tauri, way out of Greece, up beyond the north end of the Bosporus, on the north coast of the Black Sea. Today, the marvelous Scythian tombs, horse burials, golden jewelry showing the beautiful "Cossack" costumes, and the long, curly hair and beards of the horsemen tell us, more than words can do, where Iphigenia lorded it as High-priestess of Artemis.

Euripides leads up to his great scene of confrontation-into-recognition by showing Orestes arriving on that coast with his friend Pylades. They are prepared for sacrifice, which is the Taurian law. Orestes has journeyed there in order to (steal and) carry home to Argos an image of Artemis, which is to say, a fallen meteorite. As High-priestess, Iphigenia carries about this "moonstone," says Murray, for these are priestesses of the moon. Since Orestes is a firstborn child, he is all the more suitable as a sacrifice. But brother and sister recognize each other at the last moment.

Together they plot and make good their escape. They will return home and build a suitable temple where this invaluable icon can be placed.

Euripides' *dramatis personae* are Orestes and his friend Pylades, plus King Thoas of the Taurians' savage country, who will be killed by Orestes. There are a Herdsman and a Messenger, a Chorus of captive Greek women slaves, the Highpriestess Iphigenia, and the goddess *ex machina* Athena, who wraps it all up at the end, as she did for the *Eumenides* of Aeschylus.

What is wonderful about this play is the soliloquy with which it begins. Iphigenia comes out of the temple of Artemis. Imagine how it would have been had she stood before the great sanctuary of Ephesus. She walks downstage and speaks directly to us. We hear what a High-priestess would have said, how she would have spoken, according to one of Greece's finest dramatists:

Iphigenia's Soliloquy (A Paraphrase)

I was born from the line of Pelops, whose son was Atreus of Argos, whose sons were Menelaus and Agamemnon. I was the infant born to him and to Clytemnestra. It was I whom my lord father slew there beside the swirling eddies of the Strait of Euripus. He thought he made of me an offering, for the sake of Helen of Troy, to the goddess Artemis, there in the storied chasms of Aulis.

King Agamemnon had ordered assembled there the full force of the Hellenes: one thousand ships. He trusted that the Mycenaeans would win the Crown of Victory and, from the high towering city of Troy, revenge for their desecration of Helen's marriage bed and Menelaus's dishonor.

However, they were all delayed at Aulis. The grim winds blew them down and forbade them the sea. My lord father had recourse to Calchas, son of Thestor, the wisest seer we were to have before Troy. He spoke:

"King Agamemnon, Commander-in-Chief of our combined forces from all Greece, thou shall not sail from here. Land and sea prevent thee. First thou must sacrifice Iphigenia, thine own daughter, to the Queen of Light, *Artemis, Regina Lucina*. For, look, she came into the light in thine own halls. . . ."

(Excuse me, Calchas termed me "most fair," which is embarrassing for me to repeat).

"Whom thou must prepare to offer up."

It came about that by the trickery of Odysseus they carried me from my mother to Aulis, as a supposed bride of Achilles.

I journeyed to Aulis where, alas, I was lifted over the funeral pyre, up high in the air, alas. The sword was raised to slay . . . , but Artemis snatched me up and away through the blue sky. The Achaians had substituted a female red deer. She flew me straight away to the barbarians' land, where the Taurians live like barbarians.

Their King Thoas the Nimble, who rules this Tauric Chersonese, won his nickname because of his feet that bear him nimbly like the beating wings of birds. His priestess ordained me here in this temple you see.

And here I serve in the rites of dark Artemis which please the goddess. Her rites are "dark," which does not mean "fair." When I see them performed under my authority, I tremble for fear so badly I lose the power of speech.

I sacrifice, according to the ancient usage of this foreign country, whatever Greeks set foot upon this coast. I hallow this stranger and consecrate this man for abhorred butchering by my ministers.

Let me tell heaven what dreams I dream, if help there be in heaven. I dream each night the same weird dreams as Night sends down to me asleep. I dream in sleep that I have escaped from here and find myself at home again in Argos. I dream I am asleep again in my own little bed where as a little maid I slept each night. Then in the night there came the terrible loud roar of an approaching earthquake. Its tremors rippled across under me. The earth chugged, back-forth, back-forth. I fled from my bed. I went out of doors and stood there. I looked up to see the whole crown of the roof smash down upon the ground. The shaking brought down the turret from the top story, and then the whole house collapsed outwards down to the cellars. It fell as if picked up and tossed, one whole section at a time.

Only the central column still stood alone in all that dust and desolation. That was the only remnant left of my lord father's dwelling, only the shaft and the capital on its top.

But what did I see? From the sculpted capital there streamed out in the nighttime sky long, golden hair. It spoke aloud in a person's voice to me. I raised my priestess's ewer as I do when consecrating a stranger for sacrifice according to the Taurian rite. I sprinkled the golden curls, which laid a doom of death upon them. And all this time my tears ran down my cheeks.

Now let me interpret my dream for you:

Orestes is dead. I sacrificed him on the high altar. A son is the pillar of the house. Whoever is sprinkled from the priestess's ewer is doomed to death by her hand.

The man who came as his friend I cannot place. He should be a son of Strophius, but Strophius had no son, or at least, when I left Argos for Aulis he had as yet no son.

Now let me make an offering by way of a prayer and the pouring of this wine to a brother far away from a sister a far distance from him.

My handmaidens may assist me now, for they are slave girls from Greece. King Thoas gave them to me as his gift. Maidens, where are you?

My handmaidens for some unknown reasons fail to answer my summons. Let me proceed from here back to the shrine of this temple where now I dwell.

Conclusion

The reader is left to choose among these alternate versions the one he prefers, the one which suits his understanding of Mycenaean Greece. Was the dream of Iphigenia a memory or an example of second sight? He has, at least, heard a priestess speaking, dreaming, remembering, and thinking.

What makes literary dreams so very interesting, observed Sigmund Freud in his essay on the dreams of Raskolnikov in Dostoevski's *Crime and Punishment*, is that Dostoevski dreamed them, and not Raskolnikov.

VIII

DIVINITIES OF THE SEA

"A woman's countenance, with serpent locks,   *v. 38*
Gazing in death on Heaven from those wet rocks."
        Percy Bysshe Shelley
        "On the Medusa of Leonardo da Vinci
        in the Florentine Gallery" (1819).

" 'Right,' I said, 'no more Klage,'[1] *and when I looked up at the*
Vermeer girl it was Medusa I saw, flickering and friendly, trust-
ing me with the idea of her."
        Russell Hoban
        The Medusa Frequency (New York, 1987).

POSEIDON

It seems true that the Mediterranean Sea and adjacent coastlines "formed the real center of ancient life" (Semple, p. 12)
and that the ancient world was small. Beyond these immediate
hinterlands the writers refer vaguely to Scythians, Hyperboreans of the extreme north, the hot deserts behind, and even
vaguely to North Africa as almost indiscriminately "Libya." And
yet Greek Mythology arises there, in Libya precisely, which the
Romans would qualify as "Black": "Libya Africa." Thus, when
they set about writing their books on Greek mythology, they
were also mystified. But they did record the beginnings of that

---

[1] By the German word *Klage*, the author refers onomatopoetically, I believe, to the
lamentation that followed the awful death of Medusa.

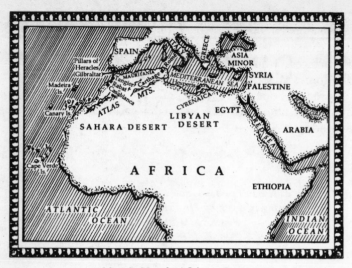

Map 5 North African Coast

mythology in the westernmost area adjacent to the Atlas Mountains, and they were able to make out the tremendous presence of Poseidon.

Herodotus makes the general ignorance of Africa very plain in his Book IV, 45:

> As far as Europe is concerned, it is obvious that none of us has obtained knowledge of its eastern areas or of its northern limits . . . or its extent . . . enough to extend across both Asia and Libya. No more am I able now to estimate the causes behind the naming of the earth either, for this entire world is divided into three parts, has three names, and why all three parts are named for women. . . .

That too must remain with the Father of History as an unsolved riddle: the naming of the continents. Great dark Africa was named for the sea god's wife: Poseidon married Libya.

That continent was named for a queen. The continent to the north was named for the Princess of Tyre, the Phoenician seaport and commercial center north of Israel: Europa. The girl was stolen away by the Kings of Crete, to found the Minoan dynasty. The third continent was Asia, named for a Lydian princess who owned in her day the eastern priestesses' kingdoms: Mysia, Lydia, Caria, and Phrygia.

Herodotus does not ask the question which immediately follows: what about the capital of the Hellenes, Attica? But he does add:

> As for the Athenian goddess Athene (Athena), they do record her as the natural daughter of (the Libyan sea god) Poseidon, and his spouse, Lake Tritonia. They say that, angered for some reason with her father Poseidon, the girl adopted Zeus as her father, and had him acknowledge her as his (adopted) daughter.

Nobody will be surprised that since prehistoric times the world has also revolved about the sea, the ocean, the moon, and woman. From the waters and from woman come fertility for both earth and mankind. The Neolithic sign for water is identical to the Egyptian hieroglyph, or sacred mark: ∿∿∿. The body of the Egyptian sea god, whose breast indicates that he has undergone a sea change from female to male, is covered with fish's scales represented as continuous parallelled lines of ∿∿∿, "water." In literature the symbols for water are frequently encountered: spiral, snail, woman, and fish (usually erotic). Water represents the Great Mother, *Magna Mater*. It is always understood as the medium by which life is born, life itself originating in water. Thus, an amphibian such as the frog is a totem for womankind, at home in both ambiances. Baptism by water leads to a new birth.

From Neolithic times to Rome and into Christianity as it spread throughout Europe, the cult of water continued, particularly among the tenacious Celts of Gaul and Britain. To this day springs, streams, and rivers are considered sacred. In France the Marne River bears the Great Mother's Latin name: Marne < Matrona.

In ancient, mythological ages prophets spoke beside a holy spring that bubbled out of the ground. Consequently, ancient temples were erected near water, either beside a spring, or on a promontory overlooking the sea. From the cliffs a fire could warn mariners to stand out to sea, just as in Crete and Alexandria the massive Pharos beamed its light out across the water. The Roman Pharos still stands in Dover, England, even though its counterpart on the opposite French coast has long since fallen into the Channel. The black-haired, black-bearded Poseidon brought it down there where the Celts called him Manannan mac Lyr, Old King Lear.

Pausanias saw priests of Apollo cut branches from the sacred (Druid) oaks and drop them in water to bring rain during periods of drought. The heroes of the Celts had only to approach the old god's castle, and strike on the shield suspended under an oak tree. Bluebirds flew up in the air. The sky rumbled. Then the rain swept down in torrents of fresh water. Homer said the Trojans cast their horses into the Scamander River near Troy, where Achilles threw the Amazon Penthesilea's corpse. For that reason perhaps the River God rose and fought Achilles. The hero Peleus who married the sea goddess Thetis cast fifty sheep into a spring. It is no wonder he fathered such a cruel son as Achilles.

Like the water goddess Thetis, the mothers of heroes were usually women who wielded supernatural power over the waters. Thus, great Aeneas, who fled safely from Troy as it burned, was the son of Aphrodite, Queen of the Sea. The ancients were warned about Nymphs. Some like Actaeon and Tiresias were severely punished for intruding upon the secret rites of the priestesses who served the sea, the springs, the rivers, and the fountains. Like their friendly serpents, priestesses preferred to remain unseen, especially at midday. Anyone bending down to look in a pool of water at midday risked seeing one of their faces. That meant death, or metamorphosis into a narcissus or a daffodil, permanently crook-necked.

The cosmos itself is represented familiarly in replica: water, grove of trees (preferably oaks), stone circle, and mountain △ as an equilateral triangle.

From deep water, and boundless ocean encircling the continents, came the mermaid or fairy priestess of the sea. Her hair fell about her body in long, tangled, wet locks. She was beautiful beyond compare. The king's son of Ireland fell madly in love with her. His infatuation was so deep that his father the king stood dismayed but powerless before her magical allure. The king's son seized Fand's fingers, and the two of them returned via deep water into the western world. Perhaps they found the Fountain of Youth. The king's son was never heard of again. Wherever he went, he no longer remembered Ireland.

When Zeus fought the African kings named "Titans," he and the Greeks, setting foot across Ocean's shore, experienced the same loss of consciousness. In that dark western Libya they entered another, older world of foreign gods. There they failed to systematize, rationalize, and categorize those they fought so successfully. Poseidon went home to Greece with them. So did his daughter Athena, that strange masculine virgin who claimed birth fully armed from the body of Zeus, without any nourishing mother to counteract her warring man's nature. There the Greeks met Prometheus whom Zeus chained but who was even then still attended by his Ocean Nymphs, priestesses of the Atlantic. Once in Greece, Poseidon fought Athena for sovereignty of Athens, but deferred to her finally as really not his, but Zeus's daughter.

Hera said *(Iliad* XIV): "He is Oceanus, from whom all the gods of Greece are descended." When displeased with him, Hera even dismissed the Sun, whom she ordered down into the deep waters of the Atlantic Ocean *(Iliad,* XVIII). It was black Poseidon, lord of waters, who held the earth in his embrace, "earth circler," "lord of the earthquake." There in the far west he raised and raced his favorite white horses of the sea. The son of Poseidon, said Plato, was Atlas, after whom the Atlantic was named. West of Atlas in Libya was the western realm of Poseidon's ocean and islands, like the Hibernia named for a sea goddess also called Eire.

The divinities of the sea, whose priestesses and temples encircled the Mediterranean, fall into an older and a younger race, the former ruled by the "powerful," the "kings" called Titans under their own King Cronos. According to this race of giants, Earth (Gaea) married the Deep Sea (Pontus):

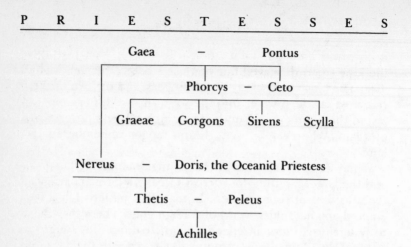

All members of the third generation were monsters of the sea, which the Egyptians and Greeks alike feared and abhorred. Nereus is the Old Man of the Sea, sometimes less murderous than the one-eyed witches called Gray Ones, or the icy-cold Gorgons, or the slippery Sirens.

Scylla's Story
There was once a King Sisyphus of Corinth. He was the son of Aeolus, the God of the Winds and ruler of the Windy, or Aeolian Islands. Aeolus was himself the son of Hellen, founder of the Hellenes, or Greek race. Through them the story of Scylla dates from one of the beginnings of prehistory.

Famous for his clever robberies, plunder, and pillage, King Sisyphus ran up against Theseus of Athens, who was so much more cunning that he killed him. When he got down to the Netherworld, Sisyphus learned what his punishment was to be, and that it would be everlasting: He was doomed forever to roll a stone to the top of a hill that would then roll it back down to the bottom.

King Sisyphus left in the upper world (and here is where the story of Scylla comes in) a blue-eyed son named Glaucus. *Glaucus* means blue-gray, or bluish green, or sea green; it is the color of sea water.

(The Romans, incidentally, disliked blue-eyed people, and, thus, were not at all fond of Celts, whose eyes they found too stern, shiny, and glaring. This blue eye coloring characterized not only water deities the world over, but was also the favorite color of Celts: Irish, Welsh, Bretons, Britons, and Gauls. All these "blue" peoples and their Druid priestesses were generally recognized as seacoast enemies, present and future, of Rome and Greece).

Prince Glaucus became the original blue merman. He frequented the waters of the Etruscan Sea west of Italy, and one day plunged into very high waves off Sicily (Ovid, *Metamorphoses*, XIV). Behind him as he swam daringly through open water, he could see the streamers of smoke rising from an eruption of Mt. Aetna. And below the peak he saw the fallow acres owned by the Cyclops, who permitted neither tillage nor the running of cattle on their lands. On the coast he could occasionally glimpse the olden city of Regium lying on its perilous strait.

His hands stroking the billows like wooden paddles, Glaucus aimed for the priestess Circe's green hills beside the Tyrrhenian (Etruscan) Sea. She came down to welcome Glaucus.

"I have come to you, beloved Sorceress Circe," he told her, "to ask a favor. Nobody but you can assist me in my madness. I am plunged into the very worst love affair you ever heard of. I know you have special magical herbs and flowers that you make into love potions. I have had experience in your magic. I stood on the Italian side of the Strait of Messina and was looking over at the Sicilian city when I first saw Scylla. I am sunk into confusion to have to tell you how hard I fell, what enchanting words of love I whispered in her ear, what sweet promises I promised, what soft pleas I pleaded. Can you believe it? Despite all that, the girl ran away from me.

"Can't you do something for me? Could you perhaps sing a song that would spellbind her? Or even better, could you fix a love potion that would work wonders on her body? Could you raise her temperature a bit? I don't really worry about warming her up, or getting burned myself. Just set her on fire for me. Let her blush red and pant for me the way I have reddened hot for her."

The priestess Circe heard him out with growing interest; for she herself was ready to make love anytime day or night, noon or evening. She was reputedly a highly sexed temptress whom Aphrodite had too richly endowed with femininity.

"Why don't you pick on somebody passionate like yourself," she advised Glaucus. "Why run after some lass who doesn't even know what it's all about? You need a real woman, warm, big-hearted, loving, amorous, and fully grown. Take me, for example. Now I," she said, "am a daughter of the Etruscan sun. I have all the charms that captivate a man. I also sing and make potions from herbs. I am ready to have you stark naked, just as you came out of the sea. Let's go to bed. Let her alone, as she has left you. When you make love to me, you will be acting as two women wish you to act."

Incautiously Glaucus spoke in haste: "Never. Priestess, I would as soon love you as see trees grow on the waves of this sea. I would as soon love you as see seaweed festoon this mountain top. Even after all that, my love for Scylla would still burn true."

Did Glaucus notice how pale with rage the witch Circe grew? She first thought to slap his face. But how do that when he was so handsome and when she panted for him? Circe turned her seething anger to a better use. She turned to her plots and her pots, and brewed up a dose. While it cooked in the cauldron, she sang it a song Hecate had taught her. Any reasonable man would have taken to his legs and run away.

Circe wrapped her sea-blue cloak about her shoulders. She passed through her golden palace, bending down to kiss her sweet pets—her pigs, her dog, and her loving lions. She let them fawn on her and lick her toes. Then she leaped onto the sea that lay over the Strait of Messina, flashing away from the rocky shores, placing her pink soles on the blue waters of the glaring, blue sea.

Beyond the first beaches of Sicily she saw the private, sandy cove that Scylla loved so dearly. It lay between two red, rocky ledges where the sand beach curved into a bow. Every midday when no shadow fell upon the clear, blue water, and she could admire the sea urchins on the bottom, Scylla went there to bathe. It was deep, clear, and cool beside the cliffs.

This noon the priestess Circe arrived ahead of Scylla. Into the crystal-clear water she poured her concoction of nasty roots and herbs. Then she closed her eyes and said the magical words nine times over, and three times more for good measure. They cast the blackest spell that Circe knew. They came from cold lips that hated Scylla.

Down to her beloved pool the maiden Scylla came at high noon. She waded in the cool water up to her waist. When she looked down, she saw to her horror that her legs had disappeared. They had vanished from her sight. Her thighs had turned into dogs' heads that stuck out barking in a circle around her hips. Scylla stamped on the sandy bottom. She splashed about this way and that trying to shake them off her. With her fingers she tried to rip them off. Then she saw that they had taken root in her soft torso. She felt as if the black hound Cerberus from the Underworld had wound himself twelve times into twelve barking dogs' heads around what had been her lower body. She sat down in the water and stayed there aghast. She had turned into a monster. No longer a girl, she had become only half a girl. Her lower half was maddened dogs ceaselessly barking all around what had been a girl's body.

Glaucus swam back to Sicily and saw what Scylla had become. He stood and looked at her. Glaucus burst into tears at the sight. He would not have cared even if he had known that soon Poseidon's white sea horses would tear him to pieces.

Glaucus never looked again at Circe. As for Scylla, she opted for revenge. She made herself a home on her side of the Strait. When Odysseus tried to pass those waters, she and her barking dogs pounded his ships for all they were worth. She would have drowned the Trojan Aeneas, and great Rome would never have been founded, except that she was metamorphosed into a gray rock cliff there on the shore. When the priestesses in their seaside temples sing her song, they are called the Chorus of Glaucus, drowned at sea. All mariners know they should steer clear of Scylla.

Robert Graves becomes very angry when he comments upon such myths of a new Iron Age mentality where the "cold-blooded treatment of women" repels him (II, p. 303). An earlier poet, John Keats, ended the story of Scylla in a modern fashion, rescuing the girl a thousand years later and uniting her with Glaucus due to the efforts of "Endymion." Glaucus becomes the father of the hero Bellerophon to whom the African High-priestess's winged horse is given as his personal steed. In order to learn about the birth of Pegasus, the winged horse of the Great African Mother Medusa, we must go back again to look at the major divinities of the sea.

The greatest sea god is still Poseidon, who Plato said ruled the lost continent Atlantis out in the ocean west of Gibraltar. He was the son of Libya herself, the Earth of Africa. After the death of Cronus, the Cyclops gave Poseidon the three-pronged trident he used from his palace in Euboea, where he dwelled and where he stabled his white sea horses and kept his golden chariot. In later days Poseidon became enraged when Athena took over Athens. He therefore deprived the Athenian women of their vote and forbade the men to call themselves by their mothers' names, as hitherto. He raped Demeter and flooded the plains of Greece. This flood occurred just before Phaeton drove madly behind the horses of the sun. Poseidon raped fully as many Nymphs as Zeus, for in the sea-god's case the rapes of these priestesses were woven by Arachne: Canace raped by Poseidon as a "bull," Theophane raped by a "ram," Demeter raped by a "horse," Medusa by a "bird," and Melantho by a "dolphin."

Poseidon killed the Amazon's son Hippolytus when the boy's father Theseus asked him to do so. He held Paris's hand and helped him aim the arrow that killed Achilles. As ruler *par excellence* of the western seas, he opposed the Asian sea goddess Aphrodite. Poseidon usually championed his Greeks against her Trojans. He approved two Labors of Heracles who performed them for him in his realm: the white cattle, and the apples of the Hesperides.

Herodotus said that despite the building projects of Poseidon, a channel in Thessaly and the walls of Troy, the sea god was really a Libyan and not a Greek deity. He appeared to be unknown to the Egyptians, who had no affection for the sea and no admiration for the bronze doors to Tartarus that Poseidon also constructed. The Homeric Hymn XXII "To Poseidon" terms him "the great god" as far as the Greeks are concerned. He was the Earth Shaker, the Tamer of Horses, the Saver of Ships, the god of the deep. He fathered the mon-

strous Charybdis, who guarded the Strait of Messina opposite
Scylla's shore. He fathered the giant Polyphemus, whom
Odysseus tricked. He loved the Ethiopians and all other Africans. He got even with Odysseus by sending the son of Odysseus born to the priestess Circe to kill his father.

The second most important divinity of the sea is the river
called Oceanus that circles the earth. Oceanus was also a Titan, also a son of Uranus and Earth, and father to the many
priestesses named Oceanids for him. One of them, his daughter Doris, married Nereus, the Old Man of the Sea. Her
daughter was a priestess Thetis, mother of Achilles. Oceanus
was also, say some, the father of the priestess Calypso.

The third most important sea god was Pontus, of the deep
sea and deep-sea channels, who later was confined to the Black
Sea alone. He too was a son of Uranus and Earth. His son was
the Phorcys (Pohorcus) who fathered Scylla, the Sirens, the
Graeae, and the world-famous African Gorgons. Son also of
Pontus and Earth was the sea deity Nereus, grandfather of
Achilles.

Although the Romans also worshipped a god of harbors,
their first sea god was Neptune, always said, perhaps erroneously, to be the double of Poseidon. Since he was a Roman
god of the sea, he can be better viewed after a study of that
great priestess whom the Romans revered, after her death, as
the beautiful Gorgon Medusa.

PRIESTESSES OF THE SEA

Perhaps as many as a dozen groups, some of young women
and some of older women, recur frequently in the stories of
Greek mythology as recorded in passing by Greek writers and
in greater detail by the Romans, especially Ovid. One hears of
these women-in-groups as haunting the sea, emerging from
the sea, moving over the sea, attached to sacred springs in the
parched land which is Greece, or residing beside the precious
sweet water of rivers. Like those individuals we know from
one of these groups, they may very well be (as Robert Graves
has said over and again in his *Greek Myths*) *colleges of priestesses,*

more specifically, priestesses of the sea and/or other waters. Their numbers are given once in a while, such as fifty priestesses of the sea goddess Aphrodite under the name of "Halcyons." In this case, their title was translated as "Kingfishers."

The "Halcyons" may have taken their name from the bird called kingfisher, or they may have been, as Latin word lists prefer to believe, simply "girls" called "birds" (priestesses). In either case, that they were priestesses of Aphrodite seats them in one of her many temples along the coasts. Temples certainly needed groups of women who possessed various abilities, levels of education, talent, and willingness to work. The myth is then elaborated to explain that kingfishers are "sea birds" that brood their young in nests close to the sea. When they do so at the winter solstice (December 23–25), the waters are safe. The myth goes even a step further: There was a (beautiful, young) wife named Halcyone, whose (beloved) husband was drowned at sea. She and her sister "Halcyons" served thereafter to ward the storms at sea off their coast, or dangerous promontory. The narrator who added the last rationalization must have seen a winter storm on the *Côte d'Azur* hurl foamy sea water over the rooftops, boardwalks completely disappearing under each monstrous comber.

We have heard again of the fifty daughters of Danaüs, the Danaïds who left Egypt for Thebes, or even for Ireland, where forty-nine of them founded dynasties and murdered their husbands. Some have seen here women ocean pilots trained, like Athena, in deep-sea, coastal, or harbor navigation. There is no reason to believe that women could not pilot a ship as well as anyone, particularly if, like Athena, they had first served as officer on a military, naval vessel.

There were also women called "Hyads," who specialized in heavy weather at sea, usually brought in by the heliacal rising of Taurus in April-May. The "Hyads," seven in number, died and are now the seven stars in the Bull Taurus's head. The daughter of the sea god Oceanus wedded Atlas on his station, the northwestern corner of Libya Africa. Her name was Pleione. She was mother of seven daughters of the sea who wished to dedicate themselves to Artemis and remain virgins in her temple. When they were pursued by the giant Orion, they prayed to be turned into "birds" (priestesses). They were twice meta-morphosed, into pigeons, and then into the seven stars of the Pleiades. Nobody writing myths was ever sure why only six were clearly visible to the naked eye.

The seventh Pleiad hid behind her sisters, either because, being a priestess of the sea, she was devoted to Troy, which she could not endure to see burned, or because she was mortal and had to wed King Sisyphus of Corinth, that stone-roller of memory. Nobody knows her name either: Merope? Electra?

The god Oceanus had as many as three thousand daughter-priestesses of Ocean. They were called "Oceanids." What is most intriguing about myths concerning the "Oceanids," whose territory was, indeed, very vast, is the tantalizing suggestion that these priestesses trained both dolphins and seals. One story relates the rescue of a suicidal sailor by a trained dolphin, which had been asked to retrieve the man from the water into which he had jumped.

Like the "Oceanids" to whom they may belong, the Sirens were extremely numerous. They seem to have been profes-sional musicians, however, in temples by the sea. Passing ships may have heard their singing from afar off as they rounded a cape or stood out to sea from some rocky island. The Sirens were accused of having lured men to death by their singing. Anyone aboard ship who heard singing at sea ought to have taken immediate action, of course, like changing course, launching the ship's boat, or jumping overboard.

The "Harpies," too, earned a very bad reputation in ancient mythology. They seem to have been old women ostracized and condemned to live below the poverty line. In any case, they were always ravenous for food. They grabbed food away from people whenever they could. They moved with such dizzying speed, which gives some idea of their degree of starvation, that they were believed to be the whirlwinds personified. Over the ages, despite growing resentment, nobody ever denied that the "Harpies" had women's faces. Their bodies were those of vultures, which ate even carrion when all else ran out.

The other women-in-groups, who tended the sea and at-tended Aphrodite, but who were also claimed as his worship pers by Poseidon, usually come in groups of three. The three

Hesperids, of course, guarded Hera's precious golden tree at the Garden of the Hesperides. Nowadays the Hesperids are often said to have lived on island archipelagos off the coast of Spain or Africa, either the Cape Verde Islands where the Romans put them, or the Canaries. Either one would also be acceptable to those who still believe in a lost Atlantis, situated not in the Aegean Sea but in the Atlantic Ocean.

Travel magazines and tour ships have made people more aware of these islands, such as the Canaries, off the coast of Spain, where the native Guanche Indians and other native people, with light skins and blond hair, still sing a strange whistling language called *silbo*. Like Atlantis, the Canary archipelago is volcanic, and some islands are volcanically active. On these various archipelagos, all tourists notice the luxuriant foliage, the warm climate, the exotic tamed birds, the marvelous fruitfulness of golden citrus trees, and the towering rocky mountains (c. 12,000′) with immense craters from past eruptions of some 4,000 years ago. The red garments and furnishings from the local red dye cannot help but remind one of Hera's favorite color, and of the red on the Lady of Elche statue found on Spain's east coast. Red dyes are not all that common.

The most important priestesses of the sea as a group were the fifty Nereids, or "wet ones," who were daughters of Nereus and the Nymph Doris. Among the group certain individuals rate separate stories, while others have such successful, popular myths that they become finally indistinguishable from the sea goddesses whom they purportedly served.

The story of Pygmalion and the sea-nymph Galatea is very popular still and is usually told by nice, English poets as a beautiful love story: Pygmalion sculpted an ivory statue of a girl. Despite his vow of celibacy, he fell in love with it. She finally came to life, loved him, and married him; and they lived happily ever after.

Ovid's account (*Metamorphoses*, X) is sinister and thus altogether different: the girl "child" Galatea wished to remain virginal. Pygmalion had, before he sculpted her, sworn off women forever. He tried his best to seduce her. She failed to respond. He tried next to buy her, first with trifling presents, then offering precious stones. Nothing availed. She would not yield. Finally he made offerings to Venus. Then he forced the girl, who ultimately "came to life" under him. Robert Graves calls it out-and-out rape, no different from those waged politically by the four dominant gods taking control over the women's temples: Zeus (Sky), Poseidon (Sea), Hades (Hell), and Apollo (Earth).

According to the worshippers of Aphrodite, goddess of the sea, their deity was also triune, divided between earth, air, and sea, a fact which would explain Aphrodite's three names: Thetis, Amphititre, and Nereis. The third goddess Nereis underwent, through some error in translation, doubtless, a sea change from feminine to the masculine: Nereis to Nereus, called Old Man of the Sea. Poseidon nevertheless claimed all three as his servitors. The case of Nereis resembles that of Athena, but the more sea changes, the better, Poseidon and Zeus would have agreed.

Aphrodite, explains the classical scholar Perry (p. 114 ff.), was originally a goddess of the Semites, brought by the Phoenicians to Cyprus, where she was born in the sea as Botticelli painted her so gorgeously. Her first and foremost temples were at Cyprus before others were constructed in Greece, where she underwent hellenization. Rising from her scallop shell, she was joined by Love and Desire, followed by wreathed Tritons blowing on conch shells, rosy Nereids skimming the waves and following her golden chariot drawn by Hippocamps. She is the Asian Queen of Love and Beauty: rosy-cheeked, golden-haired, slender-ankled, white-armed, sweetly smiling, golden-crowned, tightly belted, holding (Parma) violets, her gossamer gown trailing seductively off her shoulders. Doves and sparrows fly about her. Her other priestesses serve her as Aphrodite Urania; for her, they remain heavenly and virginal. Once when Pausanias saw her statue armed, she may have told him: "If I conquer the world when I am nude, what shall I do when I put on armor?" Under her feet her sculptors thoughtfully placed a tortoise, a symbol of Aphrodite as a homebody.

The *Homeric Hymn* X, "To Aphrodite," says:

She gives kindly gifts to men.
Smiles are always on her lovely face,
And lovely is the bright glow
That plays over her countenance.

As violet-crowned Cythera (Cypriot), Aphrodite conquered the whole world, exception made for three virgins: Artemis of Ephesus, Athena of Athens, and Hestia (Vesta) of the Greek and Roman hearth fires.

As goddess of the sea Aphrodite held sacred the myrtle bush and the dove. The myrtle, which has lovely single flowers and lanceolate leaves (it is our bilberry bush), was lately used in Israel and Greece as bridal flowers. The association with Aphrodite is therefore late, because the myrtle, long before her importation from Asia Minor, was the plant of death. The dove too must be a late ascription and better transferred, as a symbol of the soul, to the Virgin Mary.

Aphrodite was beloved by everyone: Paris of Troy, who gave her first prize among women; Hephaestus the Smith, who was her husband; the god of war Ares, who was Hera's son; Dionysus, who was Zeus's son; Hermaphroditus, who represented both sexes; and by Aeneas, who was her son by the shepherd Anchises.

That last connection, Aphrodite and Prince Aeneas who escaped alive from burning Troy, will overturn history and alter the whole world when Julius Caesar and his family, the Julian Line of Rome, declare themselves sons of the goddess Aphrodite, under her Roman name: Venus.

Not that Venus had much, if anything, to do with Aphrodite.

Thetis, or Tethys, often considered alternate names for Aphrodite, were "Nereids," priestesses of that sea goddess. Thetis was fated to bear a very great son, mightier than his father. Both Poseidon and Zeus forthwith lost all interest in Thetis. The sea maiden was richly dowered and given as a bride to Peleus. Their wedding hymn, written by the Roman poet Catullus, is one of the world's most treasured pieces.

The long-awaited child of Thetis was Achilles. Curiously, she bore seven babies in all. Six perished when she burned them too severely in the fire. This therapeutic practice on the part of Libyan women is described by Herodotus, who notes that the Greek women copied Libyan dress and manners:

> . . . to take their children at age four and smear their heads with sheep's fat in order to burn their scalps. . . . They say this keeps their children healthy (IV, #187).

One last "Nereid" comes to mind: Metis, daughter of Oceanus and Tethys (Thetis). She was Zeus's first love affair. Her name meant Knowledge-of-the-Future, she warned him. She too would bear a child greater than the father, she said. Hesiod says in the *Theogony* that Zeus therefore swallowed her. Some time later, Athena burst into life from his brain. Hesiod declared her Zeus's equal in strength and wisdom. "Equal" is not "greater." Hesiod has not explained the prophecy of Metis.

IX

MEDUSA, AFRICAN QUEEN

THE DEATH OF MEDUSA

The terrifying story of Queen Medusa now belongs to the world. The African Medusa, whose name the older generation of lexicographers defined as "Queen," today represents a feminine ideal of beauty. Lexicographers today ignore the meaning of her name. She was the High-priestess of Africa, perhaps also of Italy and Spain.

A hundred years ago the English poet Dante Gabriel Rossetti warned us, unforgettably, of wanting to see Medusa, of looking at ourselves in mirrors and pools of water. The Surrealists in our century have repeated the warning: it is death. Look twice and you will see your own aging. In his poem entitled "Aspecta Medusa," Rossetti wrote:

> Let not thine eyes know
> Any forbidden thing itself, although
> It once should save as well as kill: but be
> Its shadow upon life enough for thee.

Rossetti had said by way of preface that we are talking about Medusa's execution by the Greek hero Perseus. After he cut off her Head, he carried it, dripping blood over Europe as he flew home. On the way home from the Atlas Mountains, as he passed over southern Europe, he glimpsed another African priestess, Andromeda, chained to her rock on a headland of Libya. He rescued her from a sea monster, perhaps.

Then Perseus flew home to Greece where he gave Medusa's goatskin cape, or breastplate, to Athena. They buried Medusa's Head in the *agora* at Argos, before the goddess Hera's temple. Then they, or some emigrants from Greece, built a temple to Perseus at Chemnis in Egypt. What of Medusa's winged body?

It is obvious that this story, as we can glean it from bits and pieces of Greek mythology, is so botched that everyone must have felt that much of it was better left unsaid. The story of Medusa is still in no way complete. Even so, Medusa herself has cast her sad shadow upon the world; and, despite Rossetti's warning, shadow is not enough. Knowing can only save, not kill, us.

Rossetti's warning duplicates Andromeda's reaction, once Perseus had saved her from the sea monster about to devour her, or from the sea about to drown her. Perseus had already killed the so-called queenly monster. Then he released Andromeda from the chains that had bound her to the rock, as her parents wished. He performed these feats because Andromeda was beautiful, the story says.

Once Andromeda was rescued, she created another problem for Perseus and for women too. She demanded to see Medusa's Head. Mind you, Perseus had only just saved Andromeda's life, and Medusa's Head turns all who look upon it to stone.

In order to kill Medusa and escape from Africa with her Head, Perseus had to defeat Atlas. To do that expeditiously, he showed Atlas Medusa's Head. Atlas turned to stone. He

Figure 15. Perseus and Medusa

became the African mountain. Ovid was much impressed (*Metamorphoses* IV):

> Perseus tried to calm Atlas, but had to wrestle with him instead. Atlas would not accept calmly and reasonably what Perseus proposed to do. The Garden of the Hesperides had been invaded, said Atlas. Perseus was after the golden tree with its golden fruit. The giant refused to yield them. That tree and those three apples belonged in that Garden. They fought. Perseus was no match for an African giant. Therefore he took Medusa's Head out of his "wallet," and showed it to Atlas.
>
> "You refuse me that gift I asked you for," Perseus told Atlas. "Very well, I'll give you a permanent present." In his left, or *sinister* hand, he raised Medusa's Head. Atlas turned to stone.
>
> Trees rose up the sides of his head. Paths and tracks ran up and down his arms and over his shoulders at high mountain passes. Meadows appeared below either side of his summit. His peak gradually disappeared beneath snow that covered the boulders, once his skeleton. Higher and higher the giant rose over the coast of Africa, taller and taller, as heaven willed it, which over his rock-bare summit placed a crown of glorious stars.

Thus, Medusa also became a Mother of Mountains, which may make her a goddess creator so ancient that our prehistoric ancestors had no alternative but to cut off her Head. If she really could turn giants into mountains, then it was she who turned mere ordinary men into stone monuments. If she first ordered them to stand in a circle, then she built Stonehenge around 1750 B.C. It would have been one of her last works, just before the new men, the Celts, invaded Britain and borrowed this more ancient Neolithic religion from Medusa's people. Her stones attracted their Druids mightily, and still do.

The dragon Ladon, which guarded Atlas's Garden, birthplace of Hera said to be north of Casablanca, represented some cosmic force that circles the earth, say modern Celtic theorists in Britain. These telluric currents girdle the planet and indicate holy places to which mountain climbers aspire and at which pilgrims to Tibet worship. Thus, Medusa's Head, like the heads of her creations, aspires to heaven or is Paradise, where dwell the mother gods. In his *Illustrated Encyclopaedia of Traditional Symbols* (London, 1978) J. C. Cooper agreed, but forgot Poseidon:

> . . . and, in early traditions of the feminine godhead, the mountain was the earth and female, with the sky, clouds, thunder and lightning as the fecundating male (p. 110).

The sacred navel peaks of the Himalayas from which great rivers of India arise are named for the Mother Goddess, celebrated in Yoga by the sacred chant commencing *OM*, the hourglass sound of the earth being created by her, and ending with the buzzing of bees, her priestesses.

Medusa, as she is recalled, even in classical mythology of the Occident, resembles the Indian deity Siva Nataraja: Creator, Preserver, and Destroyer. Perseus killed her by decapitation for fear that in her third "aspect" she would destroy the earth she had created. He dreaded her "hideous" face. He mistrusted her gestures of blessing, and dispelling fear. He could not see her as Preserver. He had been ordered to bring her Head to the hermaphrodite Athena whom the thunder god Zeus had borne. Siva too had perhaps undergone a similar sex change, in her case from female to male. Athena, said Robert Graves, was a "traitress" to an old religion already being supplanted by such solar gods as Zeus and his emissary Perseus. This first took place, he also believed, in the second millennium B.C., when the patriarchal Hellenes invaded Greece and Asia Minor.

In mythology as in zoology, life came from the sea. Among the "Children of the Sea" were included priestesses of three aspects: the Hesperides (Hespere, Aegle, and Erytheis), the Gray Ones (whom Robert Graves amusingly calls "Warlike," "Wasp," and "Terrible"), and the Gorgons. Medusa was the third Gorgon. Among such monsters as the dragon Ladon, the snake-girl Echidne, and Typhon/Python were the Gorgons. They turned people to stone.

Some say the chant *OM* recalls the grief of the two immortal Gorgons, Stheno and Euryale, after the death of their mortal sister, a priestess named Medusa. The Gorgons were children of an Old Man of the Sea (Phorcys) and a Nereid Ceto. All resided at the very western edge of the known world, beside the circling stream called Ocean, renamed the Atlantic for the giant Atlas.

Aeschylus, Apollodorus, and Homer handed down to their public the key information: that nobody could survive the high ocean, that nobody could look upon the terrifying priestesses of the sea called Gray Ones *(Graiae)* and live, and that it was especially deadly to look upon the Gorgons. The Egyptians too abhorred even the moody Mediterranean. Odysseus perpetually thought during his long voyages overseas that the Gorgons were after him. Fish goddesses were generally worshipped at meals on Fridays when fish were sacrificed. Everyone remembers the Flood which almost drowned the planet.

The third Gorgon Medusa was so remarkable for her person that the black god Poseidon fell in love with her. She wore her hair entwined with royal serpents, like the heads of Egyptian queens and High-priestesses: high-crowned with rows of raised cobras' heads, adorned over the third eye with the glaring *uraeus*. Her body was circled with fishes' scales, also like the Egyptian sea god, formerly a sea priestess as can be seen by his well-developed bosom. The scales on Egyptian statues of the sea god were parallel lines of the hieroglyphs, "sacred writing," for water: $\wedge\wedge\wedge$, probably mistaken in Medusa's case for scales. But northwestern Africa, where Medusa reigned, was celebrated *and feared* for its snakes, which often grew to enormous, unbelievable size, said the Romans. And the Romans knew what they were talking about; for the Carthaginians used venomous snakes against the Roman Legions in their Punic Wars: Carthage versus Rome.

The Greeks were not entirely sure why the remarkable beauty of Medusa, who had enthralled Poseidon, was metamorphosed into what they considered hideousness: round face, protuding tongue, flared nostrils, glaring eyes, black curls entwined with serpents. Two Greek theories competed here. The one claimed Medusa had let Poseidon make love to her in Athena's Libyan temple. This desecration caused Athena to sentence the mortal Gorgon, or priestess, to death by beheading, for which sacrifice Athena dispatched Perseus. The second hypothesis suggested that Medusa had competed with

Athena in a beauty contest, or for supremacy in Libya. Neither satisfies the myth, however, nor explains Poseidon's love for a "monster" whose teeth were a boar's tusks, whose hands were brass, and whose belt was a boar's teeth. Poseidon may have loved her for her golden wings of an angel.

Unable to love the human Medusa in life, under the eye of Athena who had condemned her to decapitation, the ancients adored her in death, even the Greeks and Romans. Medusa the Gorgon was the lovely guardian angel leaning out winged from the four cornices of the Artemis temple at Ephesus. Like Protestant angels, despite Mr. and Mrs. Wood, she was female, and not male. Her Head, enhanced by clusters of curls, appeared over the parapets of Ephesus, beautiful in fragments of sculpture still to be seen at that temple today.

The Romans thought of the eldest Gorgon Stheno as *Valeria* (Valorous), Euryale as *Lativolva* (Far Flyer), and Medusa as *Guberna* (Ocean Pilot).

The oceangoing pilot is the higher trained, more expert than the harbor, or coastal, pilot. The oceangoer, or *Long Courier* (called C.L.C. in French), may handle ships of any tonnage in any waters. That "aspect" was also Medusa, whom we call Captain, or Master. Hector of Troy was said to have had her same terrifying eyes, or excellent pilot's vision. Zeus for self-protection wore her apotropaic face upon his shield. Athena wore Medusa's Libyan goatskin buckler as her *aegis* too. And angels, as Medusa, guarded Ephesus, Artemis not needing a hideous Medusa to frighten her enemies. When heifers low, they too mourn Medusa, it is believed.

Herodotus defined for us what was meant by the Libyans of Medusa's age:

> I have thus much further to say of this country: four nations and no more . . . inhabit it, whereof two are aboriginal and two are not; the Libyans in the north and the Ethiopians in the south of Libya are aboriginal, the Phoenicians and Greeks are later settlers (IV, 197, trans. A.D. Godley, 1921).

The Libyans near Mt. Atlas, he continued, call themselves "Atalantes" from the name of that mountain. The robe and *aegis* of Greek women is copied from those of the Libyan Am-

azons (IV, 188), except that the latter wear red leather clothing and red leather thongs hanging from their skin bucklers.
They wear smooth red leather vests over their dress. They are
accomplished chanters in their formal ceremonies. From the
Libyan Amazons the Greeks adopted the four-horse chariot,
which they learned to drive. Many royal Libyans claim Trojan
ancestry. The Libyan Amazons were also celebrated fighters.

The Roman poet Lucan (A.D. 39–65), who was born in Cór-
doba, Spain, placed Medusa in Libya (*Pharsalia*, IX,v. 619 ff.).
Her realm, he noted,

> was rough with the stones her eyes had turned to that state.
> Snakes pleased Medusa when they hung from her bare throat
> and hissed. She wore the royal vipers of Africa erect over her
> forehead. She was the most eager to kill of all other monsters,
> even more terrible than the Eumenides, or Cerberus in hell, or
> Heracles when he slew Hydra. Her parents Phorcys and Ceto
> feared her, and so did her immortal sisters. Birds she looked
> at dropped from the sky. Beasts dropped dead among boulders
> before her. She turned the Ethiopians into stones. She even
> turned Atlas, who was a Titan, who supports the Western Pil-
> lars, into a mountain.
>
> Athena told Perseus how to kill Medusa. He should attack
> her at sunrise. He should station himself back to the rising sun
> and fly backwards across the Gorgon's kingdom. She gave him
> a shiny bronze shield in which to watch for Medusa the Gor-
> gon.
>
> Medusa meanwhile slept on while dawn broke in the east.
> Her soft slumbering was soon to turn into death. While her
> body rested, her serpents mounted guard. Medusa's curls fell
> between her cobras and shaded her closed eyelids. She stayed
> asleep, veiled by her serpent coiffure.
>
> Athena personally guided the trembling hand of Perseus. She
> had him cut her neck down low, where it joined her Head to
> her trunk. Athena's hand steadied his arm, for he had turned
> away his face from Medusa's Head.
>
> How lay she, then, with her head severed from her body
> by one stroke of Athena's sharp blade?
> Did grim poison then drip from her jaws?
> Did foul pus run from her filthy eyes?

Athena had Perseus grasp Medusa's Head. She saw he turned
from it as he flew high up into the sky over Libya.
It is a bleak and poisonous land. . . .

(v. 700).

Nonetheless, the various cultures of the Mediterranean basin accepted Medusa as a Libyan priestess named from an ocean
goddess, and as an African queen, which Hesiod called her.
Even so, they understood that while she lived, reigned, and
died in "Libya Africa," she might have been born on a stone
mountain, a rock island, in the Atlantic Ocean. Thus, her prime
associations cling: stone, mountain, and ocean. She wore scales,
like an African queen in Egypt, and was a priestess of the sea
whose sea creatures today bear her name: *medusa, medusae.* The
Etruscans or Umbrians, who may have called her "Metusa,"
named an island for her: "Gorgon," or "Urgo," in the Tyrhen-
nian (Etruscan) Sea. Her worship was stamped out in the Greek
world by Zeus, by his "daughter" Athena, and by two solar hit-
men: Perseus first, followed generations later by Heracles. If
all this occurred in a Neolithic world, then Medusa was more
likely clubbed to death.

In the classic epic tradition most recently revived by Ian
Fleming's James Bond 007, other magical weapons were provided for the hero Perseus: winged sandals, a mirrored shield,
a cloak of darkness, and the death-dealing sword which could
not be blunted. All solar heroes have magical conceptions and
births, complete death-defying tasks in infancy, grow up to
assume labors assigned by the community, have license to kill,
will travel, and are themselves mortal.

After he killed Medusa and petrified Atlas, Perseus was believed to have overflown Europe, where drops of the Gorgon's
blood dripped from his wallet upon the earth. From this blood,
deadly African snakes were born.

Not only is Medusa remembered as both oceangoing and
also the navel mountain of Paradise; she is symbolized by
certain creatures equally ambivalent. In the celebrated painting of Medusa's Head, once ascribed to Leonardo da Vinci,
the viewer sees her dead. Only the crown of her head is visible
first as the viewer's eye enters the picture. After looking at her

dark serpent locks strewn about in the right and left fore-grounds, the viewer then sees her upside-down face, forehead first, then nose, lips, chin relaxed, composed in white death. Beside her are two creatures mysteriously dual by nature: the bat of the Tibetan bat-god Dracula, and the heraldic frog of the Celtic Gauls, the first both mammal and bird, the second an amphibian equally at ease on land and in water. Unlike Athena, Medusa's aspects are invariably feminine: children, hair, serpents, fishes, wings, islands, stones, and memorials to the honored dead.

The saddest part of Medusa's story concerns the birth of her two children, a story which has truly become one of the world's recurrent nightmares. The horrifying scene reappears in Gothic fiction, so deeply is it stamped upon the creative minds of artists and writers. The children of Poseidon and Medusa were born from the mother's abdomen, which was split open at the hour of her death.

Hesiod the poet was very sorry for this crime. He says in the *Theogany:* "Medusa, the Gorgon who suffered such pain" (v. 278). Her sons were the winged horse Pegasus, and a golden warrior named Chrysaor. Both sprang up from Medusa's corpse.

The gentle, winged horse was caught and broken in by Athena, who gave him to another of her solar champions, Bellerophon.

The royal warrior of the golden sword, Medusa's second twin son, ruled a land which he bequeathed to his sons. He sired King Geryon of Spain.

The Olympian gods then sent Heracles out west to kill Medusa's grandson, King Geryon of Andalusia. Even with this grandson slain, Medusa's line continued the war against the newer, male gods of Greece. Meanwhile her sacred mountains girdled the earth.

Hesiod recorded of King Geryon that he too was of triple aspect, like Medusa herself. Like her, he too was born on a rocky island in the Atlantic Ocean. The isle was called Erytheia, or "Red," by the Greeks, but identifiable perhaps as Gades (Cádiz) on the extreme southwest coast of Spain, just north of Heracles's Pillars, now Gibraltar.

For long centuries King Geryon continued to be recognized, before he passed into the permanent mythology of the Celts. They knew him as *Tarvos Trigaranos,* the three-headed god of the ancient Celto-Iberians. His isle was another Celtic, western Avalon, isle of the illustrious dead.

Her people said Poseidon never wooed Medusa in a temple, ← but in the green meadow which authors know from Plato's *Republic* lies just this side of "Avalon," the sepulchral isle. The isle itself is the holy necropolis intended for royal personages only. It was Heracles who met Medusa while she was still in Tartarus.

As for Perseus, he became an ancestor of "Persian" kings, it was said, but probably erroneously because only the Greeks called Iran "Persia." The land was Iran, said the Iranians at the time of their great epic, the *Shah Nameh* (Book of Kings). Perseus was worshipped by Greeks at Chemnis in Egypt, and had, said Herodotus, a watchtower built in his honor on the western Delta of the Nile. The "Persian" invaders of Egypt thought Perseus might have been Assyrian, and his wallet in Greek accounts has an Oriental rather than a Greek name, which is unusual. The text calls it a "Kibisis" (from Cyprus).

⌐ When that little is rehearsed, however, one suspects that it ⌐ was not Perseus, but Medusa as a Gorgon, who was later revered in Asia, from Ephesus eastward to Iran, and then northeast again to the Pamir Plateau, to Ariana (Afghanistan) next, and into Tibet. Mountains all along the way are named "Gorgon." Saint Gorgon was brought from the east to Rome in the fourth century A.D. The Gorgon's feast day is September 9. Medusa herself has also been called Hittite; her mountain in Turkestan is Mt. Orkhon. Medusa's "Heads" are also nomadic funeral mounds along the trails from modern Tibet to southern U.S.S.R.

There appears to be no recognized, scholarly etymology which could assist us in tracking Medusa backwards in time. Her name in Greek was Medousa. Medusa, as commonly used, is Latin, western today, and non-Greek. As a common name it is used in zoology to designate a sea anemone, or jellyfish. It also names a polyp such as the hydra. A third name from the Norwegian is *Kraken* from her snake, the *Krait,* or blue cobra. The scientific terms *Medusan, Medusoid,* and *Meduzoid* are also used to designate sea creatures like herself. The color blue appears to be freely associated with Medusa, at least in the author's personal experience.

Since there is no scholarly etymology of the name "Medusa" (*Matris* = Mother), one may either accept it as lost in time, which seems the consensus, or one may feel for some clue in language. It would seem that the name "Medusa" was Mother, which could have come into Latin from one of the pre-Roman peoples of what is now Italy. The Etruscans come easily to mind when one recalls the frequent use of Gorgons in Etruscan art. This art is also consistently funerary in character. The Etruscans as a people disappeared abruptly after their conquest by the Romans.

An ancient god of religious terror was vaguely known in later Roman times as Metus, not the usual word for fear in Latin. The noun for religious trepidation in Latin was *metus,* the gender of which, strangely enough, perhaps because it was a foreign or Etruscan word, remained uncertain. It looks masculine, but was also considered feminine. One might therefore wonder whether the name of the Mother, Queen Medusa, was altered eventually in Rome to that of a god named Metus ("t" and "d" being actually the same consonant, the former unvoiced and latter voiced).

Another myth may perhaps connect Medusa to Athena in a way that would explain why Medusa was killed by Athena, city goddess of Argos and Athens, daughter of Zeus. If Medusa was the mother of Athena, and if Athena's mother was named Metis (Metis > Medusa), then Athena joined Zeus to kill her own mother and supplant her in the hierarchy. Athena would then be most appropriately chosen to preside over Orestes' trial for matricide.

Medusa joins other Mother Goddesses of the ancient world: Hera, who was born under a willow tree; Artemis, who held a willow wand in her hand; Demeter and Persephone, who were worshipped exclusively by women and served exclusively by priestesses in temples surrounded by willows; and Medusa on her similar, willow-enclosed, sepulchral isle in the Atlantic Ocean.

Listen to the priestess Circe as she gives directions to Odysseus, said Hugo Rahner, a learned Jesuit in his book (Paris, 1954) on Greek myths and Christian Mysteries (my free translation from the French):

> After crossing the ocean waves, come to a wild grove on the shore. That is terrible Persephone's realm. You will see poplars and willows that shed their sterile seeds. Tie up there where the currents swirl, but descend then alone into the weird, fearsome house of Hades (p. 286).

These goddesses and their priestesses, said Rahner, practiced birth control. Poplars and willows are related trees which reproduce by themselves ("sua sponte veniunt"). These trees are *agonos* (childless), as is the pussy willow. Their blossoms and seeds prevent conception in women. They grew, as they grow today, beside water. Certain springs were sacred to the priestesses who used this water for sprinkling, in rain ceremonies. Thus, concluded Rahner, the sacred tree of Hades preserved a "deadly" secret, indeed.

This worship of Medusa among the High-priestesses of Africa, and this reverence for her priestesses to whom women had recourse, continued as recorded in the modern languages of Europe well through the Middle Ages. The gods of the sea in Medusa's image survive in memory, literature, and music throughout Europe. In Ireland the most ancient deep-sea goddess was called *Domnu* (Mistress) and *Fo-mor* (Under-Sea). She too was descended from Chaos and Night at a time when the world was created. The cow-faced Cyclopean god of Ireland also resembled Medusa: "cow-faced," evil-eyed, resident of the Donegal coast, whose gaze turned the beholder into stone. The sea priestesses on their bleak, northern isles were fearsome, sometimes deformed, huge, and even one-legged. They had apparently lost the Gorgon mania for sharing one eye between three sisters. They well remembered Medusa's grandson, the Celtic Trigaranos, whose sculpted image was once worshipped on an altar in Paris.

The memory of this primitive religion of sea gods and goddesses continues down the ages as unforgettable as the myths themselves. They constitute such a stimulus to reflection and such a treasury of knowledge from our most distant past that they inspire theory on everyone's part. When W. R. Lethaby finished his study on Ephesus (which we saw in Part I), he concluded fairly:

> As we go backwards in time, Gorgons, Nike, and Winged Artemis all seem to merge in one, and winged figures of Artemis were used as antefixes on some of the early Etruscan temples (p. 71).

The Ephesus Gorgons, possessed of four wings each, almost duplicate the flying Gorgons at Delphi, temple of the world's greatest oracular priestesses. Etruscan art, says Raymond Bloch (Milan, 1959), understood deities as terrifying as were their own lives. They too, like their northern neighbors in the Celtic realms, focused on the human Head of Medusa as a most sacred object of veneration and religious awe. Like her brood of affiliated sea creatures, Etruscan art was zoomorphic. Their horses from Tarquinia were also winged, like Medusa's son Pegasus.

The name of Medusa in its masculine form Metus and the peculiar masculine/feminine *metus* (religious terror) persisted for centuries after the fall of Rome, but in *only two areas:* northern Italy of the old Etruscans, and southern France. The memory of Heracles killing the triple-headed King Geryon remained alive in Spain and Narbonne in medieval epic material. The city of Narbonne (France) was the Roman capital preferred by Julius Caesar in his "Provence."

The names of the Gorgons survive superabundantly in the toponymy of Iran, Afghanistan, and Russia as "plain of Gurgan," for instance, and Mt. Gargan (more recently Mt. Stalin). When one turns to the rare book on French mythology, Henri Dontenville's *Mythologie française* (Paris, 1973), the abundance is impossible to treat, so profuse is it.

The greatest personages in all French pagan mythology are the beloved French family of the kindly giant Gorgons: Gargantua, Pantagruel, Grandgousier, and Gargamelle. From rivers, the Gorganne and the Gargonne, to fortresses ("Gurguntum's wallèd ground"), to "craig" (stone) and "karrek" (stone in Breton) and Carnac in Brittany, one finds names by metathesis from "gorgon." Such place-names and common nouns exist by the hundreds throughout France. There Gorgonio/ Gargantua is the most beloved of mountain giants, mover of dolmens, builder of stonehenges, menhirs, alignments a dozen miles long, funeral mounds, multiple tombs made of monoliths impossible to move by modern machinery. It is even sometimes remembered that Gargantua was born on the highest mountain in the east, and that he was buried on the *Mont Tombe,* our Mont-Saint-Michel.

François Rabelais, doctor of medicine from the University of Montpellier, France, remembered that Gorgons were born in strange ways. Was not Dionysus born out of Zeus's thigh? he asked. Minerva from his brain by way of an ear? Castor and Pollux from an egg laid by Leda? So then, cried Rabelais jovially, why not Gargantua born through a hollow vein into the diaphragm, left toward his mother's shoulder, and out of her "sinister" ear?

> I doubt that you believe this strange birth. If you don't believe it, I don't care, but intelligent persons always believe what they are told (by their doctor) and what they find written in books (*Gargantua,* VI).

The final question must be asked: what constitutes the particular power of the Medusa story? We doubtless feel great sadness for the sufferings of Niobe. We pity her tears on the mountain, feel horror before the crimes of Clytemnestra and her infamous son. Here in the fragments that once told of Medusa's execution, we may rather have undergone an inexplicable, mysterious charm. We know but do not really wish to understand. There lies behind those scattered "facts" some undiscovered truth. The curtain parts and closes upon the scenes. Her last minutes are played out in obscurity. We sit in a darkening theater.

Many famous persons before our day have felt this discomfort before certain myths, where the emotional content rises to the surface from a very dark, very ancient, very distant deed. In 1974 G. S. Kirk made a brilliant attempt to divide myths into seven categories. His list included those myths which, like the story of Medusa, deal with psychic material, myths where the preponderance of visceral imagery had overwhelmed both ancient and modern poets. Medusa's story was therefore often sidestepped.

Most interestingly, then, it was Sigmund Freud himself, who first seriously analyzed the myth of Medusa, addressing himself to the sense of dislocation, displacement, repression felt before her execution. The painter of Medusa's Head (once attributed to Leonardo da Vinci) compounded the reader's dream. In his case, too, time had ceased to pass by. Instead of "passing time," most fall, in Medusa's myth, into the perpetual descent into a stone stasis. We are in vertical time. It is fearful, dreadful. It is stone. We have some sense now of the paralyzing power that lay in a prehistoric, African religion, among an unknown and perhaps vanished race.

On May 14, 1922, Sigmund Freud drew up two pages entitled "Medusa's Head," which appeared to be a sketch for a work he never wrote. He began:

> We have not often attempted to interpret individual mythological themes, but an interpretation suggests itself easily in the case of the horrifying decapitated head of Medusa.

Bluntly, he said, to decapitate a person means to castrate. What the viewer or reader fears is castration, the fear of which is triggered by the sight of Medusa's severed Head. Thus, the very visualization of it "makes the spectator stiff with terror, turns him to stone" (p. 273). When Athena puts this symbol upon her chest, she wears the warning to all men that she has no sexuality, that she cannot or will not become sexually involved. "Since the Greeks were in the main strongly homosexual," he continues, they understood an Athena who had been castrated. This display of genitals upon the chest of Athena, which is what her *aegis* conveyed to the viewer, aroused such horror that it would put most enemies to flight. Rabelais, adds Freud, understood (because he too was a doctor of medicine). The work of Freud has stimulated a healthy flood of medical and literary writing, of course, both pro and con.

In 1981 an Indian psychologist, Gananath Obeyesekere, answered the problem, as stated by Freud, in his *Medusa's Hair*. This problem, added Obeyesekere, deals with a common phenomenon seen every day now in India: the matted hair of Hindu ascetics. Are not these matted locks, which appear to be deadly cobras, what cause terror in persons and revulsion in the anthropologists who have studied them? Let us study three cases in point:

> Case #1: A married woman, aged 52, became possessed after her disillusionment with a worthless husband. She became a priestess. She learned to walk on fire. She left home, studied at pilgrimage centers, abjured sex. She managed to obtain her husband's permission so that in her next birth she would be allowed to be masculine.
>
> She prayed on a sacred mountain where the priest forbade her ever to cut her hair since her matted locks were her "protector and guardian deity" (p. 26) and the "relic and essence of life force" (p. 27). Nobody should ever be allowed to touch her hair, or her head.
>
> Case #2: A married woman had become disgusted by an unfaithful husband. She went out to work and let her hair become matted until it just by itself raised up like a cobra.
>
> She began to frequent shrines. Then she learned to walk through fire. She joined pilgrimages. Then she rented a house to use as her own shrine. She cut her hair on the crown of her head. She had become an "ecstatic."
>
> (The author once saw her with her son, both rolling on burning sands.)
>
> Case #3: This woman had been married at age fourteen. By the time she was nineteen she had three sons. Her husband was lecherous and "very bad."
>
> She let her hair become matted. She "walked the fire." She knew her hair was her "life breath" and "life force" (p. 32).
>
> She blesses her clients with her hair. When it breaks, she knows that she will die.

Obeyesekere concludes (p. 32 ff.) with his own analysis of the symbols which recur in these three cases, and which have in India not only a personal meaning but which also convey a social-cultural message:

1. the loss of the husband's love,
2. a replacement by ecstasy from within,
3. the matted hair as a gift from God,

4. chastity in the exercise of a priestly vocation,
5. understanding and knowledge coming to a woman by
   means of the priesthood.

He concluded by formulating a credo, his belief that knowledge acquired by the exercise of the priesthood for these women was and is, he said, one of the most powerful and most ancient forms of knowing.

Epistemology has always so concurred. Dr. Rabelais here agreed with Dr. Freud. When medical practitioners take to literary criticism, we might add, they are marvelously adept.

Thus, the criticism by medical men has again provided convincing evidence that Queen Medusa of Libya, wife of the oceanic King Poseidon, was High-priestess and warrior in her realm. Probably she too could perform the same great feats of an ascetic: walk on red-hot coals, hold them in her hand, alter her states of consciousness at will, treat the sick successfully, fight a war, terrify her enemies, and make herself unforgettable.

Her story boils down to this: at the request of Athena in Argos and Athens, Perseus overthrew the principal shrine of the old African religion in Libya, and slew the High-priestess. Then he delivered her Head to Argos as a superb apotropaic object, which would forever ward off the evil eye from Argos and Athens.

In conclusion we might allow three Greek "poets" to speak for themselves: a summary of Dio Chrysostom on the subject of Libya as conquered later by Heracles; a summary of Hesiod on an art object, the *Shield of Heracles;* and a summary of Pindar's "Pythian Ode X" on the death of Medusa:

Dio Chrysostom, 47th *Discourse*, Vol. IV, 248, 4
(Libya Conquered by Heracles)

We heard what Heracles did, how he conquered Egypt and Libya, plus all the people who reside on the shores of the Black Sea, which is to say, the Thracians and the Scythians, and then we heard how he crossed over to Asia Minor with a small army of his own and how he stormed and took the city of Troy, and also that after he had subdued all these many peoples, he really managed to get himself crowned king over all of them; but we also heard that when, having completed all these grand, heroic deeds, he came back home to Argos, he got work shoveling manure out of Augeas's stables, chasing snakes, or shooing the birds off the farmers' crops down in Stymphalus, or any other low or odd job somebody wanted him for. . . .

Hesiod on *The Shield of Heracles*
(Perseus in the Aftermath of Battle, v. 216 ff.)

The horseman Perseus (is depicted on the shield of Heracles) wearing winged sandals and a crossed belt of bronze which holds his sword slung over one shoulder. (That way accoutered) . . . he flew fast as thought, with her Head on his back. He had it inside a silver bag decorated with golden tassels. The cap of Hades on his head rendered him invisible.

The Gorgans followed him, hot in pursuit. They had serpents slung from their belts. Fear herself sat on their Heads.

Behind them, strewn near and far, lay the dead, and behind them the bronze rampart of Tartarus. Women were screaming. Their cries bounced back from the walls, shrill ululations. Other women scarred their cheeks. Old men ran outside the gates, weeping and crying aloud for their sons. The battle was still being waged out there.

Over all their heads The Fates reached out their arms to grab the dying and lug them down to Tartarus.

Pindar
"Pythian Ode X" (v. 30, *et passim*)

The fabled course to the realm where dwell the Hyperboreans
you shall never find
    if you go by sea,
    or if you go by land.

          . . .

    There damsels dance.
Neither age, nor plague, nor toil, nor war have they.
But dwell far from the curse of bitter Nemesis,
    A band of merry men.

          . . .

    Perseus killed the Gorgon there.
      He held her Head.
        He returned.
      It shone with coiled locks.

But let me say that as I list the feats of the gods
    I find nothing too hard to believe.

THE ATLANTIC PRIESTESS

The Medusa story leads not only to the Atlantic Ocean but to a new grasp of the historical situation in the west. We see that an ancient population expansion in the east caused a war between the Olympian gods, the Titans, and the Gorgons. Territorial expansion and colonial wars lie behind the myths of Medusa, Perseus, Atlas, Zeus, Athena, and Hera. The myths of Heracles lead to Morocco, to Spain, to France, perhaps even to Britain.

Medusa emerges from some awful battle scene like the one portrayed on the Shield of Heracles. She was beheaded not only for being a priestess, whose presence remains stamped indelibly upon our collective thoughts, but because she stood out as warrior queen among a long list of such Amazons.

Medusa's title was probably "Hippo," listed as third among the catalogue of winged Amazons, having herself been "raped" by Poseidon. In death she bore his sons, one being the winged horse Pegasus, the second becoming grandfather of a king of Spain.

Such female warriors of Africa, says Robert Briffault (Vol. III, p. 454 ff.), did not vanish. They were known widely for their daring and expertise. Up to 1845–46, in West Africa, he noted, a British officer of the Life Guards preferred female warriors under his command to native, male troops. The Guanches of those Canary Islands which may have seen Medusa's birth, and her grandson's, were world-famous Amazons.

The Berber women of North Africa, famous too for their chanting, a shrill ululation in chorus, have also been feared as fierce combatants and skilled equestrians. Dressed in riding costumes of red Moroccan leather, these African Amazons are still recalled in museums and in circuses for the splendor of their dress and the elegance of their horsemanship. These Amazons equalled their eastern counterparts, whose life-style continued under Genghis Khan, Turkic nomads, and Tartars of Afghanistan. They too are described as handsome, powerful riders, habited in red or black tunics, loose trousers, and immense cloth boots.

Their dispositions were noted as "pleasant," probably because their bodies were neither corseted, hobbled, nor displayed naked or half naked before the common gaze.

Alexander the Great met such Asian Amazons during his conquest of the world. "Medusa" coiffures continue to be popular in the Far East.

Apollonius of Rhodes gives the ancient Amazons a title: "daughters of (Hera's son) Ares (god of war)." He says that if the Argonauts had

> come to grips with the Amazons, the fight would have been a bloody one. For the Amazons of the . . . (Asian) plain were by no means gentle, well-conducted folk; they were brutal and aggressive, and their main concern in life was war. War, indeed, was in their blood . . . girls who fell in love with fighting (*Argonautica* II).

History records two main contingents of Amazons in ancient times, wrote Diodorus Siculus (III, p. 52), those in Asia Minor and the group in Libya, one of whose queens was probably *the* "Libya," or "Medusa" once wedded to Poseidon. These African Amazons antedated warrior women in both Asia and Greece. Prominent among the earlier, Libyan Amazons was this "race" called "Gorgons" against whom Perseus fought. So "distinguished for . . . valor" were these Amazon priestesses that Zeus was forced to exert himself to defeat them. The hardest labors of Zeus, Perseus, and Heracles must surely prove "both the pre-eminence and the power of the Amazons in Africa."

A Medusa reincarnated was described by Gustave Flaubert (letter to Sainte-Beuve, January 21, 1863). She entered the city of Carthage in 238 B.C., he said. She was a High-priestess.

The High-priestess of Carthage made a formal appearance in her city to celebrate the defeat of barbarians and nomads by the Carthaginian general Hamilcar, called Barca (Lightning).

Medusa, as Atargatis, followed her minor priestesses down the streets to her throne. Her attendants wore transparent, perfumed gowns of yellow and black. The Medusa advanced to the sound of flutes. Her throne on the podium was of carved tortoise shell. Two black children knelt by her ivory footstool so that the priestess could rest her arms, weary with the weight of her bracelets, upon their backs.

From ankle to waist she was sheathed in fish scales carved from mother-of-pearl. A blue sash, wound tightly about her waist, opened in a crescent to expose her breasts, from which dangled pendants of precious gems. Her headdress was made of peacocks' feathers starred with gems. Behind her fell a cloak as white as snow. Elbows pressed to sides, knees together, she sat in the ancient, hieratic pose of Egyptian Queen-priestesses of the Sea. Circlets of diamonds glittered on her upper arms. She was Atargatis, the Warrior.

Before the career of his son Hannibal (Joy of Baal), Hamilcar Barca had relinquished Sicily, where Diodorus Siculus was born two hundred years later.

When Diodorus set himself (#53) to discuss the geography behind these Punic Wars, and to record a few names, he earned the plaudits of other French scholars. Since the days of Gustave Flaubert's African novel *Salammbô* (1862), they have been fascinated with Carthage, thus with Morocco all over again.

Diodorus talks about an island named "Hespera" off that coast, *or in Lake Tritonis,* which is not in north-central Africa, as mapped, but near the Atlantic Ocean itself. This island lay alongside the Atlas range, was of great extent, and bore fruit on trees of several varieties. Also, it was known for sheep and goat breeding. The inhabitants raised no cereals. The Amazons had conquered the whole island, he said, except for the active volcano. Precious gems abounded: ruby, garnet, cornelian, and emerald.

An Amazon queen named Myrina led an army of 30,000 foot soldiers and 3,000 cavalry. Her women soldiers wore snakeskins from large reptiles. They had bows and arrows to use in Parthian Shots. These women defeated other "Atlantians." The Gorgons beat them. The Gorgons were only defeated by Perseus "when Medusa was queen over them" (Diodorus, III, p. 55), but it was Heracles who later destroyed their "race" in North Africa. That occurred when he set up his "Pillars." Heracles refused to condone the practice of women ruling men.

There is no doubt, said the French academician Jacques Perret in his book on the "Trojan" founding of Rome, as opposed to the view endorsed by fellow academicians, the "Greek" founding of Rome, *that prejudice has hampered our knowledge here.* We have all been blinded by Greece and its heroes, Perseus and Heracles, "demigods" to be worshipped throughout three continents.

After these heroes, Heracles and *Heraclides,* arrived, they fought and founded colonies and cities. His *Heraclides* therefore then claimed that they alone had discovered and settled Sardinia, Sicily, Rome, Gaul, etc., and built temples to Heracles everywhere, from the red Isla de León at Cádiz to Hartland Point on the west coast of what is now England. The story of Medusa and of her children demonstrates the contrary. It was rather the Greeks who borrowed their gods and priestesses from North Africa and their plants from Hera's Garden of the Hesperides, which modern travelers have located on the coast of Africa, between Tangier and Casablanca.

X

THE DELPHIC ORACLE

"Primitive religion is perhaps the strongest and most energetic affirmation of life in human culture."
>   Ernst Cassirer
>   An Essay on Man (New Haven, 1944).

"Woe to the land where there is no religion."
>   Druid aphorism

"The word pagan *was originally applied to the inhabitants of the rural districts, who, on the first propagation of the Christian religion, adhered to the worship of false gods, or who refused to receive Christianity after it had been adopted by the inhabitants of the cities."*
>   Henry W. Ruoff, Editor
>   The Standard Dictionary of Facts (Buffalo, 1908).

DELPHI

The Delphic Oracle, who was the High-priestess of the ancient world, has been silent for fifteen hundred years now. Nobody in the ancient world wrote a history of this priesthood, although many knew some of her personal names. Her title was Pythia, Dragon Priestess of Earth.

Many writers recorded some of her oracles, which were her words. All knew her first motto: "Know thyself."

The presence of these priestesses has not faded in fifteen hundred years, even though the same disinterest continues to function against women and the idea of priestesses.

People from all walks of life and many lands go today on pilgrimage to her shrine at Delphi, Greece. For more than two thousand years this priestess was the highest religious authority in the world, and this in Greece where classical scholars insist women were objects of general contempt. The Delphic Oracles, or priestesses, must have been exceptions to this generality. So, the pilgrims throng to her ruins today, and stand there quietly, amazed and reverent.

The road from Athens to Delphi at eighteen hundred feet rises slowly at first, crossing small meadows, traversing small farmlands. Black-clad farm people ride along on diminutive donkeys laden also with black bundles, reminding one of Christ's triumphal entry into Jerusalem on Palm Sunday.

The road also traverses the town of Thebes, where the tragic family of Oedipus lived and died, even longer ago. Thus, the heart is prepared for awe and wonder.

After Thebes the road slants steeply up into the foothills of the Parnassus range, home of the Muses. Low now on the driver's side, the Gulf of Corinth parallels the narrowing course. Below lies the sea route along which ancient pilgrims, coming also to Delphi, must have stopped to rest and looked up the crags, which are black, hot, dry cliffs of stone. The sun beats down, even in the early morning hours.

The road follows a rather wide ledge running mostly west-east along the mountain's massive, bare shoulder. Off to the left the land of rock falls more sharply away into the Pleistos River bed and the distant, unseen sea. To the right suddenly rotten stone precipices crowd down to the modern paved road. Their shadows also are black. The white light is intense. The atmosphere is oddly leaden.

Abruptly huge white ruins of ancient, crumbled temples sprawl on the left. They are stone remnants of tourist stops for reverent Mycenaeans, Asians, Romans, Gauls, Egyptians of immensely bygone centuries. Around a corner of the right-hand precipice rises even more steeply a narrow gorge. It sweeps darkly black, narrowing up into the mountain's black core: Delphi.

Instantly on the right, past the gorge, also rises a crowded jumble of white stones. They lie along the narrow mountain ledge, higher and narrower in tangled rows. White ruins sprawl, strewn inertly, bleaching under a murderous sun.

There lie, higher and higher above the road, the holy ruins of the temple precinct: Delphi.

The eyes swiftly take it all in. It is a panorama not unlike inert, dead Ephesus. One glance sweeps north up the mountain: the entrance, the Sacred Way, Apollo's temple with bits of columns still erect, the theater, and going uphill always, in the northwest corner, the stadium that often seated five thousand spectators for the Delphian Games.

Every great man of our aged world for a thousand years before his time, said Plato, four thousand years before his time, said Lord Byron, worshipped here: poets, historians, geographers, priests, legislators, dictators, ambassadors, Druids, conquerors, kings, senators, prophets, seers, millionaires, and the hordes of the suffering poor who also sought an oracle (answer, pronouncement) from the Oracle (priestess) herself. Every one of them passed up the road through Thebes, or landed at the harbor Crisa down below, where the Pleistos River flows into the Gulf of Corinth.

Not only has the heart constricted and the eyes have strained to see in the fiery, hot light, but also the nostrils have dried in the white, rarefied air. The climb is slow and hard, even across the crumbled flagstones of the Sacred Way. It goes snaking up the slope to the first hairpin turn. The pilgrim to Delphi is inevitably moved by the sight of these crumbled stone bones of the centuries. "Sic transit gloria mundi."

This is the Greece the poet Lord Byron died for.

The Sacred Way leads along the side of the high foundation of Apollo's temple, makes a hairpin turn to the left, and brings the pilgrim to the megalithic entrance. The entrance is at the narrower east front of the temple. Greek, rectangular temples faced east, like the basilicas derived from them, and like the altars of our cruciform, Gothic cathedrals.

No one among the throng of tourists ventures a foot upon the temple platform. All pant and stare in silence.

Behind their backs looms the terrible precipice of the Phaedriades (twenty-three hundred feet high) from which, it is said, one of the Delphic Oracles ordered the Asian Greek writer

Aesop cast to his death. His *Fables,* or his acts, had desecrated Delphi, she is said to have decreed.

Reverence for the past rises from Delphi's sad stories. Her cliffs frown upon an impure thought. They urge pity for the dead and for the living, equally: "Where'er we tread 'tis haunted, holy ground; . . . one vast realm of wonder spreads around."

> Let such approach this consecrated land,
> And pass in peace along the magic waste;
> But spare its relics—let no busy hand
> Deface the scenes, already how defaced!
> Not for such purpose were these altars placed;
> Revere the remnants nations once revered:
> So may our country's name be undisgraced,
> So may'st thou prosper where thy youth was rear'd,
> By every honest joy of love and life endear'd!

Canto II, stanzas 88 and 93, *Childe Harold's Pilgrimage,* was written by Byron as a youth on his Grand Tour. He completed Canto II in Ismir (Smyrna) on March 28, 1810.

Delphi was originally named Pytho from the (probably Nubian) Dragon whom Apollo slew there. In honor of Pytho the Delphic Oracle herself was always called Pythia. It was Earth's priestess versus the Sun's god Apollo.

Pytho or Delphi was revered down the ages as the geographical center of earth: "Navel of the Earth." It lies at about 22° longitude east of Greenwich, and at about 38° latitude north of the equator. Modern theorists believe Delphi was knowingly built at the crossing of two major ley lines, which explains its terrific pull upon both ancient and modern worshipper: dry mouth, difficult breathing, vertigo, tearful eyes, oppressive weight, and extraordinary pull downward upon the body. Ancient writers felt its oppressiveness too.

Authors, often called "lone furrowers," may feel this special atmosphere more painfully than less solitary persons. But Celts also have generally fallen under the spell of a commonly experienced "spirit of place" that Yeats and Beckett recognized, along with Byron and Lawrence. Delphi seems to exert a powerful, downward current that the body must add to the weight of its stones, its brooding eastern precipice, its vertiginous, or seemingly vertiginous, mountain ledge, and beside it, the dark, awesome ravine that rising wide from the sea coast narrows into a dark isosceles triangle before plunging upwards into the mountain's foundation. From that dark core the Castalian waterfall tumbles into the Oracle's purifying Castalian Spring: pure, cool water from a chasm.

In front of the Castalian Spring, Pytho was slain; he had been backed up against the mountain cleft.

Chasms, above all, are fearsome places. Delphi is chasm, precipice, dark mountainside, murderous sun, with eagles' shadows overhead. Delphi soars, appears out of nowhere, is a navel situated, as were most oracular shrines, near a sea.

The sight and pull of Delphi will remain permanently stamped upon the memory. The Oracle's dark, prophetic cave must always have felt like a shrine so awesome that the feet can only stumble over worn white squares. The eyes can afford only a quick glance now and then up to the darkness of cliff sides.

They found the navel stone, or *omphalos* of Delphi, around 500 B.C., says the contemporary Greek scholar Athina Kalogeropoulou. It was the tomb of Pytho. (See "Delphi," *Temples and Sanctuaries of Ancient Greece: A Companion Guide*, Cologne, 1970; London, 1973; p. 59–73.)

Delphi is the famous "gorge," or "cleft abyss," she says, temple on its north side, overhanging cliffs on its east side. The site has always served, notes the Greek scholar, as junction for routes east-west, southwest-north, where the earth appears to have been cut in two, and where earthquakes often rumble through the chasm. This Delphi was for more than a thousand years the spiritual center of Hellenic culture, its roots and core being that cleft which narrows into the waterfall. It feeds the Castalian Spring and Pleistos River at the mountain's foot.

Each time golden-crowned Delphi and its Treasuries were looted, philanthropists disbursed fortunes to rebuild it. King Croesus of Lydia and the Pharaoh Amasis of Egypt were major donors in 548 B.C. The third temple and segments of the Sacred Way remain today, although in utter, fragmented ruins. The Roman Emperor Sulla carried away other hundreds of Delphi's celebrated, solid gold art works in 86 B.C.

The site today conveys not a whit of this antique wealth, nor a shred of the Delphi, once the world's treasure house and safest repository. The "glory that was Greece" now lies either in this strange aura of light, heat, and stone—or in the hidden memory of today's creators, artists, and poets.

As Aeschylus said, the *protomantissa* here was Themis, first daughter of Earth and Sea. Pytho guarded the mantic spring even during the Flood. Apollo then killed Pytho, had himself purified for this murder, and took over the oracle. He wintered each year, December to February, among the "northern" Hyperboreans, who may have been the Hesperides for all we know. Aeschylus adds that in all Greece only Mt. Parnassus rose above the floodwaters that once inundated the earth.

The ancient *theopropoi* (worshippers), requesting access to the Pythia herself, journeyed to Delphi, underwent sacraments such as rites of purification, asked to make an offering, and prepared to proceed up this same Sacred Way to the temple, where the third now stands, facing east. *Promanteia* (right of access) belonged as an inherited privilege, to all "males of the town of Delphi." Were lay women refused worship there? Were they being punished for that crime attributed to woman: the desire for knowledge? Apparently so.

Entering via the east steps the worshipper climbed up to the forepart of the temple floor that was surrounded by huge pillars. This *cella* area contained the hearth of Hera's virgin sister, Hestia. There burned the Eternal Flame of Greece.

Writers in the Middle Ages informed their public that this fire, this Torch of Learning, had been lighted in Greece, whence it was carried to Rome, whence it was carried by Romans across the Alps to Celtic Gaul. It burns today under the Star, *Place de l'Etoile*, where routes converge, one from the Elysian Fields, *Champs-Elysées*, Paris, France. From holy centers, worshippers in ancient times also traced "dragon lines," powerful earth currents from one holy site to another shrine of Earth. European churches were subsequently erected at their intersections, it has been suggested. Women there also have usually been treated differently, often segregated or considered dirty.

The male worshipper alone proceeded west past the eternal flame, toward the darkened, more sacred rear of the temple. There at the *adyton,* which was the inner sanctum, only the male stood enthralled before the towering cult statue of Apollo in gold.

Below this ground floor of the temple stretched an underground, most secret level, in two parts. All the ancients say so. No trace, claim modern archaeologists, of these underground rooms has been found. The *oikos*, say the ancients, was entered first; it was the waiting room for the *theopropoi* desiring, and deserving, an appointment with the High-priestess herself.

The second underground chamber was the small *antron*, which was reserved for the Pythia. She sat there, perhaps on a recessed "tripod," which Greek artists portrayed as a three-legged stool.

French archaeologists, and other members of the French School at Athens, have claimed in their books, however, that nobody has found the slightest proof concerning this "tripod." It could have been not a seat but a common symbol for an oracular center, or a zodiac in the floor, or a calendar-calculating device.

The Pythia personally conducted her priestly service there, in the *antron*. During her prophecy she rested her hand on the *omphalos*, Pytho's tomb. The sacred water of the Kassotis Spring, which once flowed into her chamber and behind her seat from the north of Apollo's temple, can no longer be seen. A part of its channel, however, *was found by archaeologists*.

Under the Pythia's feet a deep fissure dropped into the darkest depths of earth. This fissure and the recess where the priestess stood, or sat, was accessed by a steep flight of steps.

The ancients also theorized about mephitic vapors arising from the fissure. When she inhaled them, the Pythia supposedly went mad, or fell into a trance, or became ill, and then prophesied. Others speculated that she chewed laurel or smelled the smoke from burning laurel leaves, which filled her with prophetic ardor.

Various scholars, without becoming prophetesses, have tried all these suggestions, so great over the millennia was the prestige of the Pythia.

Massingham suggested that those other hills besides Parnassus, which rose above the great waste of the waters, were thereafter revered as "navels of the world": Delos, Ida, Dicte, Jerusalem, Sinai, Meru, Atlas, and Olympus.

Nothing has diminished the sacredness of the Pythia at Delphi.

The theologian Eliade explained (*Patterns,* Chapter VI) why Earth was logically, *and at Delphi,* the original Oracle. Primitive man, he says, lived so intimately related to his surroundings that he hardly distinguished between what belonged properly to Earth from what were merely manifestations of Earth: mountains, trees, waterfalls, and sacred springs. Primitive man long recognized that his true Mother was Mâ, Earth, his *Tellus Mater,* De-meter (Goddess Mother), the same deity routinely scorned by American television advertisers today as "Mother Nature." The Motherhood of Earth, Hesiod's Gaea, was man's first religious experience and, thus, his first theophany. Pausanias and Varro supported Hesiod there.

Famous personages in ancient days had as babies actually undergone abandonment on Earth's bosom, in their parents' desire to know if She would save them for great careers. Eliade listed them: Zeus, Poseidon, Dionysus, Attis, Perseus, Oedipus, Romulus and Remus, Andromeda, Atalanta, and Psyche, the latter offered to the sun on a mountaintop. All were so abandoned. Moses, Vainamoinen, Scyld, Modred, and Lancelot were entrusted to the waters; some were rescued by priestesses. Such priestesses, Eliade continued, relived daily the great human dramas of Earth: birth, fertility, pregnancy, drought, flood, storm, earthquake, and death. The care of infants, and the fear all women feel for the health and safety of all tiny infants, was another commonly experienced trauma of the priestesses. Mother Earth was once very holy at Delphi, says Eliade (p. 262), not scorned but revered by the world. We have still not found another earth.

Understanding the Pythia at Delphi, continued Amandry (Paris, 1950) in the publications of the French School at Athens (#170), implies recognizing a difference between Asia Minor and Greece, between prophecy and oracle, between Cassandra and Pythia. To the "visions" of the Trojan Cassandra we must oppose "divine decisions" uttered by the Pythia. Properly speaking, prophecy, trance, and possession were Asian in origin, while oracles were considered words sent to the Pythia from God. Asia Minor was rather the home of the ecstatic Sibyls, Cassandra, and the priestesses of Cybele, whose prophetic trances and ecstatic revelations spread through to Rome in the archaic period.

The Pythia's reception of words from God was motionless, neither passionate, nor frenzied. The words then came from her as weighed, considered, and spoken with measure, after forethought.

Their interpretation was in some cases left to the worshipper. When the Pythia wished to answer, she did so clearly. When the question struck her as evidencing cunning, she probably replied even more subtly. Socrates, whom one Pythia saluted as the wisest man on earth because he knew how little he knew, recognized several types of knowledge: prophetic, telestic, poetic, and amorous. The Pythia's answers via oracles addressed to her worshippers' questions concerning nature and society are rather telestic: planned and directed by logic and intelligent thought.

Thus, artistic practice has invariably represented the Delphic Oracle herself as always maintaining what Amandry called "a tranquil dignity." When her oracles were addressed to groups, they were usually delivered in writing by her assistants: priests, pages, and archivists, reported Plutarch.

Most scholars have stressed the serious character of worship at Delphi, where at least eight sacraments appear to have been observed before the worshipper was allowed access to the Pythia herself: 1) Abstention, 2) Exclusion, 3) Baptism, 4) Robing, 5) Procession, 6) Offering, 7) Ascension, and 8) Word. Each person interested seriously in asking a serious question of the Pythia had first to prove his honorable intent by undergoing, at the direction of her assistants, fasting; purification; isolation; the robing in proper, ritual vestments; an ascension in procession to the temple; an acceptable offering; and the utterance of his question personally, face-to-face with her, underground and in fearsome obscurity.

The fact that the Pythian Priestess proceeded underground in order to receive her suppliants does not make her a chthonic deity, but really an Oracle of Earth. Her predecessor Themis had superintended both Earth and Sea. Herodotus recorded a Pythia even declaring: "I know the number of the sands of the sea and the measure thereof" (I, p. 47).

Plato called the Pythia "our national divinity"; but it was

Plutarch who, as one of the two priests resident at Delphi, knew the Oracle best. In his essay on the virtues of women, Plutarch attempted to console the Pythia named Clea for the death of their mutual friend, Leontis. The virtues of men and the virtues of women, he told Clea, are one and the same. Therefore, barring individual differences, either male or female persons may live the same sorts of lives and perform equally well identical functions. Men and women, he told Clea, are equally brave, equally wise, and equally just.

Plutarch and his master, Plato, consulted the Pythia, the latter before he wrote *The Republic*. Writing about 100 A.D., Plutarch also estimated the age of the Pythias at Delphi to be one thousand years. Odysseus went to Delphi before 1200 B.C. to consult the Oracle about the Trojan War. Oedipus consulted her about Thebes, around 1000 B.C. Heracles visited her and was condemned, for murder, to the funeral pyre by the Oracle at around 900 B.C. Homer wrote his epics at Delphi, some say, before 700 B.C. Pindar also composed poetry there sometime between 518 B.C. and 438 B.C. The Golden Age of the Delphic Oracle fell apparently between the eighth and fifth centuries B.C.

The decline of Delphi had commenced by the reign of Philip II of Macedon, 359–336 B.C. Roman Emperors Sulla and Nero both plundered Delphi's gold and art treasures; the insane Nero, who reigned from 54–58 A.D., also carried away five hundred of the most renowned statues of classical Greece. The Gauls invaded Delphi in 279 B.C., but were driven off by earthquake and lightning. Barbarians successfully plundered the Oracle in 83 B.C.

Plutarch journeyed several times to Rome around 100 A.D. in attempts to persuade their Roman governors to restore Delphi, and he almost succeeded with the Emperors Domitian and Hadrian. Fortunately, around 174 A.D., Pausanias visited the shrine and described it and its still lingering power.

But the eastern Emperor Justinian, who himself could neither read nor write, *closed the oracle and the schools* of philosophy in Greece in 529 A.D., after which indescribably tragic date *there were no more educated women in Greece for well over a thousand years*, ergo, *no more priestesses*.

Fortunately also, Strabo studied what was left of Delphi during his wide travels in Europe, Africa, and Asia. Although forty-seven of his history books have been lost, his few records of Delphi, made twenty-five years before the birth of Plutarch, provide information from earlier Greek writers (Homer, Eratosthenes, Polybius, and Posidonius) and from firsthand observation. His works, translated into Latin in 1472 and published in the original Greek in 1516, have long been known.

Information from Strabo:

1) Delphi is most famous because of Pythian Apollo's temple there, where the Oracle must be very old, indeed, because Agamemnon went there for advice from her (1200 B.C.?).

   Delphi is situated on the southern flank of Mt. Parnassus, on a semicircular, transverse ridge, reminiscent of a half-dome. The Castalian Spring is there.

2) Delphi is so centrally located that the vigilant Amphictyonic League of twelve cities initially convened there, spring and autumn, pouring money and gifts into the holy shrine.

3) No matter how sacred Delphi is, such a wealthy shrine invites robbers. Nowadays the shrine is almost destitute, if you judge it by money alone. Most of its finest art treasures are still intact and in place, however. Homer tells us how endowed it was in his day (*Iliad*, 9, p. 404). I give you a list of the biggest thieves, etc.

4) It's untrue that the temple at Delphi had wings. The present temple was built by the Amphictyonic League. The tomb of Neoptolemus is there.

5) *The Pythia's first contests were for poets.* Later, the Pythian Games were established, for athletes.

6) My source Ephorus recounts the history of Delphi this way: Apollo conquered the Pythia because he wanted the oracle for men only, because men (more than women) need to be taught gentility and self-control.

7) My source Ephorus must have intended to confuse mythology with history. Who ever heard such a ridiculous concoction as his story that Apollo travelled on the (pres-

ent) main highway, Athens-Delphi? that he shot Pytho with an arrow? that he then journeyed over the entire earth? that Themis was a woman? that Pytho was human?

After hearing Strabo's objections it seems appropriate to ponder an explanation of the Pythia by a very wise classical scholar. His conclusions appear to have been long considered and recollected in tranquility: Introduction to *Essays Classical* (London, 1883) by F.W.H. Myers, for which reason those words stand as Epigraph to this book. The study of oracles belongs under the comparative history of religions, which addresses the problems of fear, moral government, punishment for evil, and God. Greek Oracles reflected for over a thousand years (c. 700 B.C. - c. 300 A.D.) mankind's need to connect with his distant past.

The Greeks may still claim an unbroken ascendancy over the minds of modern people. There were at least two hundred sixty practicing Oracles in the ancient Greek world, the one at Delphi being the most satisfying of all. (Their dream temples have been revived by modern psychoanalysis.)

The Greek Oracles succeeded because they offered the comfort and solace men and women needed, and because they stood up to the test of truth: that what is clear and evident, and so recognized by all people everywhere as true, is true.

The Delphic Oracle understood that "poetry is the only thing which every age is certain to recognize as truth" (Myers, p. 21). The poet and the Delphic priestess were both permitted to speak enigmatically, which puts the burden of self-knowledge upon the student, the worshipper, and the reader. Whereas a teacher's explanations are soon forgotten, the student's own struggle to understand leads to real intellectual power. Thus, the poetic and the pseudooracular style are one and the same, a style the most subtle and the most brilliantly cultivated through the ages.

Myers attributes this continued, mutual success of poet and Oracle to the influence of Socrates. The Greek philosopher Socrates asserted that there existed a close, personal relationship between mankind and the invisible world.

And to think it was Socrates, called wisest by the Pythia herself, who was put to death for impiety! His disciple Plato believed in the power of oracles as he believed in revealed knowledge, or *revelation,* as one way of knowing what we know.

The Neo-Platonists continued to support oracular pronouncements as revelatory. Some Christian Fathers also believed somewhat in oracles, since Christianity is also a revealed religion.

Myers says, "I need hardly remind the reader that the Church continued till the Renaissance to believe in the reality of the Greek oracles . . ." (Note 1, p. 103). Myers then quotes Bouché-Leclerq: ". . . qui croit à la Providence et à l'efficacité de la prière doit se rappeler qu'il accepte tous les principes sur lesquels repose la divination antique." (He who believes in Providence and in the efficaciousness of prayer ought to remember that he is accepting all those principles upon which stands archaic divination.)

Granting that ancient divination belongs more properly to the realm of comparative theology, one must even so offer a small case for literature. Literature too always asks that most difficult of questions: Why?

Therefore why have the poets continued to support divination, oracular knowledge, and why have they never ceased retelling the story of Delphi, for such is the case? Even in the centuries when the Church Militant encouraged its priests, said epic poets, to grasp golden swords and slay the dragon, the poets felt humane sympathy for the victim. More than any other persons, the poets were imprinted by the slaughter of Pytho before his oracular cave and sacred spring. Thus, readers learn about the Pythia, and reread classical eyewitness accounts with a mounting sense of *déjà vu.*

From childhood fairy tales, the reader's feelings have been aroused and educated by tales of slain giants, princes turned into monsters, and dragons that could not give up their treasures. Readers transfer, as soon as the triggers are released, all the sad burden of childhood suffering and adult grief to the slain Pytho at Delphi.

Emotions are instantly aroused by certain key words, which set off a series of reactions. Recollections of something awesome and terrible, something not understood but partially apprehended even through the author's own frustration and ignorance, begin to accumulate all over again.

The keys, which constitute as strange a phenomenon as the world of consciousness owns, are:

1) the sea, below a
2) gorge or chasm, near
3) a spring, a stream in an arid land, where
4) a guardian of an underground treasure of inestimable worth to all, watches.
5) Mother Earth is kindly repository of all goodness.
6) Dragon may be her son.
7) A cave underground and very dark, with a certain, given number of steps descending,
8) A fissure in the earth, a cleft, a furrow, with
9) terrifying sounds coming from under the earth.
10) A weird wrongness in the enveloping air, or atmosphere,
11) an absence of fellow creatures, but
12) mysterious flights of strange birds overhead.
13) The poverty of the middle world versus the wealth of the Underworld,
14) the sad inevitability of armed combat to the death,
15) the need for a memorial dedicated to the slain warrior and/or victor, the thirst for knowledge, for
16) a funeral by way of propitiation and for the purpose of exculpating the community of its collective guilt,
17) the need for women to mourn publicly and audibly some great loss all womankind has suffered,
18) the problem of how to dispose of the awesome treasure stolen from the dragon's cave, where to find it,
19) the problem of how to cleanse one's hands of it, how to think of it,
20) the possibility of restitution and reparation for humiliation, ostracism, defeat, injury, and injustice.

Poets have never tired of recreating, in disguise or openly, the story of the Delphic Oracle, of Apollo's slaughtering of Pytho before his cave, and of the confiscation of his treasure, which Pytho guarded. While not every key appears in each account, still the reader feels the same emotions aroused.

The Delphic Oracle, finally, exemplified two important routes to knowledge, teaching people to use their own intuition, as a way to self-knowledge. That women possess by birth a high degree of intuition is a theory many believe true. This attribution of intuition may more probably derive from the Pythias themselves.

The Delphic Oracle accepted and, in fact, exemplified knowledge by revelation. Ancient women of the oracles also practiced self-induced hypnosis, hypnagogic reverie, and dreams as other useful paths to self-knowledge.

The moment Plutarch dreamed of in his *Pythian Dialogue* called "The Cessation of the Oracles" *(De oraculorum defectu)* caused men also to burst into loud sobs. Some sailors were working their ship across dangerous seas. The night was pitch dark. Not a star shone to light the way or help plot a course. Suddenly a hollow voice shouted out of the darkness, "The great god Pan is dead." The oracle has been closed. The great Pythia, female divinity of the Pan-Hellenic world, has forever ceased to speak. No wonder they sobbed.

THE PRIESTESSES AT DELPHI

Three stories offer three rare accounts, which either seem to speak, or pretend to speak, of a Delphic Pythia: The Story of Phemonoë; The Story of Theoclea, or Themistoclea; and The Story of Psyche.

The first story takes its priestess's name from Pausanias (VIII), who placed her in the earliest century of the oracle, i.e., in "Pytho's day"; but the author Lucan situates this depreciatory, and clearly fictional, story during the decline of the oracle a thousand years later, in Roman days. His work can be read, and will be retold as written, from young Lucan's point of view. He intended it as a crafty piece of political propaganda that only incidentally showed considerable interest in a Pythia at Delphi. Once it is seen for what it is, one can smile at Lucan's attempt to overthrow the government at Rome, and appreciate his story of a Pythia. It is, of course, better than no story at all. Certainly Lucan met persons who had consulted the Pythia at Delphi, and certainly he had learned a good deal first-hand and from books probably no longer extant. The overt sexual symbolism which reeks throughout his pages comes not so much from Delphi as from young Lucan's fantasies.

The second story seems also to be fiction, but is also based upon some piece of written evidence. The first alleges or betrays Plutarch, and the second, Diogenes Laertius. The second author is a French scholar of the ending nineteenth century. His essay is immensely well written and inestimably valuable because he makes the connection Pythagoras-Pythia. It does not occur to Schuré to consider, however, that he had it wrong, that the link was perhaps Pythia-Pythagoras. The connection itself, if it proves correct, or can ever be proven correct, demonstrates the origin of that Pythagorean doctrine which many believe reappeared in Ireland, Scotland, Wales, and Gaul as Druidism. The connection, Pythagoras-Druidism, interests everybody.

The third story, written by the famous African author Apuleius (Appuleius), who was born around 130 A.D., tells the story of Apollo and Psyche. In fact, he is the only person ever to tell this story. Nobody has ever before connected Psyche, so far as I know, to the Pythia, or to the Delphic Oracle.

Apuleius tells her story in his marvelous book *The Golden Ass*, which recounts his initiation into a Mystery Religion of the ancient world. Such rites were secret. They were never to be revealed, on pain of death. They were also conducted and adopted entirely or preponderantly by women.

The story Apuleius tells could very well treat, it seems, the installation of a Pythia at Delphia. The reader will observe that it is a very old story, where the minor actors are neither insects nor animals, but more probably priestesses intent upon assisting poor Psyche to win through to victory. Furthermore, the symbolism of Psyche as the Soul fits a Pythia admirably. Presumably, the Pythia was initiated after the most severe of educations. Without such an initiation the Pythia could never have withstood the pressures of her ministry, one imagines.

1) The Story of Phemonoë

Plutarch (46 A.D.–146 A.D.) speaking in a "Pythian Dialogue" entitled "Concerning Oracles of the Pythia" *(De Pythiae Oraculis):*

It is true that at Delphi the air is thick and heavy (#4). The Pythia goes down into her inner shrine where she burns laurel and barley flour on the altar. Heraclitus says her words, which come from the god, will ring out for a thousand years (#6). What is inspiration, if not a light shining in the soul and creating a vision (#7)? The Pythia declares she shall continue to speak to the hearts of mankind even after her death. They will only have to look up to the moon to see and hear (#9).

Naturally we walked around the temple and sat down on its southern steps where we could look over at the shrine of Earth and see the stream of water flowing on and on.

At this very stream our ancestors founded this oracle, associating the two allied arts, poetry and prophecy, the Muses and their Delphic priestess. She once belonged solely to Earth and to Earth's temple, you know (#17). Our god Apollo has his temple here now, but he only directs affairs, without acting upon them, as she does. Her peculiar gift is the possession of a mere woman's body allied, however, to an uneasy soul that will speak out ceaselessly.

What is inspiration, if not an alliance of two opposite currents operating simultaneously, the one arriving to the priestess from outer space, and meeting the other, which arises from the depths of her human being (#21)? The Pythia is herself characterized moreover by "nobility of character." She cares nothing at all for the plaudits or censure men may care to judge her by. She is not interested in reputation. When she descends into that private chamber, she is alone with God. She is in His presence (#28).

Plutarch: De oraculorum defectu.

Our vision comes from the eye, but there must be light for the eyes to see. In the Pythia's case, the soul is the light by which her prophecy is illumined (#42).

Why was the oracle dedicated to Earth? Because the earth fluctuates. Its currents shift. We witness changes about us, calculate cycles, and watch storms collect above us. We hear and see earthquakes unleash their forces, notice hot springs shut off here and reopen there, know locations actually move, generations vanish, persons and objects disappear (#43).

In our considered opinion we soberly conclude that spirits breathing into the Pythia cause her to prophesy. This spiritual presence also changes. It waxes and wanes. It is not eternal, not everlasting, not destined to be ours forever and ever (#44).

When this prophetic priestess speaks, she sheds about her a lovely perfume, and yet she herself has no perfume on her, and is not perfumed. This phenomenon occurs only at times. Her physical condition shifts. She is not always in harmony (#50).

We had the case a short while past of a priestess who died. They say she consented to descend into her inner shrine, but that she went down unwillingly and without really wanting to perform her functions there.

The minute she answered the first questions, her voice betrayed her unwell state of health. Her voice was hoarse. She was not responding easily. She seemed to be plunging up and down like a ship in rough seas. Some distemper had her in its fierce grip.

Suddenly she grew hysterical. She lunged toward the exit and threw herself down on the stone.

The delegation left the temple at once. So did the priest Nicander, who was the interpreter present. The other attendant priests rushed out too.

After a minute or two, the attendants returned inside and raised her up in their arms. She was conscious all this time. She never lost consciousness, in fact. She lived for a few more days.

You may be sure that for such reasons of prevention, the priestess herself is very well guarded, and especially is her chastity preserved for her sake. Her person is carefully protected in every way so that she is maintained in peace and quiet, free from all physical contact with strangers and any association with the outside world.

Omens are always taken by her ministers until it is perfectly clear to them that her condition, state of mind, and inclination dispose her to preside, without injury to herself, on a particular day (#51).

2) Lucan's *Pharsalia (The Civil War)*.

The god Apollo took revenge on Delphi because his mother (v. 75) had been driven away from there after she had become pregnant. This transpired following the great flood, which inundated the earth to such a depth that even one of the cliffs over Delphi there on Mt. Parnassus was submerged. After the waters receded, a great chasm lay below Delphi. That was when Themis became queen and High-priestess of the oracle. When Apollo saw that divinely prophetic words were issuing from this chasm, he decided to kill Pytho, claim the shrine, and become a prophet himself.

What deity dwells down in Delphi's dark grottos and black caverns anyway? What heavenly divinity could endure such imprisonment? How could he stand it to be weighed down under the load of earth? How could he endure it while all the time knowing the future, events to come, secrets of earth and sky? Is he not a great and powerful god who despite all this stands ready to reveal himself to the governors of earth, and is patient enough to suffer contact with the masses and listen to their questions? Perhaps Apollo and Zeus are connected to some element of their godhead buried deep in earth and exhaled from the caves above the Pleistus River bed, a force that issuing forth to govern our world upholds it in empty air.

Perhaps this force also hides in a girl's lungs whence its exhalation loudly beats upon her soul, and thrusts open her lips, just the way Mt. Etna in Sicily under pressure bursts open volcanic vents, or as the underground fires of the Fiery or Phlegraean Fields at Cuma heat the rocks there until they burn.

Apollo's shrine at Delphi opens to all men, the world over, denies no man admittance, alone stays free from any aspersion cast by human criminality. Apollo forbids any man to pray there for any gift at all. Men there may only learn their sentence, which can never be alleviated. When the city of Tyre had to be abandoned, Apollo kindly directed the population to a new site (i.e., Carthage). He counselled Athens to meet the Persians in the naval engagement at the island of Salamis, and they won. When the earth suffered drought, Apollo healed it with rain. When the plague struck, it was swept clean away by the god.

The Pythia has lost her voice, however, which has occasioned a sad loss for men of my generation. Our kings dared no longer appeal to her, so fearfully do we all dread the future now. The powerful of our day have shut her mouth.

The priestesses at Delphi hardly grieve that divine speech is now denied them. They rather enjoy silence, the reason being that if Apollo "breathes into" them, which is to say, if he "inspires" one of them now, she is apt to die. A premature death is now her punishment for having drawn his breath into her body. Her reward is instant death. The god fractures her rib cage by the agony and size of his onrush. His mad fury, like a blast of lightning from above, explodes her tender shell.

When our Roman patrician Appius Claudius journeyed to Delphi to consult the Pythia, she had long been silent. The rock upon which she stood in later days to deliver her prophecy had long been bare of her presence and silent as a grave. Her priest was commanded to unbar the temple's inner chambers, throw open its fearsome deep, and fetch the priestess.

Her name was Phemonoë. They found her taking a stroll, carefree as can be, between the Castalian Spring and her hidden grove of sacred trees. The priest had to catch her by force and push her ahead of him into the temple. At the threshhold the maiden turned to confront the Roman dignitary.

Phemonoë remonstrated with him, "Are you not presumptuous, Roman, in your desire that the future be laid open before you here? This gorge of Mt. Parnassus must have fallen upon Apollo, and buried him alive. No voice now speaks here. No god even lives here anymore. Perhaps the current that once swept through this chasm, up into this ancient shrine, has been diverted, or redirected to some other, distant realm and worthier shrine on earth. Perhaps Apollo himself caused it to swerve from this sanctuary when he let Delphi burn to the ground under the barbarians' torches. Maybe those sacred ashes fell down and stopped up the fissures through which Apollo used to breathe. Maybe heaven has willed us to be silent here henceforth, and speechless. Perhaps you Romans should be

content to have the Cumaean Sibyl whom we dispatched to
Rome before you conquered the world. Let her unroll her
massive *Books* and read you an oracle. Even worse, suppose
Apollo finds in all the world today no man worthy of an oracle
from this once fabulous, very holy shrine."

Her fears betrayed both her and Apollo. Nothing availed
her. The fillet was tied about her head, low over her forehead.
White bands were wound around to confine her long hair at
the nape of her neck. A laurel wreath from the hills of Delphi
was prepared to crown her. The priest escorted her across the
temple to the west end. When she balked at the doorway, he
pushed her until she had entered the sanctum. She stood there
pretending to utter prophetic words. No inspiration moved
her. She stood there rigid with dread before the *antron*. Her
cries were weak and forced rather than inspired. She suffered
no divine ecstasy to enter her frame.

The noble Appius was far from being taken in by this performance, but angered that she should wilfully before him im-
pugn Apollo's divine name. He knew her words came from
lying lips. He heard her feeble voice bounce off the walls. He
saw no visible sign of exaltation, no hair standing straight up
on the scalp, no wreath lifted off her head, no rumbling of
the foundation, no swaying of the trees. She would not release
her person into Apollo's arms.

"Go down this instant into the cave beneath," Appius cried.
"Do it, sacrilegious fraud, or I myself will chastise you as you
deserve. Go down at once. Permit yourself to be questioned.

"We live in a world torn asunder by wars and by the threat
of wars. Who are you to refuse us? Let the god answer me
through your profane lips. At once."

There remained no more chance of escape for the maiden.
Down she went into the cavern. Once there, she crouched terrified beside the "tripods" (*sic*) and clung to the prophetic rock.
But the *antron* was still charged, as was the rock, with its powerful current, even after a millennium of use. She was electri-
fied.

Apollo drove as fast into her chest as ever a god was able to
do. He mastered her. He took possession. She became his thing,
then. He drove away her own life force as he thrust deep into

her body. He seized the heart out of her. Deep as he could, he consumed her until he drove her mad.

Then she whirled. Then she lurched, ran, stumbled, fell, and ran again, here, there, side to side. Her hair stood on end. The fillets broke and dropped. She tossed her head so hard this way and that she almost tore it off her neck. She careened off the walls, knocked down the tripods, bounced blindly off the partitions. Her blood seethed within her.

Apollo rode her with bit and spur and curb, whip and goad, and flame thrown to pierce her innards. He both urged her on and, at the same time, stopped her short.

She speaks but cannot utter a cry.

In one burst of light the entire past of the world became present before her goggled eyes. So many aeons crowd into her chest they stretch it to bursting. Revelation shows here events from an unknown past streaming by her memory. The future course of history parades past in sound and fury. Destiny screams its call for equal time and full utterance.

Phemonoë sees now how the earth was created and then destroyed. All knowledge is now hers. She now measures the width of Ocean and counts the length of its embrace of earth. She can do her sums of all the grains of sands. The numbers lie open to her tally. She began to sort through the endless files of names that rose before her where Fate had heaped them. Where was this Appius's name among the generations piled at random? Apollo made it hard for her to focus.

"The same occurred at Campania, our green and lovely land that lies between Rome and Naples.

"The time was when the renowned High-priestess of Rome, the Cumaean Sibyl, granted an interview. She was begged to choose one great kingdom to love among the realms of earth.

"The Sibyl consented to mount the ramps from her prophetic underground residence.

"She condescended, as begged to do, to lay her mighty hand upon the register. She actually deigned to turn its pages.

" 'Here,' she finally said. The world's rulers trembled before her. They treasured any rare syllable she occasionally let go of. They bent low before her to catch her next mutter: 'Rome,' she said."

Phemonoë finally came to his noble name: Appius Claudius, under ROMAN. Ah, yes, he went to Delphi to consult the Pythia because he knew the Greeks had founded Rome's oracle and sent out the first Sibyl to the Etruscans. Phemonoë groaned with pain and relief to have sorted out his great name from all the heap of future Romans. Her breath came harder and louder from her tortured lungs. Their rasping gasps grew shorter and shorter. In pain she cried and begged to be let go. It was no use. She saw it was no use. All she could do was wail until the walls of her cave echoed in one long cry of agony from the maiden's throat.

"Roman aristocrat," she told him finally in gasps of breath. "You shall live. You shall escape the wars. You shall survive the wars in peace. You shall find a haven . . . for yourself . . . beside a private cove . . . on the northeast coast of Greece . . . renowned for priestesses."

The god Apollo closed her throat for her. He shut off her air. He stopped up her words. He had finished.

Appius's Paean to Apollo and Artemis
Oh, gods of oracles, be praised, who preside over our fate! Oh, oracles! Oh, mysteries of earth! Oh, master and mistress, from whose all-seeing eyes no truth, no occurrence, no life, no future, is unrevealed, tell me now. Let me hear the awful truth from you now. I can endure if I know. Have no fear, you gods!

Is it not true that empire after empire shall fall? Shall not great Generals of Armies die? Shall not our Emperors fall, stabbed to death? Shall not nations self-destruct? And green Campania, our beloved Italy, bathe in blood from wars and ever more wars?

Is all that not yet decided, oh, ye gods? Have you not yet resolved how it shall be? Will the awfullest crime take place? And what of their stars? Is great Pompey's fate still being tested in their stars? Or has he already been doomed to eternal death? Does our life hang by a thin thread before Atropos? Why are you still?

You have fallen silent, have you not, to allow blind, bad Fortuna her free hand rummaging in our affairs? Some sword will have to avenge us.

Ambition has been let run mad at Rome. Our leaders have become our tyrants. We are oppressed, not governed, but oppressed. Ambition among the highest must be chastised. Tyranny will meet, otherwise, another sword of Brutus.

Who will die? Not I, says this priestess. I shall find a safe corner to hide in.

Praise be to Apollo and to Artemis.

Phemonoë escaped, barely alive. She managed to gather enough breath and strength to rise. She steadied herself, and made one leap toward the outer door. This time she crashed it, made it swing open to permit her exit. So doing, she bruised her numbed body. Wildly she plunged across and away from Apollo's temple.

Her prophetic fury still rode upon her. He had not let go of her because in there she had lied. *Appius had not heard the full story.* She had tricked him at the end. She had lied, and Apollo knew it.

Rolling her eyes in an effort to clear her head and rid herself of the frenzy, the Pythia glared up at the white skies over Delphi. Grimace after another stretched her muscles into hideous grins. Her tendons almost snapped. She tried opening wide her mouth, spreading wide her fingers to release tension. She tossed her head and faced into the wind to cool her cheeks. The whiteness of her hands and limbs frightened her. She felt like lead. Her whole body obeyed but still stayed numb. Her heart beat so strong she thought it was the sea driven by a norther, whipped by winds into monstrous combers that tumbled roaring on algaed rocks. She sighed to calm it, but no sigh came from her chest that still seemed under water, full of seawater. Her voice was hoarseness, not sound.

Then the daylight vanished in one swoop of wings from the heavens above her. Like a blackbird hit by a hawk she dropped to earth and fell quiet.

Apollo had turned off her light. He had shut off her enlightened interval of prophecy when the divine knowledge of the universe had poured freely into her. He withdrew from her his blinding presence, his shower of gold like that of Zeus when he wooed Danaë. Phemonoë dropped to earth and lay fallen into sleep there, a natural sleep. When she awoke at his command, she would not remember; for the waters Apollo had poured into her had come from Lethe's amnesiac stream. No drop of truth remained in her now.

In a flash of light Apollo withdrew. Back to the tripods inside the mantic cave flashed all truth, all knowledge of the future, all records of the past.

Phemonoë slowly came back to life, opened her eyes, rubbed her palms together and her feet, tested her chords and tendons, stretched out her sore muscles and returned alive among the living.

Ah, Appius, in your arrogant haste, you forgot the final appeal is not to the gods of light, neither to Apollo's sun nor to the moon's silver beams. Ah, Appius, you were careless today.

Your fear blinded you. It sent you in final search to the Pythia. That was an error.

You should have asked *the priestesses of the dead*. You only heard today at Delphi a *priestess reluctant to be asked*. She gave you what you deserve: a riddling reply. When she could not turn you from your purpose, reluctantly she let herself be used, but recovering, refused you the sum of her knowledge, in the last analysis.

Appius, you will now foolishly follow her vision as far as it went. You will find your refuge along the shore of northeastern Greece. There in Euboea you will huddle in what you think is your domain. Think, man. Where is there a safe refuge from civil war when Rome itself totters on the verge of collapse? How can sequestration save you then?

When madmen seize the reins of government, they will sweep all that is not gold down into common dust.

Your tomb will probably be splendid, perhaps, as befits a Roman patrician of the Claudian Line. You will find your sheltered cove, but where? No domain in Euboea can save you, Appius! No shelter will be yours!

The directions of Phemonoë blinded you, Appius. She sent you to reside between the very pits where the marble for the temples of Nemesis was quarried from earth. You surely recall that Nemesis hates proud men. She will cut you down, Appius.

The directions of Phemonoë have not yet sunk into your head, Appius. You have been deceived by the Pythia whom you abused and forced to prophesy against her will. She really directed you, although she said "Euboea" vaguely to you, *to Aulis!* Surely you remember Aulis? Surely you remember Chalcis, chief city of Euboea, where the Greek ships made rendezvous. They were bound for Aulis, where they awaited fair winds for Troy. Surely, Appius, you have been easily deceived by a Greek today.

At Aulis Iphigenia was sacrificed by her father, their chieftain Agamemnon. She sent you there, to your death also.

The Furies await you, Appius. You will be charged with the desecration of sacred Delphi, compounded by aggravated assault upon the High-priestess of Hellas. The Pythia has spoken.

The lessons learned by C. Julius Caesar still obtain for our other tyrants ruling Rome today: 1) once a Caesar draws the sword for war, it can be turned, by his own men, against him, and 2) a leader of men fears the men whom he leads as much as they fear him.

3) Conclusion

Marcus Annaeus Lucanus (39 A.D.–65 A.D.) "Lucan," has referred much too plainly here, in this poem on civil war, not only to the Roman Emperor C. Julius Caesar, assassinated by Brutus and Cassius in Rome (44 B.C.), but to his own then ruling Emperor C. Claudius Nero (37 A.D.–68 A.D.).

Lucan's hero Appius was related to both Caesar and Nero.

This poem by Lucan defends the Delphic Oracle whom and which Nero desecrated and plundered.

Nero had murdered his mother and his wife; set Rome on fire so he could, against a background of red flames, recite a poem he had written on the conflagration of Troy; probably put to death, among many Roman notables, both Saints Peter and Paul; and he promptly ordered Lucan to commit suicide.

In his poem, when Lucan says "Appius," he really means "Nero."

Nero committed suicide three years later, proclaiming, "What a poet the world is losing when I die!"

As final irony, the promising young poet lost to the world at the age of twenty-six was Lucan.

The Story of Themistoclea, or Theoclea, and Pythagoras
Introductory Note

It was very difficult, even in the ancient world, to learn and be sure about the teachings of the philosopher Pythagoras. Plato himself spent a great deal of money to acquire three rare books about Pythagoras. The Sage had migrated from Delphi to Italy, and died there. The biography of Pythagoras by the Greek Diogenes Laertius is therefore invaluable.

This story involves name dropping. It is thought that the very name of Pythagoras magnifies and validates the Delphic Oracle.

Diogenes Laertius, who lived in the third century B.C., wrote this biography of Pythagoras, in which he said that Pythagoras *was at Delphi* and that he had *studied under the Delphic Oracle:* "The same authority (that Plato read) asserts that Pythagoras took his doctrines from the Delphic priestess Themistoclea."

Such a statement by a learned biographer deserves great attention, for it has surely not occurred to anyone today that the Pythia at Delphi was more learned than Pythagoras, nor that she was the last of his renowned teachers.

The people of Croton, Italy, reverenced Pythagoras because, having descended into the Underworld, he thereafter spoke infallible truth. He took his name "Pythagoras" at the time of his studies, from his teacher's name, the "Pythia," at Delphi:

> Aristippus of Cyrene affirms in his work *On the Physicists* that he was named Pythagoras because he uttered the truth as infallibly as did the Pythian oracle.

The Story

Before he completed his formal studies at Delphi, Pythagoras had already worked under the best teachers of his day. He spent twenty-two years in Egypt; there he underwent his first initiation into the Mysteries (i.e., he descended into the Underworld, and/or suffered a cataleptic death) and was reborn into a more powerful, second life.

While Pythagoras was studying in Egypt, he witnessed a hideous sight. It marked him for life. He actually saw the Persian conquest of Egypt by Cambyses, who sacked Memphis in 525 B.C. The horror and inhuman cruelty of that carnage haunted that Sage of Greece, Pythagoras, all his life long.

Leaving Egypt after his graduation, which was the initiation, Pythagoras went next to Babylon. There he studied twelve more years, this time under the Magi.

After these thirty-four years of advanced study, Pythagoras journeyed to Delphi. There he formulated and expressed those doctrines which spread widely over Europe during his lifetime. His teachers and their students continued this dissemination of doctrine.

Pythagoras considered himself a mere messenger to the Pythia, and the Pythia herself as the source of his wisdom. At Delphi he served as a teacher in her college.

His best and most adept student at Delphi was a young girl named Theoclea whom he singled out in the college of novices preparing for the priesthood. It is fairly certain that Pythagoras chose her, and not the other way around, because his students were not allowed to look at their teacher while he lectured. Pythagoras lectured behind a curtain to those students whom he authorized able to continue their education with him. He could see them, but they could not see him.

Delphi was founded, he had learned in Egypt, by the Ethiopian dynasty of Egypt. Their queens were all High-priestesses, like the Pythia. The Pytho, also known as "Python," was assigned by the Africans to Delphi for the purpose of guarding the sacred Castalian Spring.

The defeat of those "Pythos," or celebrated *black warriors from Upper Egypt,* after which Apollo took over the oracle, cut the direct link between Egypt and Delphi. Their deaths left the Pythia dependent upon Apollo and his solar heroes. The latter, including Heracles, the Pythia sentenced to death whenever she could, for their string of murders and seizure of priestesses' sanctuaries and territories by one excuse or another.

As he commenced his teachings at Delphi, Pythagoras also established the rules he insisted upon as requisites for admission to his lectures. Among his students he noticed that Theoclea, more than any other student, adopted these rules willingly and practiced them as natural, healthy, and in no way burdensome.

As he taught, Pythagoras watched his students' faces and recognized at once, as experienced teachers always recognize, the one most brilliant member of any group: quiet, concentrated, reserved, thoughtful, shining, still, and inspired.

Pythagoras advocated self-knowledge, which was the first Maxim of the Pythia: "Know thyself." He also advocated self-criticism and, wherever necessary, self-reproach. He taught that every student at Delphi was responsible for her own life. Every student must administer to herself praise for her good deeds, but also censure for her failings. This is her responsibility. She can be judged, and must be judged, by her deeds; and her judge is herself.

Pythagoras also gave a Golden Rule for those girls who wished to continue their education; that they should train their memory by two daily practices:

1) at bedtime, review their day, evaluate their performance that day, and make a plan for the following day; and

2) at bedtime, rehearse what they have learned that day, before falling asleep.

Such practicing, taught Pythagoras, would facilitate learning and develop the memory. Upon awakening, the student would find the material already mastered and safely committed to memory.

The soul of every human being, he taught, is divided into three parts: intelligence, reason, and passion. Only mankind, and no animals, possesses reason to any high degree. Only reason among the three faculties of the person is immortal.

The soul is invisible, like wind and the outer atmosphere.

My students will wear white robes like my own, he said, and like the Pythia's white robe, which symbolized purity, pure thoughts, continence, and abstinence.

My students will respect the law and wage war endlessly on

the lawless alone. So the Pythia disputes Apollo every inch of the way, Pythagoras taught, just as spiritual power disputes brute force and criminality every inch of the way.

The impersonal desire for knowledge-for-the-sake-of-knowledge, like the practice of art-for-the-sake-of-art, is the rarest and most admirable of all desires and all practices. The Pythia and her priestesses in training are chosen for their single-minded pursuit of wisdom and beauty. Such women will be found among the future teachers and poets of mankind, at all times and in all places. The world will also use them.

My students at their teaching centers will represent the human manifestations of Pytho's force, which belts the earth as currents that meet at sacred intersections. The source of true wisdom rises from and lies under the earth. For this reason the Pythia's oracular chamber is underground.

The world's Great Initiates first pass examinations and then undergo the trials of rebirth, or initiation, underground. Their names are secret.

Divine beings are reborn upon the earth at irregular intervals. Such persons reincarnated are called "avatars."

The story of how Pythagoras, because he was the greatest teacher then alive in the world, initiated Theoclea into her rebirth as the next Pythia, and how he remained with her thereafter for the period of a year, has been admirably told by the French scholar Edouard Schuré in his *The Ancient Mysteries of Delphi: Pythagoras* (Paris, 1889; New York, 1971), pp. 54–62. By initiating Theoclea as the new Pythia, says Schuré, Pythagoras ensured the continuance of Greek thought over the Western world:

> By forming the magic chain of wills, initiates in this way prolong the life of nations, (for) the future of Greece and the destiny of the whole world were at stake (pp. 60 and 57).

Schuré concluded:

> It was only after . . . preparing Theoclea for his ministry, that he took his departure for Greater Greece (p. 62).

Historians say that many legends concerning Pythagoras grew up in the centuries following his death, but Diogenes Laertius is convincing when he reports a Pythia named Themistoclea from whom Pythagoras received his final knowledge, and perhaps his final initiation.

Thus, it was probably Themistoclea who prepared him for his ministry. The Pythagoreans, such as Theoclea, who were his pupils, and their pupils after them, formed a separate group of philosopher-teachers, experts on mathematics, astronomy, and also on political reform. This last specialty caused their dispersal and/or perhaps their continuance as a secret fellowship.

The Delphic Oracle, on the other hand, was not secret. Her responses to monarchs of Asia, heroes of Greece, and Roman rulers were generally plain, open, and recorded. Only when she was asked to reveal the future destiny of individuals and nations, were her replies usually guarded and obscure. While the Pythagoreans scattered, after the suicide of Pythagoras, the Oracle at Delphi continued for another thousand years to furnish replies, direct colonists to favorable sites abroad, pacify the Greek cities whenever possible, and unite Greece at this common shrine and commonly shared altar. There officiated a line of priestesses controlling the entire, known world. It was probably, after all, the Pythia who taught Pythagoras.

Much as the Oracle respected Pythagoras, the Sage of Samos, she has over long centuries merged rather with the greatest of the early Seven Sages of Greece, Socrates. His moral teachings are hers. His first favorite admonitions to his students are said to have been carved upon the temple at Delphi: "Know thyself," "Nothing in excess," and "The proper study of mankind is man." When Socrates spoke of his guardian spirit, who guided him, watched over him, and maintained him in right and profitable actions, he may have had the Pythia in mind.

Edouard Schuré believed that the Druid priestess (of his play *La Druidesse* [Paris, 1914], which he prefaced by an essay entitled "The Awakening of the Celtic Soul") descended from the Pythian priestess at Delphi.

The controversy concerning the origins of Druidism seems likely to continue unsettled for some time, but many scholars have already gone on record by declaring that Druidism, to the best of their knowledge, derives from the doctrines of Pythagoras. If he studied with the Pythia at Delphi, then beliefs in reincarnation, for one example, are, indeed, far older than the Druid priestesses, and may derive from the Pythias. If this is true, then we are able to take one step backwards in time.

The Pythia was a priestess of Earth. One notable historian of *The Celts in Pre-Christian Times* (Chicago, 1906) was Edward Anwyl, who wrote:

> This predominance of the earth in religion was in thorough keeping with the integrity of religion . . . a factor . . . that gave the Druids at some time or other in the history of the Western Celts the power which Caesar and others assign to them (p. 67).

It is Lucan who informs us categorically that the Celts also believed in reincarnation:

> This gives the (Celtic) warrior his eagerness to rush upon the steel, his courage to face death, and his conviction that it is cowardly to be careful of a life that will come back to him again (I, v. 447 ff.).

Before turning to the actual words of the Delphic Oracles, as they answered questions and offered assistance and counsel, we might turn to one other story from an ancient priest. This is the story of Psyche, which has haunted the western world since its discovery in the Renaissance. We look to it now first because it was written by a priest who was a brilliant scholar and a wit, secondly because it has haunted Western thought, and thirdly because it contains geographical and symbolic material that, in my opinion, connects it to the Delphic Oracle.

The Story of Psyche

> "The situation of the patriarchate—known to us particularly from its western development—is characterized by a recession of feminine psychology and its dominants; now feminine existence is almost entirely determined by the masculine world of consciousness and its values."
>
> Eric Neumann
> *Amor and Psyche* (Princeton, 1956).

The story of Psyche's arduous initiation into the priesthood comes from only one source, *The Golden Ass*. The author, Lucius Apuleius, was an African priest of Asclepius. Apuleius was born in Africa, educated first at Carthage in North Africa, then at Greece, and then at Rome.

In his story of Psyche, to my mind clearly an initiation into the priesthood at Delphi specifically, he is pretending to write a fable. What he is really doing is defending Paganism against Christianity. Amidst sly allusions to Delphi and the Oracle, he is admiring Psyche's heroism during the ordeal of her initiation. He makes his every word count. He includes enough errors to mislead any uninformed reader. In other words, he is a master of irony.

As an example of the curveballs Apuleius threw with such glee, one has only to consider the title *Amor and Psyche*. Apuleius apologizes, explaining the error by way of a non-explanation. You see, he says, I know that *Amor* is Latin for the Greek god Eros, and I did learn enough Latin in Rome, although Latin is so hard to learn for an African, to know that Psyche is a Greek name. But, you see my problem: I am an African telling a Greek story partially in Latin. But really, it is an Asian type of oral story from Miletus. But, to tell the truth, I heard a crazy, old woman tell the story. It was too bad I didn't write it down.

The Story

Psyche was the youngest of three sisters, and the only one of them to be acclaimed as beautiful, more beautiful even than Aphrodite. Her second handicap was that she had no husband.

Her parents consulted the Oracle of Apollo who told them to lay her out on a rocky peak. Psyche dressed for her wedding with Death, veil and all. Parents and mourners escorted her to the top of the rock, staked her out a place, and withdrew.

As she lay there, more dead than alive, the West Wind raised her, veil and gown like sails, and bore her down to the purple palace of Eros, son of Aphrodite. It laid her in a gorgeous, nuptial bed inside a golden chamber. Eros came in darkness and took her virginity. Psyche welcomed him and enjoyed herself immensely.

Next day she found herself deserted in an empty palace. But she had fun wandering over the grounds, counting the gold in the Treasury, and admiring the artwork.

Eros came again as soon as it was dark, and they made love. Psyche enjoyed herself immensely, but afterwards she sighed and complained about being left alone all day. She told Eros she could get sick of a husband who went out before dawn and didn't come back till after dark, and who came into her bed without ever giving her a chance to see him. She also complained to him about not being able to show all her wealth and her handsome spouse to her older sisters.

Eros delivered some very stern warnings. "I forbid you," he began each prohibition, "to see your sisters, to visit your parents, to leave this palace and these grounds, or to see me, or to light a lamp at night."

Again, on another night, as Psyche felt more and more imprisoned, she recommenced her complaints. Then Eros warned her again that disobedience on her part would bring dire consequences, enough to crush her. But Psyche still argued she wanted to know him, and she wanted her sisters to know she was alive, well, happy, and very wealthy. Eros replied that her sisters were hags and that they hated her and wished her ill. Psyche begged and begged him. She repeated her desire to know, until he finally consented to let her bring her sisters there.

Her married sisters arrived at the rock, each one by ship. They were wafted down to the valley. Psyche welcomed them and showed off her palace and its Treasuries. Far from admiring all these, the sisters berated Psyche for having allowed her husband, who they believed must be older and more impotent than theirs, to hoodwink her so long. They suspected he was some black Dragon, or Pytho, and they told her so.

Again Psyche pleaded to see her sisters, who again were wafted down to her palace where again they scorned Psyche's account of a dear husband whom she adored. They told her he must be some evil Snake. They also failed to share her joy that she was pregnant. "Your husband," they told her, "will probably eat you alive some night."

When Psyche refused to believe them, they told her, again

for her own good, to wait until he fell asleep, then to light a lamp, and see him for herself. While it was still daylight, Psyche prepared a lamp and set it where she could lay her hands on it, even in the dark. Then she examined her husband's weapons because she wanted to know how they worked. While handling his knife she pricked her finger.

Her husband came after dark, and they made love. Psyche enjoyed herself immensely. As soon as her husband had fallen asleep, she found the lamp, lighted it, and stole up close to the bed. She saw him. He was gorgeous—young, handsome, curly-haired, blond, and winged! In her love and ecstasy, she leaned over him. Then, horror of horrors, a drop of hot oil from the lamp fell upon his chest. The pain awakened him. Inflamed, he jumped out of bed, yelled farewell at her, and flew out the window.

Psyche had barely time enough to grab him by one leg. She hung on tight as he soared into flight. Despite her love and sorrow, Psyche had to let go. She fell back to Earth. He would never consent to see her again. He would never forgive her.

In desperation now, Psyche returned to the world of her childhood and begged each sister to help her. In each of their palaces she pleaded with the first and the second sister to save her and her child, and to reunite her and her darling, young husband. She explained how wrong they were; her husband is really the god of love, Eros, son of the goddess Aphrodite. She threatened to kill herself. She told them how on her way to their palaces, she had already thrown herself once into a river, but that the river feared Aphrodite so much he tossed Psyche back on the bank, taking care neither to drown nor damage her. She also went to consult the Great God Pan, but he was of no help to her. He said these days he was only a shepherd.

Psyche finally convinced each sister to return to the rock. Each took ship again and climbed up the mountain to the rock. However, this time, when each one expected to be wafted into the palace, she crashed down the precipice and died. What was Psyche to do? Where could she go for help now? She had a baby to think of now, and not herself alone. She began to wander over the world. Hers was a long search for knowledge.

The first thought she had was to consult the Mother at her

own temple, which was situated on the summit of a very steep hill. Poor Psyche labored up it, ridge after ridge. She entered the temple to ask Demeter for assistance during her pregnancy and at her lying-in. Demeter answered her humble plea: "Leave." Under her breath she probably added, "Grow up."

Then she decided to visit one of Hera's temples, for Hera was reported always ready to help a pregnant girl. She went to one of Hera's shrines—not the greatest one at Samos, of course, nor the well-known temple of Hera at Carthage on the coast of Africa, and not, of course, her celebrated shrine at Argos. Again Psyche was turned away.

When she heard that welcome news, Psyche's mother-in-law, the goddess Aphrodite, sent Hermes, who always escorts the dead and the souls of the dead, to fetch her. As soon as Aphrodite laid hands on Psyche, she paid her in equal currency for having seduced Eros and then for having burned him with hot oil. She told Psyche that her darling boy was still in bed, nursing his wound. She was not at all sure he would ever recover. Psyche had probably caused his death.

Aphrodite sent Psyche away to a safe place where nobody could hear her being whipped, beaten, scourged, and then tortured to within an inch of her life. Psyche did not succumb, however. She clung stubbornly to life and somehow protected her baby. So Aphrodite summoned Psyche to her presence again. "So we have a survivor," Aphrodite said to herself. This time she set Psyche Four Labors, one for Demeter, one for Poseidon, one for Zeus, and one for Hera's husband Hephaestus.

Labor I

"You slave," Aphrodite told Psyche. "Here is a job fit for you, mother of a bastard brat." Then she slapped Psyche, tore off her clothes, pulled out her hair by the handful, and set her to work. She showed Psyche a pile of seeds all mixed up together. There were grains, legumes, poppy seeds, and meadow grasses all piled indiscriminately. "I will give you until night," Aphrodite stormed. "Let's see how cleverly you can work those fingers of yours. I want this entire pile of seeds sorted and each variety placed neatly in a separate pile."

After the goddess had taken herself off, it was quiet there in the meadow. Psyche sank down and looked at the pile of seeds. She saw no reason to begin sorting. The task was impossible. She would await death, her final punishment.

But then along came one insignificant, little, six-legged ant, who took in the situation at a glance. As fast as she could, the ant rounded up her sisters. "We must help this girl," she told them. "She is pregnant with a love child." All the ants in the area heard the challenge and rushed to offer their services. The first ant explained the problem. Before long the little ants had separated the seeds and stacked each kind neatly in a separate heap. Then they went about their business on earth.

When Aphrodite came to inspect Psyche's handiwork, the goddess was in high temper. Angrily she tossed the girl a crust of bread and stalked off. Psyche was glad to have the bread.

Labor II

The next day Aphrodite set Psyche a second task, which also had to be accomplished by nightfall. She took her to a grove beside a gentle stream fringed with tall reeds. There along the bank of the little river grazed a flock of golden sheep.

"Go down there, my girl," said Aphrodite, "and gather for me a lapful of precious golden fleece."

As soon as she was alone, Psyche looked at the problem and the fearsome, yellow creatures and decided it would be easier for her to jump in this river and end it all. Hardly had she approached the bank, however, than a Reed by the river spoke to her. "Don't even think of it," he said. "Your suicide would pollute this clear water, which incidentally is sacred. Furthermore, do not go among these sheep during the heat of the day, which makes them so irritable they will gore you, stomp you to death, or butt you to death. Go over to that plane tree (Helen of Troy's sacred tree) and rest under its cool branches. Then, when evening approaches, you will see that the sheep will doze by the river bank. Then you can slip quietly among them and gather their golden fleece from all these thorn bushes."

Although Psyche performed her Second Labor as it had been assigned her, still Aphrodite continued to berate her. She gave

Psyche not one word of encouragement. "Toughen up, you," she muttered to herself.

Labor III

Psyche must now have gone to northwestern Greece, for the mountain the goddess points out to her now overlooks a most dread entrance to Tartarus. At that spot the Rivers Cocytus and Acheron pour into the marshy Acherusian Lake. The oracle near which presence she must seek water stands on the rocky pinnacle where the rivers fall and thunder down a precipitous bluff. This is the ancient kingdom of Hades (*Odyssey*, X, pp. 509–15), where priestesses of the dead and of the goddess Persephone had their grove of poplars and willows. They reign beside these rivers of fire and lamentation. As Robert Graves wrote *The White Goddess* (p. 135):

> The dreadful waters of Styx burst out from half-way up an enormously tall, steep, precipice . . . On both sides of their outlet she saw fierce dragons crawling, never asleep, always on guard with unwinking eyes . . .

Psyche could only look up at this terrifying spectacle. She was stunned by the noise of the thunderous waterfall.

Aphrodite had ordered her to fill a jug with water where it fell cascading over the falls. Psyche made herself impervious, like stone. No human being, she knew, could approach the margin where the rivers broke and fell. The labor would have been impossible to perform if not for the eagle of Zeus who volunteered to fly over the waterfall and fill Psyche's jug. Otherwise, Psyche would have failed at this point. The eagle knew how to soar and swerve, he said, so as to avoid the dragons' jaws.

Although Psyche succeeded again and carried the sacred water to Aphrodite, she still censured and assigned an even more terrifying ordeal. The next time she must personally consult the final tribunal, the High-priestess of the dead, in person.

Labor IV

The final and most terrifying ordeal through which a candidate must pass is the descent into the Underworld from which very few have returned alive. Those few, who descended and returned, became Great Initiates, persons of high ability and high achievement on earth. Aphrodite handed Psyche a box. "Take this box down to Queen Persephone in Hades. Ask her to fill it for me with her potion which maintains youth and delays the signs of age."

Psyche took the box, but she had no idea where to go nor where to find a lava tube or the white rock near which Odysseus descended. She understood that she was being sent to undergo the sleep of death, and that she risked never awakening from it. When she came to a Round Tower, she decided to climb to the top of it and then jump to her death.

To her astonishment the Tower advised her against it. "How can you lose hope, you foolish girl, just when the end of your trials may be in sight? If you jump from my height, you have no hope whatsoever of escaping from Tartarus. Let me guide you to the vicinity of Sparta, which is in southern Greece, on a peninsula. When you get to Sparta, ask directions to the nearest descent. Somebody there will guide you. Vents to the Underworld are dark tunnels. The candidate lies down, puts his feet in the vent, and then closing his eyes, gives a push, and slides quickly and smoothly down the tube.

"There at the exit, after you land on your feet and can stand upright, you will see the road to Queen Persephone's audience chamber. When Heracles descended, he wore his lion's skin to frighten the dog Cerberus. You too will need protection and gifts. Take in each hand a chunk of bread dipped in honey. Put two coins in your mouth before you slide down the vent. You would have died if left to your own devices. You could never have survived a plunge headfirst.

"Now follow these instructions carefully," added the Tower. "First you will meet a lame man driving a donkey. The beast has lost part of his load. The driver will ask you for a length of rope so he can tie the load back on the donkey's sides. Refuse. Do not answer. Pretend not to see or hear. Sharing a cord is bad news.

"Next you will come to the river Styx, dread stream of Tartarus. There you will see a dilapidated boat of sorts and beside it King Hades's son Charon. He is the boatman. Approach him. Open your mouth. Let him take one of your coins for the ferry passage across the river. Do not hand him the piece of money. Without this fee no person is allowed to proceed. The river must be crossed in his craft, with this boatman, and in no other way. A poor person without a cent to his name will have to wander through all eternity this side of the river. He can neither die nor find rest.

"While crossing this turgid river you will see a floating corpse, that of a man. You will not see his face, but his skeletal hand will reach up for you to pull him in. Do not touch or pull him in. Thus, again, you must prove that you can steel your mind against misplaced pity until, like a judge, you have heard all the evidence.

"Once you have set foot on the opposite shore, you may proceed on your journey. Soon, however, you will see three women. They will be engaged in a weaving process. You will see their tools and their product. Now, tread carefully past them. Do not under any circumstances touch their cloth.

"Probably you realize by now that these persons are all creatures of your long dream. They were not real, but only ghosts, or apparitions, or phantoms, or figments of your own imagination. Perhaps you can remember that during your trials you will incur a series of temptations. You must not yield to them, no matter how cruelly you desire their touch. These figures beg you to help, to assist, to fraternize. You are being examined, weighed, and tested. Do you understand? Were you to pull, to touch, to pay your passage, you would have dropped the honeyed bread in each hand. Control of your random impulses will ensure your safe return to earth. The descent is the easy part; the trick is to return.

"The sugary bread is for the black hound Cerberus, who will otherwise not let you pass. Give him the bread from one hand when you enter and the other when you exit. This sop will stop his three heads from barking and biting until you have slipped past his guardhouse. You must not let fear defeat you here. Control your emotions. Stand firm before him, for he really hates only ghosts that in their silliness twitter and fly from him. They fail to realize they are only shadows.

"Once you have mastered yourself and know your own power

you will have passed these minor trials and come into the presence of the High-priestess Persephone in her palace. She will welcome you, invite you to be seated in a splendid cathedral chair, and have served to you a lavish dinner. Beware of all these last temptations. You are not preparing yourself to sit in majesty on hers or any other splendid chair in any rich palace. Wealth and comfort are not your goals. Nor are you preparing to lead a life of ease and luxury where rich foods will be served you as if you were a worldly potentate.

"Sit down before her on the bare ground, humbly.

"Eat nothing but a piece of dry bread taken by your empty hand.

"Then give her the message directly, as you were instructed to do. Then leave her palace. Make your way up to the surface of Earth, giving your second candy to Cerberus and your second coin to Charon. Watch your step on the road ahead of you. Look up from time to time. Finally you will see the twinkling lights of the stars above the tunnel mouth. Then you will know your fatal trip has ended. You will have won through to knowledge of yourself.

"One final warning, however. You were sent to bring back to the goddess Aphrodite a box filled by the goddess Persephone with the essence of all beauty. DO NOT OPEN IT. This box contains knowledge which you are neither to seek nor to learn. That box will have been shut by Persephone, secretly."

Psyche followed all his directions, commands, injunctions, and prohibitions to the letter and arrived safely back from the Underworld. That is to say, she followed each instruction except the last. SHE OPENED THE BOX containing KNOWLEDGE. There was no beauty secret in it at all, nothing except sleep and forgetfulness of all her past trials. Her love rescued her and closed the box, which was given to Aphrodite.

Then the Muses of Mt. Parnassus, for they alone possessed a roster of the gods, called them to a formal conclave. The Muses let Zeus propose that Psyche, whose name means "moth" or "butterfly," be declared an immortal soul. Psyche then celebrated her marriage to her heavenly lover. At this ceremony Apollo played his lyre and the Muses themselves sang the wedding hymn. The steward of souls, Hermes, handed Psyche the cup and said to her, "Drink." In due time Psyche bore a daughter named Pleasure, who was in her own image and after her own heart.

Afterword

Erich Neumann agreed with Apuleius: this is a woman's story because it reaches back to a lost matriarchate, and illustrates feminine psychology.

It can also be viewed, which was the manner of its summary here, as an inauguration of a Pythia at Delphi, and as perhaps the only archaic or ancient text which assures us that women also underwent and withstood a rigorous initiation similar to that undergone by male heroes over the centuries.

Radical departures make this tale a record of a woman's initiation: the emphasis upon sexual love (for male heroes spurn love), the failure to murder her way through her trials (for male heroes possess dread weapons, which they use unstintingly), the emphasis upon humility and humble assistants (for male heroes hold back the sun and are supported by legions of secondary heroes), Psyche's awareness of the sorrows of the poor and the oppressed (for male heroes struggle to dispossess and kill such persons as monsters, even mothers of monsters), Psyche's dependence upon her own intelligence (in lieu of male strength and aggression), and, finally, her intuitive grasp of the fact that any injunction against knowledge must always be disobeyed.

The candidate's love for her child's father does not present a problem here. We may recall that Pausanias, who reported on his visit to Delphi around 174 A.D., said that the first Oracles were very young girls (IV, p. xi). After one of them was abducted, the priestesses were chosen among women who were at least fifty years old and virginal. The early Pythias did bear children and called themselves brides and wives of Apollo.

Another clue to the persistence of oracular practices, and to the prominence of later women priests practicing illegally, comes from the religious wars during the Renaissance when the Catharist priestesses were put to death. Interestingly, in those days, when the Protestants were obliged to leave France to avoid death, their secret name for "Dissenter," or "Protestant," and their secret symbol or badge was *psyche:* a moth or butterfly.

NAMES OF THE DELPHIC PRIESTESSES

"Delphi was, in some respects, such a religious center of Hellas as papal Rome was of medieval Europe. It was the common altar of the Greek race."

Philip Van Ness Myers
Ancient History (New York, 1904).

The following list of names rehearses our entire memory here of the Delphic Oracle. The *Pythian Dialogues* of Plutarch are the only authoritative, lengthy, firsthand accounts of her ministry. Plutarch noted considerable evidence of prejudice and hostility to these priestesses, and particularly on the part of Herodotus, Father of History. Because Herodotus was not born a Greek, Plutarch pointed out, he failed to show the same reverence for the Pythia that a native felt. Herodotus was an Asian, from a Greek family. Aside from Aeschylus, Hesiod, Pindar, and Homer, who make references and write some short lines about a Pythia, other ancient scholars, some of whom visited the shrine, saw it in its last declining period.

Therefore the names, and the circumstances surrounding these priestesses, must speak volumes in place of the volumes which nobody has cared to write.

Dates		*Authority*
?	Gaea was the first Pythia, or Pythoness, at Delphi	Aeschylus and Hesiod
	Her daughter Themis was "queen of oracles"	Ovid
c. 2000 B.C.	Indo-Europeans were passing the Bosphorus, on their ways into western Europe	Modern author: H.G. Wells, *Outline of History*
c. 1500 B.C.	During the tenure of Phoebe, Apollo killed Pytho at Delphi	Aeschylus and Homer

c. 1447 B.C.	Volcanic eruption of Santorini, and destruction of Minoan Crete	Modern authors: Galanopoulos and Bacon, *Atlantis*
Before 1200 B.C.	Warrior heroes at Delos and Mycenae coincide with monumental architecture, open sanctuaries such as Apollo's temple at Delphi	Modern author: F.W.H. Myers, *Essays Classical*
	Phemonoë was the fourth priestess at Delphi	Pausanias
	Herophile of Erythraea (descended from Noah) was named Sibyl	Plutarch and Lactantius
	She expanded the oracle into Italy	Pausanias
	Hyperochus followed her, and then the Hebrew prophetess from Palestine, whose name was Sabbe	Pausanias
	Manto, daughter of Tiresias from Thebes, prophesied in the streets	Ovid
	A daughter of Tiresias named Daphne also prophesied	Diodorus Siculus
	The Delphic Oracle predicted the Trojan War	Strabo
c. 1200 B.C.	Trojan War	Strabo
	Agamemnon journeyed to consult the Oracle	
	Return of Heraclides	Diodorus Siculus
1200 B.C.	The Aegean world was plunged into Dark Ages	Modern author: Stuart Piggot, *Ancient Europe*
Before 1000 B.C.	The Oracle predicted the crimes of Oedipus	Homer
	Odysseus was wounded near Delphi	Homer

	Thebes was settled	Homer
c. 970 B.C.	Solomon built first Hebrew Temple at Jerusalem	*Samuel, Kings, Chronicles*
Before 900 B.C.	The Pythia Xenocleia ordered the Twelve Labors of Heracles	Plutarch
	She also ordered Heracles to be burned	Diodorus Siculus
776 B.C.	First Olympiad (Greek chronology begins)	Timaeus of Sicily
753 B.C.	Cuma (Cumae) in Italy received another "first" prophetess, or Sibyl	Vergil and Livy
750 B.C.	Cuma is now colonized	Strabo
c. 725 B.C.	Messenians received an oracle at Delphi	Diodorus Siculus
c. 700 B.C.	Homer composed his *Iliad* and *Odyssey* at Delphi	Pausanias
600 B.C.	Lycurgus received the code of laws for Sparta from the Pythoness	Diodorus Siculus and Plutarch
c. 582–507 B.C.	Pythagoras studied at Delphi with the Pythia Theoclea and/or Themistoclea	Plato and Diogenes Laertius
c. 560–540 B.C.	Croesus, King of Lydia, consulted the Pythia	Herodotus
556 B.C.	Chilon of Sparta carved three inscriptions at Delphi	Diodorus Siculus
548 B.C.	Delphic temple burned, restoration, and polygonal wall built	Diogenes Laertius
c. 535–438 B.C.	Heraclitus said the words of the Delphic priestess then reached back one thousand years	Plutarch
c. 518–438 B.C.	Boeotian Pindar composed Odes at Delphi	Pausanias
c. 500 B.C.	Aesop was killed at Delphi for the crime of sacrilege	Plutarch

	The priestess Perialla was found to be corrupt and was deposed. Aristonicé prophesied harshly to Athenians *in re* the Persian Wars	Herodotus
c. 458 B.C.	*Eumenides* attested to the antiquity of the oracle	Aeschylus
c. 427–347 B.C.	*The Republic* called the Oracle "Our national divinity"	Plato
c. 359–336 B.C.	Philip of Macedon and his son razed Thebes	Demosthenes
c. 357 B.C.	War among Greek states, lasting ten years, for possession of the oracle	Pausanias
c. 330 B.C.	The present temple of Apollo was built by an architect from Corinth	Strabo
306 B.C.	Cult of Epicureans scorned the oracle and were not allowed near it	Lucretius
279 B.C.	Gauls (or Galatians) under Brennus attacked Delphi and were repulsed Brennus died in Macedonia (278 B.C.)	Pausanias and Cicero
200 B.C.–A.D.	Maccabaean (Apocalyptic) Period	*Maccabees*
c. 150 B.C.	Stoics defended divination (Panaetius and Posidonius of Greece and Spain)	Cicero. *De divinatione*
146 B.C.	Greece fell to Rome	Livy
116–27 B.C.	A Roman writer listed the Oracles of his day	Varro
82 B.C.	Burning of the Capitol at Rome and destruction of the *Sibylline Books*	Livy
80 B.C.	The Roman Emperor Sulla plundered Delphi	Plutarch

60–59 B.C.	Celtic War in Greece	Diodorus Siculus
45–44 B.C.	Rome's Golden Age	Cicero, *De divinatione;* Horace, *Epodes;* Ovid; Vergil.
46 A.D.	Birth of Plutarch, priest at Delphi	Pastor Hermas
54–68	The Roman Emperor Nero removed from Delphi five hundred gold statues	Tacitus
67	Nero was in Greece when Plutarch was twenty years old. Nero declared Greece free and immune, at Corinth	Plutarch. *Lives*
69–79	Plutarch journeyed to Rome to plead for the restoration of Delphi. The Pythia foretold the eruption of Vesuvius (79 A.D.)	Plutarch
70	Destruction of the Temple, Jerusalem, by Roman Emperor Titus	Flavius Josephus. *Antiquities of the Jews*
88–97	Clea, Leontis at Delphi	Clement of Rome, *Pseudepigraphia*
117	The Roman Emperor Hadrian planned the restoration of Delphi	Plutarch
126	Plutarch spoke of a holy island off the coast of Britain. There officiated only women priests	Plutarch
c. 150–230	Pagan authors	Lucian, Tertullian, Celsus, Lucius Apuleius
c. 174	Pausanias visits Delphi and is initiated (reborn)	Pausanias
185–285	Famous Christian authors	Origen, Clement of Alexandria

c. 250	Birth of Lactantius; Sibyls are recognized by Lactantius	Lactantius
	Diogenes Laertius writes concerning Pythagoras and the Pythia	Diogenes Laertius
288–337	Constantine the Great robs Ephesus to build Hagia Sophia (Istanbul)	Modern source: Jacob Burckhardt, *The Age of Constantine the Great*
	His mother, Saint Helena of Britain, becomes Christian	
May 3, 327	Helena finds the True Cross at Calvary. She then builds the Holy Sepulcher in Jerusalem	
331–363	The Roman Emperor Julian the Apostate sent to the oracle and was answered. Delphi still functioned	Modern author: H.W. Parke, *Greek Oracles*
339	Saint Ambrose of Milan in Rome	E.K. Rand, *Founders of the Middle Ages*
354	Early Christians respected the priestesses	St. Augustine
395	The triumph of Christianity at Rome	idem
529	The Roman Emperor Justinian closed the schools in Greece, thus suppressing the Delphic Oracle and other educated women	W.G. Holmes, *The Age of Justinian and Theodora*
600	St. Columba of Scotland founded Iona: Feast Day—June 9	

10th century	Plutarch is discovered. Scholars begin to learn ancient history anew
11th century	Destruction: Church of the Holy Sepulcher. Crusades commence
1099	Fall of Jerusalem to Christian nobles
12th century	The works of Plutarch now translated into the modern languages of Europe
	Other translators began work upon Arthurian literature, which bore witness to the continuance of women priests even after the suppression of both Delphi and Cuma

XI

ORACLES FROM THE DELPHIC PRIESTESS

"But the prophetess at Delphi . . . entirely gives herself up to a divine spirit, and is illuminated with a ray of divine fire. And when fire . . . invests her . . . , she becomes filled from it with a divine splendor."
      The Syrian philosopher Iamblichus (d. 300)
      The Mysteries of the Egyptians, Chaldeans, and Assyrians, trans. Thomas Taylor (London, 1821).

What sorts of oracles the Pythia delivered objectively to her pilgrims, either personally or by way of priests, can perhaps be judged by Psyche's performance during her initiation as High-priestess. She enraged her sponsor Aphrodite, abandoned her parents without a backward glance, wounded her husband so severely he was thought not to recover, caused the deaths of her sisters, defied her instructions until others served her, and disobeyed the final injunction. Single-minded, tough, and hardheaded, she had become a High-priestess.

The Pythias must have resembled this personality profile, if judged also by the oracles they handed down century after century. Substantiating their pronouncements, Herodotus said they gave directions to colonists; handed down the laws of Sparta; established funeral customs for the known world; extended their authority over large areas of Asia and Africa; acquired vast wealth from such millionaire kings as Croesus; amassed unbelievably huge collections of art treasures; supervised foreign and domestic relations between states; felt free to deliver ambiguous answers when it suited them; caused the deaths of persons and peoples whom they considered criminal, sacrilegious, or dangerous; and ordered their words transferred to hexameter verse and recorded for posterity. As Pindar said in his "Fourth Ode": ". . . the priestess throned beside the golden eagles of Zeus gave for them an oracle"; she was the Queen Priestess over all such famous priestesses.

The maxims of the Pythias are recorded as follows:

Edouard Schuré:	1) "Know thyself."
	2) "Let no one enter here with impure hands."
Diodorus Siculus:	1) and 3) "Nothing overmuch."
(Book IX)	4) "A pledge, and ruin is nigh."
Alexander Altmann:	1)and 5) "Know that you are but man, not divine."
	6) "Do not turn back while on a journey."

Both Diodorus Siculus and Alexander Altmann explain the profound significance of her maxims, but the latter's evaluation takes the Delphic Oracles from Greece in order to trace their continuing influence upon medieval Islam and Judaism.[1]

The Prophet Muhammad quoted the Delphic "Know thyself," said Altmann, in two pronouncements:

1) "He who knows himself knows his Lord";
2) "He among you who knows himself best knows his Lord best." Their "Know thyself" reappeared in Hebrew mysticism as "He who is incapable of the knowledge of himself will naturally be incapable of the knowledge of his Creator. How will he consider what is reliable in the science of any of the things, being ignorant of himself?"
3) "Know thy soul, and thou wilt know the Lord."
4) "Whoever possesses the knowledge about the intelligent soul, recognizes his essence," and such a man "is able to recognize God." The idea that self-knowledge leads a person to God passed into medieval Islam and medieval Judaism. Therefore the soul itself was like God, it was

[1] See Chapter I of Altmann's Studies in *Religious Philosophy and Mysticism*, pp. 1–5.

Figure 16. Consultation with the Pythia

said. As Diodorus Siculus also stressed, the Delphic maxim #3 recommended moderation and temperance.

Plato had further reversed the Oracle's first maxim, believing that he who knew God also knew himself, because "like knows like." Cicero in Rome was to agree that the mind cannot know itself until it has become fused into the divine mind of God.

Therefore Psyche can be adjudged correct in her search for knowledge, for no one without intellect can hope to know himself and God, and reach up to the angels. Muhammad and Dante thus journeyed up, from sphere to sphere, until each man reached God. Psyche had achieved no less.

In his Book IV *(The Greek Gods)* Diodorus Siculus lists and comments very astutely upon a great many oracles given by the Pythia:

1) Heracles. She ordered his Labors and promised him immortality as his reward. When she considered the sufferings he had caused and incurred, she ordered his

funeral pyre to be built, and him and his weapons to be burned upon it.

2) Telephus. He asked her who his mother was. The Pythia told him where to sail. In that land Telephus found her and married a king's daughter.

3) The Corinthians. They asked the Pythia what they were to do with the bodies of Jason's children. Their mother Medea had slain them and departed in her Dragon Chariot. Jason had then committed suicide. The Pythia replied: "Bury them in Hera's precinct and pay them heroes' honors at their funeral."

4) King Laïus of Thebes was childless, for which reason he consulted the Pythia. The priestess answered that having children would not be in his interest, since a son sired by him was destined to kill his father, and bring misfortune upon all his house. King Laïus had not forgotten the oracle by the time his son Oedipus was born. Laïus died unexpectedly, and the mother of Oedipus took her own life.

5) Lycurgus of Sparta consulted the Oracle (well before the First Olympiad, 776 B.C.), said Aristotle, concerning a Constitution for that city. The Pythia gave Lycurgus the Constitution of Sparta, which was to last for 500 years (c. 871 B.C.–371 B.C.). The Pythia, said Plutarch, advised "Lycurgus" to gain the consent of the governed for:

(a) A *Council of Elders* made up of twenty-eight senators and two kings, each having one vote apiece. The senate, she said, is intended to balance the state between the kings (tyranny) and the people (democracy).

(b) Her Covenant required the Spartans to:
1. build temples to Zeus and Athena,
2. divide all the people into clans and brotherhoods,
3. establish and maintain the senate,
4. assemble all citizens *out of doors* to introduce or rescind measures,
5. allow the people a voice in all affairs.

(c) The Pythia also recommended the equal redistribution of all land and all wealth so each citizen could make a fresh start. She pointed out that the poor and destitute must share the wealth and the property. She also recommended the seizure of all gold and the substitution of iron coins. That should devalue the currency.

(d) In order to abolish illness due to gluttony, the Pythia recommended that all meals be cooked, served, and eaten in common at a common table.

After Lycurgus had established these and her other recommendations, at the cost of an eye which he lost to an angry youth, he returned to Delphi to ask the Pythia if his laws were good, and if Sparta would prosper and be honored. She replied, "Yes, so long as these laws are obeyed." Satisfied, Lycurgus then abstained from food until he died. The Pythia said he had been more god than man.

6) Messenians, c. 725 B.C. A messenger was dispatched to Delphi on behalf of the Messenians, to ask what they were to do. The Pythia replied that they should sacrifice a maiden. (Diodorus says he found a *lacuna* here. This happens not unfrequently in manuscripts. But Pausanias says here that the Elders among the Messenians found a way to avoid her sentence.)

7) Spartans, c. 675 B.C. They sent to ask what to do after their defeat by the Messenians. The Oracle replied cryptically in verse that they should keep their territory the same way they got it in the first place, i.e., by strength and cunning.

8) Mysellus of Achaia (Diodorus, VIII) asked the Pythia about begetting children. She replied that Apollo intended to send him children, but that he should first found the fair city of Croton (Italy). Men who seek what the gods deny them usually reap tears, she told him.

9) Epeanactae, c. 705 B.C. The veterans of the Messenian Wars, who had been assigned to the surviving widows, wanted to be given lands between Corinth and Sicyon and requested them of the Pythia. She said no, that they should settle other pieces of land overlooking a certain harbor "where the goat first catches the scent of the sea

and wets his whiskers and the tip of his gray beard with its salt smell."

The helots go to her again, protesting that they cannot understand her oracle. The Pythia gives them a short reply, "I have given you a gift of fertile land. You heard me."

10) Chalcidians. They ask where to found a city in Sicily. The Oracle replies, "At Gela, found a home for men of Crete and Rhodes."

11) People of Sicyon. They ask the Pythia how they shall be governed. She replies, "By a scourge."

"Whose scourge?" they inquire.

"By the first man who has a son born after you land on shore." (That man was Andreas, father of the Tyrant Myron, adds Herodotus, VI, 126).

12) Aristotle the Stutterer (c. 675 B.C.) asked the Oracle about his plans to found the city of Cyrene in Cyrenaica, west of Egypt. The Pythia gave him fourteen verses of elegant instruction, to which she added hers and Apollo's blessings. He was, indeed, to set forth for Libya, where upon landing he would be attacked by "barbarian warriors . . . clad in leather from wild animals." Aristotle was to offer prayers at once to Zeus, Athena, and Apollo, and win the fight. Apollo declares he will prevail. He shall rule "fair-crowned Libya." He and his heirs shall be blessed. He is to take Apollo as his guide to that end.

(Diodorus adds: "For envy by its very nature builds an ambush for the successful, and therefore causes the ruination of those preeminent in glory.")

13) King Arcesilaus of the Cyrenians complained to the Pythia about life in his kingdom. She lashed out at him, accusing the complainer of both tyranny over his people, and impiety toward the gods.

14) King Perdiccas of Macedon (c. 640 B.C.) expressed his desire to extend the boundaries of his kingdom. The Pythia resorted to verse to sanction his requests. She directed him to a site where he would find goats with white horns and fleece as bright as snow in the early

light of a dawn. There he should set up an altar, make a sacrifice to the gods, and, because he is noble and god-fearing, build his capital city (Aegae).

15) Greeks. They ask permission to sack a certain city. The Pythia forbids it. They may neither plunder the city nor tear down its tower until the raging waves of Aphrodite's dark blue sea rise up the "holy cliffs" of Mt. Parnassus and deluge the "sacred precinct" of Delphi.

16) Son of Miletus (590 B.C.) asks what to do with a golden tripod that was found in the sea and recovered. The Pythia replied that it should be bestowed upon the wisest man in Greece.

Or she replied that this gold stand, which had been forged by Hephaestus himself, should be delivered to that man's home who had "in his wisdom . . . foreseen" what is and also what is to be. Thales of Miletus declined the gift, and so did the six others among the Seven Sages, or Seven Wise Men, of Greece.

The gold tripod was presented to Solon as a reward for his "wisdom and understanding." Solon also refused it; he advised the bearers that the tripod should be dedicated to Apollo.

17) The Spartans, who are on the verge of invading Arcadia, ask for an oracle. "What do you want?" she asks them. "If you make great demands on me, I shall refuse. Arcadia is a land rich in acorns and strong fighters whom you cannot defeat. I can offer you Tegea as an alternative. Go dance your war dance there, on that rich plain. Plot out your fields and crops there with your stakes and your cords."

The Spartans also ask her where Orestes is buried. She replies that he lies there, on the grassy, flat plain of Tegea in Arcadia. Two contrary winds still blow over his grave. Blow versus blow still rain over his guilty head. His crime causes him still to rest unquiet. "So first, before you plant your crops on Tegea's plain, bring the son of Agamemnon to Delphi. Then you can lord it over Tegea."

(Diodorus read this oracle very differently. He thought

the Pythia was talking about a blacksmith's forge, that the winds were bellows, that the blows were strokes of a hammer upon the anvil, and that the "unquiet" stemmed from the discovery of iron ore, which has been a "bane" to mankind.)

18) The Thurians (434 B.C.) from Italy (Thurii) asked the Pythia to settle a violent dispute between them as to who had founded their city. The priestess gave them a one-word answer: "Apollo." Thus, she restored peace to their city.

19) General Tiribazus (385 B.C.) was imprisoned for having secretly consulted the Pythia . . . (record not completed).

20) War (383 B.C.) broke out between two rival cities (Clazomene and Cŷme). They laid down their arms and brought their case to the Pythia. She decreed the winner to be those citizens from the city that got to Leucê first and sacrificed first. Each city should choose representatives, and each group should set out promptly at the same hour. The first group lived nearer to Leucê, but the second outsmarted them by founding a new town near Leucê and sacrificing there first.

21) The Ionians (373 B.C.) send an embassy to Delphi to request aid. The priestess assists them in their religious duties and helps them build altars.

22) King Philip II of Macedon sent to inquire if his war against the Persians would be successful, or not. The Pythia replied:

> The bull wears a garland.
> All is preordained.
> Another will strike him down.

(Diodorus understood by hindsight, better than did King Philip II beforehand, that Philip himself would be assassinated in the middle of a festival, and during a holy religious ceremony at the altar. He would be wearing a garland like a sacrificial bull. He would fall stabbed to death. His son Alexander the Great was also reassured falsely by the Oracle of Zeus Amon at the Libyan Oasis.)

23) The Thebans (335–334B.C.) sent a delegation to Delphi to ask what would happen. Alexander of Macedon and his army were approaching. Their temple at Delphi had its roof covered with blood. That was a portent.

24) Carcinus went to Delphi (before 317) to learn the fate of his unborn son. The Pythia replied his son would cause calamities. When the child was born, he was therefore exposed to die. The baby did not die, however. He lived to become a gigantic hero.

25) The citizens of Delphi consulted the Oracle, 279 B.C.

26) King Attalus of Pergamum (133 B.C.) consulted the Oracle. The first king of that name was told that he and his descendants of the "bull horn," they who worshipped Dionysus, would reign as kings for three generations, but no longer than that.

Answers from the Pythia were computed by Joseph Fontenrose in his book *The Delphic Oracle* (Berkeley, 1978), pp. 436–443 and Tables, pp. 21–52.

The following lists have been simplified from those computations. Fontenrose found that four-fifths of all questions addressed to the Oracle concerned historical subjects.

I. Types of Answers Made by the Pythias

1. Commands (simple, complex, clear, obscure)
2. Sanctions (largely approvals)
3. Prohibitions
4. Warnings
5. Information concerning past history and traditions
6. Future predictions (clear, obscure)

II. Topics

Divine, Domestic, or Profane, Public/Political (2/3 of the total)
Religion
Recommended sacrifices

Laws/Disputes
Customs (explained, upheld)
Rulers (throned, deposed)
Colonies allowed
Wars/Possession of lands
Human Affairs
    Births, Marriages, Origins, Sex, Death, Funerals, Careers,
        Professions
Rewards/Punishments
Gnomic wisdom, Aphorisms
Personal advice requested

III. Occasions Legendary and/or Historical

Catastrophes (drought, plague, flood, fire, famine, earth-
    quake)
Exile
Crimes by others
Welfare of city/state
Sterility
Testing of the Oracle
Orphans/Parents
The future of children
Death
Missing persons
Career advice
Advice during pregnancy
Whether or not to marry

IV. Numbers of Answers

	Questions of prime importance	Of secondary importance
Divine Subjects	81	102
Public Affairs	66	116
Domestic Affairs	120	150

V. Tallies

	#1	#2	Total
Plague/Famine	41	37	78
War	20	53	73
City founding	11	20	31

Omens	7	18	25
Exile	16	6	22
Rulers	6	14	20
Civic good	2	18	20
Illness	9	9	18
Sterility	7	4	11
Crime by worshipper	7	3	10
Enterprise	3	6	9
Worship	5	3	8
Disappearance, loss	2	6	8
Crime by others	4	3	7
Origins	3	1	4
Death	1	2	3
Test of the Oracle	1	2	3
Pregnancy	1	1	2

Father Hugo Rahner, S.J., throws considerable light upon the rituals practiced at Delphi and such texts as those three telling stories about the Pythia. Such stories give us, he says, the lost words from the Greek religion called "pagan," or mythological, because they bear the unmistakable mark of *Mütter Erde* and the mother-religions. They show us a common set of symbols and speak a once-common language understood then only by initiates into the "Mysteries" (<*ministerium* = ritual).

Such tales open the teachings of the Pythia and her friend Pythagoras. The latter casts pearls of wisdom only to acolytes. How communicate with souls that have not been purified? he asked. How lavish upon every ordinary stranger a wisdom that has been so hard to come by? Should the sacred mysteries be revealed to the profane? Can the scoffers be trusted with arcane knowledge? No. Let us, urged Pythagoras, keep a silent tongue before low intellects.

Magical circles intersect about us, taught Pythagoras, at the equator, in the ecliptic, across the dome of heaven, at Delphi. The Mysteries, said Father Rahner, led into the first- and the second-century Christianity of the primitive Church as established by Saint Paul.

These words from the Pythia reach out into the western world, for her immigrants will take them into Italy, where her priestess, the Cumaean Sibyl, will reign supreme for more centuries. The thousands of pilgrims from around the world who daily toil up the slopes of Parnassus to meditate upon the Delphic Oracle and her influence upon the world pay tribute to her presence and to the power of her ministry.

XII

ROME

LXXIX
"The Niobe of nations! there she stands,
Childless and crownless, in her voiceless woe;
An empty urn within her wither'd hands,
Whose holy dust was scatter'd long ago.
George Gordon, Lord Byron

LXXVIII
"Oh Rome, my country! city of the soul!
The orphans of the heart must turn to thee,
Lone mother of dead empires, and control
In their shut breasts their petty misery.
What are our woes and sufferance? Come and see
The cypress, hear the owl, and plod your way
O'er steps of broken thrones and temples, Ye!
Whose agonies are evils of a day—
A world is at our feet as fragile as our clay."
George Gordon, Lord Byron
Childe Harold's Pilgrimage,
Canto IV (Venice, 1817–
18).

THE FOUNDING OF ROME

The dates corroborating the founding of Rome have occasioned much controversy and long calculations from solar eclipses. Whereas myth and legend furnished a prehistory for Greece, they were lacking at Rome except for legends concerning priestesses and their circles. The Romans themselves blamed the Gauls for this loss of their records, myths, and legendary history. The Gauls sacked Rome in 390 B.C. and left off their destruction only after being paid one thousand pounds of gold. The Romans set themselves one great task, which was eventually to conquer Gaul.

By 300 B.C. the Romans had at least the story of heroic, Trojan founders, Aeneas and Antenor, who were allowed to escape from Troy. Carrying his aged father on his back, and holding his wife, the Trojan Princess Creusa, by the hand, Aeneas made his harrowing escape amid falling walls and collapsing roofs of Troy. Unfortunately, in the din and fury of conflagration, Aeneas let go of Creusa's hand.

The Julian line, family of the Caesars and High-priests of Rome, was perhaps, then, descended directly from Aeneas's putative son Iulus, in whose honor the seventh month is still named "July." The navigation of Aeneas alone caused endless difficulties to historians, particularly since the harbors of Asia Minor face west, toward Greece, while the best harbors of Greece face east toward Asia. To compound the problem, the best harbors of Italy face west toward the vast, more or less unknown Atlantic Ocean.

The question of Rome's founding is further fraught with unsolvable, ruder problems. If, as the Greek historian Timaeus claimed, Rome and Carthage were both founded in 814 B.C., then how many hundreds of years old was Aeneas when he reached Italy? If Aeneas was in Italy founding Rome in 814 B.C., then how could he have spent so much time in Libya, making love, and watching the Tyrian queen Dido build Carthage? Instead of seducing Queen Dido, so that as a result she lost her status of High-priestess (if that is what happened) and had to throw herself on the funeral pyre, why did not Aeneas conquer Carthage at its founding and save future Rome its disastrous Punic Wars against Hamilcar Barca and the truly dread Hannibal?

Was it not perhaps the Greek hero Euander with his mother Carmenta, a prophetic priestess, who arrived at Pallanteum on the Tiber River *sixty years before the Trojan War*? And does not great Rome stand on the site of Pallanteum, which was named for Euander's native home in Arcadia, Greece? Roman historians founder here also.

Was it not the prophetic priestess Carmenta who supervised the actual disposition of Rome, and laying of Rome's first boundary stones? A city gate was always named for her: *Porta Carmentalis*. An annual festival was named for her, the *Carmentalia* in January when Carmenta, patroness of mothers, foretold for them the fortunes of their children.

History textbooks usually make easier work of this, saying Romulus founded Rome in 753 B.C., that date established by Roman historians and the gods as A.U.C. (from the founding of the city): AB URBE CONDITA.

Livy agrees that the greatest priestess of Rome was the Cumaean Sibyl, who settled at Cumae (now Cuma) on the north hook of the Bay of Naples in 753 B.C. during the reign of Romulus. She is said to have settled at Cumae as a result of the burning of Ilium, district of Troy. The greatest of Roman poets, the beloved Vergil, said Crete was the cradle of Rome, and that the Cretans also migrated to Italy around 1200 B.C. Thus, contradictions abound and will not go away.

The best Roman historians could make of historical evidence seems to have been to declare by fiat that Troy fell, as Eratosthenes said, in 1183 B.C., that Rome was really founded in 751 B.C., that the monarchy lasted 238 (or 244) years, and that the Roman Republic was established in 506 B.C. The orator Cicero said one of his friends had arrived at a proper calendar date for the city's founding: April 21 (Easter Sunday!). The Consul C. Sulpicius Gallus worked out two eclipses of the sun, one when the foundation stone was being laid, and another when Romulus was miraculously wafted out of his city into heaven. Some astronomers placed a year 0 between B.C. and A.D., altering Rome's corrected date of founding to 752 B.C.

This dating problem assumed a very great urgency after Julius Caesar declared himself descended directly from the goddess Venus (Aphrodite) and the Trojan shepherd lad Anchises, parents of Aeneas, ancestors of Iulus or Julius. The confusion regarding dates had to be hidden so as to make Rome's chronology conform to the celebrated Julian calendar made by Caesar, assisted by two scholars, after his election as Chief Pontiff, Rome's *Pontifex Maximus*. As the earliest priest-

esses knew, the only person able to change a date, or the calendar, is the most important religious in the land. The rise of
Julius Caesar was only slightly less meteoric than his fall, but
some of his books, and his calendar, survived it.

This revisionist history completely ignores the early preva-
lence and the prominence of goddesses and their priestesses
not only in widely separated regions of Italy, but in Europe,
and Gaul, to the north of it.

The Etruscans, for instance, remained rulers in Italy until
100 B.C. Two of their goddesses remained widely venerated
while Rome was a mere settlement on the Tiber River: Fortuna in the city of Praeneste and Diana Nemorensis (Artemis
of the Woods) at Aricia under the Alban Mount, sixteen miles
from future Rome. Aricia itself honored the wife of Hippolytus, son of Theseus and the priestess Phaedra from Crete. Sir
James Frazer commences his great *The Golden Bough* by a long
discussion of the worship of Diana there, so close to Alba Longa.
Frazer also laid down the law about priestesses: they take the
name and identity of the goddess they serve, and dress in her
prescribed, traditional costume.

The goddess Fortuna reigned for centuries as good *(bona)*
and evil *(mala),* along with her priestesses, in her temples. Her
temple site at Praeneste is vast, indeed. There she was adored
by her priestesses as *Fortuna Primagenia,* the "firstborn" daughter of Zeus, elsewhere in Italy as Fortuna, *mother* of Zeus (Jupiter) and Hera (Juno). Another of her temples stood on the
west or right bank of the Tiber River at Rome. There the goddess's name was reduplicated: *Fors Fortuna,* which indicated
some marvelously unexpected piece of good fortune. Teachings of her priestesses survive today as common superstic-
tions, like "Fortune's child," the child born wealthy, or with a
"silver spoon in her mouth," "blind Fortune" (like Justice), "a
mainstay of fortune," a "lucky chance," a "stroke of fortune."
The word "chance" itself may refer to an ancient pre-Roman
ritual, for "chance" means the "fall of the dice," and the *roulette* or "wheel of fortune." Thus, the millions who frequent
the gaming tables of Las Vegas, Deauville, and Monte Carlo,
to name only the ones declared most "glamorous" (which in

turn means "magical spell"), are all modern devotees of an ancient, pagan worship. Every great writer of the Middle Ages tried to argue for or against Fortune, Destiny, Chance, and Predestination, so overwhelmingly was she adopted from ancient Italy.

Considering the prominence of such widely adored ancient goddesses whose priestesses carried on, sometimes in isolated spots like Aricia, pretty much as they saw fit, it is no wonder the public worship at Rome lent itself so eclectically to goddesses from foreign parts, adopting Isis from Egypt, Artemis (renamed Diana) from Ephesus, Hera (renamed Juno) from Samos and Argos, and Hestia (renamed Vesta) from Apollo's temple at Delphi. In days of the Punic Wars, when it seemed all Rome would fall to Hannibal, the women further insisted that Cybele herself also be brought to Rome from Asia Minor, and her sacred black stone, which fell from heaven. One of the most beautiful temples to the Egyptian Isis, whom Lucius Apuleius so dearly loved and so wholeheartedly venerated, stood at Pompeii under the shadow of Mt. Vesuvius. Nor is it any wonder such Romans as Appius Claudius could have journeyed to consult the High-priestess of them all, the Delphic Oracle on Mt. Parnassus. Every poet who ever dreamed of composing real poetry has doubtless thought of her Muses as the wellsprings of inspiration.

Another account of Rome's founding can be read in the pages of a Greek historian, Dionysius of Halicarnassus in Asia Minor. He wrote around 25 B.C., under the Augustan Principate. His compilation from long-lost annals and masterpieces, he claimed, is considered excellent evidence concerning the "early history of Rome" *(Romaike Archaiologia)*. He begins his Book IX (p. 29) authoritatively: "This city mistress of the whole earth and sea, which the Romans now inhabit. . . ." Then follows his exhaustive list of what peoples, tribes, immigrants, and leaders these Romans are, as of that date when their empire had still not ceased to expand.

Dionysius agrees with Plutarch and Diodorus Siculus that the Greek Oracles dispatched settlers to western Mediterranean shores, and he tells why. The annals at Delphi, as recorded by Diodorus, have spared the reader these painful facts: drought, massive crop failure, famine throughout Greece and Asia Minor. What could be done to save mankind?

The corollary is even more daunting. If measures that will save mankind in Greece and Asia can be advised, who in the world would have had the courage to implement such measures? As the modern world has proven in the States, intelligent people are a dime a dozen. But courage is another matter. Administrators commonly say, "I can find all the brains I need and want to hire, for peanuts. But I can hardly ever find a courageous human being who will stand up, and lead, and act alone. People are too scared of their peers."

The only persons then living who had the intelligence and the courage to save mankind in the east were the priestesses who directed settlers to the shores of the western Mediterranean.

Each High-priestess at Delphi was tough. She had survived unheard-of hardships in preparation for her mission. Having died once and been reborn, she was fearless. Owning nothing herself personally, she could be neither blackmailed nor threatened. Most of all, the High-priestess at Delphi had grown accustomed to respect. Her personal life had been fulfilled by a first love, and the birth of her daughter. All the mighty of the world had bowed before her wisdom: Homer, Hesiod, Pindar, Aeschylus, Pythagoras, Lycurgus, Socrates, Plato, plus the evil solar killers Heracles, Theseus, Philip of Macedon, and Alexander the Great.

Dionysius of Halicarnassus, where Herodotus also was born, says the Oracle at Dodona near Delphi also instructed settlers to embark for Italy (p. 63), to set forth, and to settle a new land that lay under the aegis of a country (i.e., "pagan") god named Saturn. Once they were established, they were henceforth to return a tithe *to the Delphic Oracle.*

The emigrants followed directions. They made the journey, which enough survived to struggle ashore. They first erected a temple in the Falernian district of (what is now) Italy. They organized worship in the manner and according to the rites, rituals, and practices long sanctioned by the Greeks on both sides of the Aegean Sea, i.e., the ancient ceremonies at Hera's temple in Argos (p. 67):

1) "holy women served the sacred precinct,"
2) an unwed girl "performed the initial rites of the sacrifices and"
3) "there were choruses of virgins who praised the goddess Juno (Hera) in the songs of their country."

This emigration was ordered in detail by the Oracles at the oak grove of Dodona and at Delphi on Mount Parnassus.

The emigration was not only specifically and geographically directed. The oracles were delivered as orders. The emigrants were ordered, as follows:

1) they were to select their most stalwart and most necessary citizens,
2) they were to take along the very best of all their increase (seeds? livestock? children?),
3) the rest were to be slaughtered so that the best people might survive.

When famines occurred in ancient Britain before the discovery of America opened a vast land for the immigrants from the poorest lands—Ireland, Scotland, and Wales—the women and children, of their own free will and accord, would walk to a sea cliff and throw themselves down into the ocean.

The Arcadians from the southern peninsula of Greece in the year 1243 B.C. or thereabouts, says Dionysius, chose a leader named Euander, who would be called Evander once he arrived in Italy. He was to take his "inspired" mother, whose name was "Delphian Themis," to safety and long life in the new land. The immigrants would have to learn a new alphabet and a new language, Latin. Their leader would henceforth be called "Evander," and the Latin-speaking natives who worshipped under his mother, knowing that "Themis" was a time-honored title of the Delphic Oracle, changed her name too. Evander's famous Greek mother is very well remembered, and still highly honored, in her new land.

Her new name is Carmenta, which gives us the common

Latin noun *carmen*. Carmenta was so named because, as High-priestess in her new land, she could sing or recite for each worshipper admitted into her presence a "carmen," which is a song, or a poem, or a prophecy.

Historians have commonly told us that the Delphi priestesses were mere nothings, mere women unable to make their own oracles, for which reason they employed priests. Priests are supposedly more able at delivering hexameter and other verse. Men alone write poetry, according to most historians.

Dionysius of Halicarnassus says no. Carmenta delivered oracles which *she sang or recited in verse*. The Romans called her Carmenta because of her many *carmina*. They called her a prophetic singer "possessed of divine inspiration," who foretold the future, not only for great warriors and rich men like Philip of Macedon and King Croesus of Lydia (everything he laid eyes on turned to gold, of course), but for "the people" (p. 99).

Possessed by divine inspiration Carmenta one day told "the people" to choose "a hill, not far from the Tiber (River), which (hill) is now near the middle of the city of Rome" and to build a village there. They were instructed to call their village *Palatium*. This is now called the Palatine Hill, one of the seven hills of eternal Rome, *Roma aeterna*.

The Capitoline Hill also dominates Rome today, its massive white marbles like a crown over the holy city, holy today as it always was holy for all people of all faiths and denominations. It was the Oracle Carmenta herself who first saw the beauty of this hill for future Rome. After her death, the ancient Romans built a first temple as her personal crown on the Capitoline Hill. They dedicated this first, and original structure in memory of the priestess Themis, called in Latin Carmenta.

Themis/Carmenta had ordered—and "ordered" is a sign of her own estate and rank in the new world—a temple built for the earth deity Pan of Arcadia because at home in that most fertile valley of Greece Pan had from time immemorial been the most cherished of the male earth gods. She chose the Lupercal site, which is to say, a temple site at the base of the Palatine Hill. By their god called Pan the Arcadians perhaps meant Zeus.

This first temple, which Carmenta ordered, was "a large cave" (p. 105) like the cave at Delphi where the cleft narrows up to the waterfall, or Castalian Spring. The temple was further described in terms of the Delphic Oracle, as a large *cave*, under a high *cliff*, or steep hill, "overarched" by dense forest, where a constant spring emerged from large rocks, below a "glen" beside a "cliff," the whole shaded from the sun by a "grove," or dense growth of especially tall trees. The altar was placed there adjoining the spring of the cool, fresh, pure water that comes only from springs and forests. All the doctors of the really olden days prescribed such drinking water to their patients. Country children always know where they are to be found.

Carmenta, as befitted only a priestess of Greece, also established the high, holy days for the Romans. She set aside days in February for purification after the hard winter solstice: the *Lupercalia*, traditional holidays (holy days) in honor of the Arcadian Pan. She also established the festival of spring, decreeing the *Ideo*, meant to be the middle day of the month of May, or the Ides of May, as the public festival celebrating the vernal equinox (April 23 thereabouts). She called for another holy day called *Parilia*, April 2, to celebrate the arrival of spring. She called for the middle of August to be set aside forever as the *Calends*, the day when the new Consuls governing Rome would assume their office.

Sacrifices were always made to the gods from the summit of the Capitoline Hill in Rome, adds Dionysius, and they dated back, according to that book, to that High-priestess who in Italy replaced the Greek, Delphic Oracle: the Cumaean Sibyl at Cumae (Cuma) on the Bay of Naples.

Her *Sibylline Books*, Rome's permission to live, as it were, declared that such rituals on the Capitoline Hill dated from the passage through Italy of Heracles. The High-priestess Themis, now called Carmenta, ordered a memorial for Heracles, because he had become immortal, as the Pythia permitted. Themis directed her son Evander to erect a "greatest" altar to this god Heracles, an *ara maxima*, in the *Forum Boarium*, or Cattle Market of Rome! Thus, the immigrants remembered Greece.

Heracles had also married Lavinia, daughter of Evander, and also a Hyperborean girl he had brought with him (from

Spain?). He had built the port city Herculaneum for his fleet, between Naples and Pompeii.

Aeneas also followed custom; he married a girl named Lavinia, it is said, and there were fifteen generations, or seventeen generations, between him and the Romulus who founded Rome.

The Trojan Aeneas, who was always called a religious man, consulted an Oracle before he set sail from the Troad altogether. Confusion has not been cleared as to which Sibyl he consulted, whether the Erythraean Sibyl in the Troad; the Erythraean Sibyl in Ionia, Greece; or whether he went overland to the famous oak-grove oracle at Dodona.

RHEA SILVIA

The legend of "Rhea Silvia," also known as "Ilia" (Trojan princess), was told by two of the greatest Romans, Livy and Ovid. The historian Livy relates the priestess Rhea Silvia to the Trojan founders of Rome whose genealogy fitted, or was made to fit, into a founding of Rome by exiles from Troy (Livy's Book I, pp. 3–7). Livy gives the best historical account. Ovid treats her story poetically, and from a religious point of view (his *Fasti,* or account of the Roman calendar's holy days, Book III, pp. 1–164).

Thus, the Romans themselves honored Rhea Silvia, even though little is known of her, for two reasons: because she was their prehistorical, legendary Trojan princess and mother, and because she was a very holy virgin and a priestess. They saw no contradiction here.

The story of Rhea Silvia gives us the first mention of ancient Rome's greatest priesthood: the Vestal Virgins.

Livy

The son of Aeneas, Ascanius, settled Alba Longa and accepted the Tiber River as boundary between his Latin peoples and the Etruscans. Then reigned his descendants: Silvius, Aeneas Silvius, Latinus Silvius, Alba, Alba Atys, Atys Capys, Capys Capetus, Capetus Tiberinus, Agrippa, Romulus Silvius, Aventinus, and Proca, who begat two sons, Numitor and Amulius. The latter expelled his brother Numitor, killed his sons, and raised his daughter Rhea Silvia to the priesthood as Vestal Virgin. Thus, her enforced virginity henceforth precluded any male issue from her to threaten Amulius's claims to the kingdom.

The Fates decreed otherwise, however, having already planned that a great city would arise around this small beginning at Alba Longa, and that it would grow until it became Rome, the greatest empire the world had ever seen.

Ovid

The month of March derives its name from the Roman god of war, Mars (the Greek Ares, son of Hera). This is also important for poetry, because Mars fell wildly in love with a "Roman" priestess. He also desired to found a city from a source worthy of its future greatness. Why not tell it from the beginning?

One morning the Vestal maiden-priestess went down to fetch water for temple use in washing sacred utensils and preparing all for the services that day. She took the easy path down to the riverbank and lowered her lowly, ancient earthenware pitcher from her head to the ground. She felt tired from her walk. She sat down on the riverbank and loosened her dress to let the breeze blow on her bosom. Then she began braiding her hair and rewinding it around as a crown to her head.

Without realizing it, she slowly sank into a soft sleep. Her eyes closed. Her hands slid down her sides. She slept.

This is the way the god Mars first saw her. From his eyes rose his desire. From desire he moved to enjoyment. Because of his divinity he was able to depart unseen and unknown.

The priestess awakened none the wiser. But she was already pregnant. Already the renowned founder of Rome grew inside her body. Wearily she arose to her feet with a prayer on her tongue: "May my vision prove true."

"I saw myself in a vision," she realized. "But perhaps it

was too clear to have been a vision. I saw myself standing before the altar where the eternal fire from Troy, the Ilian fire, burns in our temple.

"Suddenly the fillets of wool (symbols of her office) dropped from my head to the floor! So did my hair fall too!

"Then I saw a wonderful sight. Two palm trees sprang up before my very eyes. I saw them emerge from Earth, and grow. The one was taller and greater than the second. Its leaves began to uncurl and its trunk to branch and leaf out and spread over all the earth and grow with ever renewing branches wider and wider until it spread its shadow between heaven and earth and reached its topmost foliage to the stars.

"My Uncle Numitor comes then, swinging an ax. I thought he would cut down my trees! My heart began to throb and pound!

"Then came two defenders of my trees. The first was the woodpecker, sacred to the god Mars. The second was a female wolf. They fought off the danger to my trees."

The priestess raised her traditional, earthenware pitcher and returned to her temple of Vesta.

Livy

The Vestal Virgin Rhea Silvia was raped. She gave birth to twins. She named the god Mars as their father, probably thinking that she could thus escape punishment, or that her crime would be considered less wrong if she accused a god of it. Nothing availed, however. Neither god nor man helped the Vestal. King Amulius ordered her thrown into prison and her sons entrusted to the river.

Ovid

The sun had only nine months to shine before Rhea Silvia's twin sons were born.

The priestesses of Vesta threw their hands up to hide the sight from their virginal eyes.

The altar of Vesta quaked inside her temple.

The sacred, eternal fire from Troy took fright, flickered on its hearth, and died! Catastrophe!

Then King Amulius ordered those brats of hers drowned

in the river. But the water drew back from such injustice and stranded them on dry ground.

Livy

By chance, the Tiber had spread into shallow pools along the banks so that the orders of Amulius could not be executed exactly. The men found it impossible to reach the main channel. They hoped the twins would be drowned anyway, even in the backwater where they hastily dropped them. They exposed the babies in their basket where the Ruminalis or Romularis fig tree (altar) stands, a then uncultivated shore. (Rumina was the Roman goddess of nursing mothers.)

The rest of this story is accepted by everyone as truth—that the basket floated down the Tiber. It came to rest on the riverbank where a female wolf came down to drink. She heard the infants crying. She nursed them herself and groomed them with her tongue until the royal herdsman found them, took them to his hut, and gave them to his wife Larentia. She brought them up.

Ovid

Is there anybody who has not heard or read the rest of this story, how a woodpecker flew down with food for the twins, and how they were nursed by a wild animal, even while they were exposed, and before the shepherd Faustulus rescued them and carried them to his wife Larentia?

Oh, I shall not pass you by, Larentia, nurse to this powerful race of Romans! Nor shall I fail to give you your due, Faustulus, poor and humble though you are! All Rome honors you both at the Festival of Larentalia, every December.

Livy

The boys grew up tending the farm and the livestock. They spent their free hours roaming the countryside, however, and hunting. After having learned to kill wild animals, they next set upon highwaymen, took their loot, and divided it among the poor shepherds, who enjoyed hearing about the lads' adventures.

Soon a band of young hoodlums joined the twins' gang. This turned out badly, for, to make a long story short, the boys were all apprehended. When they were turned over to Amulius for punishment, they killed him. Then Numitor became king of the Alban state.

Romulus and Remus then set off to found a city of their own, near the very riverbank where they had been exposed as infants. And also, their Latin shepherds and common folk far outnumbered, even then, the citizens of either Alba Longa or Lavinium.

What happened next is shameful enough. It came about because the twins had been cursed by both grandfathers. It came about secondly because the brothers were greedy for sovereignty. It came about lastly because of a quarrel between them.

Since they could not decide the question of seniority by themselves, they turned to the gods to decide for them which one could give his name to the new city they planned to found. Which one was the older?

In order to receive an augury from the gods, Romulus took over the temple on the Palatine Hill, and Remus, the one on the Aventine Hill.

Remus received the first reply, an answer signalled by the flight of six vultures.

Romulus received the next augury, an answer signalled by the flight of twelve vultures.

Each brother declared himself king and founder, Remus supporting his claim by his prior omen; Romulus, his claim by the greater number of birds. From words they passed to taunts, and from anger, to blows. Remus was "felled" in the fight.

The more usual story is that Remus mocked his brother by leaping over the walls that Romulus had built about his future city. Angered, Romulus slew him, declaring: "Death to anyone who leaps over these walls!"

Ovid

When the twins learned who their father was, they felt ashamed to be followed by a band of poor peasants only. So Romulus with a sword killed King Amulius, which restored the kingdom to their elderly grandfather Numitor. Romulus then built new city walls, which, however low they might have been, should not have been jumped over by Remus.

In that desolate area, where only yesterday cattle had roamed the forests, there now stood an "eternal city," the ruler of which proclaimed: "I rule by means of my weapons, and by the martial blood that bore me. Henceforth, let us observe the first month of every year in honor of my father Mars and name it 'March.' "

But really, don't you know, the ancient Latins were a warlike people who had always worshipped Mars, the god of war, before all others, anyway.

Livy

In this way Romulus took all power into his own hands, founded his city, and named it for its founder. Then he fortified the Palatine Hill. Next he made the laws and established the customs for religious services and worship. Next he summoned all his people and laid down their laws because he believed that only a body of laws would bind them into a union. After that, he attended to his own magnificence of dress, richness of ornament, ceremonial appearances, impressive personal guard of three hundred men, and mighty, noble attendants.

In my opinion, he drew all this pomp and circumstance from the neighboring, very wealthy Etruscans.

Romulus ruled for forty years, during which his city grew and prospered, stole the women they needed from the Sabines, and defeated their enemies. One day while Romulus was reviewing his army on the Field of Mars, a great storm swept over Rome. A cloud hid Romulus from the view of all. Then came a loud clap of thunder. When the cloud lifted, not a trace of Romulus could be found, or ever was found.

Ovid *(Metamorphoses,* XIV)

The Sabines fought the Romans and the Romans slaughtered the Sabines, and after them, their Sabine wives' fathers. They finally declared peace rather than wipe each other out. They decided they should save a couple of kings.

When Mars took off his helmet, he spoke to Jupiter, reminding his father of the promise he once made: that

Mars should be able to have his son Romulus declared immortal. Jupiter gave a great clap of thunder to show he remembered and consented. Mars jumped back in his bloody chariot, cracked the whip, and sped over to the Palatine Hill. Genial Romulus was already there, hard at work passing out with great pomp new laws to those poor citizens that were standing in long lines before him.

Mars reached down, raised him by one arm, and shot him up into heaven; just like a ball of lead. When shot from a sling, it gets smaller and smaller until it becomes a nothing.

So Romulus soared out of Rome and disappeared before he got there.

His heavenly name is Quirinus.

Up there he lolls at his ease, in beauty all the time, able every day to dress up in gorgeous clothes as good as any worn by those other immortals.

THE VESTAL VIRGINS

Rome in the monarchy was divided into four regions, supposedly named for four commanders under the Argive hero Heracles. One bridge, *Pons Sublicius,* crossed the Tiber eastward into the city-of-seven-hills. The bridge led first to the Cattle Market; the road then passed Tarpeia's Rock, with the Capitoline Hill on the left and the Palatine Hill on the right. The Citadel *(Arx)* stood further left or just north of the Capitol. The road into the city passed between these hills, as it does today, bifurcating at the round Temple of Vesta, Hera's sister, and the Roman goddess of the hearth fire and of the state. Egeria's Vale lay far to the southeast.

The city was protected by being built on hills, where its principal altars were located, and inside a large earthwork to the northeast. The rampart *(Agger)* had been begun by the first Tarquin, an Etruscan king, and continued under King Servius Tullius. Roman fortifications were usually set on a hill, mound, or embankment surrounded by a palisade *(vallum),* and that encircled by a ditch *(fossa).*

The Roman historian Varro says that the Capitoline Hill was formerly "Tarpeian" after the Vestal Virgin Tarpeia. This patrician Vestal from highest nobility, as were all or most Vestal Virgins, threw open the gates of the citadel to let in her own people, a hostile Sabine army. The Sabines were an Italian people, neighbors of the Latins; their daughters were the ones kidnapped and married by force. Tarpeia's reward for this betrayal of the Latins was death. The Sabines themselves killed the traitor by burying her under their shields. They hurled their weapons upon her so as to crush her by the weight, says Varro, and bury her. A constant reminder of her death is the high "Tarpeian" Rock from which thereafter criminals in Rome were cast down by way of execution. A most ancient citadel, then, overlooked Rome from the Capitoline Hill and Tarpeian Rock, said Varro (V, # 41, 46).

The cult and order of Vestal Virgins was not indigenous to the Latin peoples but a religious institution founded by the legendary Sabine King Numa Pompilius. It was called *Vesta publica populi Romani Quiritium,* which meant that Vestal Virgins were the national, public religion of the federated Roman peoples (originally Latins and Sabines).

The priestesses of Vesta were drawn from the highest aristocracy of the kingdom, then the republic, and then the empire, for the sole purpose of serving the Roman state. They were mere functionaries, to put it plainly, who were respected, honored, and highly regarded—*but* powerless figureheads otherwise. Their estate resembled that of many Roman women; they were considered superior, but not equal before the law.

It would not be too great an exaggeration to conclude that the Roman religion was more ancestor worship than deference to any female deity. This cult of male ancestors appeared in every Roman home as their private, family religion; the father of the family officiated as its priest. All sacerdotal functions, all ceremonies of worship, were performed and only performed by the father of that individual family, at *his own hearth.* The state religion mimicked the private, male-only, family religion.

The honored Vestal Virgins, like Rhea Silvia a.k.a. Ilia, actually washed the dishes and swept the hearth. Their "father" too was High-priest of Rome: a *Pontifex Maximus*, like Julius Caesar. All these fathers, from father to son, inherited the priesthood, for the purpose of worshipping male ancestors only. Each and every father had unquestioned, instant power, of life and death. His daughters were totally expendable—creatures who could be legally slain at any moment, sold into slavery, sent into prostitution, or turned over to the High-priest as his chattels, the Vestal Virgins.

The rare statue of a Vestal, who was more often painted than sculpted, shows a pinched, careworn, deeply lined face, with dead and hopeless eyes (See Fig. 17). She looks out blindly, shut inside a worthless body that has been togged out in a ritual costume. She wore only white, which is the customary garb of a minor priestess, a bride, and a corpse. Vesta's round

Figure 17. Vestal Virgin

temple adjoined the court of the High-priest's residence, originally the *Regia* of King Numa Pompilius, *Pontifex Maximus.*

Thus, from earliest times in Rome, church and state were one and indivisible. After Celtic Gaul yielded perforce to Roman Law, its later kings of France likewise claimed kingship "by the will of God." No such ruler, so kinged, could be either questioned, or modified, or deposed. The father's power there too was absolute, and his eye lay upon all his daughters.

There were no statues and no images inside Vesta's temple, only the "unextinguished fire," as Cicero termed it, and it was "sempiternal." An inner *penus,* or curtained area, sheltered several sacred objects, those talismans upon which the safety of Rome depended. Nobody but the High-priest and his Vestals saw them, or cleaned them, if cleaning was required, or protected them from the elements. Nobody else knew what these objects were. They must have resembled other such items, like the "Thirteen Treasures of Britain." Once a year, on June 9, labelled a fearsome day of ill omen, the curtain was drawn aside for housekeeping duties performed by these "patrician" Vestals. The day was publicly called *Vestalia,* but probably only the naive public honored these tragic virgins. In ancient days the Vestals had an atrium for their use, and perhaps also once their private grove of shade trees.

The High-priest alone chose a future Vestal from among twenty little girls, aged six to ten years old, whom he had requested to appear. He pointed with a finger, and said: "Te, Amata, capio": "Darling, I seize thee." These priestesses, whom he had so honored, remained usually under his tutelage until age thirty, at which time they were dismissed and free to wed. Very few, it is said, or none, so desired. The Vestals could receive other, signal honors, such as being emancipated from bondage to their natural fathers. When accused of a crime during their years of temple service, a Vestal could be exonerated only through some act by Vesta herself. Throughout their years of service, each Vestal wore the same, old, ritual or sacral dress of a bride. There tended to be "clusters" of miracles, which occurred at this temple in particular, but which scholars have dismissed as due to the natural "hysteria" of women. The word "hysteria" comes from the Greek *hysterikos,* which means "uterus," but the miracles reported by Vestals are considered psychoneurotic symptoms due perhaps to repressed emotion.

Vesta's round temple *(Aedes rotunda Vestae)* was adjudged an anomaly in Rome, where temples had to be square so as to face the four cardinal "regions" of the sky. Otherwise, the augur's wand could not get a true response from the south sky (side #1), the west (#2), the north (#3), or the east, *the fire side* (#4). These four sides corresponded to a mythological universe: 1) civilization, or Egypt, 2) death, or western ocean, 3) Hyperborean or frozen north, and 4) birthplace of religion, the Orient. Vesta's temple was round, on the contrary, which pointed to its extremely antique origins as a navel and center of the earth. It was likely eastern, or Greek, and at least as old as Delphi and Heracles. Others said it was round in souvenir of primitive wattled huts built by the aborigines.

A French authority on comparative religion differs, however, attributing Vesta's temple in Rome to a forgotten cult, the symbols of which we are now almost totally unable to read. We do preserve, says Georges Dumézil in his book on Indo-European rituals at Rome (Paris, 1954), some inkling of this particular worship of Vesta if we look at associated, ritual colors (p. 45 ff.):

Colors	India	Celts	Rome	Greece
White	Brahmans	Druids	Vestals	Pythias
Red	warriors	Cuchulain	Jupiter	Demeter
		Lancelot	Mars	Cybele
			Quirinus	Ares
				Zeus
Yellow	priests	Govannon	Vulcan	Hephaestus
	farmers			
	merchants			
Black	Kali	Bran	Saturn	Cronos
Blue	Indra	Morgan	Neptune	Hera
Green	—	Bridgit	Mercury	Aphrodite
		Bards, poets	Venus	
		Druid ovates		
Multi-colored	—	High-priest or High-priestess	Flora Cumaean Sibyl	Medusa

The three colors red-white-black, together, always indicated to Romans a religious ceremony, or a sacrifice. The same was true for Celts as in the adventure of Perceval, where he falls into a trance because he has seen a black bird and red blood on white snow.

Scholars expert in comparative theology point to the ancient book from Tibet, the *Bardo Thôdol,* which shows how much symbolic language the Western world recovers only with the greatest difficulty. The reason for this is that such symbols, taught during initiations, were never to be revealed, on pain of death. Thus, when the Pythia condemned Aesop, it may well have been because his *Fables* reveal some of this lost, symbolic language. The Pythia and other Greek initiates knew what we have not entirely recovered, such as the meaning of lamb, dragon, dove, the triangle with the eye in its center, fish, eternal fire, risen sun, temple orientation, colors, and designs. When Medusa brings Mt. Meru, Everest in the Himalayas, to mind for no conscious reason, the Tibetans tell us: both Mt. Meru and Atlantis were centered inside concentric rings of mountains and seas.

The Vestals and their cult were instituted by the second King Numa Pompilius, a Sabine monarch said by legend to have reigned from 715 to 672 B.C. He entrusted to their care, said Plutarch in his biography of Numa *(Parallel Lives,* IX), attendance upon the perpetual fire. This was strange, observed Plutarch, because at both Delphi and Athens, the holy fire was maintained by elderly widows. When it was extinguished during warfare, it was rekindled by sun and mirrors. The first Vestals were named Gegania, Verenia, Canuleia, and Tarpeia. When Vestals were being carried in their litter, they could commute any criminal's death sentence; if anyone passed under them, however, he was executed.

For any minor offense, the High-priest had the Vestal stripped naked. Then he whipped her, usually behind a curtain, and in a dark place.

When a Vestal, such as Rhea Silvia, whose son Romulus founded Rome, broke her vow of chastity, she was executed. Inside the Colline Gate stretched an earthwork alongside the city wall, what the Romans called an *agger.* Under this wall was a small chamber with steps going down to it. Inside this chamber were placed a couch with its coverings, a lighted lamp, a piece of bread, and three bowls, one of water, one of milk, and one of oil. In other words, nobody could say that a Vestal who was sentenced to death had died of hunger. That would have been unsuitable for a lady of such high birth and so consecrated to such a sacred, public office. The "culprit" was laid in a litter. Many covers were then thrown completely over and around her. Then the covers were tied tightly with ropes wound round and round so that no sound from her would be at all audible.

The Greek historian Plutarch, priest at Delphi, wrote: "No other sight makes everyone in Rome shudder as this one does; nor can any other day make people so downcast as this day can" (X).

Everybody who sees this litter going by, he adds, drops everything and stands aside in complete silence as it passes. They all stand rigid there, and speechless, in absolutely silent horror at the sight.

When they have carried the litter to its destination, Plutarch continues, the bearers unfasten the ropes and unwind the blankets. Then the High-priest raises his hands to high heaven, and recites some incantations that were to Plutarch completely non-understandable. After he has "apparently prayed," the bearers open the litter, and lead the "culprit" down the stairs; for, being heavily veiled, she cannot see where she is going. The High-priest and his fellows have meanwhile averted their faces. After the priestess has entered the room, the door is closed, the stairs are removed, and the stairway is quickly heaped up with earth. Workers hasten to make all level with the rest of the earthwork. That is how Vestals who broke their vow of chastity were "punished."

King Numa did not order a round temple built because he thought that site the center of the earth, but because he had adopted the Pythagorean notion that fire burned at the earth's center. Numa established priesthoods to regulate the periods of mourning allowed, others to guard the peace, others to arbitrate disputes and decide when or if to declare war. When the Gauls conquered Rome, their victory was blamed on the citizens who had disregarded these priests. Numa also adopted the Pythagorean idea that worship should take place when people were free to attend and able to devote their undivided attention to the services. They tell a story about this, that one day Numa's messengers broke in upon him to say an army was attacking Rome. The king turned to them, smiled, and said, "But I am in church."

Numa also rescinded the law allowing fathers to sell their sons, if the latter had already married with his consent. King Numa felt it too hard on the wife who had married a free man only to find later that her husband was a slave. He also changed the calendar, making the first month March the third month and the eleventh month of Romulus's calendar, which was January, the first month of the year. During his reign the double doors to the temple of war were kept closed at all times, and peace reigned.

What others [will] say about King Numa and the Sage Pythagoras, decreed Roman Livy, is totally wrong because anachronistic. The Sabine King Numa lived some two hundred years before Pythagoras (c. 582–507 B.C.). Numa could not have understood him anyway, because of a language barrier. Numa's virtues stemmed from his noble nature. It was he who founded the order of Vestal Virgins, a priesthood he endowed with stipends from Rome's public monies so that their offices could be continued in perpetuity. He laid down their rule of virginity so that these priestesses would be invested with all the awe and majesty that their purity of life guaranteed them. He had Numa Martius inaugurated as first Pontifex Maximus, supplied by the king with written laws stating his rights, obligations, and regulations *in re* the performance of his duties.

Because of these holy priestesses and priests, the neighboring people in Numa's day laid down their arms and began to respect Rome as a religious center divorced from conflict and threats of weaponry.

It was King Numa himself, however, who served as model for his people. The king was understood to be a deeply religious man. He often withdrew from the cares of state to a thick grove of trees watered by a spring of pure water. In the center of this grove there was a large, very dark cave. Into this grotto Numa frequently withdrew. He claimed he went to consult "his wife, Egeria."

King Numa's wife, Egeria, was one of the three *Carmenae*

who, like the three Muses at Delphi, were old Italian goddesses of poetry, literature, writing, and the arts of prophecy.
What King Numa told his public was that his wife, Egeria,
consulted the *Carmenae*. King Numa found it convenient to
refer infrequently but allusively to his "wife" and her sister
priestesses. He hoped by such veiled references to instill fear
or dread into the hearts of those people closest to him.

Therefore Numa pretended to meet a renowned priestess,
Egeria, by night so as to receive advice from her concerning
the establishment of those rites and rituals most acceptable to
the gods, and those appointments most likely to serve the state.
He took care never to have witnesses present either during his
"consultations" with Egeria, or his journeys to and from her
mantic, Delphian grotto.

One ritual established by Numa has never been explained.
He had seven or even thirty puppets made of straw thrown
into the Tiber on certain holy days, March 17, or May 15, for
instance.

That Numa consulted a priestess who may have been Evander's mother from Greece could not surprise Sir James Frazer.
In Volume I of his monumental *The Golden Bough* he informed his readers that "the kingship at Rome was originally
a plebeian institution and descended through women," from
Carmenta to her son Evander, for example. The early inhabitants of Italy "worshipped a Mother Goddess, not a great Father God. That goddess was Diana," the Latin counterpart of
the goddess Artemis from Ephesus. The Italian goddess Diana
at her temple of Nemi outside Rome "stood for the older principle of mother-kin, or the predominance of the wife in matters of inheritance over the husband." In Numa's case his wife,
Egeria, if she was his wife and not a priestess only, settled in
addition matters of religion, but also customs, and protocol
for the Sabine king (pp. 45–46). In such ancient times priests
had to resign their office at the death of their wives, or in
Diana's temple, after a tenure of seven years.

First comes the hero's introduction into the presence of the
goddess, their marriage, and his departure outside her "palace" in order to defeat succeeding aspirants over a period of
(seven) years. This same pattern reoccurs in medieval fiction,

but barely disguised from legend, which in turn has been barely disguised from myth, the actual ritual at Nemi. A very faithful repetition, which adheres literally to the Diana worship in Rome, is called *Yvain ou le chevalier au lion,* a medieval work in Old French, but which also exists in the Welsh *Mabinogion.* Yvain is the youthful hero being auditioned for the job of future king-consort. His first interviewer is a moon-priestess identified as "Little Moon" (Lunette). Yvain has already slain the reigning, old king, whose tenure has that day expired. The priestess introduces Yvain to Diana, here called "Laudine," or Lothian. She is the eponymous queen of Scotland. Yvain is reluctantly accepted because, of course, he is a murderer. Consummation takes place immediately, however, after which Yvain departs to take up his stand out by Laudine's precious oracular spring. Laudine and Lunette politely mourn his passing—in anticipation of his younger replacement seven years later. These particular texts are mistakenly called "romances;" they were once all too real.

In this same connection Livy said King Numa was not real, that he drew his theology from a Pythagoras who was not yet even born, and, of course, Livy would have staunchly contradicted Plutarch anyway. How could any Greek come along after Livy's death and write biographies of Numa and Lycurgus, and then dare to compare their lives? Both were not historical, but legendary only. Ah, but look here, Plutarch would have replied, what I also find interesting to write is "history heard at the gates of legend."

The true history of certain Vestal Virgins can be found in Livy's scattered, brief sentences in the volumes of this historian: Titus Livius (59 B.C.–17 A.D.). Well over one hundred of his books have been lost, but about three dozen remain. His title instructs his readers that he is going back to the founding of Rome: *Ab urbe condita libri* (books).

Postumia's Story (B.C. 420)

Livy IV, 64.
In the year A.U.C. 334–35 charges were brought against the Vestal Virgin Postumia, who was detained and ordered to stand trial. As it turned out, she proved inno-

cent of all charges. It was decided that she had been at fault, although not actually guilty of unchastity.

Her frivolity laid her open to suspicion. She customarily dressed herself all too fetchingly. Furthermore, she had a sharp tongue which she used too freely in "unmaidenly" impertinence.

Postumia was acquitted of the principal and only grave charge, which was loss of her virginity. She was released from custody, but censured for her fancy clothing and freedom of demeanor.

In the name of her College, the Pontifex Maximus then ordered her in future to forego comedy and to dress as befitted her office and not as demonstrating a compulsion to attract attention.

This year Cumae fell to the Campanians. It had been a Greek city up until this year.

Vestals and the Sack of Rome (390 B.C.)

(Historical explanation by Philip Van Ness Myers, *Ancient History*, p. 390: While the Romans were occupied in the conquest of the Etruscans, tribes from Gaul moved to within eleven miles of Rome, where they so frightened the Romans that they ran to cover. Consternation resulted. The Vestals buried their sacred objects and fled to the Etruscans at Caere. No attempt was made to resist the Gauls, who sacked Rome.)

Livy V, 39.

When they lost all hope that they could defend the Capitol, the Roman men of military age, and those senators who were still alert and fit, gathered their families to shut themselves up in the Citadel and the Capitol. Having laid in a goodly supply of weapons and provisions, they determined to hold fast, sit tight, and save the honor of Rome.

They ordered the Vestal Virgins to remove all their sacred objects, reminded them that the State depended upon them, and cautioned them not to betray their sacred trust by letting their Order become extinct.

The elect decided that the State could survive if the sacred Citadel and sacred Capitol were saved, and if those young men and older senators who were strong enough kept up their health and resolve. The State should not regret the loss of the rest of the population, old men in particular, they told themselves.

In this state of utter apprehension, those older men who had already made a great success of their lives in government and elsewhere announced to the general public that they would ease their approaching ruination and death by sharing it with them. They planned to stay behind rather than, unreasonably, to expect protection from the superior armed men and noble senators who had shut themselves up in the Citadel and the Capitol.

The old men who were thus abandoned and left to die consoled each other that at least they would not burden the young with their care. They cheerfully escorted those chosen to live up to the crowns of the two small, circular eminences of the Citadel and Capitoline Hills. They entrusted the young, they told them, to uphold the military might of a great city which for the last three hundred sixty years had never known defeat. The young upon whom all hope and help resided said farewell and shut themselves inside the gates.

The scene was really painful to see, however. There were women running back and forth, clasping loved ones, calling pitifully, and sobbing. They kept appealing to their husbands and sons, asking them if they were to be left outside to die so cruelly. A few were let in at the end, after all. It would have been inhuman to leave them all out there to die.

The greater part, the common citizens of Rome, simply picked up whatever they could carry and trooped out in long lines, as far as the eye could see, across the *Pons Sublicius,* and out into the country. These plebeians understood that whatever grain there was left in the city was needed by the younger men of military age, by their close families, and by the senators. Furthermore, they had no chance of finding even a foothold on those two, small hilltops. Most headed for safety up on the long slopes of the Janiculum hills to the west. Others went for the western cities nearest Rome. This disorganized, silent mob had neither leader nor evacuation plan. Each person was alone now,—with neither resource nor aid to expect from the government.

The Vestal Virgins milled around in a dither, trying to decide which of their sacred objects they might be supposed to transport out of the city and which ones they might be better advised to bury or leave. Some were simply too heavy for them to lift, to say nothing about carry any distance. So they worried about future reprisals, and they tried to decide where they might safely hide the treasures that they could not bear with them.

They finally hit upon a plan, deciding it unanimously, so that all future blame could be shared equally. They decided to place some in storage jars and bury them near their Burner's *(flaminis)* dwelling.

Note that it has been forbidden, since that day, for a person, or persons, to spit anywhere near that Burner's house.

Then the Vestals too set out, burdened with the sacred treasures of Rome, which they took turns carrying as they staggered out from the city to the Sublician Bridge and Janiculum hills.

As they plodded wearily up the first slope, they were overtaken by a commoner named Lucius Albinus. He was leading a horse and wagon stored with goods, and conveying his wife and children to safety. They constituted only one family amid the throng of poor misfits unable to fight for Rome, and therefore forced to flee from the terrible, lordly Gauls.

This man Albinus was shocked to see Vestal Virgins among the mob. He could hardly believe his eyes, that the most holy, ordained priestesses of Rome should be allowed to wander on foot, and, in addition, burdened with heavy loads upon their backs and shoulders, and slung between them! That these holy maidens should bear these venerated objects upon which, as everyone knew, the safety of them all depended, was simply not conceivable. He ordered his wife and children at once out of the vehicle, loaded the priestesses and their relics inside, asked them where they wished to go, and took them as comfortably and as speedily as he could, to Caere in Etruria.

(In memory of their love of and service to the Vestal Virgins, whom the Etruscans sheltered during the sack of Rome, the Romans afterwards, in 353 B.C., decided not to wipe out the Etruscan city of Caere, but to declare a peace with them and to inscribe its terms on a bronze tablet.)

The Gauls sacked Rome to their wild hearts' content and then withdrew after receiving a supplementary offering from the senators of one thousand pounds in gold.

"Vae victis," they told the Romans: "Woe to the conquered!" The Romans remembered this taunt. How could they forget it?

Minucia's Story (B.C. 337)

Since according to Roman Law a person accused of a crime is arrested and considered guilty until he, the accused, from his prison cell proves his innocence, the Vestal Virgin Minucia was taken into custody as soon as accused. In her case her accuser was known. It was one of the Vestal's own personal slaves.

The Vestal Minucia had come under suspicion, to begin with, because of the richness and wealth displayed by her dresses. This display failed to become her station as a holy priestess, in holy orders. Her slave (perhaps a captured Gaul, a princess) brought this offense to the attention of the High-priest.

Before the Vestal was able to release her slave, which would have rendered her free from torture and made her a free citizen, Minucia was ordered by the Pontiff to refrain from this manumission, and to remain in her cell, without attending to duties or appearing during services.

Whether or not her slave, or slaves, after more torture, informed further against Minucia, the Vestal was in any case tried and found guilty (of unspecified crimes).

The Vestal Minucia was buried alive near the Colline Gate, to the right of the paved route, in a field called "The Polluted Field." It was *probably* called that because she was another Vestal who lost her virginity.

The Story of Vestals Opimia and Floronia (216 B.C.)

The Senate that year fell into a panic over the unsuccessful outcome of the war so far, and ordered home the Fleet Commander from Ostia. In the midst of their panic at the disasters their forces were suffering, they became very distraught by the other bad news of portents and prodigies signalling utter catastrophe.

That very year already two more Vestal Virgins had been apprehended, accused, and proven unchaste. One of the pair had already been buried alive at the Colline Gate, as per custom. But the second girl had committed suicide.

An investigation was ordered. It was discovered that one of the pair had been deflowered by a lesser priest, who in those days was considered a mere private secretary to the pontiffs.

When the Pontifex Maximus was so informed, he took action. He instantly ordered this secretary to be severely scourged, and publicly, in the Voting-ground. The guilty man's name was Lucius Cantilius. The fellow died under the lash, so severe was his punishment.

These three deaths, occurring so rapidly together, obviously constituted a further omen of disaster.

The Ten Commissioners for drawing up laws commanded *The Sibylline Books* to be consulted. It was done.

The Cumaean Sibyl out at Cumae on the Bay of Naples took a very unfavorable view of Vestals who broke their vows. An ambassador was dispatched posthaste to Delphi to beg the Pythia for her advice, counsel, and recommendations in such a dire emergency (since the Cumaean Sibyl, as frequently occurred, was as noncommital as she pleased).

A Vestal Scourged (206 B.C.)

It was a frightful year. Two snakes slithered around Jupiter's temple. Reapers discovered ears of grain that appeared to be stained with blood. A pig was born with two heads. A lamb was born hermaphrodite. Two suns shone over Alba. A strange light appeared in the nighttime sky. Out in the country an ox spoke some words about Rome.

In the city Neptune's altar dripped sweat. The temples of Ceres and Romulus were struck by lightning.

The Consuls ordered the necessary worship and prayers, which were performed.

Then a worse calamity struck at night. It caused more terror than all these other dire prodigies moving from the country into Rome itself: the eternal fire in the temple of Vesta was allowed to go out.

The Pontifex Maximus then was Publius Licinius. He took prompt action, ordering the Vestal who had been on duty that night to be scourged, sacrifices offered, and a day of prayer observed at Vesta's temple.

Addenda *from Livy* (B.C. 178)

The Forum at Rome was burned, and the holy fire in Vesta's temple went out. Marcus Aemilius was then High-priest. He ordered the Vestal on duty when it died to be whipped. She declared it would not happen again.

(B.C. 114)

When Publius Elvius was returning home from the Games, his maiden daughter was struck by lightning. She sprawled lifeless on her horse, but her dress exposed her groin. Her tongue also protruded.

The soothsayer predicted a disgrace to all other Roman virgins also, as well as to the father's noble ranks.

Three Vestal Virgins, in fact, from most aristocratic families, underwent the punishment for loss of virginity, and several men of equestrian rank were also disgraced.

The Miracle of the Vestal Aemilia

Somebody let the sacred fire go out, and the Vestal Virgin Aemilia was held responsible. She protested her innocence. Before the temple members, who quickly assembled, she tore a strip of fabric from her gown, and threw it upon the ashes of the fire.

Lo and behold: the fire blazed up again.

By the time of Rome's most grave emergency, when the Carthaginian General Hannibal had crossed the Alps and was ravaging Italy, Second Punic War 218–201 B.C., it was patently clear that the priesthood of the Vestal Virgins was by and large a failed priesthood. Too many lapsed priestesses, too frequent executions of priestesses, too much unreliability proved more than the citizenry could bear. They called for a radical change. The Africans were inside the land. Rome was about to fall to Hannibal. Something had to be done, beginning with religion and religious observances.

By the terrible days of the Hannibalic War, the Romans saw their Vestal Virgins as no longer able to absorb collective despair. Scapegoats for several hundred years, once acceptable in primitive Sabine and Etruscan terms, they could absorb no more burdens of fear and guilt. A positive, enheartening, newer religion was needed, urgently.

Plutarch was to put his finger on the problem: fire and maidens are not compatible. The veneration of fire is not womanly. Women staffed temples dedicated to the moon, to the earth, to the waters, to the ocean, but definitiely not to the sun, ergo, not to fire.

What Rome needed, with awful war *inside her gates*, was not weak but aristocratic maidens for wrapping up so their mewing cries remained inaudible, and for burying alive.

What Rome needed was a dauntless Medusa, fierce warrior

Amazons, belligerent and undaunted Mother-goddesses flashing the much more ancient banners of War: Mâ-Bellona. They
needed an image of strong women, like the Italian warrior
maiden Camilla, whom Aeneas met in combat when he stepped
ashore on Latin soil. She was fearless and so strong that men
trembled before her. She was so athletic she ran on the tips of
the blades of grass, barely skimming the earth.

Their Roman maidens, Vestal Virgins, never grew to maturity. Like packaged goods, they were handed mutely from one
father to the second husband-father. They never even once
were allowed to take responsibility for their own lives. The
majority knuckled down to authority and hunkered down quietly enough in their dormitory adjacent to the High-priest's
Regian palace.

Clearly there was trouble, witness the executions and whip-
pings recorded. Those few records testify to the severity of the
problem. Nor was the problem solved. Scourging and burials
alive merely exacerbated the dilemma. A few maidens, even
wealthy, aristocratic maidens spoiled by their doting parents
from babyhood, eventually showed some spirit.

For fire is a masculine sexual symbol, like the "ascending
fire" of Heracles's funeral pyre, said Northrop Frye, or the
Promethean fire of male revolutionaries like Lord Byron, Gustave Flaubert, and Victor Hugo. A myth such as these myths
of fire can be studied, Frye added, as "a structural principle
in literature." He wrote these words in his Introduction to a
psychoanalytic study of fire by the noted French surrealist
Gaston Bachelard.

Bachelard makes perfectly clear the anomalous situation
caused by six or so maidens spending thirty of their young
years tending an *eternal* fire. Obviously this task went against
the grain. Fire is perhaps the strongest, most painfully enforced of "general prohibitions" (p. 11 ff.). Every baby is taught
not to approach fire, which is elevated in childhood to a trau-
matic and life-threatening, emotional experience. Interdiction
is the human person's "first *general knowledge of fire.*" This taboo, this stern command, was delivered over and over again
in the gigantic father's angry, loud, male voice. Even so, children die every day from handling and holding fire, and setting fires during their parents' absence.

Bachelard locates the problem which faced the Vestals also, for they too were young girls, initially chosen between ages six to ten: *the problem of clever disobedience.* What parent and what teacher has not faced it endlessly? The more intelligent the child, the more stubborn the child, the more she will defy authority but mask *clever disobedience.* Every schoolteacher has seen the anguished faces of fathers who could not believe how their daughters had elevated disobedience into self-destruction.

The Vestals faced both a social and a personal problem, which overwhelmed them sexually and emotionally. Bachelard scorned Sir James Frazer for not having grasped certain sexual implications. The sacred fire was rekindled at Athens and Delphi by sunlight and mirrors. At Vesta's Roman temple, it was relighted by friction. What a human disaster!

In mythological thinking common to most peoples, fire represents the Sky Father Zeus-Jupiter in contradistinction to the Earth Mother Cybele-Medusa-Atargatis-Mâ-Bellona. The sun evokes volcanoes, impregnation, the seeds of man and bull, sexual power, passion, and the wedding torch.

This torch escorted every Roman bride, with its fire, from her own family and family gods *(lares et penates)* whom she will never see again or *worship ever again, by force and sham combat,* to her husband whose ancestral adoration she must henceforth observe and share, in silent participation, every day of her life from that moment forward. Her family hearth and her married hearth brought comfort to fathers and their sons only.

The public fire gods were Marduk, Kali, Agni, Zeus, Perseus, Heracles, Ares (Mars), Hephaestus (Vulcan), and Mithra. Vesta was that anomaly, a fire goddess: Euripides's "Lady of Fire."

At the Second Punic War the Roman people demanded Cybele, the Levantine Mother Goddess from Mt. Sipylos: "Meter Sipylene, matar Kubile." She came smiling, her Medusa-face composed into beauty. But she was resting her hands upon lions.

The Romans then defeated Hannibal. Carthage was razed, and salt was sown on its ground.

· XIII ·

THE CUMAEAN SIBYL

*"For a long time it was regarded as a sign of great sagacity and
high critical acumen to spurn tradition as a tissue of lies."*
    Giuseppe Consoli-Fiego
    Cumae and the Phlegraean Fields,[1] trans. Alma Reed
    American and British Club (Naples, 1927).

THE DISCOVERY OF THE CUMAEAN SIBYL

For a thousand years, or perhaps for more than that, the Cumaean Sibyl of Rome when it was a kingdom, and then a republic, and then an empire, was considered legendary only.
Thanks to the positive attitude, hard work, and determination
of the Italian archaeologist, his colleagues, and his American
supporters, the Cumaean Sibyl was finally recognized as the
High-priestess of Rome, and as a member, one priestess after
another, of a priesthood venerated for centuries by Romans.

Modern peoples have long assumed that only what can be
held in the hand is real. Everything else, such as literature,
can be dismissed as mythical, legendary—ergo, unreal. Thus,
as Consoli-Fiego remarked sadly, to many people, even established tradition is labeled a "tissue of lies." He disagreed. He
believed that a line of priestesses, each called the "Cumaean
Sibyl," had ministered at Cuma (the old Cumae) on the Bay
of Naples.

This is the way Consoli-Fiego narrates the legend of the Cu-

[1] Also called the Forum of Vulcan.

maean Sibyl, as he heard it in Italy. This legend set him to excavating alongside the Bay of Naples.

The Story of the Cumaean Sibyl

Centuries ago, concurrent with the Fiftieth Olympiad and the Founding of the City, an old woman arrived *incognita* in Rome. She came to see the king named Tarquin.

Which king named Tarquin she went to see is a moot question; for the generations of tellers of legend, who are the world's writers, sometimes recover the long distant past with considerable difficulty. However that may be, whether she went to Rome to see *Tarquinius Priscus* or *Tarquinius Superbus,* she went to see *one* of these legendary Etruscan kings of Rome, and, more likely the Former rather than the Proud.

She told him she came on business, which she then clarified for him: she came to see him on the business of the state.

She offered to sell him nine books. Her price was three hundred pieces of gold.

The king couldn't believe his ears. Nor his eyes. "Books? What books?" She was such an old woman.

"I want to sell you nine books," she told him. "They contain the destiny of the world."

The king could not believe his ears. "The what?" he said.

"The future of the world," she told him in simpler terms. "My books contain the destiny of the world."

"Even so," said King Tarquin. "The price seems too high. . . ."

A few weeks later—for the old woman had to journey all the way from Rome to Cumae, which is on the north hook of the Bay of Naples, and then, all the way back, crossing the farm lands of Campania—she presented herself again at the audience chamber of King Tarquin.

"What now?" he asked, for she was really an old, old woman.

"I offer you six books for sale," she said.

"How much?" he asked her.

"I told you," she replied. "Three hundred pieces of gold."

"Too much."

Some time later, for the old woman was not as young as she used to be, and the roads between Cumae and Rome are very long roads in any century, she presented herself again at the court of King Tarquin.

"I can offer you three books," she told him.

"How much?" he inquired.

"Same price," she said.

"What happened to the other six?" he asked.

"I burned them," she said.

King Tarquin bought the three remaining books, which contained the destiny of the world, for three hundred pieces of gold, from the old woman. She was the Cumaean Sibyl in person.

Then he asked her to rewrite, or to have reconstituted, the other six books.

"No," she said.

After he had read his three books, he asked her again. "No," she said again.

Thus, great Rome rose to be a kingdom and subsequently flourished as a republic, which conquered Gaul under Julius Caesar. Then Rome inaugurated its worldwide empire. That Caesar was stabbed to death in the Roman Forum. And all these centuries Rome expanded but never knew its destiny, thanks to King Tarquin the First, for it was more likely he who had failed to worship that worshipful, old woman, who was the High-priestess, in perpetuity, of Cumae and Naples.

The Roman Senate ordered two Roman patricians of highest birth to rewrite the lost *Sibylline Books*. They were called the "Two Men," the *Duumviri*. Later, their ranks were increased to Ten Men charged to reconstitute the lost *Sibylline Books*. Their ranks in turn were increased to Fifteen Men, whose ranks later became a whole College of Priests charged to reframe the lost *Sibylline Books*. Nobody else was ever allowed to read Rome's three original *Sibylline Books*. Marcus Atilius was sewn in a sack and cast into the Tiber River for having authorized a copier.

During his short term as dictator, and as *Pontifex Maximus,* Julius Caesar gave a copy of the *Sibylline Books* to the High-priests (Pontifices) under him. These High-priests were the only public servants of Rome, all men of vast wealth and high birth like Caesar's, legally permitted to read the *Sibylline Books,* as supplemented and/or revised. These *Sibylline Books* were guarded, stored, and preserved in subterranean chambers of the Capitoline Hill. Those chambers and temple on the Capitoline had been completed and were consecrated in 500 B.C., to commemorate the union between Rome and the Etruscans.

The *Sibylline Books* were at last completely destroyed in 83 A.D., when the temple of Jove Capitolinus burned.

The Emperor Augustus Caesar at once authorized a High Commission to seek out capable authors worldwide, who were to rewrite, edit, and reestablish the *Sibylline Books*. They may now be read in *The Apocryphal Literature,* edited and introduced by Charles Cutler Torrey, who was Professor of Semitic Languages at Yale University. As he says, the present Books IV and V were written by the Sibyl who introduced herself as the daughter, or as a granddaughter of Noah. This should not surprise anyone. The celebrated Delphic Oracle whose Rock may still be seen at Delphi, was a Jewish priestess from Jerusalem. The place just below Apollo's temple at Delphi, where she stood to address the multitudes, is still called "The Sibyl's Rock." Plutarch sat there while he composed one of the *Pythian Dialogues.* And furthermore, the books of the Bible were written by Jews, perhaps the book of *Esther* by a priestess. In any case, the *Sibylline Books,* as we have them today, resemble apocalyptic literature like the books by Daniel and John of Patmos. Both Jewish and Christian theologians wrote the books we have today.

The *Sibylline Books* and their troubled history may also be traced in the extant books of the Roman historian Livy (Volume III). He follows their thread from the year 461 B.C., when the two commissioners *(duumviri)* consulted the *Books* because of a terrible earthquake when the heavens also blazed; and again in 443 B.C., when an epidemic struck men and cattle. The *Books* warned Rome of all multiples of three, for Jove had foretold it: Aeneas shall reign three years, Ascanius shall reign thirty years, and the Alban kings of Rome, three hundred years only. The Senate had recourse to the *Books* again in 399 B.C., a year of catastrophic distemper in men and livestock. The following year, in such awe were the gods held, only high noblemen were elected as military tribunes. In 343 B.C. they were consulted again because of a fearsome prodigy: a shower of stones fell on Rome.

Livy says it was the Cumaean Sibyl who told the Romans

their gods and goddesses had been imported from Greece:
Jupiter and Juno, Neptune and Minerva, Mars and Venus,
Apollo and Diana, Mercury and Ceres, and the deities of fire,
Vulcan and Vesta.

When a pestilence decimated the Romans in 292 B.C., the
Books instructed them to send for the healer Asclepius; and
one of his "snakes" (priests) came over to Rome two years later.
War had delayed his departure (Vol. IV).

During the winter of 218 (B.C.) the populace became terrified because of large numbers of prodigies:

1) a baby of six months suddenly cried "Victoria!"
2) an ox climbed three stories and jumped,
3) phantom ships gleamed in the sky,
4) the temple of Hope was struck by lightning, and
5) a wolf snatched a sentry's sword.

When the *Books* were consulted, they gave counsel and provided remedies, *which much comforted the citizenry:*

1) Rome was cleansed and purified,
2) forty pounds of gold were collected and offered to Mother
   Juno's temple,
3) Roman matrons raised the money and dedicated a bronze
   statue,
4) a prayer service was held to the goddess Fortuna,
5) vows were ordered,
6) two thanksgiving feasts in honor of and for gods and
   goddesses were prepared and served.

It is interesting to see hidden in Livy's pages that it was
women who seemed both most afflicted by their religion and
quickest to propose active remedies: a *supplicatio* (prayer service) and two *lectisternia* (feasts of thanksgiving). Even so, it
was the corporation of priests who officiated here, and not
Roman matrons.

The situation at Rome grew most precarious in the spring
of 217 B.C. when the African Commander Hannibal moved
out of winter quarters to finish his so-far highly successful
conquest of Rome. That spring in both Italy and Sicily, the
heavens warned of impending death. First, the orb of the sun

decreased in size. Then it appeared to be colliding with the moon. Then two moons appeared in the daytime sky. Then the sky split apart. Through this rift a brilliant light shone. Then the sky appeared to catch on fire. Then in the city of Capua, during a rainstorm, one of these moons fell to earth.

As the Roman Commander Fabius took the field, or rather, as he drew Hannibal from one battlefield where he failed to meet him to another where he also failed to show up, the Romans grew more and more hysterical. The same portent which had signalled the fall of Thebes happened: a holy spring ran blood. Crimes were committed by the Vestals Opimia and Floronia. A pontiff was whipped to death in 216 B.C.

The Cumaean Sibyl finally ordered people to go sit at the crossroads and pray to Triple Hecate, and, last of all, to bring from Asia the Black Stone of Mother Cybele, and then Cybele herself, as their protectress in this great emergency.

Despite these records, and despite this long tradition of sanctity, the Cumaean Sibyls were considered fantasy until the archaeologists proved their actual existence. They made this proof by discovering sticks and stones, tunnels and slabs of quarried rock, and the cave in which each Sibyl lived at Cumae. In other words, which are those of principal archaeologist Giuseppe Consoli-Fiego (Naples, 1927), "archaeological remains" supported "classical texts."

Although Livy must have known that "Sibyl," the Latin *Sibylla*, was a title and not a name, he made no effort to list these priestesses. The Roman historian Varro did list ten Sibyls, not by origin but by place of prophecy: Persian, Libyan, Delphic, Cimmerian (Italian), Erythraean (Ionian?), Samian (Isle of Samos), Cumaean, Phrygian (Trojan), and Tiburtine (Latin).

The first Christian to list the Sibyls was L.C.F. Lactantius (c. 260–340), who was, like Saint Augustine, born in Africa. In his book on holy, religious institutions (Book I, Chapter 6) he lists the Sibyls as follows:

1. Persian (or Chaldean, who answered Alexander the Great),
2. Libyan (her name was Lamia, meaning Snake or Medusa),

3. Delphic Oracle (Delphi, Mt. Parnassus, Greece),
4. Cimmerian (located near Lake Avernus, i.e., Cumae),
5. Erythraean (from Babylon, and she predicted the Trojan War),
6. Samian (Isle of Samos near Hera's temple complex),
7. Cumaean (so named from Cumae in Campania, Italy); Sibyls named: Deiphobe, Amalthea, Herophile, Demophile, Taraxandra,
8. Hellespontian (Trojan, born at Troy during the lifetimes of Solon and Cyrus the Great),
9. Phrygian (priestess of Cybele who prophesied at Ancyra [Ankara, Turkey]),
10. Albanean or Tiburtine Sibyl (Latin town of Tiburs, Latium), whose statue was on the Capitoline Hill in Rome. It was found in the Anio River at Tiburs.

Since the designation "Cimmerian" refers to priestesses who lived underground near Lake Avernus, it probably duplicates #7, or refers twice to the Cumaean Sibyls. An oracular shrine dedicated to Apollo, as at Delphi, stood on the Acropolis of Cumae (modern Cuma). An underground Roman road ran three-quarters of a mile from the southeastern part of Cumae, through Monte Grillo (the wailing mountain) to the shores of Lake Avernus (Vergil's celebrated *"facilis est descensus Averni"*).

The comic writer Petronius has his hero say he saw the (one) Sibyl at Cumae. She was then so old they had to hang her up in a bottle. She had prophesied by then seven hundred years. When children asked her what she wanted, she replied, "I want to die." Here Petronius is making fun of priestesses who received from Apollo the grant of one wish: to prophesy. The gift of prophecy did not imply their immortality.

France's greatest author, Dr. Rabelais, paid back Petronius by setting the record straight. When his hero asked the Oracle whether or not he should wed and if he would be happy, she answered him by only one word: "Drink." That is, she meant him to understand that the secret of a happy life is "Know thyself." But clever Christian evangelist that he was, Rabelais informed his readers that the Sibyl was not *in* a bottle after all. On the contrary, that was her name: *Bacbuc*, which is Hebrew for "bottle." Rabelais's hero had addressed one of the Jewish Sibyls, from Jerusalem, or Babylon, or Alexandria in Egypt.

The word "Sibyl," which was a title of these priestesses like Bacbuc derives from the Greek, and Cumae was founded by immigrants from Greece: *sios* or *theos* = God + *bola* = advice. Saint Augustine, who admitted that the Sibyl spoke words received from the Judeo-Christian deity, from God, considered that there had been only the one Sibyl. As more persons looked into the matter, however cursorily, the number of Sibyls had by the Middle Ages reached twelve. Other oracular centers were found: Colophon, Rhodes, Ephesus, and Sicily. Other names of Sibyls were also found: "Hera" (i.e., priestess of Hera), "Lucana," "Demo." Now in the National Museum of Naples, an oracular disk, looking like a bronze medal, warns: "Hera does not permit oracles to be given out in the morning."

When they obliged by answering questions, the later priestesses employed several methods, either vocal, in writing, or by arcane signs and symbols. Sometimes they transcribed their answers on palm leaves that the wind blew about, to the great distress of the suppliant. This also may be a misunderstanding, because if the priestess's words were in Latin, their order would make no difference or furnish no impediment to understanding them. Furthermore, to say that leaves blow in the wind may also be misleading, for the pages of books are also called "leaves," and we speak of "leafing through pages." And paper came from papyrus leaves. When the priestess wrote neither Greek, Hebrew, nor Latin but hieroglyphics only, then one understands the worshipper's consternation.

It is known that their oracles at Cumae commenced and ended properly and according to a due and duly sanctified ritual: "The spirit of god indicates . . ." and ". . . Do not forget to honor River Achelous, the oldest mother of the waters. . . ."

The Sibyls were still believed to be only legendary even after Michelangelo painted them beside the Prophets on the vault of the Sistine Chapel, at the Vatican, Rome. Commissioned by the Medici popes, Michelangelo worked there from May of 1508 to October of 1512. Rabelais arrived in Rome for the first time on February 2, 1534, and there he saw the face of Bacbuc, his Jewish Sibyl, on the new ceiling. There in the spandrels of the ceiling Michelangelo had painted in colors as brilliant as polished stone:

The Sibyls, or Oracles	The Prophets
1 The Libyan Sibyl	1 Jonah
2 The Persian Sibyl	2 Jeremiah
3 The Cumaean Sibyl	3 Daniel
4 The Erythraean Sibyl	4 Isaiah
5 The Delphic Sibyl	5 Ezekiel
	6 Zechariah
	7 Joel

David and Solomon are there also, among many others; Rabelais's Bacbuc is usually referred to as "witness" David with the Sibyl: "teste David cum Sibylla."

Both Prophets and Priestesses are seated on alternate thrones in their paintings, and each is identified by an ornamental scroll. The official book by the Vatican Press identifies the Sibyls as follows:

1) The Sibyl of Libya turns gently toward her open *Book;*
2) The Persian Sibyl is immersed in reading the *Book,* her "worn features mocked by the harsh light";
3) The "Cumaean Sibyl, face lined with age, absorbed in meditation";
4) The Erythraean Sibyl "youthful, serene, about to open her *Book";*
5) The Delphic Sibyl "with limpid, wide-open eyes straining into the void."

The paintings were unveiled on October 13, 1512, which was All Saints' Day.

The art historian Charles de Tolnay understands these works as illustrating the Platonic philosophy of the Delphic Oracle, human existence conceived as innately tragic except that the human soul reaches upward from the prison of earthly life through the architecture of the Sistine Chapel, past the Sibyls and Prophets, or via them, to God. "No detailed iconographic program," says Tolnay, "was given to Michelangelo in advance for the execution of the Sistine Ceiling." He therefore took his interpretation directly from the *Sibylline Books*.

The Delphic Oracle resembles earlier portraits of the Virgin Mary whom Michelangelo conceived also as a Sibyl, a priestess, or "kind of prophetess." He painted the red-haired Erythraean Sibyl as the Jewish daughter of Noah, and represented her dressed in multi-colors, i.e., as a High-priestess. He used for her sweet figure a bouquet of lovely colors: pink, red, white, green, golden yellow, yellow, and ultramarine. She makes a gorgeous picture of loveliness and radiant beauty. But her studious concentration is unbroken. Her pallor indicates nights of study and reflection.

The golden-haired, youthful Libyan "Medusa" is shown as Pausanias described her, some daughter of Poseidon, or some snake goddess Lamia, as some African enchantress from the Atlantic Ocean. Her former snake locks are now neatly coiled around a pale chiffon scarf. Her face is averted, and her body twisted away as she raises her huge *Book*. Despite her lovely rose and violet petticoats, peach-colored overskirt and her bodice of peach with blue buttons, her muscular, strong body and massive shoulders betray her as an athletic, Amazon warrior in *négligée*. Michelangelo was right to use a male model in her case; Libyan and Egyptian sea gods were interchangeably masculine-feminine: petticoats and a man's nose.

The Delphic Oracle holds a scroll or roster, for, as Apuleius told us, she alone knew the names of the gods. On her forehead she wears the white fillet of a priestess, and over her head a green Druidic veil. Her dress is rich: green, sea blue, and topaz. Dark golden hair hangs in uncombed curls down her back, and her eyes and brows are a dark golden color. Her nose is flared, her lips curled, and her eyes haunted, apprehensive. As Tolnay observed, she looks far away, out of this world. It is an unforgettable image, at once innocent and disturbed.

The masterpiece among these Sibyls is the Cumaean, whom Michelangelo painted wide, large, huge, filling her space. Her hands and arms holding her *Book* form the base of a triangle the width of the picture, while her crowned head tops the apex, right of center. Instead of a coiffure she wears a white wool scarf nicely draped about her braided hair and tucked charmingly in above her left ear lobe. We see her in left profile: brown, deeply wrinkled folds of aged flesh, leathery-textured skin, mouth slightly agape, raised eyebrows, but very alert eyes, scanning the pages. She appears to be wearing a pale blue nightgown piped in acid green, and she is not concerned with its décolletage. Over her gown she has draped her body in a voluminous bronze-colored shawl, perhaps of a heavy, raw silk. Her muscled forearms and throat are bare, but her hands draw the eye again. They are very elegant, with the long, slender, squared fingers of a creative person. All else about her, except her massive strength of swelling back and powerful shoulder, is aged. Overall she exudes great personal power. Standing, she would be six feet tall and weigh two hundred pounds. Michelangelo thought highly of this ancient priestess-person. He made her, constructed her, a Titan. She could have held up the world, he said of her, even Rome.

In this sixteenth century the glorious members of the Medici family, bankers to the world, financed expeditions to the Americas on the one hand, and commissioned Michelangelo to create his windows into the lost past of ancient mankind. His priestesses spurred authors and scholars to write new consultations with the Sibyls, to study the three Roman authors who had specialized, while the memory of her was fresh, in the Cumaean Sibyl. Perhaps due also to Michelangelo's paintings, and while Rabelais was still in Rome, the major archaeological discovery of the century was made: Nero's Golden House. By 1600 archaeologists had trained their shovels on Cumae.

First Michelangelo had come in to show the world that he too believed in Roman tradition. He too believed that the great Roman poets spoke the truth when they described a Cumaean Sibyl's oracular shrine at Cumae, when they recorded her words, and described her methods of prophecy. Michelangelo believed in her *Books*, that each Sibyl read and wrote biblical literature, that their *Books* also contained the destiny of the world. He believed that they had been its mistresses.

What Michelangelo achieved was a miracle and a revolution in world thought. People today seem to enjoy debunking Michelangelo, as they often enjoy belittling such superior achievements, thoughtlessly and perhaps without malice. They now say Michelangelo used male models for his priestesses because he was homosexual. Such a judgment clarifies nothing and moreover skirts the issue. The point is that he chose models, or selected parts of various human bodies, to convey the idea and shape of great priestesses.

The only priestesses most of us have ever seen are these women imagined, reconstructed architecturally, and colored symbolically by Michelangelo. He had to imagine a priestess, in a world where there were none. He had further to construct a woman scholar, an intellectual, in a world where they were so rare as to be nonexistent. What does a woman prophet look like? Well, thought Michelangelo, she had to be strong enough to carry nine huge *Sibylline Books*.

Secondly, his Cumaean priestess had to be hardheaded enough to lesson the Etruscan King Tarquin I, or II. She had to be wise enough to counsel Rome century after century in times of earthquake, falling comets, floods, volcanic eruptions, plagues, droughts, famines, and, worst of all, hideous wars. She had to be able to look with equanimity upon entire peoples, Greeks and Carthaginians, bound into slavery regardless of their upbringing, financial position, learning, or rank. In catastrophes Roman people looked desperately to her for advice, for encouragement, and for comfort, which she provided.

Michelangelo painted these priestesses who were also judges in the court of last appeal, priestesses of the dead. Is it not wonderful to have been told by Michelangelo, whose pictures remain there high up in the Sistine Chapel of the Vatican, always available to us, that for centuries on earth there were great priestesses who could not be bribed, could not be humiliated, could not be frightened, could not be corrupted, and who could not be silenced? His priestesses are as strong as men, as professional as men, as dedicated as men, as authoritative as men, as learned as men, and as resourceful. For these reasons Michelangelo created their pictures out of male and female body parts.

A necessity to search for the Cumaean Sibyl and her shrine

at Cumae was stressed in Strabo's forty-seven books of *History of Rome,* all now lost. Even in his *Geography* (V, 4, 5–6) he was much impressed by the site. Cumae faces west across the Etruscan Sea. The Bay of Naples is a huge, semicircular harbor, deeply indented, with Cumae on its northern hook, built high on a volcanic hill, affording a far view of the sea. Safely crowning this eminence—and Cumae means hilltop, eminence, or summit—rose Apollo's temple and the Acropolis.

Strabo first developed the theory that French scholars have called "exoceanism." Cumae was the refueling site for another leg of the long voyage: Naples to Gibraltar, after which came Gibraltar to Casablanca, or Tangier to Cádiz. No geographer as sharp as Strabo could miss Cumae and this vast Bay of Naples where the place names come straight from Homer's voyage of Odysseus. This bay gave the Greeks major harbors along their way to Cádiz: Circe's Promontory, Calypso's Isle. It was then also a celebrated entrance to the Underworld. Worship was required by priestesses of the dead. Nobody could pass it by otherwise, and hope to live. Every traveler had informed himself and dutifully sought Lake Avernus and the Sibyl.

Heroes precede men, said the archaeologist of Cumae Giuseppe Consoli-Fiego. Therefore, to commence a new search for the Sibyl and her entrance to dark Tartarus, excavators start at Cumae's acropolis built on what the original Greek builders called a height: *Kyme.* Strabo called the date very early, perhaps as early as 1049 B.C., greatly antedating the Roman A.U.C. of 753 B.C. Just as a magpie led Jason and his Argonauts, so a dove led the early Greek mariners to Cumae's hill. It could be seen, and can be seen, from far out at sea. The deep blue bay crowned on the port side by Cumae's red volcanic acropolis, beside the red fumaroles of the Flaming Fields, and directly ahead of the ship the magnificent harbor of Naples, Cumae's center, enchants the traveler. Who found it first?

It was not the Greeks, replied the ancient myths of mariners. Cumae was discovered and colonized as early as 1200 B.C. by Daedalus from Minoan Crete. He flew there on wings he built for himself and his unfortunate drowned son, Icarus. Daedalus built Apollo's temple and cast its celebrated sculpted bronze doors. Myths counter myths, alleging it was Heracles, the greater hero, who navigated the Straits between Sicily and Italy and nightly sailed in his golden cup from Cumae west past his Pillars to Cádiz, Ogygia, and Tingis on the African coast. He was the Taurus who made the trip to steal King Geryon's cattle and kill Medusa's Gorgons.

The *Odyssey* tells on the contrary how after the Trojan War, or c. 1184 B.C., Odysseus sailed into this unforgettable Bay of Naples, which is closely described in Homer's poem: the Cyclops' dwelling near the volcanoes at Naples and the Phlegraean Fields, Vulcan's Forge and Forum, the one-eyed monsters seen as the pitted craters of fumaroles. The priestess Circe required Odysseus to descend into the land of the dead, where he would consult the ghost of Tiresias, Prophet of Thebes. Odysseus started this trip from Circe's Promontory *(Promontorio Circeo)* to the land of the Cimmerians underground and the Lucrine Lake *(Lacus Lucrinus)*. He passed the river of fire, performed his ritual sacrifices, and upon returning to earth he dedicated a helmet to the Queen-priestess of Tartarus, Persephone.

Odysseus too observed the marvelous blue Bay of Naples, Cumae on its volcanic cliff, the snow-clad Apennines to the west of him, the Promontories of Minerva and Circe; and he entered the Sibyl's Cave, which had been hollowed out from trachyte rock. When Plutarch considered all this dangerous trip under the earth, he concluded: "No way back for the foolish. No way in for the wise."

Throughout all antiquity, it appears then, Cumae was kept sacred and it was dedicated by the priestesses of the dead to their Queen-priestess Persephone, who had been abducted by Hades in Sicily. Its volcanic craters, which were the dread Lakes Lucrinus and Avernus, were actually two retreats from the sea, explained the ancient geographers. Vulcan's Forum and the black lakes over which no bird dared fly, so toxic were their exhalations, formed the *locus niger,* dreadful black place, where dwelled the Cimmerians underground. Like all aborigines they were held to be "K-M-R," obscure men, underground peoples dispossessed of their habitats on the upper crust.

Strabo insisted he saw this terrain that today resembles a lunar landscape, but which in his day was a dark, heavily wooded and sacred forest. In its center was the black tarn of Lake Avernus, an entrance to hell. The deciduous trees have long since disappeared, one cut to make an image of Calypso, most cut to build a Roman invasion fleet for Augustus Caesar.

The archaeologists found an inscribed gravestone there: "Nobody but initiates may be interred here." It has no date, and the Romans had no date for Cumae before 524 B.C. By 180 B.C. Cumae had been romanized and the neighboring Etruscans also. There were no more Gorgons in the area by 915 A.D., when Cumae was destroyed by landing parties from a Saracen fleet.

Archaeological activity by the early 1600s had uncovered in the Cumaean area valuable treasures in buried statues, cremation tombs, beehive tombs, cellars and other underground structures, vaults, and niches for cinerary urns. Massive excavations were led by H.R.H. the Count of Syracuse, between 1852 and 1857; these finds and the description of his works are in the Naples Museum.

The excavations of 1924–32 brought to the world's attention the proof that the Cumaean Sibyl had been a priesthood which flourished over the centuries just as three Roman poets had tried to persuade everyone during the Golden Age of Roman letters. Thus, since 1932 it has been known but not widely or openly admitted that the Cumaean Sibyl once lived and that she, and others of that title, had been High-priestesses of Rome. The archaeologists by May, 1932, had cleared what they described as a "grandiose subterranean gallery" cut into the rock summit of Cumae, so that this passage crossed the hill, the *Monte di Cuma,* and afforded via this tunnel an access to the Acropolis and two temples at its summit.

"This gallery," says Consoli-Fiego (p. 111), "is one of the most extraordinary, evocative monuments not only in Italy but on the entire territory of the Mediterranean civilization." After twenty-five meters one enters a "vast underground passage" into the heart of Mt. Cuma. Unbelievably, the tunnel is not round but trapezoidal (now known to be more resistant to earthquake) and, moreover, lighted diagonally from above by means of windows cut through the rock into galleries above each side of the passage: 131.50 meters long, with a median height of five meters. Once cleared of the earth and debris that for millennia had blocked the entrance, the Sibyl's passageway was still clean and well ventilated, its walls, floor, six galleries, and ceilings cut smoothly into the tufaceous banks.

The galleries opened overhead in the direction of the sea. To the east the passage was cut by lateral arms that went to cisterns for the Sibyl's use. The main passageway led to her audience chamber, which also had been cut into the tufa bank. The stone masonry is archaic and of Greek workmanship, identified as Minoan and Mycenaean in type.

An unidentified early Christian visited the site just after the Sibyl ceased to perform her priestly duties (i.e., before the end of the Republic and death of Julius Caesar). This tourist said he saw a massive "basilica" that had been cut out of rock. It lay concealed under a mountain. It was, he declared, a "magnificent" piece of architecture. They took him on a tour of this temple, showed him three cisterns also cut out of the mountain's heart. They told him the Sibyl purified herself there. Donning a long, ceremonial robe, she proceeded solemnly to her chamber, seated herself upon a throne, and delivered her oracles. At the end of her chamber was the holier *adyton,* or sacred inner chamber. The tourist probably saw Christian tombs there, for the Cumaean Sibyl was venerated by early Christians for her prophetic gift but also because she had specifically prophesied the birth of Christ.

Archaeologists also found another crypt which connected Cumae to Lake Avernus and the entrance descending into Tartarus. This *crypta* was a vast, vaulted tunnel one kilometer long, and wide enough to allow passage to two vehicles side by side. An aqueduct formed a second gallery within this gallery. This long subterranean passage with its aqueduct was also lighted, but dimly, by loopholes high in its sides.

The traveler comes out upon the canals connecting the Lakes Avernus and Lucrinus with the sea beyond Cumae, and upon Lake Avernus itself. Its black, dull waters lie in the closely wooded crater of an extinct volcano with precipitous banks. Another tunnel connecting Naples to Pozzuoli was constructed by this same architect named Cocceius. By the steep shores of Lake Avernus, there is a bubbling hot spring where again the

Sibyl stopped her worshipper, who was determined to pene-
trate the Underworld, if she consented to guide him safely to
and fro.

The volcanic eruption of Monte Nuovo in 1538 considerably altered this area. By forming the new mountain on the
shore of Lake Lucrinus it caused the water of Lake Avernus
to retract and destroy the Roman naval fortifications and ports
built on those lakes. The active volcanoes of the area, the hot
springs, and frequent subsidences have maintained in rather
constant terror persons visiting Cumae today. Even Hannibal
offered gifts and attempted there in 209 B.C. to placate the
deities of Tartarus.

Consoli-Fiego concludes:

> When the cult of the oracle closed with the triumph of Chris-
> tianity and the whole region fell into a state of abandonment
> and silence with the disintegration of the Empire, and the dar-
> ing passages through the hills were slowly silted up and flooded,
> popular belief, returning to its Italic roots, placed here the Grotto
> of the Oracle, transferring the Sibyl from the Cumaean *antro*
> (cave) to the shores of Avernus (p. 137).

It is therefore fortunate that the Cumaean Sibyl's person
and her voice lived on in the magical poetry of three Romans,
two of them among the greatest geniuses of the literary world,
who in person first and then in immortal poetry "responded,"
says Consoli-Fiego, "to the tremendous mysteries of the earth
and the invisible" (p. 141).

KATABASIS: DESCENT INTO HELL

> "The refugees from the drowned continents fled to the high
> places . . . and some . . . , like Druids or Etruscans or Chal-
> deans or Amerindians or Chinese, refused to forget, but taught
> the old wisdom, only in its half-forgotten, symbolic forms. More
> or less forgotten, as knowledge: remembered as ritual, gesture,
> and myth-story."
>
>   D.H. Lawrence
>   "Fantasia of the Unconscious" of 1921
>   from *Psychoanalysis of the Unconscious*, ed. Philip Rieff
>   (New York, 1949).

Foreword

In our language of the twentieth century, to descend into the Underworld, or to journey into black Tartarus, is to go to hell. This is really what the Cumaean Sibyl told the frantic Romans when they asked her what they should do in their life-threatening emergency: go consult the triple goddess Hecate, who sits where three roads *(trivia)* meet. In other words, go to hell. She knew they would have forgotten what must not be forgotten: that her name was Trivia, a.k.a. Hecate. Priestesses took the names of the goddesses they served. The Cumaean Sibyl was a priestess of the dead. She was Hecate personified.

Inside hell every traveler glimpses the silver-footed Queen of the Night: Queen Persephone and her husband Hades, Queen Titania and her husband Oberon, and Mozart's Queen of the Night from *Die Zauberflöte*. The Roman *Luna* was another such queen, merely one more manifestation of Artemis-Astarte-Diana-Phoebe-Cynthia-Hecate-Selene. When Aeneas descended, in Vergil's pages, he met his jilted lover who had committed suicide, Queen Dido of Carthage. She claimed, in Ovid's pages, to have borne Iulus to Aeneas. The founder of Rome, Aeneas saw Dido as a wan moon, a Phoenician manifestation of Astarte.

Katabasis seems to be a common experience, common today, if we can allow a conclusion drawn from everyday, American speech. Katabasis, judging from our daily vocabulary, may have become a semiosis, a semiotic or deep structure of the human mind.

Our lingo betrays us. When we say, "Go to hell," we mean "perish." When we say "hell," we are also referring to the place: a den of thieves, a den of gamblers, or some infernal region.

We further associate hell with the discord, the din, the noise, the turmoil of a modern metropolis (William Faulkner's Memphis, Jean Giono's Paris). When we conceive of someone defying death, we say he is "hell-bent" for perdition, suicidal and damned. We call certain women "hellcats," "hellhounds," "hellhags," when to understand ourselves better, we probably mean that such a woman has come to resemble a "fury," *recte*, a Fury, one of the *Eumenides*.

What we need now to remember is what the ancients knew

about hell and the descents thereto. The believed such descents were real, that the Underworld really existed, that real human beings, when guided by the Cumaean Sibyl or other sacred persons who also were real, could descend and return to the upper world. The soul of man—and of woman in Psyche's case—was also thought to have a bodily existence. Such beliefs stemmed from Egypt, India, Asia Minor, Persia, Babylon, thence into Judaism. They came into Christianity from Israel and from Rome.

The persons who descended did so for punishment. To reap the benefits of this experience, they descended to a real place. Others could stand and look at the entrances to the Underworld. The entrances also were real and can be mapped. In the accounts which follow, the hero descends because he is a sun god, like the Egyptian Ra who nightly rode his solar boat into the western darkness of sunset. Such journeys form a branch of theology called eschatology, about which there are many studies available to the interested.

The Middle Ages depended largely upon Ovid and Vergil for their orientation. The account by Silius Italicus brings us directly into the history of priestesses and a real, Roman hero. In all three cases it is perfectly wonderful to see this great, aged priestess in action, and to hear words from her lips which the ancients heard before us. Now in 1988 volcanic activity in the Flaming Fields where her temple still stands, or lies underground, is likely to sweep her even farther away from us all.

A major function of the Cumaean Sibyl, a living priestess, was to guide travelers to hell, personally, to direct their steps in this darkness they had elected to see, to allay their natural fears, to escort them, lead them by the hand, console them, explain what they saw, heard, and felt, and most importantly, to ensure their safe return to earth's surface. Without her guidance, such a return was impossible. The Sibyl was also nurse to the hero Aeneas.

Since the first Delphic Oracle was taught by the Muses, and since poetry and prophecy, song and *carmen*, are one and the same divine gift divinely bestowed upon the very few, we now turn to the three Roman poets who composed and narrated ancient descents into hell:

Vergil (70 B.C.–19 B.C.), Book VI of the *Aeneid;*
Ovid (c. 43 B.C.–17 A.D.), Book IV of the *Metamorphoses;*
Silius Italicus (25 A.D.–101), Book XIV of the *Punica (Punic Wars).*

The Myth of the Golden Bough (from Vergil's Aeneid)

Vast is the cave at Cumae. Greeks settled the ancient place. They cut a hundred wide passageways through the mountain's heart with a hundred portals where, standing outside, you can hear the Sibyl's rumbling voice uttering prophecies.

"Aeneas! Trojan Aeneas! Have you landed at Cumae at last? Then come hear your fate. Ah, the god is upon me!"

"Apollo," he prayed, "forgive the wrongs we committed at Troy." Aeneas bowed his head and waited. The Sibyl also kept silent.

"You are most holy, Priestess," he began again, "for you know the future. Grant us a home in the Latin land .We are weary of wave and water." She was still silent.

"I will build a great city and deposit your sacred *Books* in its capitol. . . . Look kindly upon us. . . . Do not give us your words on leaves to blow off in the wind. . . . Priestess, I beg you."

Deep in her *adyton* the priestess shook under the stress of her genius. Then she mastered her body.The gates to her shrine swung open, before Aeneas, all by themselves. Her reply thundered from below and rushed quivering out into the air of day. Aeneas was overjoyed that she knew him, that she would speak to him, and in words of encouragement.

"Oh, Virgin Priestess," he prayed, "grant me my urgent request. I can do no more unless I pay my respects to my worshipful, departed father, Anchises of Troy. When the city burned, I raised him first, like a dutiful son, to my shoulders; he was my primary concern, recipient of my tenderness. I brought him safely through the streets of that burning city. I tended him faithfully, every day during our long sea voyages. He left me suddenly, Priestess. He stepped down without warning. I must honor him at once. My father comes before all else. I am his only son. He is my only father. Pity us, Priestess. He sent me to you. He had learned and remembered that Hecate gave you sovereignty here also, in these dark groves of Lake Avernus. . . . Help us, Priestess.

"I know Orpheus descended to Tartarus in order to bring back his wife Eurydice. And Helen of Troy's brother Pollux descended to ransom his twin brother Castor. No need to remind you of Theseus's descents, Priestess. Or how Heracles went down safely and lived. . . . I too, Priestess, am descended from the king of the gods, by my mother Venus."

"Child of Anchises," the Sibyl began, "the descent into hell is easy, for the gates of Persephone's realm stand always ajar; but the ascent is so heavy as to have been rarely achieved. Very few survive to breathe the air on earth again—a few heroes perhaps, or a god of music like Orpheus.

"Are you very sure you desire to cross its black waters twice in one lifetime? Is your love of your paternal ancestor so integral that you will chance it now, although without certainty of exit? If so, I must teach you the procedure."

v. 137

"The route midway falls into the gloom of a virgin forest so dense that no light pierces the foliage of these patrimonial trees. Grown to one of the noblest foliages you will espy a Golden Bough ("aureus . . . ramus"). The bough, its leaves, and its buds are entirely gold; but it is not plain to see. It is hidden. This Golden Bough was consecrated to Juno, queen of the gods. It was enfolded in foliage, buried among tree trunks, and encircled by dark valleys.

"That being alone who has first broken from the tree its Golden Bough will successfully win the way down to hidden depths of earth.

"Persephone has said it: this must be offered to her. It must be ceremoniously presented, and she must accept it. . . . Have no thought for the gold branch itself. Another such will grow in its place on the same tree, and it will be equally golden and gold. Only the eyes of a man destined to go into hell will pierce the dark forest's huge trees and catch sight of the glint of gold. Whoever sees it must pick it at once. If he does so, then he will know that The Fates have summoned him, and nobody else. Strength of fingers and arms alone cannot pull it from the tree. Nor can it be cut by iron." v. 148

v. 179

Leaving the Sibyl's doorway, the weeping Aeneas leads his crew out to the forest to cut logs for his altars, as the Sibyl has commanded him to do. He must first superintend the funeral rites for his dead trumpeter Misenus.

They soon step carefully into deep darkness and silence. It is a primeval forest so hoary, so deep, so still, so dense no light shows them at first even where to set foot.

First they cut some soft pines and then roll out enormously hard ash logs; and then they fell the holm-oaks which they are able to split open by driving in wedges. From time to time Aeneas lifts his head from his labor. He hopes sadly all will go well and that he will catch a sight of the Golden Bough.

Then as he hauls logs and swings his ax, he suddenly sees a pair of white doves fly down, as chance would have it, between the branches. They alight on the moss almost close enough for him to touch them.

At once this greatest of heroes ("maximus heros") recognizes them as his mother Venus's birds, and he prays.

"Oh, twin doves, please guide me into that grove where the Golden Bough also casts it slender shadow to the forest floor.

"Fail me not, Mother Goddess. Let not Fortuna turn aside from me."

Princely Aeneas followed the doves as bending to feed and advancing they hopped through the undergrowth until they arrived at that steep slope which plunges into Lake Avernus. Loudly then they beat their wings and swooped safely up and away from those mephitic waters. Then they perched side by side on a leafy branch. As Aeneas followed their swift ascent, and as his eyes adjusted, he caught one quick glimpse of gold.

It happened fast. It was just the one glint of gold there in the deepest woodland foliage above his head.

It happened to him as it sometimes happens in the darkness of a December day, when not a touch of brightness remains among the trees, when not a single rosy flower lifts its colored face above the fallen leaves. There in this chilled and rigid forest gleamed the golden branch of the mistletoe. There it thrived and glowed on the alien oak, saffron and gold against evergreen holly. Aeneas climbed the tree. He broke off the Golden Bough easily. He carried it to the Sibyl's grotto.   v. 211

v. 390

Fearfully then, Aeneas followed the Sibyl in her dangerous descent into the Underworld.

They were stopped both by the barking of Cerberus and by the ferryman Charon. "This is the land of Sleep, and Ghosts, and Night," he warned. "Personally, I want no more heroes here, not another Heracles or Theseus roughhousing in our kingdom."

v. 407

"This is the royal Trojan Aeneas," the Sibyl protested, "a man celebrated for religion, conduct, and warfare. He goes down to encounter his father; perhaps this branch will convince you."

The boatman is impressed. He defers to the priestess. He takes her and Aeneas aboard ship. He steers for the opposite mud bank.

v. 450

Along the myrtle groves where gathered those poor ghosts who still after death wept for unrequited love, they met the Carthaginian Queen Dido. Aeneas bowed and spoke to her although he could hardly be sure it was she. This dead queen still wept. Her death wound continuously oozed blood. Aeneas couldn't help but think she looked as wan as a new moon low in the western sky.

v. 539

"Night falls fast here," the Sibyl warned Aeneas. "Let us hasten and court no more weepers. We have come to the fork in the road. We take the right-hand path here that leads past the city of Hades and goes to the Elysian Fields."

They rush past Titans suffering eternally their eternal torments.

v. 628

"Hurry now," cried the valetudinarian priestess. "I can see the ramparts above us. There is the archway before us. Look. There is hell gate. There you lay down your offering. That is their custom."

Aeneas bent down to the pure fountain and sprinkled his hands with clear, fresh spring water. Then, before the gateway, he carefully planted the Golden Bough.

v. 679

He found his father Anchises relaxed and waiting for him in green meadows. "Ah, my son, you have made this great journey to see me."

v. 893

"Twain are the gates of shadowed dreams, the one fair-framed of burnished ivory and the other all with silver overcast."

Anchises told the Sibyl and his son, as he shepherded them toward the exit and said good-bye, to go by the Ivory Gate.

Afterword

Two points in these summary selections from Vergil's *Aeneid* direct us toward the future rather than back to the Trojan and Carthaginian past of Aeneas: that this same, ancient story of the Golden Bough was also told in Old Norse, and secondly, that the business of the gold-colored mistletoe directs us to Druidism, thus directly to our last great priestess Velleda, the only Druid religious who is historical.

In his commentaries on the *Gallic War*, which he fought and won, Julius Caesar, who was a near contemporary of both Vergil and Ovid, claimed the Romans had no knowledge of Druidism until he had conquered Gaul and mentioned it, more in passing than in depth. Either his statement was untrue, or he was sadly misinformed.

The story of mistletoe had long been told among the northern peoples of Europe, Germans and Norse: that the Love Goddess and/or Earth Goddess Freya or Frig bore a lovely son named Balder. His mother adored him, of course. Hoping to make him immortal, which was Thetis's wish for Achilles, she forced every object capable of harming him to promise never to do so. She thought of weapons, sticks, and stones that might break his bones. But she forgot to exact a commitment from the mistletoe because she thought it so insignificant a plant. When the evil Loki gave a branch of mistletoe to an idle god, maliciously suggesting he throw it at Balder as a joke, the Golden Bough pierced Freya's darling son, and sent him down to Hel. (Goddess of the Underworld, Hel was obviously the northern equivalent of Persephone [Proserpina in Latin].)

From this familiar northern myth, we see that what Aeneas underwent was that final initiation which brought him, as it had brought the future priestess Psyche, through death to rebirth and a new life.

Similarly, the references to a holm or holly oak, which stays green even in dead of winter, and to the logging operation, which customarily took place in winter when sleds could be used over snow, place the initiation of Aeneas properly at the winter solstice. It also sets it correctly on the sixth day of the new moon, also per age-old calculation. Such a use of arithmetic was considered holy and was called gematria.

The word for Druid was DR, from the Greek word *dryas* for "oak." The Elder Pliny, Rome's foremost naturalist, explained in his *Natural History* that the mistletoe was connected to the Oak Cult practiced by the Druids of Gaul. "Visci tria genera," he begins: three varieties of mistletoe (a viscous plant). One grows as a parasite, one grows on hard oak and holm-oak, and the third also grows on another kind of oak tree. Both berry and leaf of the mistletoe are bitter. "The Druids *(Druidae)*— that is what they call their magicians *(magi)*—hold nothing more sacred than mistletoe and the tree on which it is growing, provided it is a hard-oak."

> Mistletoe is, however, rather seldom found on a hard-oak; and when it is discovered there, it is gathered with great ceremony, and particularly on the sixth day of the moon

because the tribesmen in Gaul measure the month and the year by the moon and consider thirty years the cycle of generations. When they find a mistletoe plant growing on a hard-oak, they consider it to have been divinely sent. They hold a religious ceremony under this tree during which they hail the new moon as all-healing.

> A priest *(sacerdos)* dressed in white vestments climbs up this oak tree and cuts the mistletoe branch with a golden sickle *(falx aurea)*, and catches it in white (linen) cloth *(candido sago)*.

The Gauls also use mistletoe, or its dried and pulverized berries, as medicine, considering it an antidote for poisons, and either an aphrodisiac, or a fertility drug.

The British Celts also administered strong medications to their heroes and rulers on several occasions, witness illnesses cured and/or aggravated, as reported in Arthurian texts. Lancelot, Yvain, and Tristan were among those given potions and drugs in either liquid or powdered form. On one occasion Gawain underwent what seems like Aeneas's mistletoe-harvesting rite, and in Gawain's case the instructor was a highly revered woman, by analogy a Druid priestess.

Both Elder Pliny and Vergil reported use in religious ceremonies of another sacred plant now thought to be extinct—an *herba sacra,* which is related perhaps to our verbena *(Verbena officinalis).* The verbena or vervain, thought to have been used in solar worship and in fertility rites, used to be sought two hundred years ago near stone circles, then thought to have been Druidical temples. Velleda will wear it as a crown.

Whether he sought a Golden Bough, as Vergil thought, or cut a branch of mistletoe with a golden sickle, as Pliny thought, Aeneas's experience authenticates the last test in Psyche's initiation. Both texts situate a test near a primary oracle of the dead and a Cimmerian shore, the one on the northwest coast of Greece, and the latter on the west coast of Italy. Both stress the whereabouts of dangerous waters. Both feature particularly sacred birds, eagle and dove. Both narrate sequences with the river of hell and the boatman Charon, without omitting the barking, fierce dog Cerberus. Both initiates bear a gift for Hel/Persephone. Aphrodite/Venus is a parent in either case, mother or mother-in-law. Psyche reemerges at sacred Delphi, the first oracular shrine of Greece, while Aeneas emerges at the same sort of prime oracular shrine, at Cumae. Psyche presumably rises to the supreme achievement for a woman of any age: Oracle or Pythia. Aeneas too reaches supremacy as "founder" of Rome.

He will be claimed by the Julians as ancestor of Caesar.

Oracular sites in western Europe will be found to duplicate the geography, first, and the high rank of these initiates whose teachers are priests and/or priestesses of earth and death.

In symbolic language Vergil's mistletoe, and the Elder Pliny's, mean immortality. Thus, today, mistletoe and evergreen holly most appropriately stand for the winter solstice, which ushers in New Year.

The famous Roman orator, lawyer, and senator Cicero came in to support Pliny's association of Cumaean Sibyl and Druidess from Gaul.

In his treatise concerning divination *(De divinatione)* Cicero says the proof that divination is practised can be seen in at least three such practitioners, and especially in a Cumaean Sibyl named Herophile, once the Erythraean Sibyl before she transferred to Cumae. You must grant, argues Cicero, what cannot be contradicted without distorting the whole *record of history:* the Pythia was inspired by the power of the earth *(vis terrae)* and the Cumaean Sibyl also by the power of the very terrain *(natura)* . . . because soils and sites vary in type and influence. One has only to read Vergil's *Aeneid* to conclude that geography plays a large part in prophecy, priesthood, and history.

It is also true, he continues, that the Druids in Gaul prophesy, which is to say, they communicate so well between god and man that they really can know and explain divine will well in advance. This we call the power of divination *(vis divinandi).*

We Romans certainly can testify as to how frequently our Senate has ordered the *Sibylline Books* to be consulted by our "ten men" *(decemviri).*

Any number of Stoic philosophers, drawing their authority from Pythagoras, Socrates, and Plato, have refuted those thinkers who considered divination a superstition to be uprooted.

The Stoics have replied that divination effects a union between religion and philosophy. It proves that the nature of the gods is so adapted as to reveal divine will via divine prophecy.

As far as the Druids of Gaul practicing prophecy, Cicero affirmed, *there can be no doubt whatsoever on that score.* I myself received into my own home, as my guest, the distinguished Aeduan prophet from Gaul, Divitiacus. *He became my personal friend.*

Our forefathers passed down to us as much, he continued his Dialogue, believing that when a person fell into an intermediary state, without conscious thought or knowledge ("animi sine ratione et scientia"—*De divinatione* II), when the mind moved in its own free associations and unbound impulses, it could receive the power of divination either as ecstasy or as dream. For this reason, because the *Sibylline Books* represent free utterances from divinities, they have to be interpreted by our learned experts.

Divination such as that performed by the Delphic Oracle and the Cumaean Sibyl is the effect; but god, environment, and fate are its cause. The human soul then receives an emanation from the divine soul because both souls are equally divine and equally eternal. If and when purely physical controls can be circumvented, a flow of sympathy, a current of "feeling with" will connect person to god. This current, this mutual sharing, this fine connection, becomes apparent in sleep and in ecstasy. Then the link is joined between cause and effect, mover and moved. That is called omniscience. The science of reading its signs, hearing its message, and relaying its words is called "divination;" god, fate, and the nature of the world are its source.

The Stoic philosophers like to define divination as "the fore-knowledge and foretelling of things that happen by chance," Cicero concluded. That was the theory of the Stoic Posidonius (c. 135 B.C.–51 B.C.), he added.

It was our ancestors who told us all about Cumae and that Sibyl, Strabo confirmed:

> These are the tales my ancestors told me, but nowadays, since Agrippa felled the forest that bordered Lake Avernus, and since the country fields have all been built up into houses, and now that the subterranean passages too have been cut, such as that tunnel between Lake Avernus and Cumae, why, all these tales have been found to be merely mythological (*Geographia,* Book V, pp. 4–5).

The Sibyl's Own Story
(from Ovid's *Metamorphoses,* XIV)

v. 101

After his ship passed on the starboard side the walls of the Neapolitan city, Aeneas came finally within sight of the shore-lines of Cumae, and its marshy indentations. They hauled up and settled in.

Aeneas himself entered the caverns of the Cumaean Sibyl, who was so very ancient, to pray her to allow him passage through the realm below Avernus in order to pay homage to his father's ghost.

The Sibyl sat silently for some time, her vision fixed upon the stone pavement. Finally she raised her eyes to him, as soon as the ecstasy came upon her, and spoke: "Great achiever of heroic deeds, your hand has proved its strength by sword and through fire, and your duty to the faith has been well tested and likewise proven solid. Yes, noble Trojan, your wish is granted.

"With myself as guide, you will see the Elysian palace, which is the last great fortress of the world.

"I say: you shall see your beloved father once more. Virtue deserves such rewards."

Thus, the Sibyl addressed Aeneas.

With her to lead the way, the hero Aeneas plunged into the dark forest beside Lake Avernus. There he found the Bough all shining bright with gold. The Sibyl instructed him to break it from the tree. The hero obeyed her command.

Then he went down to stern Hades's kingdom under earth and saw that lord's piled-up riches. Next he saw the shadows, who were his own paternal ancestors. He saw at last the feeble, white-haired ghost who in life had been his father, lordly Anchises.

There in hell were revealed to Aeneas his future life, the laws of hell under which he ultimately lived, the perils on earth he must face and overcome, and the wars he was destined to win.

To while away the weary journey uphill to earth again, he conversed with the priestess, even as his eyes strained to see the steep path by which they climbed.

"I cannot say who you are," he told her. "I cannot tell whether you are a goddess, or not. Perhaps you are some maiden, who enchanted the gods. I can only say that I consider you divine, and I always shall. I understand, and I freely confess, I owe my very life to you, Priestess. Without your care and guidance I could never have reached death's kingdom, nor ever seen its walls, nor ever put my heart at rest concerning my noble father Anchises, who was taken from me. Thanks to you, Priestess, I have escaped death myself, and now am almost safely past its major perils.

"Priestess, if I return safely all this dark way to the upper world of sun and air, I vow to build thee a temple and in that temple to burn offerings in thine honor."

The Sibyl turned to look him in the face. She sighed as she replied, "You may not call me goddess. Nor does mortal deserve the honor of a temple and its incense.

"However, let me say, for your information, that I was once offered immortality by Phoebus Apollo himself. He several times proposed to me, that is, to grant me eternal and everlasting life. May I explain so as not to leave you unenlightened: my maiden state in all modesty declined advances.

"The god Apollo then offered me gifts, saying, 'Maiden Priestess of Cumae, come choose whatever presents you like.'

"There before me was a pile of sand. I pointed with my hand to the sand and, without thinking it through, I asked him for as many years at Cumae as there were grains in the pile. As you see, and doubtless sympathize, I did not have the presence of mind to request youth as well as years.

"But Apollo thought of it. 'You may also have eternal youth,' he told me 'if you will yield to my passion.'

"I spurned his second gift, because of that condition. I took only years from him. I chose to remain virginal. I have never married. . . . As you doubtless have observed, I am no longer chasing youth's rainbow. My young years have fled like a first breath of spring. I totter now when I walk. Every day I grow weaker. I shall have many more years to endure this wretched old age of mine . . . before my years can catch the grains of sand.

"Three hundred years of a feeble body growing weaker every day stretch endlessly before me: three hundred harvests, three hundred vintages. As the scroll of time unfolds, it will shrink me down, melt more of my flesh, shorten my bones, melt my marrow until from this still large body that you now see I shall have shrunk to a tiny, weightless, wisp of a 'thing.'

"Before that happens, people will doubt I ever could have turned heads or aroused a god's ardor. When that day comes, Phoebus Apollo himself will gaze at me as if he sees me for the first time. Should I remind him he once found me beautiful, he will protest.

"What will be left of me then? What will be left to me? For I shall dwindle down to a nothingness alive, wind down to an unrecognizable shade of my formerly robust self. No eye will know me then. What comfort then?

"This comfort: the world shall still hear my voice. The Fates have allowed it. The Eumenides have granted me this."

v. 153

Scipio's Descent into Hell (from the Punica *by Silius Italicus)*

Foreword

Today classical scholars say Silius Italicus "invented" a poor work about how the Roman Commander Scipio descended into the Underworld. Scipio, Silius wrote, went there to pay his respects to his father and his uncle, Scipio Africanus Major and Minor, those brilliant generals who had fought the first two

Punic Wars, Rome vs. Carthage. The poem is important because it demonstrates clearly that Romans did believe they once
boasted a real priestess who could accomplish the hardest
priestly task, to descend alive into the Underworld, to escort a
famous Roman warrior and veteran there, and to bring him
back alive.

Silius had become, by the time he retired, an immensely successful, high functionary of the Roman Empire, from being
Nero's adviser promoted to august proconsul of Asia. He had
long awaited retirement and free time in which to write this
longest poem in the Latin language. Silius Italicus survived
Nero's friendship and prospered so well he rose to eminence
in politics and amassed a treasure in gold and precious art
works. Apparently, he did all this legally. As soon as he had
retired, Italicus commenced buying up real estate in Campania. He bought most of Cumae, parts of Naples, the coastline between the two cities, and including Vergil's tomb (now
lost), after which he spent another fortune in its restorations.
His Cumae is real.

One can hardly blame Italicus for loving Vergil, Ovid, and
Cumae to that degree. He was a passionate antiquarian, a col-
lector of ancient memorabilia, antiques, art of all kinds, property where the great had sat, objects the great had handled,
but especially rare books. Having lived also in Asia, where he
had been governor, Silius Italicus collected manuscripts, scrolls,
pieces of paper, carvings, statues, busts, and all the oral testimony his secretaries and other minions could transcribe. Then,
like Vergil before he wrote the *Aeneid*, Silius Italicus walked the
terrain until he became too feeble and ill to walk it lovingly
once again. He too loved the aged Sibyl.

Very few have praised him, and even Martial, who praised
him, thought old Italicus had no genius; he was merely indus-
trious. Critics have found him lacking Vergil's charm, and Lucan's power. Most of all, his critics have found Italicus ma-
cabre. The old man was a ghoul, they said.

But was it so ghoulish to describe Cumae again: the Sibyl,
the descent to hell, and especially to put Scipio there? He was
Rome's great, last conqueror of Hannibal. When the Carthaginians lay prostrate in defeat, even then, they refused to sur-

render. Scipio had to kill them, house by house, before he razed Carthage and strewed it with salt. He needed to descend in order to be absolved.

Italicus made a final error. He should have made Scipio the hero of his seventeen books of epic poetry, the *Punica*. But he let African Hannibal be his hero. In retirement Silius grew very brave. Before he died, he spoke his mind:

XIII, v. 385

Young Scipio was home at Pozzuoli on the Bay of Naples for rest and a visit when the news of his relatives' death was brought to him. At this loss of his august father and uncle, young Scipio tore his robes and beat his breast in a fury of grief. He could not get their dear faces out of his sight. He therefore decided, since his villa was so near Cumae, to consult Apollo's priestess Autonoë in her cave there and ask to descend to Avernus.

The priestess made no objection but instructed him as to what sheep he should sacrifice before dawn and how to let the blood of a black sheep, a black bull, and a virgin heifer drain from their living throats so the dead could lap the blood. She said she would then call up from hell the High-priestess of the dead, the ghost of the Cumaean Sibyl, who had passed away. He was also to take honey and wine.

Scipio arose from his bed and presented himself with his offerings, exactly at midnight, at the storm-swept gate of black Tartarus. There the priestess sat in her dark cavern.

Scipio saw the earth crack open. He smelled sulphurous breath.

He dug his trench and cut the animals' throats. The priestess sat and chanted words he could not comprehend at all except that the third realm of the world, after Heaven and Earth, was Hell, she said, which was even then opening to him.

"Let no one drink the blood," she cried, "until the Sibyl comes."

While Scipio fought off the thirsty ghosts, he could not help remembering what he had learned during his military service abroad: how in Spain they let vultures devour the dead, how in Persia they throw them to the dogs, how in Egypt they stand them upright in coffins and then invite them to banquets, how on the Black Sea coasts they extract the brains and embalm the bodies, how in central Africa they bury the corpses in sand, and how in Libya they commit their dead to the Atlantic Ocean. The bearded Celts up in the north are the most barbarous: they encase the skull in gold and use it as a drinking cup. In

Athens they passed the law that all soldiers who died in battle were to be burned on one funeral pyre. But the Scythians tie their dead to trees and let time dispose of them.

"Be still," Autonoë warned him. "The Dame of Cumae is approaching. Ah, here is her ghost. Here comes that wellspring of truth, she who received in her lifetime more revealed knowledge than Apollo himself ever had. Now your followers and I must leave you. Place your victims upon the fire."

First the Dame of Cumae touched her lips to fresh blood. Then she, repositor of all the lost knowledge of earth, stood studying young Scipio's face. "While on earth I joyed in heaven's light," she began. "My voice was heard from Cumae to the ends of the earth.

"I prophesied your career also," she continued, "and I recognize you. But King Tarquin paid little heed to my warnings. Your own ancestors lacked the intelligence to acquire the *Sibylline Books* when they were for sale. Now you come here, young man, to hear your destiny, do you, and the destiny of mighty Rome? Very well.

"Although not much more than a boy, you will command in Spain, and you will conquer Carthagena, that other Carthage. You will live to wipe the smiles from Carthaginian faces altogether and forever. You will pursue them out of Spain and herd them back into Africa. You yourself will conquer Hannibal. I feel shame for those who, when they should be grateful, will haul you, after all your heroisms, into court on personal charges that will tarnish your name forever."

Although she had already turned away from him, Scipio begged her to stay. "I will endure it all, as destiny allots me my sorrows, but, Priestess, grant me to see my dead fathers. In your life, Priestess, you came to the aid of mankind in all his perils. . . . Call up for me my mute and ghostly dead departed."

Although she seemed inclined to grant this wish, the priestess first warned Scipio: "This third kingdom should not be so ardently desired. Here in total dark the countless hordes of dead generations twitter and flit, shadows among shadows. Here they are all alike finally and all made equal. There to that empty void, beneath our feet descend all who were ever born in Earth, Air, or Sea from the beginning of the world's creation. That naked wasteland stretches so far it can accommodate them all, side to side, or end to end."

v. 531

"The kingdom of Pluto has ten gates for persons to enter, in this order: 1) warriors, 2) law-givers, 3) pagans (country dwellers), 4) artists, 5) shipwrecked sailors, 6) sinners who have confessed, 7) women, 8) babies and maidens, 9) the just, who dwell beyond the Ocean and beside the Fountain of Youth, in the Elysian Fields, where they drink to forget their life on earth, and 10) the souls who have risen to heaven, where after five thousand years of paradise they will enter new bodies and spend another lifetime on earth.

"Outside Hell's realm, pale *Morta* wanders with her deathly jaws avid for rejects, pacing back and forth outside Hell's gates."

v. 561

"Every Figure of man's destruction glides through Hell and lies in wait: Grief, Illness, Sorrow, Pallor, Remorse, Insanity, Betrayal, Regret, Age, Envy, Poverty, Error, and Conflict. They roam beside the monsters and the Furies, the Centaurs, the Giants, and Cerberus, the Hound of Hell.

"You would see lines of guilty rulers of men there, standing there in chains, awaiting Pluto's judgment, and Prometheus in chains with the vulture devouring his liver."

v. 732

"If you wish also to see the Carthaginian general Hamilcar Barca, you must first allow him to taste blood. Then he will stand still and speak to you, although I doubt he will relax his usual fierce frown, even after death, or put aside his bitter, fierce hatred of Rome and all your kin."

Scipio called up the Carthaginian father of Hannibal, and let him drink all he wanted. Then he chastised him roundly, "Tell me, you father of traitors, why did you break your nonaggression treaty with Rome? Why did you break your agreement with us, who released you from captivity, and guaranteed you safe-conduct out of Sicily?

"Look at what your son is doing now! He has broken all his sacred treaties with us! He has brought the war into Italy. Yes, to the gates of Rome. He has broken over all borders and crossed all frontiers. He has brought his elephants over the Alps. (He has enlisted the Gauls against us.) Now he falls upon our citizens. He lays waste our lands. He has set fire to country and cities alike. He has so choked our rivers with our own dead that they run upstream rather than down to the seas."

The Carthaginian general replied to Scipio, "My son Hannibal was a boy, barely ten years old, when he swore a solemn oath, as I bade him do, to continue the war against Rome. There is no way he will ever betray his gods, who are my gods also.

"If this is true and if my son Hannibal is now wreaking havoc upon your Latin land, then, hail to thee, my dear son Hannibal! Thou art truly my son, truly a good and honorable son to me, thy father, and faithful to the oath I had thee swear. . . . I pray my son will recover all the lost glory of Carthage."

Holding high his head, Hamilcar Barca turned away from Scipio and proudly went his way alone. The farther he went, the taller he seemed to grow.

v.751

Next the priestess *(vates)* pointed with her finger toward the illustrious military men, and then to the lawgivers who had shaped Rome's laws from those of Athens. Scipio admired the Ten Men entrusted with interpreting the Sibyl's *Books,* and would have stood there overcome with admiration if she had not remonstrated with him again.

"You may well stand spellbound here," she said, "but please consider how many thousands of spirits have descended to this hell over the ages. How many are there, would you say? Not a minute goes by but Charon ferries another load of them to this farther shore, and still they crowd down for passage. Even his spacious craft does not suffice to afford them rapid transit."

The Dame of Cumae wanted him to see Alexander the Great because of his military might, and because he too had honored with his presence the Oracle of Zeus Amon in the Libyan Oasis.

"Act now," Alexander advised Scipio curtly. "Be bold," he added. "Attack is the watchword. Black Death's behind you."

Scipio was thrilled to see Homer, whom he recognized because of his shining, broad forehead. "Ah," said the Sibyl, "Homer raised Troy high enough to become the mother of Rome."

Scipio also saw the heroes Achilles, Hector, Ajax, and Castor.

Then the Sibyl reviewed, as they passed, the ghosts of the most famous Roman women. She showed him Aeneas's Latin wife Lavinia. She showed him Hersilia, the peacemaker and wife of Romulus, for she it was who brought peace after the Romans stole the Sabine women. She showed him Carmenta, mother of Evander, who prophesied that Rome and Carthage would wage three bloody wars. She showed him another priestess, Queen Tanaquil, who was married to King Tarquin I. She could foretell the future by studying the flight of birds into or from the four "regions" of the sky. He also saw that model of chastity, Lucretia, whose rape caused the expulsion of the Tarquin kings and the establishment of the republic.

Standing by her was the ghost of Virginia, whose breast still bled; her father killed her rather than have her raped by Appius Claudius.

She also showed him the virgin Cloelia who, when she was given as hostage, jumped into the Tiber River and swam to safety, thus halting an Etruscan army. She exemplified in life the triumph of Roman womanhood.

Scipio also saw a guilty woman being castigated. "That is the ghost of Tullia," the Sibyl told him, "who smashed her father by driving her chariot wheels back and forth over his body. She will have to float forever on the river of fire.

"There beside her you see another wretched girl, the wicked maiden Tarpeia who loved gold so much she let the Sabines into Rome. They had promised to 'reward her,' and so they did. They dealt her sudden death.

"There is the dog Orthrus whom Heracles killed. Do you remember? Orthrus guarded the Gorgon's cattle in Spain. . . . They use him here to yank out the bowels from guilty women, whose crime is beyond any other punishment. Over there is one such, a Vestal Virgin who broke her vows."

v. 890

"Could you, as a last favor, tell me what will happen to Hannibal?" Scipio asked.

"He will have to leave Africa," she said, "and he will lose both wife and son. When Rome has him at her mercy and demands his surrender, he will take poison. . . ."

Then Scipio returned joyfully to his comrades-in-arms; and the Sibyl, to her cavern below Cumae.

THE ROMAN CONQUEST OF GAUL

"Led by Vercingetorix they collected all their forces and tried to expel the foreigner from central Gaul. By the utmost exertion of his activity and a series of well-planned manoeuvres, Caesar suc- ceeded in surrounding the Gauls at Alesia and inflicting upon them a decisive defeat. His business in Gaul was finished, and all that Gaul could give him he had got—military reputation, an army, and money."
        Mikhail Ivanovich Rostovtzeff
        A History of the Ancient World, Vol. 2 (Oxford, 1927).

"Yet so strong was the unanimity of Gaul as a whole for the maintenance of their liberty and the recovery of their ancient re- nown in war that no benefits, no memory of friendship could influence them, and all devoted themselves with heart and strength to the campaign before them" (p. 489).
        C. Julius Caesar
        Commentarii de bello gallico, trans. by H.J. Edwards.
        The Gallic War (New York and London, 1930).

JULIUS CAESAR VERSUS THE CELTS

The real question that looms very high now as Celts of ancient Gaul mass again to resist conquest by Rome is this: how to find the High-priestess of Gaul who, say Roman historians, once led that resistance? Like other priestesses sought so far, the High-priestess of Gaul, sometimes called Velleda, seems impossible to find. How are we even to dream of finding her, after two thousand years of virtual oblivion? Reconstituting so lost a past seems an impossible dream. We must begin by reexamining what little we think we know.

Everybody knows who Julius Caesar was, but who were the Celts he conquered? Opinions differ. Irish historian Douglas Hyde wrote in 1906: they were "vainglorious" clansmen who once ruled about one-quarter of Europe. The Greeks first called them Hyperboreans, among whom, they said, their god Apollo regularly retired. Their eastern branch was known as Galatians. In their western realms, such as France and Spain, they were known as Celts, or Celtiberians. But what of a leader-priestess?

Imagine the well-trained Roman generals, supported by legions, failing to exterminate all the Gauls! A Roman general was once stopped by a priestess? The Gauls say it was Ireland, including Gaelic Man, which furnished their priestesses.

The first three Roman victories over the Celts took two hundred years, until 300 B.C. They learned first lessons there about their new subjects, whom they also recognized for what they admittedly were: defiant and *titanic* Celts. After having swept a clean swath through Italy, Spain, and the Danube River regions, the Romans turned and wiped out Carthage. It had absorbed remnants of defeated Celts. Druid priestesses should probably have known better than to defy Rome. It was these Druidesses who had negotiated payments and indemnifications from Hannibal in exchange for his passage into Italy. This is a first reference to learned priestesses who were Druids, and empowered to negotiate on behalf of their warriors.

Century after century Roman Legions, well armed, well paid, and superbly led by brilliant military men commissioned in Rome, moved millions of tons of Celtic soil in order to encircle the Celts of western Europe, clan by clan, hill-fort by hill-fort, tribe by tribe, province by province, until the last survivors *welcomed surrender and death.* This is fact; they welcomed it. After a while the Romans saw whom they were up against: the Celts led by their Druids had no fear of Death. Death, the Druids preached, was father to them all because he had created them.

Death was a father of theirs, to whom they would return. For centuries historians have relied on Julius Caesar's account of his conquest of the Celts in Gaul; he slanted it for one purpose only, to glorify himself as a military genius. As soon as he won that last siege at Alésia, Gaul, he hastened to cease his lying words and hunkered down in winter quarters. He had finally seen enough dead Gauls in that "one" war of his.

Caesar misrepresented the facts, firstly because it was far from having been one war. Those he defeated at Alésia in northern France were confederated, it is true, but only recently so. Caesar exaggerated the numbers of Gauls he defeated. The French claim he killed not more than 268,000 Gauls there, from a total population not exceeding five millions in 52 B.C. The women customarily killed their children and themselves before the surrender. Caesar's bonus at Alésia was made up of men only: one as slave for each legionary. That was after young Prince Vercingetorix surrendered.

Prince Vercingetorix of Gaul was no King Arthur, and no Roman. He also lacked a powerful, canny Merlin behind him. Vercingetorix expected that his unselfish gesture of sacrifice would persuade Caesar to grant his people amnesty. He boyishly expected a hero's generosity, but what he received was chains for himself and slavery for his followers. Vercingetorix failed to realize how unreasonable and how unwordly his chivalry appeared to others who considered themselves more civilized.

Today the dead Gauls and their landscapes are hard to imagine, so daunting are their size. The primeval forests of Gaul then covered that rich land. The wealth of modern France, in resources, metals, foodstuffs, animals, textiles, timber, but especially in industries based upon metal still astonishes the modern historian. Nor do they exaggerate the easy living, nor the opulence and elegance of warrior and priestess in Gaul, nor the quiet, watchful power of Druidism.

French historian Albert Grenier turned to the Roman Emperor Julian for a more honest impression of ancient Gaul: "I happened to be in winter quarters at my beloved Lutetia—which is what the native Gauls there call the capital of the tribe called Parisians. We lived on their small island, which lies in

the middle of the Seine River. The citadel is entirely surrounded by a wall. They have built wooden bridges, which
afford access on either side. The river flow is more or less
constant, summer and winter. What a delight to have such pure,
clear water at hand! The winters there in Gaul are mild. The
Gauls allow no heat in their quarters, and so one gradually
grows quite healthy while hardening oneself to the cold. . . ."

The ancient Gauls who fought Caesar were so tall, so gallant, so splendid, and their priestesses so solemn and so virginal, that it is no wonder the Roman military genius Caesar
put down his pen after having slaughtered hundreds of thousands of them at Alésia, and given the rest into slavery and
chains.

The Gallic warriors wore their hair long. They had had it
bleached and curled. Then they gathered it into a tuft atop
the head, much in the style of the Amazon warrior-priestesses
as they are depicted at Ephesus. The Gauls were bearded, and
wore long, drooping moustaches. Julius Caesar was himself almost emaciated, for he had long suffered from epilepsy, and
he was bald and clean-shaven. He wore the short leather skirt
of the Roman legionary. The Druidesses, on the contrary, covered their bodies completely except for hands and feet, which
were bare.

The Gauls went into battle naked, if it was summer, and if
they were fighting near a river. Usually they wore superbly
tailored trousers that had been adjusted until they fitted the
limbs snugly, like modern bluejeans. The Gauls did not wear
the loose, baggy riding britches of Afghan or Scythian or Tar-
tar. They also wore either a short, full cloak fastened at one
shoulder by a penannular kilt pin, or a pleated plaid they could
wrap up in at night or in daytime secure at the waist by a large
black leather belt. Their blouse was the same loose, linen
shirt cut full at sleeve and shoulder, which is worn commemor-
atively by Scots around the world today. Their shoes of tanned
leather were waterproof, with thick soles. They called them
gallicae. They were excellent for kicking, as every French
schoolboy who still prefers feet to fisticuffs knows today.

The wool fabrics of the ancient Gauls resembled our modern tartans, as they are woven today in Hawick, Scotland. The

cloth was and is tightly woven worsted plaids of brilliant, intersecting bands of color for dress wear, but muted squares and bands of subdued and faded browns, blues, and greens for camouflage, hunting, and war.

These costumes adorned with eagles' feathers, hares' feet, fur purses, leather hawking gauntlets, gold, and precious gems were the costumes of both men and women. It was an aristocratic society, a sort which usually supports, encourages, and admires beautiful women also. The Romans in Rome were much taken by the tall, handsome women from Gaul, and by this warrior ethos such as George Rawlinson referred to when he tried to understand Asia with its superb Amazon warrior-priestesses:

> The Arian races seem in old times to have treated women with a certain chivalry, which allowed them the full development of their physical powers, and rendered them specially attractive alike to their own husbands and to the men of other nations.

Julius Caesar could not possibly have fought the Gauls so many years and seen so many hundreds of thousands of dead bodies, and neither known, nor met face to face, a princess or a priestess of the warrior Gauls. He was thirty years old when the then High-priestess of Gaul was seized by Romans and executed. Although this shameful deed was hushed up, Caesar too must have heard of it. Later Roman historians knew of it and recorded it. This High-priestess is historical, but still unknown.

The Celts of Gaul were particularly expert metalworkers. They loved swords, daggers, dirks, and kilt pins, but also emeralds, sapphires, topazes, and rubies. Over their dazzling costumes their princes of the blood royal wore characteristically ornate jewelled pieces: solid gold bracelets, kilt pins, collars, huge gold torques across their chests, and fibulas. None of their splendid armor or jewelled and chased weapons has been found in France, any more than King Arthur's sword, in Britain. A few pieces from the Clan Chieftains indicate the metals which separated their ranks: bronze, silver, and solid gold. Some gold torques, as worn by priestesses, and by men, have surfaced (see Fig. 19).

Their light, very fast war chariots were recorded by the Romans and perfectly described in Irish literature; they were the best in the world of their time, and so were each team, charioteer, and warrior or priestess. The Gauls practiced, as did the Scythians and Britons, the cult of the severed head. They beheaded their opponents, carried them slung on their chariots, or hung on their horses' chests, to be displayed later at home.

His largesse indicated the leader's rank—his hosting of banquets before combat being truly Lucullan, lasting for weeks. The genius of their artisans is proverbial, for the Gauls built five different wheeled vehicles for easy travel on the roads, and a superior navy off the Breton coast: flat-bottomed, oaken hulls with high keels fore and aft. Even so, the Romans beat them.

Common signs betrayed passage by the Celts over Europe: the single-bladed ax designating royalty, the sheathed sword indicating peace, the *carnyx* or three-tubed war trumpet held vertically, the torque of Druidess or Druid with knobs at each end of its arc, the bardic harp as at Tara's Hall, the cauldron of inspiration with its braided metal handle, the king's mallet as in Camelot (*caer* + mallet), the yoke with upraised palm in its center probably symbolizing truce, the masted ship of war, and a holy plant with one small, round berry. Duval thought this tiny plant was a *fleuron*, which is an ornament designed from flowers, and a common typographical ornament used at the beginning or end of a chapter in a book. The Celtic design in question is not made of flowers, however. It is a delicate sprig of thin, spare leaves with one berry at its top, and it looks very much like the European mistletoe *(Viscum album)* commonly seen in northwestern France.

The torque, which was worn by both royal men and royal women, is found primarily in the graves of the latter sex. The word is of Latin origin, from the verb *torquere:* to twist, turn, bend, or wind around. The torque itself is of unknown origin, say French dictionaries, which often prefer not to know—for reasons of harmony. The torque was a symbol, then, usually worn by a woman of enough distinction to have it buried with her. Texts refer to it as being worn by persons of exalted rank and immense wealth. It was a twisted collar, often of heavy gold, and of great size so that it covered the neck or came down into a ∪ or a ∇ on the chest. There is definitely more to it than that, however, despite the reticence of French dictionaries.

"Torquatus," a wearer of a torque, was the Roman T. Manlius whose cognomen derived from the fact that he wore the torque of a Gaul whom he had slain. The Latin dictionary thinks it was of twisted (or braided) gold: a neck chain. But "to twist" also means in Romance languages "to torture" or "to be put to the test." Therefore, it seems possible that the women who wore most of the torques found in Gaul were priestesses who had successfully undergone an arduous initiation into the priesthood.

When Caesar says a few words about religion in Gaul, he should again be dismissed, say French historians. The Gauls possessed in common two sacred cults: water and trees. A Roman should have seen the connection: Lake Avernus and the Golden Bough, the maiden *Dryad* imprisoned in an oak, and the Druid Priestess of the Oak.

A Roman Consul in Toulouse in 106 B.C. found in a lake that had just been drained a large quantity of gold, which by weight and description could well have been that taken by King Bran from the Delphic Oracle centuries before. The British Lady of the Lake represented a water deity such as the ones in Gaul, like the Mother Goddess Matrona for which the Marne River was named.

This homogenous, ancient culture which Edward Gibbon called "German," especially after the Germans withdrew from conquered Gaul and refused to submit to Roman rule, once embraced more than a third of Europe. After Gaul fell, the German Celts continued independent east of the Rhine and north of the Danube, until eventually they "overturned . . . the western monarchy of Rome" (I, p. 208). Their Teutonic religion continued to venerate priestesses, says the German scholar Jan de Vries (pp. 217–19).

The greatest priestess of them all was the High-priestess of Gaul, Velleda, who was born in 70 B.C. in Teuton, Dutch, or Germanic territory, but who led the Gauls in a major rebellion against Rome. Her case needs closer scrutiny, but she herself stands out so prominently because no other such warrior priestess was recorded by historians until the career of Jeanne d'Arc, also born in ancient, Germanic lands. The Germans remember their priestesses' title, however; they called their Druid priestesses "Gertrudes."

Before turning to the religion of ancient Gaul and the territories ruled by their ancient kinfolk, the Germans, it might be appropriate to recapitulate evidence concerning Gaul and its conqueror.

Gaul *(Gallia)* is a term first applied by the Greek colonists in Marseilles and then by the Romans (c. 600 B.C.) to designate the large geographical area south and west of the Rhine River, west of the Alps, and north of the Pyrenees Mountains. This land, ancient Gaul, now comprises: (1) France, (2) Belgium, (3) Luxembourg, (4) a part of Holland, (5) Germany, and (6) Switzerland.

Between 100 B.C. and Caesar's Gallic Wars (58–51 B.C.) Rome acquired Aquitania in the southwest of this territory, Gaul in the center, and Belgium in the north. Caesar divided it thus, but Augustus reorganized it into four provinces. Approximately thirty-six tribes or Celtic clans occupied what is today France; each group settled around a large citadel or fortress city.

Caesar's Wars (58–51 B.C.)

	1) Helvetii (Helvetians) stopped from crossing out of Switzerland to S.W. Gaul, defeated at Bibracte.
	2) Aedui (Aeduans) asked Caesar to help whip the German Ariovistus. Done.
	3) Belgians were pacified.
56 B.C.	4) *Veneti* on the Gulf of Morbihan, had a fleet. Caesar built a fleet and defeated them.
55 B.C.	5) Caesar crossed the Rhine near Cologne. Then he crossed the Channel to Britain.
54 B.C.	6) Caesar invaded and "conquered."

The Celtic chieftain Ambiorix with Belgians rebelled and destroyed one legion. Caesar had to intervene personally in order to defeat him. The Celtic chieftain called "Dumnorix" by Caesar (*ri an domhain* = King of the World) rebelled against Caesar and died.

53–52 B.C.   The Belgians again rebelled and were again defeated.

c. 52 B.C.   The Gallic chieftain called "Eporedorix" by Caesar (*ri echraide* = King of Horses) was also defeated.

Prince Vercingetorix (*uer-cinget-rix* = over warriors king) of the *Arverni* (Auvergne in France), who was born in 73 B.C., rallied almost all Gaul in 52 B.C., causing Caesar to recross the Alps and take command personally. The Romans cut off the Celts from their reinforcements and shut Prince Vercingetorix in the hill-fort of *Alésia* (Alise-Sainte-Reine, near Dijon). Caesar then starved the besieged. Vercingetorix, aged twenty-one, rode out in his own chariot and surrendered to Caesar, then aged forty-nine. Caesar took the prince in chains to Rome and obliged him to walk behind Caesar in his ceremonial march, or Triumph, through the capital.

Prince Vercingetorix was kept chained in an underground dungeon, which is still shown to tourists in Rome, for six more years. Then, after being reduced to a skeleton, he was publicly beheaded, as Julius Caesar accepted plaudits.

The Druid High-priestess of Germany and Gaul, Velleda, had led a rebellion against Rome in 70 B.C. She also was defeated, probably taken to Rome, and executed there.

The twentieth century has seen a number of excellent books on Druidism and one which offers considerable positive proof that this religion was followed throughout Celtic lands. After listing again all the ancient authors who mentioned Druids, and after giving again their names or titles in Gaelic and other Celtic languages, A.L. Owen (Oxford, 1962) finally found a way to prove that Druids really existed.

This proof came from Roman Law, which duly recorded that the Emperors Augustus, Tiberius, Claudius, and Valerius Maximus *forbade, persecuted,* or *suppressed* Celtic Druids. Valerius Maximus expressed astonishment in 31 A.D. that such crude barbarians, *actually clad in barbaric garments called "trousers,"* should share the beliefs of the lordly Pythagoras. By 400 A.D., in other words, the Druids had already been rigorously suppressed for at least the last three hundred fifty years. It was even forbidden to name their names.

French historians have never been able to decipher the attitude of Julius Caesar concerning Druids, whose Arch-Priest he placed vaguely inside "Britain." His charge was one that modern English historians such as Piggott, Kendrick, and Chadwick have been obliged to deny. How could Caesar have elevated Druids, and then refrained from granting them a role in Gaul? And Gaul was the very place where their High-priestess had been, in Caesar's lifetime, actively engaged. Yet, in Caesar's terse military moves, not even the name Druid appears in opposition. And yet one hundred years after him, the Druids of Gaul are still preaching and fomenting rebellion against Rome. Caesar referred to Druids in Britain, against a mountain of evidence that where they continued their ministry was Ireland and Scotland, says Lavisse (p. 55), and that until the beginning of the Middle Ages.

The Druids were the ancient equivalent of university professors, trained as educators of young aristocrats. They were also learned astronomers and mathematicians to whom the calendar and its holy days were entrusted. They appeared at religious and political assemblies of the noble Gauls and other Celts who yearly held tribunals for the nobility only.

The Druids built no temples and seem to have worshipped no idols. They met in secret at forest clearings, oak groves, and on mountaintops. We are sure of this, for the Roman Commander Suetonius Paulinus in 61 A.D. scattered the Druids in Brittany by setting fire to their sacred groves. Some French scholars prefer to believe that Druidism was not universal among the Celts, but restricted to parts of Great Britain, which included Ireland and the Isle of Man, and to central and northern Gaul-Germany.

It is generally agreed in France that the Druids believed in life after death, therefore in grave goods, and in metempsychosis. The vision of a transatlantic Elysium haunted them all. They looked to an overseas journey into the Atlantic at their life's end, and believed that the dead return for a period of millennia to the autochthonous western land of their ancestors. Thence, after long forgetfulness, uninterrupted bliss, and purification from all the sorry emotions of life, they return in new bodies to earth. Each comes "trailing clouds of glory" from the exoceanic, "western" cradle of his race.

Many continental scholars, and including Salomon Reinach in his *Orpheus* (1909), also believed that Druidism originated in Ireland, to which land even the Druids of Gaul, national treasures though they were, eventually returned. The Greek and Roman pantheon died, he said (p. 177), because they had never come alive, while the ancient Druidical beliefs of the Celts had taken root so deeply into native soils that they could not be eradicated. Even their secret priestesses were not burned until the case of Jeanne d'Arc, burned by the English in 1430. Their kings were tabooed, and so the princes were educated by their aunts and uncles, who were Druids. To them, the cock, hen, and goose were sacred, the hare was an augural creature, and gold booty such as was carted away from Delphi was cast into a lake as eternally untouchable. Inside Britain, even in King Arthur's declining years, a prince like Perceval was educated by a Druid priestess, Cundry, noted Jean Markale (Paris, 1971).

Was not that education the Socratic system of question-and-answer? asked T.W. Rolleston. And also, was not the Druidical belief that each Celt alive had returned unto a new life after a long rest in Elysium, taken from and echoed in the Druidical symbol of three circles, also representative of Atlantis, whose concentric rings reduplicated the novice's path to wisdom: *Abred, Ceugant, Gwynfyd*? Were they not the three circles of being on the path that lasts twenty years from primary school, to secondary, to university?

Question:	Where was thy beginning?
Answer:	In the Underworld.
Question:	Where art thou now?
Answer:	In the Little World; I am now a man.
Question:	Through how many forms hast thou progressed?
Answer:	Water, Earth, Air, in all suffering. I must know it all before I reach the next circle of knowledge.

Two very important French works on Druidism stress the importance of women in this priesthood, but many others disagree. In his Preface to *La Druidesse,* Edouard Schuré develops further his initial discoveries concerning the Pythia and Pytha-goras. Whence came all this emphasis upon love, if not from Druidism? he asked. There was no romantic love in Greek and Roman letters. Before Druidism, women were objects to be kept inside the house.

Celtic history, observed Schuré, acts like a riptide. The phe-nomenon is curious, indeed. Every time it is silenced and re-futed, it surges back again twice as powerful, four times faster. Celtic history must go all the way back to the K-M-R, the un-derground Cimmerians who beside the Sibyl's grotto acted as psychopomps. They were sacred, hellish creatures. Their priestesses sacrificed strangers, as Iphigenia waited in Tauris to do, on the altars of unknown gods.

The Gauls were not so different from the other Celts be-yond the Rhine and below the Alps. One and all, they were the terrors of the ancient world (Schuré, p. 23) everytime they loomed on the horizon, armed to the teeth. Their chief traits were a thoughtless impetuosity after which, exhausted, they collapsed into contemplation and deep reverie. Such opposi-tion defined their hereditary temperament. Either the Scots raced into battle madly, as they followed Jeanne d'Arc, or they sat dreamily staring into space. Those Celts who followed her lie buried now in her own cathedral at Orléans.

Julius Caesar had them pegged: kill their chief, he opined, or take Vercingetorix prisoner, and the rest will eagerly follow him into death *of their own accord, with no exception.* Caesar had reasoned correctly, and history bore him out, that the Gauls ran unhesitatingly to their death as soon as their prince left them. Schuré argued that this confrontation pitted Vercinge-torix against eight centuries of Roman military discipline and hard experience learned in the field. Thus, he left Vercinge-torix to suffer the long punishment for his lack of caution, in the Mamertine Dungeon at Rome.

The priests and priestesses of the Druids appeared to have been defeated by their own teachings. These wise "oak" prel-ates, dressed in white linen and crowned with garlands, ap-peared powerless, despite their knowledge of astronomy, bot-any, medicine, prophecy, augury, thought, and ethics. They appeared to have vanished before such a war machine as Caesar maneuvered endlessly, effortlessly. Their precepts—worship the gods, do no evil, and practice bravery—Caesar thought had been turned against them at Alésia. Caesar thought he had judged the Gauls correctly; they were more than "half in love with easeful death." He therefore reported that they believed themselves created by Dis Pater, god of the dead. If a Gaul reached *Gwynfyd* at the center of the circles, he would finally remember all his former existences and all his reincarnations. At Alésia, in the real world, he was beaten, killed, given permanently into slavery. What was not immediately apparent was the new lease on life the Roman population signed when the Gauls were brought into Rome. Nor had Caesar reckoned on all those heroic warriors and statesmen waiting in the Atlantic Elysium, ready and eager to enter the political arena in new bodies.

Every spring equinox the Druid priestesses in Gaul threw aromatic branches of sacred herbs, verbena, primrose, clover, and their mysterious "golden herb" upon the fires around which the Gauls collected. On Mother Night the mistletoe which grows only on the dormant, snow-covered oak and which blossoms only on that shortest, darkest day of the year, was harvested year after year by golden sickles while the priestess held her linen cloth to receive it.

Therefore the peaceful Druids, as still as ghosts upon bare feet, prayed: Be not dismayed. The human soul comes from elsewhere, becomes again a body in other flesh. It survives Rome and the death of winter. As the mistletoe blooms only in the snow, falls only to gold, and drops only into this holy priestess's pure linen cloth, it brings us all a promise of renewal. It promises to all a New Year. It beckons to all a return this night of all the dear, departed souls who once lived beside us here, in our Gaul. It signals to you and me the immortal life of man and his continuous renewal. It announces again the victory of man, not over Rome but over death. This night our priestess becomes the Moon. She will rise now and escort the souls who await reincarnation back upon our sacred earth again.

This was the doctrine, declared Edouard Schuré, which has fired and dominated the Celtic race, and which has persisted across the centuries. It underlies and informs the ancient history of France.

That there were always hundreds of priestesses in Gaul was reported by Strabo, Polybius, and Plutarch among others. In addition, there remain scores of stories still told about the heroism, the battles fought, and the ingenuity of Gallic heroines and Queen-priestesses. One such comes from Polybius (XXII, XXI):

The Story of the Galatian Queen Chiomara

Somewhere between the third and second century B.C. the Romans defeated the Galatians and subdued almost all of them. Roman Consul Manlius took credit for the final, terrible battle that ended in his victory over three allied tribes. The Galatians made a last stand on the slopes of Mt. Olympus.

These eastern Gauls lost everything, their loot which they were hauling with them, their goods and provisions, plus their supplies and valuables. Their Chieftain escaped up the mountain. The survivors who remained on the field of combat were taken prisoner.

To his surprise the Consul Manlius recognized among the lines of hostages none other than the Chieftain's wife, Queen Chiomara. She was captured, still fighting after the retreat had sounded.

The Centurion in charge of the prisoners also saw the holy lady of Celtic royalty among the prisoners. He started out by rolling his eyes and attempting to please her. He strutted up and down before her. When she would not flirt in return, he injured her. Then he abused her. After this, when he considered her thoroughly humiliated, he offered her freedom in exchange for one Greek coin in gold.

The queen asked permission to contact her parents and ask them to meet her and the Centurion that night, and to bring money. She asked to dispatch one of her slaves on that errand. The girl was instructed to set up a rendezvous at the river that night. The queen agreed with the Centurion that she would purchase her freedom. He made her swear, and she swore it.

The parents of Queen Chiomara met their daughter and the Roman Centurion by the riverbank that night. The queen handed over gold to the Centurion, who had brought a scale so he could be certain to get his promised weight.

As he bent down to weigh and measure the gold, he turned his back to Queen Chiomara. "Now," she told her two parents, "kill him."

The queen's trophy was his severed head. She carried it up the mountain and threw it at her husband's feet.

She recited for him the tale of her injury and her abuse, but only after she had shown him her sweet revenge.

Various fragments from classical history and Celtic literature speak of the intelligence and heroism of aristocratic women, and of the Celts' veneration for priestesses:

1. It was a Chieftain's daughter who at a banquet for Greek mariners chose as her future husband the Greek Captain. This royal daughter, whose name is given differently in Aristotle and Thucydides, was named either Gyptis or Petta. She and her Greek husband founded Marseilles. Founders of cities were venerated as gods.
2. Two tribes of Gauls quarreled as they were campaigning in Italy (sixth century, B.C.). Their wives threw themselves on the ground between the armed groups. When they arose, they negotiated a mutually acceptable settlement of the dispute.
3. When Hannibal, who was an ally of the Gauls, prepared to cross their territory with seventy-five thousand foot soldiers and ten thousand mounted troops, Druidesses of Gaul forced him to agree beforehand that complaints by any Gaul would be heard without delay by Carthaginian magistrates, but that all complaints by a Carthaginian would be heard by a court made up of the "sacred women" of Gaul.
4. When the troops of the Gallic Chieftain Ariovistus were drawn up to meet Julius Caesar, they had to await their marching orders from the holy priestesses of Gaul (Plutarch's *Life of Caesar*).
5. When the Roman general Marius met the "Germans" in his final battles, he defeated them twice. He had not expected a third battle to follow. In that battle the Roman legions met and defeated an army of women only. Thus, they wiped out the entire population (Plutarch's *Life of Marius*).

   At Aix the Gauls in chariots fell upon the Romans after they had halted for the night and were digging in. Those charioteers and warriors again were all women.

This battle raged through the night. The Romans did not succeed in killing all these women until the next day.

6. Saint Jerome is reported to have said there were three hundred priestesses in Gaul. When those women who pleaded to become slaves of the Roman Vestal Virgins were refused, they promptly killed themselves.

7. Gallic coins prove that priestesses and Celtic women went to war in ancient times.

8. The evidence concerning a battle at Verceil horrified Rome. The Gauls had chained themselves together so they would die as one man. They were trampled by their own oxen.

Their women then mounted the men's war chariots and continued the battle. As soon as they faced certain defeat, they strangled their children, *whom they had brought with them,* and then cut their own throats.

One woman was found afterwards on the field, hanging from the shaft of her chariot, her two dead children tied to her ankles. They had been dragged along behind her corpse.

Strabo has testified that when defeat was imminent, the Celtic women, and these were probably their High-priestesses, assumed responsibility for killing everyone, themselves last.

9. The women of Gaul remained usually inside the circle of the chariots until the battle was lost. Then they took up arms. The weaker and ill women usually remained in a circle at the center of the fray. Plutarch tells how at one battle they were finally all hacked into pieces.

10. Scholars among the Bretons testify as follows from their traditional lore:

a. The Druids of Gaul came there *from Ireland* about 300 B.C.

b. The western isles off the coasts of Brittany were sanctuaries reserved by the Gauls for Druids and Drui-desses.

c. There were also colleges for Druid priestesses situated along the Loire River. No men were allowed.

d. Nine priestesses resided permanently on the *Isle de*

Sein. They forecasted the weather and lighted fires along that isle during storms at sea.

11.   When the Gauls assembled for a declared battle, they were preceded on the field by their High-priestesses, persons of first rank in all Gaul. These were white-haired women *carrying swords,* walking barefoot, dressed in long white robes with sashes of finest white linen, and belted with copper.

The Irish recorded the words of their prophetess, after the battle of Mag Tured, as follows:

> I shall see a world that will not suit me
> summer no bloom
> cow no milk
> women no modesty
> men no courage
> captives no king
>
> . . .
>
> trees no fruit
> sea no fish
>
> . . .
>
> bad advice from elders
> bad opinions from court
> everyone treacherous
> every boy thievish
> father in son's bed
> son in father's bed
> everybody a father-in-law's brother
>
> . . .
>
> a bad time

This poem, chant, or charm (the Latin *carmen* of the priestess Carmenta comes to mind) uttered by a Druid priestess gives us a glimpse into her psyche.

RESISTANCE AND THE
HIGH-PRIESTESS VELLEDA

The illustrious historian Edward Gibbon advanced a theory concerning the demise of Druidism, and therefore of its priestesses. It was a pagan religion, he explained, that was stamped out by laws promulgated and enforced by the Roman Empire. Druidism collapsed as soon as its priests and priestesses, religious services, and customs were forbidden by law. Had the Druids written theology, their form of paganism might have survived. In his *Decline and Fall of the Roman Empire*, III, p. 147, Gibbon wrote:

> But the imperial laws which prohibited the sacrifices and ceremonies of Paganism were rigidly executed; and every hour contributed to destroy the influence of a religion which was supported by custom rather than argument . . . but the victors themselves were insensibly subdued by the arts of their vanquished rivals.

A fascination with Gibbon's cryptic conclusion, that Rome stamped out Druid priestesses only to fall under their influence, introduces a new topic: the High-priestess Velleda.

The Druid priestesses themselves vanished, perhaps. This seems true if understood conditionally. That they disappeared from sight might more accurately express what happened. They stage-managed their own disappearing act, in other words.

Once when Roman soldiery, ordered to do so, massacred a band of Druids, including women, an event which has been supposed to have occurred on Anglesey Island, contiguous to the coast of North Wales, the Druids there offered no resistance. Or rather, what they presented to their murderers was a passive resistance. Note how soldiers killing in the line of duty become branded as murderers of innocent persons.

This failure to fight for their lives on the parts of Druid dignitaries garbed in long, white, priestly robes effected the most damaging sort of passive resistance. What Rome had created were martyrs. The propaganda value was immeasurable.

When the Druid band refused to fight, even to cry out, or speak, or plead, or run, they struck terror into Roman hearts. The Druids had another purpose: to light anew the fires of resistance in their noble pupils' hearts. Thus, they bound in tighter resolve a confederation of warrior aristocrats, with followers.

Now, since aristocratic societies alone invariably venerate and champion women, what Druidism needed next was a great priestess, preferably a Druid High-priestess, who would inflame the blaze already kindled. The Celtic peoples of northern Europe supplied the necessary climate and customs: an aristocratic warrior elite, *and* an unparalleled exaltation of Woman.

News of the mass martyrdom spread like wildfire. In death the martyred Druids lighted the torch they intended. So dying, they became next to immortal, which they also certainly intended. In such ways, as a result of such a public spectacle, "victors" are "insensibly subdued." They and others suffer the pains of guilt.

That massacre was recorded. It has become an often-quoted part of history. More significantly, it established for the Gauls a terrifying pattern of resistance.

Thus, in 1429 another priestly figure in white, a "White Maiden," *puella gallica,* from the eastern forest land of "White Gaul" emerged, hailed as a Druidess by the local peasantry, to strike rigid terror in her English foes. Jeanne d'Arc was, unbelievably, announced beforehand by cryptograms passed from hand to hand, decipherable by the use of Roman capital letters which, when added, gave *in advance* the year of her martyrdom: 1430. English sailors in Bristol harbor mutinied when they were ordered to embark for war in France against Jeanne and her allied Scots.

This Maiden from Gaul, who was burned at the stake at Rouen in 1430, has become a Saint. Incredibly, the first charge against her was that *she wore Celtic trousers* under her armor (to keep it from chafing her, she said, when she had to wear her armor several days in a row). *Sainte* Jeanne d'Arc now has her own cathedral, *Sainte Croix* (Holy Cross) at Orléans, France. One could also be tempted to consider her a Druidess in Velleda's image, fourteen centuries after the Druidess's death.

Such inclination may perhaps seem ridiculous, but also, perhaps, not so farfetched. Before Jeanne was captured, and she had just suffered a first defeat outside the walls of Paris, the chancellor of the University of Paris wrote for her a list of charges that would be laid at her door if she were ever captured alive. He warned her: You will be accused first of being

Figure 18. Celtic Warrior

unnatural, asexual and not feminine, *because you wear trousers.* Your answer to this charge should be: The warrior maiden Camilla also wore trousers centuries ago, near Rome itself, when she fought Aeneas and his settlers from Troy. She was a warrior. Warriors in Gaul also wear trousers. There is your "precedent."

The tragic death of Jeanne d'Arc also set people an unforgettable precedent, i.e., a repeated pattern of events. Victor Hugo always said that we may forget what happened in a book, and who did what, but the structure remains filed away in our minds. This pattern, which has been repeated to us as children in our textbooks, is peculiar: maiden, warrior, defeat, capture, immolation, martyrdom, sainthood. It is probably by now a deep structure of the human mind.

Jean Gerson, that unforgettable chancellor of the University of Paris, saw that such a pattern of events was being set in motion. "Camilla," he wrote Jeanne. "Velleda," we now say, and her armed resistance to Rome: white maiden, Druidess clad in white robes, a warrior *in extremis,* a High-priestess of Gaul captured, perhaps tortured, and martyred. It was bound to be heard by some author somewhere, but it was the Roman historian Tacitus who heard and recorded it.

Tacitus felt for Velleda as he felt for the Celts of Germany and Gaul. We Romans desolated all western Europe, he charged, and called it "peace." We killed truly admirable people.

Why might one have expected a Druid priestess to resist the Roman conquest of ancient *Celtica?* First of all, women are by their education at all times, in all cultures, in every century, specialists in the methodology of resistance. As small children they have all had to resist abuse and increasing discrimination. As she matures (if she matures) every woman has had to adopt firmly, and repeat to herself daily some such modern axiom: *"Je n'ai que l'idée que je me fais de moi-même pour me soutenir sur les mers du néant":* I have only the idea I have made of myself to sustain me on oceans of nothingness (Henry de Montherlant). Thus, man's weapons differ considerably from those used most commonly by women, and with such consummate skill as to be detectable only by other women: secrecy, guile, disguise, stealth, craft, dissimulation, and even Agatha Christie's expedient *in extremis*—poison.

Roman Vestal Virgins, doctrinally related to Saint Bridget's Vestals in Ireland, since both maintained the eternal, holy fire, exercised clever disobedience as most useful, but which turned out to be also a most dangerous form of resistance to authority. The more openly aggressive members of their Order foolishly underwent, in full view of Rome, the supreme penalty. The most intelligent beat the system, disobeyed as they pleased, and survived.

The most openly aggressive priestesses on record remain the ancient Amazons from the Hittite Empire, the days of Mycenaean Greece, and the Libyan troops of Queen Medusa. They worshipped the warrior goddess Mâ-Bellona, and Atargatis, the Syrian goddess. Later followers of Artemis-Diana also used weapons offensively and defensively. The tradition of warrior priestesses reached back to times immemorial. Those Druid priestesses who took up arms against Rome were descended from a long lineage of such heroines. When Vergil so lavishly praised Camilla and blamed Dido for cohabiting with Aeneas without having been wedded by him beforehand, he was also praising Druidical and warrior women, athletes all.

Another, and certainly the most formidable weapon employed by these priestesses of the Druids, was also the combative Cumaean Sibyl's chosen weapon: prophecy. The inspired words of the Irish priestess chanting after the carnage at Mag Tured may be memorized easily and are easily employed by poets (Villon) with variations upon a theme, by those close allies of all priestesses, the world's poets.

Priestesses resembled poets in the same tradition reported of Delphic Oracles themselves, pupils of the Muses. Few words reach the heart faster than those of an Oracle, a poet, or a priestess. By the same token, no words are more feared than her anathema. Delivered in solemn contralto tones, a priestess's prohibitions and curses can today perhaps be heard only in Grand Opera, but they are unforgettable.

The Druid priestess had yet another advantage, which was the cold of her northern territories and the open enjoyment of this cold by the Celts. Before deep snow and ice the Romans recoiled. Gibbon reported as much (III, IX, p. 210 ff.): the "severity of a winter campaign . . . chilled the courage of the Roman troops." But the Gauls, said Plutarch in his "Life" of Marius, often threw down their shields and upon them slid down the snow for pleasure. These "Gauls" were the Teutons and Cimbri whom Marius annihilated in 101 B.C., a total of three hundred thousand killed plus sixty thousand taken into slavery.

The High-priestess Velleda's war against Rome took place at the end of the great slave rebellion in Rome. The rebel gladiators led by Spartacus, one hundred fifty thousand strong, had defied Roman troops for three years then, and had just been slain the year of Velleda's capture. The year she probably entered Rome saw sixty thousand crosses hung with as many corpses of her countrymen erected along Rome's Appian Way.

Velleda must have considered, while she was still safe in Gaul, what measure she could possibly take if she were ever captured alive. All her adoring Celts must have envisioned it, and made up their minds as to what they could do in such an eventuality. Thus, suffering the worst beforehand, a person steels his or her courage. The measure of Velleda's position in Gallic society suggests the magnitude of her final solution. It would show Rome the full measure of her resistance, as made in public formally by a holy priestess.

In any case, said Gibbon, the admirable women of the Gauls and Germans lived secluded from the evils of Roman society as Romans themselves grew more and more licentious and depraved. The northerners treated their women "with esteem and confidence, consulted them on every occasion of importance," because of their own, peculiar belief concerning women.

The Gauls and Germans firmly believed that women possessed a "sanctity and wisdom more than human," that they were the true priestesses and by nature also the true visionaries:

> Some of these interpreters of fate, such as Velleda in the Batavian War (Tacitus, *History*, IV, pp. 61, 65), governed in the name of the deity the fiercest nations of Germany (Gibbon, III, IX, p. 222).

As much as they respected a priestess, they scorned an adulteress; she was driven out of their camps while being whipped.

The camps of the Gauls and Germans were shared equally by men and women, the latter fearless and "undaunted" even by the din and horror of battle. More than once, the women forced their men back into combat, so terribly did these Celtic women fear capture and resultant slavery (see Fig. 20). When that was true of ordinary women, the fear of their priestesses must have been tenfold; for what all men revered first and foremost in a priestess was her virginity, and this for both conscious and subconscious reasons. Priestesses were considered inviolate.

> Conscious pride taught the German women to suppress every tender emotion that stood in competition with honour, and the first honour of the sex has ever been that of chastity (p. 223).

Gibbon blames the martial spirit of these Celts not upon any Druid priestesses but upon a somewhat lower order of Druids, the bards or harpers. As priests, they too were maintained and rewarded by the aristocratic Clan Chieftains. These bards were the authors of the North, whose main tasks were the maintenance of genealogical records and, secondly, the composition of songs and epic poetry celebrating heroes. The great battle champions were preceded upon the field of combat, and their corpses escorted from it, by singing bards. Perhaps Velleda's story was first remembered in this way. Surely, the poets magnified it as they championed resistance.

Priestesses tend to characterize aristocratic societies, also concluded Rostovtzeff (I, p. 287): when aristocracies ruled Greece and Ionia, as always in Sparta, women played important roles, but they gradually declined in importance, privilege, respect, and power under democratic governments:

> Democracy banished women from the street to the home: the kitchen and the nursery, and the *gynaeceum,* a special part of the house reserved for women and children, now became their sphere.

This domination of Greek women forms a startling contrast when compared to ancient, Celtic Ireland, where women and daughters legally inherited land at the death of parents, where priestesses were both seers and Vestals, and where certain women, indicated as such by titles beginning with the initial syllable "Brig," were magistrates. A certain Brig Ambui, daughter of Senchad, even pleaded a case of a woman's right, says Eugene O'Curry in his *Manners and Customs of Ancient Ireland* (I, pp. clxx–clxxxi). Such "women of judgment" resemble others described by Strabo as a "class of druidesses." O'Curry adds:

> The Prophetess Velleda mentioned by Tacitus was no doubt one of them. The name must be generic, as it is related to the O(ld) N(orse) *vola, völva, fatadica.* The *Matres Familiae* (Mothers of the Family) were called in the Gaulish *lingua rustica* (country speech) *Matrae, Mairae* (Mothers) . . .

Mother (mara) is the last syllable in the names of the Galatian warrior heroine Chiomara and the British battle queen Guanhumara (Guinevere). O'Curry hammers the point home.

I may also refer to the position which women held in the councils of the Gauls of Italy and Gaul, to show that the *Brig Bretach* (Druidess of the Judgment) was not an isolated instance of a woman pleading the cause of women, but the representative of a very ancient and important institution, which has been the source of many customs and traditions.

An English Lady, imprisoned on the Isle of Man in the aftermath of Jeanne d'Arc's death, lamented the passing of Druidism. Elinor Cobham wrote in her letter (recorded by A. L. Owen):

They say that *Druides*, once lived in this Isle,
This fatall *Man*, the place of my exile,
. . .
O that their spels to me they had resign'd,
Wherewith they raised, and calm'd, both see and wind,
And made the moone pause in her palid spheare,
Whilst her grym Dragons drue then through the ayre. . . .

The Scots have placed the massacre of the British Druids on Man, and not on Anglesey (both islands called "Mona" by the Romans). If Gaelic Man was the British headquarters of Druidism, then the priestesses of Gaul and the *Isle de Sein* were probably educated there. It was in King Arthur's day the site of his religious center, the Castle of the Holy Grail. Since Druidism also believed in avatars, their custom of "raising the name" of a dead aristocrat by renaming a child with his name, would have given any number of "Gertrudes" to Germany, and "Velledas" to northern Gaul. Many Druids claimed reincarnation from Pythagoras. The Irish heroine Etain was an avatar, and so was King Arthur, considered an avatar of Heracles.

The Druidesses of Gaul like those of Ireland were probably divided into four categories:

	Gaelic
druidesses	*bandruaid*
seeresses	*banfhdith*
poetesses	*banfhilíd*
prophetesses	*faith* (Latin *vates*)

As first conservationists they taught respect for nature, especially water and trees. As doctrine, they all preached the immortality of the soul. Any Druidess of Judgment would have been feared by a Celt like no other person on earth. Her curse could doom a man to hell.

Diodorus Siculus also seems to have thought that not Ireland proper, but the Isle of Man, which was also Gaelic-speaking, was the hidden, sacred precinct of the Druids. They were the same peoples once called "Hyperborean," he thought, where Apollo retired because his mother had been born there. There stood Apollo's precinct (II, 47, pp. 1–5), he added. The *Boreadae* resided there, he continued, a hereditary family of priests and priestesses. They celebrated there every year the rites of spring, with Apollo present every nineteenth year.

If the Isle of Man, with its triskeles, which is an oracular symbol, was the actual British center of Druidism to which Julius Caesar referred, then it was safe during Velleda's lifetime as refuge, as place of training, and as center of the resistance to the Roman Occupation. Isolated in the middle of the Irish Sea, the Isle of Man can be reached by small craft from Ireland and from the continent. Aside from the one massacre there, or at Anglesey, the Romans left Man strictly alone, and probably for good reason; for otherwise it would have made, as it does today, the perfect vacation area.

Edouard Schuré believed, as he wrote his *Druidess* tragedy, that Velleda was probably one of the last High-priestesses of a dying religion already almost annihilated, as Gibbon also said, by imperial decree. As heroine, Velleda captured his imagination and that of Chateaubriand, father of French Romanticism. She also captured Gustave Flaubert's love.

Sir James Frazer was also captivated by Velleda whom, he found, the Germans must have confused with a goddess and therefore worshipped as divine. Velleda's power, he saw, extended far and wide. She herself resided in a tower by the Lippe River, tributary of the Rhine. Ambassadors from upriver were not even admitted to her holy presence, but were obliged to communicate by means of her minister acting as mouthpiece. He reported her comments, which she delivered first in oracular form.

The farther east she is found, the more mythological Velleda becomes. Jacob Grimm explains in his *Teutonic Mythology* (Chapter XVI) that any high and prestigious northern priestess like Velleda, who cannot be derived from a known genealogy of royal ancestors, stands dependent upon higher divinities. Such a priestess is only and forever mortal, after all, and not herself divine. Such women were obliged to earn reverence, amounting in her case almost to deification, by wisdom alone, not by heroic and martial exploit.

Grimm believed that the name "Velleda" was not a personal, private name, but an appellative that defined her functions combining prophetess and prietess. She resided in a tower like Queen Brynhildr (Brunhild), and so was probably a Norse Valkyrja (one of the Valkyries, German Walkure). Living in a wood beside a great river, she also much resembled one of the Three Fates, or weird-sisters in *Macbeth*. In Germany she was also considered a "weirdelf," whose conservation efforts caused her to travel widely and inspect her forests closely for damage and crimes committed against nature. Everywhere in the far North she was venerated in her lifetime.

"Mistresses (Mothers) of families practiced augury," adds Grimm (p. 417). Their names ended in "mara." They were also, perhaps, women selected for a mission or special purpose: they were persons of superior and godlike repute, like Velleda. In war a minor priestess's prime function was doubtless to choose among the dead warriors those destined to become members of the divine body of heroes. Such a northern maiden is the Norse *Valkyrja*, which translates priestess of Mâ-Bellona, or Alecto, one of the Furies. In other words, Velleda in Germany also commanded mounted warriors, was one of the death maidens, there described as *gorgonae*, equestrian Gorgons. And Medusa also may mean Mother (*Matris*).

Such a northern battle-maid resembled a Druidess: white, beautiful warrior, shield-maiden, white handed, an Amazon (Grimm, p. 418). They also removed to fairyland, where they pricked their fingers on spindles and fell into the sleep of beauty. They rode to war as "mothers" too and "mistresses" of victory.

Sometimes this Velleda-figure resided on a high mountain where she too slept in a hall, magically protected by encircling fire, which her prince broke through. As one of the Gallic maidens, or *Gallicenae*, she held in her hand the sacred pentagram, ancient symbol of Pythagoras, but revered also in both Gaul and Germany as a Druidic symbol. It too surfaced centuries later on the Isle of Man as Gawain's five-figured Pythagorean, Druidical, and Christian virtues: generosity, kindness, abstinence, courtesy, and reverence. Beside the hero, as certainly beside Velleda's tower, stretched the primeval forest. There was the sacred tripod, mountainous cleft, underground chamber, and sheltered Oracle.

Thus, the Druids' last but not least form of resistance was mythological. Druidism vanished for a time, if it vanished, only to reappear as primitive Christianity.

Teachings of ancient Druidism, as delivered in free verse by another northerner, a Scandinavian priestess, have survived in the ancient poetry of the North. The priestess Völva, whose name reduplicates that of Velleda, said as soon as she awakened to prophesy after a long beauty sleep *(Völuspa):*

> I remember there were giants when time began
> who first gave birth to me and to my people . . .
>
> I have known nine worlds, in concentric circles,
> each overshadowed by the World Tree,
> which in its wisdom has forced its
> roots down to the heart of earth.
>
> I know this is the Ash Tree called Yggdrasil:
> its foliage crowned with clouds,
> its valleys damp with dew.
>
> Yggdrasil standing forever tall and verdant
> towers above our holy Fountain.

Yggdrasil was the axis around which, the Druids taught, the earth revolved. It was also oak and ash logs, which Aeneas and his Trojans felled, said Vergil, in order to construct the altar ordered by the Cumaean Sibyl. This also points to an origin of Druidism farther removed in the past than has been thought.

When he felled these trees, apparently sacred as early as the fall of Troy (for Vergil is still an impeccable witness, venerated by the Christian Church at least until, or perhaps throughout, the Middle Ages), Aeneas was constructing a navel center for his new colony in the new world. He was building, as directed by a priestess, an oracular center. Such a center, another navel of the world, was the Grail Castle on the Isle of Man. Also situated on a western-facing coast, it too symbolized the center of the sea. At each earth- or sea-center three units stood in conjunction: stone, tree, and altar. The Greek stone of Hermes, the *palladium* of Athena, the black stone of Cybele (brought to Rome per order of the Cumaean Sibyl in the dark days of Carthaginian invasion by Hannibal), the pillar stone of Apollo, the *omphalos* of the Delphic Pythia, the *bethel* of Jerusalem, the *perron* of the Isle of Man, and the Stone of Scone have all been held holy.

No historical people has revered stones more than the ancient Celts, who found themselves surrounded. They lived and live today among the largest collection of stones in the world and among earth pyramids as large as the Great Pyramids of Egypt. Stone as an object of worship, as memorial and funeral monument, as altar, as earth center, and as meteorite fallen from heaven have followed all our priestesses and their stories. But the Gauls especially found themselves haunted because they were beside Carnac, which is the largest megalithic stone complex—thirteen miles in length alone—in the world. See Map #6.

The Gauls too therefore fell under the spell of their megalithic monuments: fan-shaped alignments such as at Carnac, circles, cromlechs, menhirs, perrons, henges, omphaloi, thunder-stones, meteorites, rain stones, witness or judgment stones, fertility stones, woman stones (as at Avebury), ring-stones, gravestones, coronation stones, and the slabs of coffins under which their heroes and priestesses died during initiation and were reborn. For centuries the Catholic church battled to close down paganism by forbidding the worship of stones, and such initiation ceremonies also.

No gravestone on earth can compete in beauty, enigma, and sculpture, it seems, with that of a Celtic priestess, King Arthur's Queen Guinevere, in the Women's Museum of Meigle, Scotland. Her cairn stands outside the church door there, but her monument is now sheltered inside the small museum in the churchyard, a fact which does not mean that she is honored yet either as pagan or as Christian priestess. In fact, it

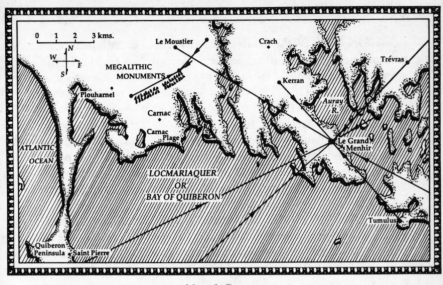

Map 6 Carnac

does not even mean that anyone except women will even recognize the monument as hers, or recognize her as priestess, queen, or historical personage.

Celtic monsters guarded these stones and these oracular centers. They themselves descended from the Nubian Pytho who had guarded the Delphic Oracle *before the coming of Apollo to Greece*. Monsters like Medusa, who was called "monster" by her Greek conquerors, but Mother Atargatis by her own Libyan Amazons, served to guard the sacred centers of Druidism for western Celts. For this reason monsters are honored in Celtic numismatics.

The sacred tree with its five-fingered palm fronds comes again to mind (Figs. 9, 10, 11) in representations of priestesses at their altars on Minoan Crete. The tree was universally accepted as a pillar or column which held up the sky. That the sky would fall upon Chicken Little, another woman or "bird"-priestess, was the only fear from which the Celts suffered. Otherwise, they were death-defying. The warrior Celts so trusted the gods of the Underworld that they even lent money casually before committing suicide, saying, "You can pay me later." The Golden Valley of Wales is glorious when its golden oaks bloom; the Celts and their priestesses adored such trees.

A prophetic priestess like Velleda would have solemnly approached the sacred ash, or oak if it was Yuletide, before she prepared to prophesy by entering along its axis into an uninterrupted communication with earth-axis-heaven. The electrical or other kind of current passed, she thought, along the axis as it rose from earth's core to heaven's vault. That current triggered her prophecy, said the Druids.

Were her forest to be burned—and the Roman commanders learned this lesson quickly—the priestess too would expire, along with the source of her prophecy. If the priestess died, or even before she died, her warriors would leap into the arms of death, "without exception," said Julius Caesar. Thus, the sanctity of the German Yggdrasil, the Anglo-Saxon Irmunsul, the Roman Golden Bough, and our Yule Log becomes apparent.

Water symbolized for the Celts not only birth and therefore the *Magna Mater* or Matrona who named their rivers, but also purification, rebirth, baptism, wine and eucharist, and resurrection. The *Magna Mater*'s own plant was the grapevine. The island Elysium stood surrounded by water. There grew the sacred pomegranate of Hera, and also the golden apple of rejuvenation and regeneration. The water or Castalian Spring on that island was therefore the Fountain of Youth in flowered earth, *Terra Florida*.

The Gauls, their Druids, and their priestesses resisted their conquest by Rome with all the means that came to hand. Velleda's solution was the most terrible of all. They missed the one method of resistance most needed: history. The Romans made Velleda historical, ironically.

Nothing daunted, as soon as modern French historians had by 1800 rediscovered Gaul, their great author Chateaubriand, who was a Celt, rediscovered Velleda: *Les Martyrs*.

The Roman historian Tacitus, whose name was probably Publius Cornelius Tacitus, and who lived from c. 55 A.D. to c. 117, recorded the priestess Velleda. Tacitus was a prominent

Roman, and like Silius Italicus, a proconsul of Asia. He spoke of Velleda in his work on the origin and location of the Germans, a book now called *Germania*. He also spoke of her in Book IV of his *Histories*. Fortunately for the posthumous reputation of Tacitus, archaeologists have approved his work on the Germans, whom the historian praised as highly as he condemned Rome. He felt great admiration for the Germans and Gauls, who lived healthy, respectable lives far from the decadence, immorality, depravity, and mass slavery he saw every day in Rome. He placed Velleda in Gaul during the year 69–70 A.D., when Vespasian ruled Rome. This would give us the historical situation of Velleda's life.

The Flavian general Cerealis, under the Titus Flavius Vespasianus who founded the Flavian dynasty, was duly prosecuting the conquest of Gaul along the Rhine River. In the territory, now Holland, of the Rhine River delta he met Gaius Julius Civilis, a noble of Gaul and Germany. Civilis was an educated military leader who had secretly been fomenting rebellion. Under the pretext of supporting Vespasian, this Celtic chieftain dared to attack *Castra Vetera*, which was the main army base for the Roman invasion of Germany. Two Roman legions were always stationed there in permanence. (The headquarters buildings and magnificent Roman Legate's palace have been excavated.) Civilis managed, unbelievably, to destroy *Castra Vetera* in 70 B.C.

In that winter of 69–70 he had enrolled more tribes under his standard and had persuaded them to swear allegiance to All-Gaul, *imperium Galliarum*.

Tacitus adds (*Germania*, #8):

> In the reign of Vespasian we realized Velaeda [*sic*] had been treated as a goddess by many natives and for a long time; but in ancient German lands they also worshipped an Albruna or Aurinia along with many other such women, and neither to flatter them, nor simply to create holy women.

> .   .   .

> Tradition informs us that . . . women reversed defeat during battles, praying and baring their breasts (before their warriors) so that their men understood the women would not accept captivity . . . , and as a result we ensured the loyalty of the tribes

in Gaul by taking from them their maidens of noble or royal birth and carrying them down to Rome. . . .

.   .   .

Further, the Gauls and Germans conceive that in women resides a certain, mysterious power of prophecy, and so as a result of this belief they consult women and take great stock of their replies to questions. . . .

.   .   .

Civilis planned to become king of a united Gaul and Germany. . . .

French history books have accepted as common knowledge that Velleda was a prophetess of a tribe of Gauls called "Bructeri," and/or "Batavi," who resided in Batavia, now the Netherlands. The *Batavi* were a Celtic people who inhabited the *insula Batavorum* (island of the Batavians) in the delta of the Rhine River, and near the confluence of the Rhine, the Maas, and the Waal Rivers. The chief town of the *Batavi* was *Lugdunum*, now Leyden, Holland.

Velleda was not only a prophetess, common knowledge reports, but also a Druidess and High-priestess of Germany-Gaul during the reign of Vespasian (69–79 A.D.). She was widely venerated as a holy virgin.

During Vespasian's reign the priestess Velleda, who was a principal inspirer of the uprising by Civilis in 69 A.D., was captured by Caius Rutilius Gallicus, while he mopped up operations after the defeat of the *Bructeri*.

Velleda and Civilis were both seized by the Romans and taken to Rome. (Or Civilis surrendered first and then signed an honorable peace with Rome—or their fate is unknown.)

Tacitus expands upon this uprising in northern Gaul; summaries follow of his *History*, IV:

XII. When citizens in Rome heard about disasters in Germany, they showed no sorrow at all, despite our armies cut down, our winter quarters seized, and all Gaul in rebellion.

The *Batavi* belonged to a very warlike tribe called the *Chatti*, and both had defied the injunction to stay on their side of the Rhine, and so had come down into northern Gaul. The *Chatti* had trained with Roman recruits, and had also gone over to Britain under their chiefs, who are their most noble warriors.

They also kept on home ground their special body of performing equestrians; they surpassed any cavalry by actually swimming their horses, and the riders were dressed in full battle dress, across the Rhine River, while never breaking formation.

XIII. Their leader of insurgents was that same aristocrat Civilis, who had once before been hauled in chains down to Rome. But he was clever beyond your average Gallic chieftain, and he also capitalized upon his hideous appearance, suggesting he was another monstrous, one-eyed Hannibal. He was a terrible fellow.

XIV. These *Batavi* were extremely tall people. . . . They gathered in their sacred Druid groves, where Civilis loudly harangued them, privately urging rebellion against Vespasian in Rome, which empire he meanwhile publicly pretended to support. . . .

LIV. When the insurgent Gauls heard that the Capitol at Rome had burned, they were inflamed with new courage. The Druids recalled for them how they had once seized it. . . . Their Druids prophesied. . . .

LV. Civilis had the Gauls swear to die for their empire. . . .

LXI. Civilis cut his hair after his first massacre of Roman legions. Previously he had made a public vow, in accordance with Celtic custom, never to cut his hair until he had defeated Roman legions. Then he had his hair dyed red so that the new growth would be shockingly visible to all. (He was a horrible-looking man.)

He sent a prisoner to Velaeda, none other than the Roman legionary commander, Munius Lupercus. But he was killed on the road. He also sent gifts to Velaeda.

"This maiden of the tribe of the Bructeri" ("Ea virgo nationis Bructerae") wielded very wide authority among the Germanic peoples because of their ancient reverence for priestesses. As the powers of prophecy residing in such women flower, and as soon as their prophecies come true, these priestesses are offered deference which approaches that accorded goddesses.

"At that time the power of the prophetess Velaeda [*sic*] had reached its height. It was she herself who had foretold the

Figure 19. Celtic Priestess

recent victories of the Celts and their massacre of the Roman legions."

The last ancient word concerning Velleda seems to have been written around thirty or forty years after her death by the poet Statius. He wrote some occasional pieces, one to the famous Roman general Caius Rutilius Gallicus, so-named "Gallicus" because he had distinguished himself by successful campaigns in Gaul, and had captured Velleda alive.

Statius dedicated a poem to the sick commander, congratulating him on his victory in Gaul *and* on his capture of the "Gallic" priestess:

> Time allows me no opportunity to tell about
> Our victorious armies in the North,
> By the rebellious Rhine, or to repeat here
> The imprecations of your captured Velleda;
> Rome's greatest glory and our last was
> Due to you who brought her here
> In custody.

Before she died, Velleda anathemized her captors. The Romans were subjected to her condemnation and subsequent execution. That was regrettable, from their point of view, but a great stroke by the priestess, who thereby achieved martyrdom. If the priestess of the Celts failed to observe her vows, she was put to death as had been the Vestal Virgins. In Scotland, many tiny cells were found, one in the Abbey of Coldingham, and a tiny skeleton inside that had been immured, said Sir Walter Scott (Appendix to *Marmion*, 1808). The priestess was left at the words: "Vade in pace." Go in peace.

The ceremony of imprecation at which Velleda seems to have officiated in Rome can also be recovered from Scotland. Similar ceremonies performed by priestesses were witnessed in 1900 by Rev. John Gregorson and reported in his book *Superstitions of the Highlands,* published in Glasgow.

First the priestess threw the veil from her head, tossing her hair into disordered (snake) locks. She lifted her robe above her knees and fell to the ground in such a way that her shins touched the earth. She then raised her hands in an attitude of prayer, while from her lips came a torrent of curses, or wishes, such as:

Figure 20. Chieftain and Wife. Gaul

Sian do ghonaidh ort! (The spell of the death-stroke be yours!)
Sar du do ghonaidh ort! (Your certain death stroke to you!)

The Druid priestess, like Velleda, had been ordained, adds Sir Walter Scott. She walked bare-footed before the warriors because her feet had been anointed. When they followed in her footsteps, they were assured paradise after death. Thus, she had blessed them all. We recall how Martha had anointed the feet of Jesus shortly before His death.

Young Vercingetorix, one might assume, followed Velleda's example. Both forced the Romans to kill them, publicly, and before all Rome.

What ends Velleda's story is a last example of her resistance to the Roman conquest of Gaul. She forced Rome to execute the martyrdom of Gaul's High-priestess, who was in her lifetime adored by "all Gaul."

PRIESTESSES

"One day a woman that I know came face to face with heroic beauty, that highest beauty which Blake says changes least from youth to age, a beauty which has been fading out of the arts, since that decadence we call progress set voluptuous beauty in its place."
William Butler Yeats
"And Fair, Fierce Women" from
The Celtic Twilight (Dublin, 1893).

The historical Velleda sacrificed herself, as the fictional Druidesses have always done, to fight Rome. She died heroically after having cursed her enemies. Other high-ranking women of the Celts bore sons, among whom King Arthur and Merlin are the prime examples, so that as Romano-Celts they would bring victory to their mothers' peoples. A British royal princess bore Constantine the Great. Julius Caesar fathered a Gaul and an Egyptian son.

The fictional Velledas demonstrate what happened to priestesses at the advent of Christianity: they rushed in to martyrdom, and so continued the tradition of heroic careers. One of the earliest texts in Old French, or in the French langauge (c. 900), is the poem of the martyrdom of Saint Eulalia. The most famous account of Velleda's life and career was written by Viscount Francois-René de Chateaubriand, in *Les Martyrs* (The Martyrs), which was published in the spring of 1809. He placed Velleda in Brittany near that greatest of megalithic monuments, Carnac.

In the three texts featuring a Druidess by French authors, the priestess herself always dies. The French tragedy of *Norma*, now the famous Italian opera of that name, stars perhaps the best known Druidess. There again appears Chateaubriand's Druidess, who has seduced a Roman commander. Norma dies like Velleda. What halts one there, however, is an interesting etymology. The original, French story of the Druidess Norma, which only seems to have no antecedent, and which appears to be negligible historically, may not be so. Interestingly, the name "Norma" is not Latin, as one might expect, but Egyptian. It means "Abbess" of a Christian, religious house, a woman who originated a monastic *normula,* or rule. Thus, it may have had a basis in fact that would take it back to the earliest origins of Christianity in Egypt.

It is not possible always to dismiss fictional truth, as in this case of Chateaubriand's Velleda, nor in that of Bellini's Italian *Norma;* both of these Druidesses have so long been approved, admired, and feared, the first as a Celtic Carmenta or Scandinavian Völva, and the latter as another White Goddess, or "casta diva," priestess from the "chaste wood." Arthurian literature, and particularly the German *Parzival,* bears out their truth: that the aristocratic maiden of the Celts was instructed in seduction for the sake of male heirs of first quality. In King Arthur's day (c. 500) they were still being dispatched from the Grail Castle, for that purpose. Thus, young priestesses, very much like Psyche, very much like Parzival himself, created a child to continue royal bloodlines.

In their book (1964) on Hebrew myths, Robert Graves and Raphael Patai began by theorizing (Introduction, p. 15) that the major theme of Greek myths was "the gradual reduction of women from sacred beings to chattels," following another prototype of Eve's guilt and perpetual punishment. "The Greeks, too, made woman responsible for man's unhappy lot," they continue, despite the fact that by their scapegoat, named "Pandora," the Greeks meant the woman who created the universe. Scholarship has noted the fall of woman, her curse, and prolonged punishment. It has faltered when prompted to assign blame.

The opposite current, which also runs along lines of priestesses, from Asia Minor, Greece, Libya, Rome into Gaul, continuously exalts certain outstanding women, and especially priestesses at Ephesus, priestesses of Hera, Asian and Libyan Amazons under heroic queens, the Delphic Oracles, and the Cumaean Sibyls. While the Vestal Virgins appeared to have represented a sorry priesthood where many failed to live up to their role in the Roman hierarchy, still they inspired hundreds and hundreds of Vestals over many centuries in both Gaul and Ireland. New Vestals in Celtic countries rose to preeminence in their medieval societies as they did later in the Church as Abbesses, Prioresses, and Mothers Superior. Royal daughters in both Ireland and France presided over royal religious houses such as Fontevrault, where kings of England and France were interred. The continuity seems apparent.

Other evidence of continuity exists in European poetry and literature where the *carmina* of the founding priestesses of Rome became the *charmes* of the poets. Prosody continually duplicates ritual verses by priestesses and by Druid poets like the Welsh Taliesin, as one might expect, but recurs surprisingly in confessionals by François Villon, in fifteenth-century France: "I know flies in the milk . . . ," begins the poet, who goes on feverishly to list all the mundane, mysterious, prosaic but necessary bits of knowledge a person needs in order barely to survive an impoverished, everyday life. But he concludes in the awesome words of the Delphic Oracle:

"Je connais tout fors de moy-mesme . . ."
(I know all, save for myself.)

Both Villon, and his admirer Rabelais after him, disappeared mysteriously, never to be heard of again. And Rabelais confirmed *Parzival* and ancient Celtic lore: there were once (Druidical) schools for the education of women along the Loire River. And, said he so fervently, the Hebrew Oracle of Bacbuc herself was to emigrant Protestants the ultimate authority and source of knowledge in the Renaissance world. At least, he wished it true as we have done after him and with him.

The priestesses we have found, who continued sometimes at one sacred site for many generations, mothers to daughters, passed along, wherever they set up their shrines in the ancient world, a set of beliefs which must have comforted their worshippers and made their lives less intolerable. Had their teachings failed, we should not have been able to trace their passage and their transmission. Each center of their world constituted a shrine made around units, which remained invariable: water, stone, tree, and altar.

Thus, Chateaubriand, creative artist and self-taught historian in an age before History had become an academic discipline, placed his Druidess Velleda accurately: the megalithic alignments of Carnac, the priestess educated on an isle in the sea, the sacred oak called Irminsul, and the sacrifical stone and dolmens still visible at Carnac, France. Such a holy combination carried its message worldwide of sanctity and priestliness: India, Mesopotamia, Minoan Crete, Greece, Phoenicia, Asia Minor, Rome, Gaul, Britain.

Every March 27 the Vestal Virgins at Rome washed the black stone which represented the goddess Cybele, also called the Trojan goddess, Mâ-Bellona, and Magna Mater. Her cult had been introduced into Rome at the suggestion of the Cumaean Sibyl, and her fallen stone from heaven brought there by ship, carried ashore in a ceremony Ovid included in his Calendar, and prayed to *by women* during the fearful days when Hannibal was ravaging Italy.

The Greeks originally adored undressed stones such as those at Carnac which a Velleda walked among, mile after mile, in long fan-shaped aisles. Some sacred stones, like that of Cybele, had literally fallen from the sky. Athena, and Hermes, and the Oracle at Delphi had their own stones in their temples tended by priestesses. Many of the megaliths at Carnac, like those at Avebury, England, seem to be "woman-stones" because they are diamond in shape but rather wider than tall, quite suggestive of a pregnant woman. Sacred stones, and especially the *omphalos* at Delphi, were geodetic markers, considered navels of the earth. They indicated an oracular center where priestesses officiated.

The Libyan Medusa and her Amazon priestesses, whose Gorgon tribe may once have populated not only North Africa but the coast of Spain, and which can be traced from Europe east into Afghanistan, were also closely connected to stone at mountaintops. The reason seems to be that the summits of the highest mountains were originally sacred to the Mother of mankind herself. Robert Graves pointed out in *The White Goddess* that this seemed true for the Israelites, who had placed God's mountain in the far north. The god Bel, or Zeus, or Thursday's god, had inherited "the rule of the north from his mother Belili, the White Goddess" (Note, p. 364).

After we hear that the priestess Velleda of *Les Martyrs* has climbed upon a dolmen to deliver her harangue to the Gauls, we have the second reference to the sacred site where she officiated. It was the oak tree where the Gauls hung their weapons. The hanging of dolls and assorted objects on sacred trees also refers us back to the priestesses serving Helen of Troy at Sparta. The priestesses of Dodona, near Delphi, officiated in an oak grove, whence they also directed Greek settlers into western lands. The Golden Bough that the Cumaean Sibyl required Aeneas to discover was his key to safe passage into Tartarus.

Besides the oak trees of Dodona, there were the fir tree sacred both to Attis and the epic heroes of Ireland, the myrtle of Artemis, Hera's willow, the laurel of Apollo, Helen's plane tree, the Magna Mater's grapevine, and the olive tree Heracles brought into Greece. Trees were so sacred to goddesses and their priestesses that monsters, or dragons, or lions guarded them. Hera's Garden at the Hesperides enclosed priceless trees, and perhaps the golden apples of eternal youth. The tree symbolized knowledge for it too, like the mountain, reached into the cosmos. There at its base the priestess drew from heaven the beamed message she would relay to her people. To the Celts, who always feared the heavens would fall, the oak tree was the axis which upheld them. Trees and plants helped sanctify spring and resurrection, July and the fires of summer, Christmas and a new birth, and the birch switches of February for purification. Children were once "birched" for Artemis.

The Orientalist W.M. Ramsay had noted, as he studied ancient Cappadocia, Lydia, and Phrygia, that it was the point of departure for the later determination of venerated priestesses. The development went, he said, from the city centers of Asia, Magnesia and Smyrna, for example, to Delos and Samos, and from the isles of the Aegean to the Peloponnesus. From there it spread from the ancient Mycenaean centers to the cele-brated priestesses at the Delphic Oracle, and to the authors of classical Greece two thousand years later. The great historian from Glasgow, O.G.S. Crawford, in his book on ancient reli-gion, *The Eye Goddess,* endorsed this same line of diffusion. The oldest priestesses in the Western world have been found in Asia Minor, both among the Hittites and in their vassal kingdoms to the south of the Anatolian plateau.

The worship of Cybele, as conducted and transmitted by her priestesses, has been traced back in time to another moun-tain range. The northern slopes of Mt. Sipylos are a mere four miles east of Magnesia, where one of the ancient fonts of wis-dom, the traveler Pausanias, was born. On the mountainside Ramsay found ruins there of an even more ancient citadel one thousand feet above the Hermus River valley. There he saw the rock-cut image of the goddess Cybele (Niobe) gazing over the sheer precipices of her rocky pinnacles. The area once sheltered priestesses who chanted and spoke of their august Mother Goddess: Meter Sipylene, Matar Kubile, Cybele. The priestesses there, added Ramsay, also worshipped not only the Midas who was their primitive Apollo, but also Medusa, the Gorgons, and Aphrodite. The Mother Cybele was so named thereabouts for her rock on the mountaintops. This is the same Cybele who centuries later was transported into Rome during the Second Punic War and whom her new priestesses there renamed *Magna Mater.*

One of her reliefs carved upon a cliff face of Mt. Sipylus is now called Niobe, the Mother who weeps constantly for her dead children. This daughter of King Tantalus, himself con-demned to a life sentence in Tartarus, lived to see her seven sons and seven daughters slain by Apollo and his sister Ar-temis.

The wide diffusion of Niobe's story speaks volumes for the skill of the priestesses who told it. Even after Niobe's grief turned her to stone on Mt. Sipylus, she wept ceaseless and defiant tears down her stone cheeks. A mother will not be de-nied. There she still stands, as Pausanias and Ramsay saw Niobe, crudely outlined on a square of unlit rock, her mother's hands clasped in agony across her breast. Above her, but at no great distance, are the hot springs dedicated to Apollo where scores of the most ancient priestesses sternly commanded pilgrims to cleanse themselves.

Other Asian priestesses of Cybele may well be the prototypical fairies who sit spinning their webs, for the *Kedêshôth* of Cybele spun and wove the Mother's *péplos,* her sacred peplum. Other priestesses seen as figures in the moon spun webs which nobody could ever touch. They worked in Egypt for their goddess Neith, in Asia for Ishtar, in Greece for Athena, in Scandinavia for Holda, and in Italy for Circe. Poor Arachne in Asia Minor worked so skillfully it was the death of her; while Penelope wove too for her life. Clytemnestra wove for revenge the web she threw over Agamemnon. The mother will not be denied her children, although one Greek mother did once allow her son to be sacrificed. She was told that that alone would save the city. Even so, she was a most exceptional woman.

In Greek art Cybele still kept her Asian dress and appearance, also holding, when she was carved in the round, a phial from which she would have poured a libation during services at the altar. She wore a mural crown, as did female goddesses in Asia, presumably to signify that she ruled inside the walls of cities. Like Hera and Aphrodite she carried a flower, probably from her own sacred plant or tree. Her figure so carved at Magnesia furnished an iconography for Greece, her hieratic representation. Her other attributes down the ages were two lions, which she caressed, or which climbed up to her knees, or which lay in her lap. In some cases she rested her feet on them, as medieval lords and ladies were depicted on their coffin lids resting the soles of their shoes on dogs. Even in her native mountains of Asia, Cybele seemed a composite of Indo-European and Oriental traits.

Similarly, King Tantalus of Lydia was naturalized as King Tantalus of Thebes in Greece just as their Niobe was a borrowing of Cybele from Asia. The Greeks knew of a Heracleid Dynasty ruling Lydia from c. 1192 B.C. for a period of over five hundred years. That Lydia resisted Greek immigrants to the point of conflict only repeats the history of the Trojan War a little farther north in Phrygia. Historical accounts in Lydia place the Heracleids upon their throne in Sardis. The

Magnesians in 245 B.C. ratified a treaty with Smyrna by swearing upon Hera and the Mother Goddess of Sipylos, Cybele.

The Asian Amazons, we have agreed, were priestesses and devotees of Cybele when she was worshipped as Mâ-Bellona. Thus, Chateaubriand's Velleda as warrior, and the historical Velleda from the Rhine River delta, were only separate manifestations of a tradition thousands of years old. Like all warriors defending their own goddesses and their homelands, the priestesses, both Amazons and Druidesses, were willing to die in battle, to be raped, and to be imprisoned.

Neither group of women worshipped fire, and neither were they expected to remain forever Vestal Virgins. Without daughters how could they have propagated their faith? Cybele herself, this Great Mother of the Trojans, abhorred fire worship, and for good reason. A fire god had once pursued her. During her flight the black stone of Pessinus fell from a blazing sky. Her priestesses recovered it, declared it sacred to their Mother, and centuries later escorted it to Rome. There the Asian Mother accomplished the impossible by driving Hannibal out of Italy.

The Romans subsequently complained, however, about the unbridled license and wild abandon of Cybele's priestesses. Even Julius Caesar felt compelled by these rumors. He divorced his second wife because of her role as priestess.

Only small fragments of their services were recovered by Henri Graillot (pp. 2, 195):

> "La terre fait sortir des fruits du sol; appelons donc la Terre du nom de Mère."

> (The priestesses of Cybele at Dodona sang: "Earth brings forth fruit from the soil; let us therefore call Earth by her name of Mother.)

> "Accorde-nous la douce puissance de parvenir jusqu'à toi."

(They prayed, as recalled by the Roman Emperor Julian the Apostate: "Grant us the sweet strength to come unto thee.")

Graillot concluded: Cybele descended from an ancient Matriarchy, witness her worship and her priestesses. It may have been a Matriarchy of backward peoples, he admitted, and it certainly preceded historical time. But Matriarchy it was.

Henri Graillot's long book, *The Cult of Cybele, Mother of the Gods, at Rome and in the Roman Empire* (which would be its title in English, had it been translated), concludes in words what our study of priestesses has only corroborated: the religion of Cybele "constitutes the first conquest of Rome by the Orient" (p. 556). Rhea and Cybele were one and the same: deities of mountaintops and the Underworld, and tamers of lions and serpents.

This religion attracted women particularly, for the goddess Cybele in her aspect as Mâ-Bellona symbolized courage. Graillot believed that another of her cults, as Virgin Mother, originated in the old Matriarchal system of Crete. In any event this cult from an ancient Matriarchy spread widely among the women of Egypt, Greece, Syria, Anatolia, Chaldea, Phrygia, Lydia, and finally to Rome. Herodotus said the Matriarchy which spawned it was still a thriving society in Lycia of his time. As the *Vierge Noire* (Black Virgin), Cybele is still enthroned in France today, at the pilgrimage center of Le Puys.

Her priestesses were the original psychopomps, or Psyches, who escorted worshippers to and from the Underworld. Thus, the Cumaean Sibyl herself was a priestess of Cybele and Hecate. In fact, only such ordained priestesses could enter the grotto of Cybele in Arcadia, where her son Attis was brought into the world (as Zeus). Two villages on Mt. Ida in Crete were also named for her: "Sipylos Idaia." Eventually, in Greece proper, she was deemed to have been Rhea Cybele, mother of Hera, Poseidon, Hades, Hestia (Vesta), and Demeter. Graillot concluded (pp. 554–56):

> The worship of a divine Mother is one of the oldest we know from the Aegean Basin. It was the first of those cults upon which Greco-Roman paganism based its last hope. Thus, we can follow the course of its destiny for about twenty centuries, six of which belong to the history of Rome.

This religion shows everywhere traces of an origin from Matriarchy, a rule by women of women. The Mother received throughout Asia Minor the services of women, priestesses, and eunuchs dresssed like women, in robes embroidered with gold (such as one finds for sale widely in Greece today, and particularly at Thebes and Delphi).

Why did the religion so appeal to women everywhere that they finally overcame massive male resistance and insisted it be imported into Rome? Graillot answered. Women adored:

1. the imposing ceremonies observed on the Feast Days;
2. the moving ritual of the Passion and Resurrection of Cybele's son Attis;
3. the solutions offered individually and collectively to the problems posed by destiny;
4. the easing of the conscience by pleasant rites of purification, in cases of illness and sin;
5. the promise of happy immortality for the cured and the blessed; and
6. the wide knowledge by resident priestesses of astrology and necromancy.

These Phrygian Mysteries and the priestesses who performed them impressed upon their congregated listeners the utter, wonderful dignity of woman.

The eunuchs and priestesses who served Cybele carried her cult throughout the ancient world. These missionaries depicted her as *Optima Maxima* (Best and Greatest of Women), who held in her hand the scepter of world domination. She was queen over all. The white eagle sat beside her, guarding his mistress, *Domina*. She was "Ourania" (Urania), governess and regulator of the vaults of heaven, the rain, the storm, the stars, the springs, and the waters of ocean. When her peplum floated in the wind over her image, it described a blue semicircle studded with stars, the vault of heaven. The Druidess Velleda's veil recalled Cybele's peplum. The Mother wore a mural crown and the crescent moon of the Egyptian Isis. The brightest jewel in her crown was the brilliant planet Venus, the morning and evening star. Her four-wheeled chariot represented the four faces of the Earth-Mother: spring, summer, autumn, and winter. As supreme magistrate she handed down unquestioned judgments under her name, Nemesis. As leader in war, she dispatched her trained Amazon priestesses, servitors of Mâ-Bellona, and ordered them to guard and die for her realm.

What a sorry change in the position of women, cried Walter Copland Perry, between Asia, Mycenae, and the days of classical Greece (*Excursus,* pp. 220–32)! Between Homer's age and that of Pericles, what a fall! By the days of Attic drama the word "love," and even that love and reverence for a mother, had totally disappeared. In the drama of the Greek masters "love" between a man and a woman is a *disease.* Antigone prefers her brother. Orestes declares over and again: A mother is only a uterus! A mother is not a parent of the child. A mother is merely its wet nurse. If we could only get children without having to use a woman, cried the Greeks! Apollo and Athena agree. . . . That was not love the Greek Eudore felt for the fictional Velleda. He could not love her, and he said so *(Les Martyrs).*

Dedicating his scholarly work on the women of Homer—for they alone were admirable in all Greek letters—to Queen Victoria, Perry expressed his consternation (p. 221):

> The men (by the age of classical Greece, c. 500 B.C.) have ascended to intellectual heights never attained before or since; the great mass of the women have become mere household drudges, without part or lot in the great affairs of life, disregarded and despised as necessary evils.

Another answer as to why women disappeared as worthy and respected human beings comes from the Orientalist Jean Przyluski at the Collège de France: In agrarian communities of the Neolithic Age women were elevated because, as symbols of fecundity and industry, they answered the need of small, scattered populations. Once society changed from a gynocratic to the evolved religion of an androcratic society, where large draft animals were domesticated, the Mother Goddesses and their priestesses were gradually supplanted. Many Indo-Europeans, Semites, and Chinese very early transferred their allegiance to a God-the-Father. But India, Iran, and the Celts held out longer for a God-the-Mother. Przyluski lists for us again the various names of the same Mother Goddesses (Chapter II, p. 35 ff.):

Assyria	Mylitta
Arabia	Alitta
Persia	Mitra
Greece	Aphrodite, Anaïtis
Afghanistan & Iran	Anahita
Lydia	Artemis
Semites	Nanaï, Nana
Carthage	Tanit
Rome	Venus, Cybele
Phoenicia	Astarte
Scythia	Tanaïs
Ireland	Danu
Etruria	Turan
Phrygia	Cybele
Africa	Medusa (Matris)
Hittites	Atargatis
India	Aditi

The altars of these goddesses and their thousands of priestesses of various specialties and degrees varied from the splendor of Ephesus and the royal courts of the Hittites and Egyptians, from the lone, almost lost Egyptian Oasis at Siwa, to the Garden of the Hesperides near modern Casablanca. In Italy principal shrines at labyrinthine Cumae speak movingly today, as do the grandiose pilgrims' marble way at Ephesus, and the fragmented angels from Artemis's temple, about the high status and reverence in which women were once held.

Greek dramatists wrote several tragedies featuring Choruses of Priestesses, individual, tragic figures like Cassandra and Iphigenia, and the dread, mortal Furies, whose real name (Erinnyes) could not be uttered.[1]

Both Pasiphaë and Helen of Troy had memorial shrines, or

[1] Authors become, in any case, very angry during periods of the suppression of women, like the Reign of Terror in France, when multitudes of innocent women and girls were beheaded. Balzac in particular bemoaned the passage of the primitive *Code Napoléon*, which effectively sentenced French widows to starvation. Balzac and Hugo both thought France was lost! And Balzac grieved deeply. He wrote a short-story collection in a futile effort to protect women. Nothing availed. William Faulkner, Jean Giono, and D.H. Lawrence are all three excellent examples of contemporary novelists who over the decades, and with great courage, continued, despite the most vicious attacks against them, to champion contemporary women. All three portray priestesses.

temples, built for them, where priestesses conducted services. The former queen, or queens of this same name and title, officiated in the *hieros gamos* rite, and one Pasiphaë bore a son who became a priest of Zeus Amon's oracular oasis. Was not the abduction of the beautiful Helen, like the rapes by Zeus, the unseating of a goddess of love? If not, then her story and Paris's abduction are more idiotic than childish.

There would have been no point searching for priestesses in any ancient society so "advanced" that it was served uniquely by male priests serving male gods. The discovery of priestesses, on the other hand, has enabled us to determine those areas of life, culture, and interest that women control, whether or not they are recognized as priestesses.

The terrible beauty of Medusa has marked every woman alive, it would seem, for even in dying she gave birth to her children, and so completed her destiny, which is that of Everywoman: the willing acceptance of death in order to give life to her child. Thus, the mother countries—Crete, Asia, Britannia, Russia—show their ancient religion, as do the Idaean Mother Cybele; the Mother of Sipylus Niobe; the Mother of Gorgonio Medusa; Pyrene, Mother of the Pyrenees; and Matrona, Mother of the Marne River.

Priestesses have also been located at all shrines dedicated to the fertility of women and earth, where the myths of Hera accumulate, as at Argos and Samos, the myths of Europa and Pasiphaë in Minoan Crete, and those of Juno Lucina at Rome. In such temples medicines were manufactured, and midwives especially practiced in reproductive arts were trained. Descendants of such women doctors were targeted by the millions during the witchcraft trials of the Renaissance; they were tortured also and put to death by the millions. As a profession, they have never recovered.

Arthurian literature, which is often seconded by its prior and alternate version, the fairy tale, tells of women practitioners of the healing arts. The Arthurian heroes, and Arthur himself, fall ill after long periods of imprisonment or from the stress of battle. Both Lancelot (King Angus of Scotland) and Yvain (the Gaelic king's son of the Isle of Man) suffer bouts of madness when they reject the world and go mad in the forest. On two occasions a mysterious "donor" accompanied by a young girl (nurse? apprentice?) administers medicine to both heroes, who consent subsequently to come to their senses and undertake their careers as warriors again.

Of a different sort is the medical practice of Yvain's mother, Queen Morgan le Fay of Man (and Ireland?), who was King Arthur's half-sister. Her specialty was the dressing of wounds, their care, and the ability to return to life young men so torn apart by combat that they were thought to be dying.

What makes one think all three older women were priestesses is that each was disguised from any such interpretation. The first two are nameless older women. What they ordered administered to Lancelot and Yvain was a small dose of a "powder." The case of Morgan is different. Her history exists in no manuscript. In other words, it may have been destroyed. Furthermore, accounts say openly that for centuries it was forbidden, on pain of sanctions by the Church, to mention aloud or in writing the name "Morgan le Fay." Thirdly, "Fay" means "fairy," which, we have also hypothesized in Velleda's case, meant *Druidess*.

As some writers of detective stories know (for example, Mary Roberts Rinehart and Agatha Christie), women are often priestesses of death. Priestesses of dread Persephone specialized in necessary, healing rituals for grief-stricken survivors. Like the Cumaean Sibyl they tended the crossways under their aspects of Hecate and Trivia. Mother Nox (Night) had her cult statue at Ephesus and her children clustered about her: Day, Air, and the Fates (Nine, Ten, and Death). The Fury Alecto had snakes for hair because she was a Medusa-style priestess like her modern followers in India today. Priestesses of a minor order wailed in solo, obbligato, or chorus. In Ireland one such professional mourner was called Old Woman of the Fairy Mound: *Banshee*.

In his book on the genesis of myths Alexander Krappe (Paris, 1952) wrote at length (Chapter III, p. 100 ff.) on the moon and its significance to ancient peoples. The moon, he says, was known to foster the growth of certain marine plants and to cause white flowers to bloom at night, like the perfumed epiphylla of Hawaii. The old moon's days were said by the priestesses to be unhealthy, and seeds were therefore to be planted with the new moon. Trees and crops were to be harvested, or cut, only at the waning. The moon goddesses, whom he argues were Ishtar in Babylon, Anaïtis in Persia, Europa in Crete, and Helen at Sparta, promoted animal and vegetable growth, while their priestesses brewed moonshine, universally an alcoholic drink. The sun's wife was the old poplar tree, or moon woman, Hiawatha's mother: "the wrinkled, old Nokomis," who nursed the little Indian corn-child. In Egypt, Ishtar and Neith spun the moon's web, forever untouched by human hands—until flown through by our modern astronauts.

Aside from the temple of Artemis at Ephesus, where six thousand priestesses found useful employment, the greatest accumulations of such religious functionaries were probably employed by the queens of the ancient world. The Ethiopian Dynasty of Egypt honored queens above male sovereigns, and could have originated in an African Matriarchy somewhere along the Upper Nile. Those handsome queens were perhaps the persons who dispatched their giant warrior Pytho to guard the sacred Castalian Spring at Delphi. Many other queens have stamped their names upon history: Chiomara and Guanhumara (Arthur's Queen Guinevere), Ireland's Queens Morgan le Fay and Isolde, Libya's Medusa, Crete's Europa and Pasiphaë, Sparta's Helen of Troy, and Lucian's Stratonice.

A very large category of priestesses has been found, with the aid of the poet Ovid, among women metamorphosed, suicided, and reincarnated. One Velleda so believed, like all the Celts, in the Druidical promise of another, better life that she unhesitatingly cut her throat. Antigone was entombed, Arachne hanged herself as did Erigone, the aged Queen Hecuba of Troy threw herself into the sea, and so did Sphinx. Evadne and Queen Dido died on funeral pyres, like the Christian Saint Jeanne d'Arc.

The priestesses of Nemesis deprived the too fortunate. The Norns of Doomstead oversaw human destiny. Priestesses of Fortune smiled as their handmaidens spun the roulette wheels or tossed the dice before greedy gamblers.

Colleges of priestesses chanted meanwhile like bees (Melissae); sang like Gertrudes (Druidesses); wore white veils like Mermaidens; guarded mountains as *Oreades* and rivers and seas as *Naiads, Nereids,* and *Potamids;* protected forests as *Dryads* and *Hamadryads;* oversaw valleys as *Napaeae;* sang their *Carmina;* and lent a hand to overworked women "pagans," as beneficent Irish fairies.

Greek myths, which Ovid delighted to tell, abound in metamorphoses of priestesses: Phaeton's sisters dissolved into tears of amber; Daphne into a laurel; Clytie into a sunflower; Helice and Callisto (often called King Arthur's heavenly mother) into bears; Arachne into a spider; Mintho into the trailing garden mint; Io into a heifer beloved of women in all farmyards, but especially in Scotland today; Lotis into the flower Lotus, symbol of virginity to the priestesses at their altars in Minoan Crete; Syrinx into a reed pipe in honor of the goddesses' musicians; and Psyche into a priestess of a very high order such as the Delphic Oracle. The Druid priestesses sang of metamorphosis: "I have been . . ." and "I know a . . ." from and in their previous incarnations. The Indians say the god Vishnu will descend in his tenth avatar on a white-winged horse (like Queen Medusa's son Pegasus).

While the priestesses of fire seem to have been very successful only in Ireland under their aristocratic Saint Bridget, the priestesses of medicine, other than specialists in childbirth, prospered for centuries, unmolested until the witch trials fomented against them in the sixteenth century—after which men took over the medical profession.

Evia had formerly taught healing to the Norse gods and heroes. The Cumaean Sibyl had drugged Cerberus with opium although Psyche had had to stuff his three heads with bread dipped in honey. Circe's drugs turned Odysseus and his men into pigs. Velleda charmed Eudore with verbena. Isolde seems to have made Tristan impotent, so that during their sea voyage from Ireland she kept her virginity, as during their flight through the woods. Isolde of the White Hands was very likely a Druid priestess, another White Goddess.

The most highly educated, most beneficial, most powerful, and most highly honored of all priestesses, even above those tending the Great Mother who were the most numerous and apostolic, were the priestesses revered and consulted for centuries by the entire ancient world as prophetesses. They may be womankind's greatest claim to honor.

The many specific references to priestesses and trees make it fairly apparent that priestesses were original conservationists, who apparently looked upon trees as sacred to the earth, or Mother Earth. Nymphs called Hamadryads not only protected certain trees but enjoyed also the privilege of punishing desecrators who had willfully damaged these groves. Dryads were also conservationists whose especial care was oak trees—Druid Oaks and each Irminsul. Scandinavian priestesses watched over the Grove Glasir in the Norse Asgard, a forest so precious that its leaves were all of red gold.

Some say all trees were considered by the ancients to be the hair of those wonderful, lost giants who had once protected the earth.

In any case, the Hesperides were three priestesses who owned an orchard of the most treasured golden fruit trees. This grove was so unforgettable that travelers have thought to have found its site in present Morocco, there also the place where Heracles slew its guardian giant Antaeus. That a queen-priestess named Pyrene guarded the (Oriental) Pyrenees, but was seized by Heracles, makes sense, for a place featuring golden apples, lush meadows, and heavenly trees is surely a paradise on earth. Pyrene could have been another fruitful Pomona herself. Beside the Cumaean Sibyl and her Golden Bough in Campania, as lush a garden area as any in the world, there were Colleges of Oak Priestesses at Dodona in Greece, and, one supposes, miles of rows of plane trees along the roads of Sparta, as sacred there to Helen of Troy as they once were in Provence to the east, or ancient Occitania to the west of the Rhône River. The tract of land between Athens and Megara, say classical scholars, was once a protected forest of sacred trees. They also inform us that there once stood, where the ruins of ancient Rome rise from the modern city's subcellars, two hundred-thirty sacred groves!

The *Midgard,* or Middle Garden of the Scandinavian Earth, was also guarded by a sleepless serpent, the *Midgard Sormen.* There the Norse Iduna—who was a sparrow, a bird, i.e., a priestess—kept golden apples in a treasured box. She permitted the very gods themselves occasionally to take a taste. Otherwise, they would long since have lost youth, health, and looks.

Surprisingly a great number of priestesses in ancient Asia and Africa probably were warriors. Today it seems odd that the priesthood should so early have been intimately connected with war, even defensively, as seems to have been the case. To be sure, it was so connected in the Dark Ages when the Archbishop Turpins of France fought on behalf of the Franks and Charlemagne. In Britain also, we are told in Arthurian manuscripts, Archbishop Merlin led King Arthur's assaults so long as the king was a boy.

But that mounted priestesses trained in hand-to-hand combat fell into ranks, charged, wheeled, and fought to the death, that they had mastered metal weapons and archery, astounds a modern woman who might, if she is wealthy, spend only three or four hours a week working out in a gym. Such ancient women soldiers had been trained from childhood for such a priesthood under the Mother Goddess Mâ-Bellona, say French Orientalists, the goddess herself being depicted in art as holding in one hand a lighted torch, and in the other a whip, or crop. Syria, Troy, Anatolia, and Libya knew such armies of Amazon warriors. The river in South America was named for them, whom early explorers like Sir Walter Raleigh longed to see in the flesh. Athletic Amazons and youthful queens were lovingly portrayed by the Greeks: long-limbed lasses riding astride or sidesaddle, without even the use of stirrups; slim, ponytailed girls, heels nonchalantly capable of kicking their mounts into a cavalry charge.

Penthesilea, Atalanta (?), Chiomara, Guanhumara, Antiope, Hippolyte, Myrene of Smyna, the Gallic Epona, Camilla the Volscian Maid, the squads of three, nine, or sixteen Walkure (Valkyries), the raped and humiliated Brunhilde, Queen Medb of Connaught, and Queen Boudicca of the chariot who alone defeated a Roman legion in pitched battle were women to fear and admire.

Most of all, one must bow to the evergreen memory of Queen Medusa, a priestess so brave and so holy her Head was buried before Hera's temple in Argos.

Last of all, we imagine a young Druidess Velleda wheeling swiftly, driving her chariot. In her person she represented the Celtic goddesses who rode their steeds along the forest paths and city streets: Epona of Gaul depicted on the Stele at Agassic, and the Welsh Rhiannon, described as clothed in gold and mounted on a large, snow-white horse. Those white horses were already sacred in the ancient Persian epic, *The Shah Nameh.*

Why has the world lost all this knowledge of heroic women, asked Alexandre Krappe (Paris, 1952). His answer: because of "certains savants passés sous silence par la science officielle"— certain scholars who were officially ignored, or whose books were given the silent treatment by the chiefs in power in the academic world.[2]

The key to these Amazons, claimed Krappe, is their domestication and dressage of the horse.

Most tiny girls in the United States today go walking beside their mothers while wheeling a doll carriage. But some small girls do not naturally take to dolls. On the contrary, all the way to womanhood—in fact, beyond old age—they long for a horse to ride. . . . In ancient days the deities of the Amazons; Medusa's husband, Poseidon; and Persephone's husband, Hades were magnificent horsemen. The Erinnyes themselves, dread goddesses also, because priestesses of the dead, rode horseback about their business. The Scythian funeral mound was called *Colline du Cheval,* where their horses were interred in a circle about the Scythian horsewomen. Persephone on horseback (Ovid to the contrary) tasted death and survived. Brimo rode horseback, as did Lady Godiva in Coventry, and bareback at that. When an Irish lady today dreams of a white horse, say our grandmothers, she interprets it as a precursor of death. To see a British royal princess ride horseback is emotionally to understand an Amazon priestess defending her realm.

That extraordinary queens, who were revered as Highpriestesses, founded cities and realms is not completely unprovable either. The heroine Danaë founded Ardea in Italy. The priestess Egeria gave Numa Pompilius the formulae used

[2] The Englishman Rendel Harris, the German Eduard Hahn, the Belgian Robert Briffault, and two French scholars: Charles Clermont-Ganneau, and the Orientalist Salomon Reinach.

in rituals of worship in Rome; or she was a later Norma. The "shepherdess" named Pales, for priests are also called "shepherds of flocks," founded the ritual ceremonies of the Palilia in Rome, or the rites of spring celebrated on April 21. Both the priestess Carmenta and the Vestal Virgin Rhea Silvia, because she bore Romulus and Remus (even thugh she was executed for it), may be said to have founded Rome. The mother of Saint David of Wales was named *Nonne,* which is both the diminutive of Norma (Abbess), and also the French word for nun. Merlin's mother, who never would name her lover, and who was *said,* but certainly as a whitewash, to have been saved by her son, was sentenced to death. After her baby was weaned, she was most assuredly executed. One Velleda saved the executioner the trouble by killing herself.

Gyptis, whose name sounds like "Egyptian nun," like Norma (Normula), founded Marseille. Myrine founded Smyrna. Alésia in Gaul was founded by a priestess whom Heracles "wedded." Even the wicked Medea, who slaughtered her children, as did Norma, rather than allow them to fall into enemy hands, was said to have founded Media, land of the Magi. And Medea's story stands still today as the prototype of a priestess tale. Relative of both Pasiphaë and Circe, Medea herself is the magical, medico-priestess par excellence. Morgan le Fay takes up her terrible story again in the Irish Dark Ages.

Last of all, into this brief recapitulation, comes the large group of priestesses dealing not with fire, which is preponderantly a male domain, but with waters, which are feminine symbolically and, in many ways, really so. We recall this as we admire today the sea-coast temples to Aphrodite, Circe, Calypso along the Mediterranean shores. The Norse guardian of coastlines Egia was another giantess like the Atlantians and the Fathers Atlas and Poseidon. The horses of the sea come crashing upon the rocks of western Ireland, wrote James Joyce, in powerful verses. The mermaids came ashore often, said the Manx, to beg for apples, in between their priestess chores and washings up.

The fifty Nereids of the sea, in their Colleges, said the Greeks, possessed powers of divination. The Naiads, who were priestesses of fresh water, could sing so charmingly they won the hearts of men.

Matrona named the Marne River for herself, and why not?

Priestesses at altars in Minoan Crete held aquatic plants, symbolizing virginity, in their hands.

Libya, who wedded Poseidon, overlooked a realm in the vast Atlantic. Medusa too fell in love with him and his Ocean. The priestess Fand crossed the Atlantic to woo the King of Ireland's prince. Medusa wore scales like all Egyptian deities of the sea. Morgan le Fay was called Muirgen, a sea-born British priestess. Velleda was believed to have been educated on the Druids' sacred island in the sea called *Isle de Sein,* which could have been Man. Three things were the most sacred to all priestesses: stone, tree, and water. But because it bore life, water came first.

She looks a sea Cybele, fresh from ocean,
Rising with her tiara of proud towers
At airy distance, with majestic motion,
A ruler of the waters and their powers.
And such she was;—her daughters had their dowers
From spoils of nations, and the exhaustless East
Pour'd in her lap all gems in sparkling showers:
In purple was she robed, and of her feast
Monarchs partook, and deem'd their dignity increased.
                    George Gordon, Lord Byron
                    Childe Harold's Pilgrimage, Canto IV, II.

This book is the result of readings in various disciplines concerning religions in the ancient world and their possible connections to priestesses, women of exalted rank and profession.

Before beginning a program of reading and rereading ancient literatures and modern scholars, the author held two notions as incontrovertible: that priestesses must have lived in very ancient times to have been so forgotten, and that they must have served under the protection of a Matriarchy.

Neither notion was necessarily correct, it seems. While no priestesses come to mind either in the Middle Ages, nor until very recently, which is to say, none in the last fifteen hundred years, priestesses still officiated in Britain, Gaul, and Scandinavia around 500 A.D. By 600 A.D. the ancient temple schools were closed, and the oracles were closed. Women desiring to become priestesses were unable to find either an education or an altar that would accept them.

The pleasant thought that there was once a wonderful Matriarchy where young women were cherished by hordes of doting ancestresses is probably false, we are *now* being told by sociologists. But what of yesterday's scholars? Because of yesterday's scholars who disagreed, and in view of this present inquiry concerning priestesses, it should be interesting now, in conclusion, to follow a controversy of the last hundred years. Was there a Matriarchy? Today we are being asked even to replace "Matriarchy" with looser terms which more aptly fit the case: matrilineal, matrilinear, matrilocal, and matriarchates. We may still keep the term matricide, a crime of our century also.

Most recently, books tend to be entitled *Patriarchy*. They are attacks against patriarchal government, complaints about the lamentable conditions of contemporary women, and pleas for radical change.

Let us commence by availing ourselves of an unbiased explanation: how a Patriarchy works today. It has been made perfectly clear by Professor of Economics Carl Mosk of the University of California at Berkeley: *Patriarchy and Fertility, 1880–1960*, p. 18 (New York, 1983).

Decision Making

Household member	Motivation	Control instruments	Constraints
Patriarch	Maximize his income and continue his family	Bequests and dowries; arrangements of marriages and jobs	Children can leave home
Son	Maximize his income and marry young enough to continue his family	Working for or denying work effort to patriarch	Alternative forms of employment available to him
Daughter	Maximize her income by marrying a male with earning power, and ensure her old-age security by marrying at a sufficiently young age	Working for or denying work effort to patriarch	Alternative forms of employment available to her

We should now review some important books on the subject of Matriarchy and Patriarchy in order to allow experts in religion, anthropology, sociology, economics, and ethnology, among other disciplines, to speak for themselves, if only briefly. It is important to consider some of their most striking conclusions, in chronological order, so as to perceive modifications and especially trends.

In his book on the higher aspects of Greek religion (London, 1912), Lewis Richard Farnell told his readers categorically that the patrilinear was the only type of family organization known in Greece, and that it was moreover the only system that "confronts us" in every "Aryan race" and all "Semitic communities" (Lecture II, pp. 25–47). Any "supposed matrilinear system" left no mark at any time. Anyone asserting the contrary is ignorant of modern evidence. Goddesses were not ancestresses. Their societies were not ruled by queens. Their religion was not in the hands of women. The Furies who opposed Athena in the trial of Orestes were not evidence of any Matriarchy. The Greeks worshipped the hearth and were content.

Brief Definitions (Oxford Dictionary)

1. *matriarch* = "supposed analogy of Patriarch." Sometimes "jocular." Used from 1606.
2. *matriarchy* = social organization where mother heads family, where descent is figured through mothers. Used from 1885.
3. *matriarchal, matriarchalism* = pertaining to maternal rule, condition of life under a matriarchal system. Used from 1863.
4. *matrilineal* = based on kinship with the mother, descent through female. Used since 1904.
5. *matrilocal* = applied to custom where married couple settle in wife's home or community. Used since 1906.

In Boston Dr. John Harris (1858) judged the effect which the patriarchal system had caused in Greece:

> The estimation in which women are held in a country, supplies a just criterion of the degree of its civilization. The degraded condition in which Solon[1] found and left them—viewing the

[1] Athenian legislator, one of the Seven Wise Men of Greece.

wife as a mere household drudge with whom rational intercourse and friendship were impossible—gradually led to a de-
pravation of manners, not in Athens merely, but in the states
of Greece, generally, which could not but sow the seeds of social dissolution (p. 298).

This judgment is reinforced by a book entitled *Thatcherism*
(London, 1988), in which author Robert Skidelsky finds that
women in Britain today experience a profound sense of inferiority and physical shame. They feel helpless under a system
where they have no control over their lives, where they lack
power, pride, self-respect, money, and medical care. They fear
to break the bonds of a sexuality that clouds their reason, and
love which holds them cowed, abused, unassertive, and dull-
witted. And this sad report emerges from a country led for
well over a decade now by Prime Minister Margaret Thatcher,
who reportedly thinks men are "wimps," and who is commonly said to rule successfully via a method called "fear at
first hand."

The first and most important book to date on Matriarchy
appeared in Stuttgart in 1861, written by Johann Jakob Bachofen, jurist and historian of Roman Law. According to his
findings in social development, the first period in human history *was clearly matriarchal;* he called his theory of this philosophy of history "Amazonism." How shall we reconstruct the
inner life of dead civilizations if not by their literature, language, rituals, allegories, and myths? We must *by them* come to
understand the ineradicable, changeless, and religious nature
of all men and all women. All past life rises from oblivion via
Myths, Religion, and Mother-Right, he said. Whether what the
myth records for us really happened or was only thought in
the minds of this earliest society makes no difference. Since
legend and myth preserve for us all a collective memory from
the past, *they are historical.*

The liberation of woman is ongoing, he believed, and will
continue because it emerges from the very nature of our cosmic
and physical life. We may suffer periods of stopping, but since
abuse always leads eventually to social progress, one step ret-
rograde will bring about two giant steps forward. The natural
right of a mother will never be nullified, neither by nature,

nor by law. This is universally true. The knowledge of this truth, which binds us together, will set us all free.

Four years later John F. McLennon presented evidence supporting Bachofen in *Primitive Marriage* (Edinburgh, 1865). The ancient kinship (Chapter VIII, p. 63 ff.) was a Matriarchy, he agreed, which is the oldest of all ancient systems of blood-relationship, through females only. Females were the original heads of houses, proprietors, and they practised polyandry. This was true for the Britons, the Germans, and the Picts. Among all early peoples of northern Europe there was no certainty of male parentage, as seen in the cases of both Merlin and King Arthur.

Matriarchy was superseded by modern civilization, which employs a system of kinship through males only. Thus, he continued, the original barbarians mentioned by historians entered the arena using ruder modes of law such as marriage by capture and/or rape. But the *descensus per umbilicum*, descent through the umbilical cord, continued in isolated Ireland and among the mysterious Picts until at least 731 A.D. There brothers, and not fathers, succeeded each other. Sons never inherited from fathers, and never had, like Lancelot, either house or name until they won both.

The German Bachofen and Scotsman McLennon were soon joined by a powerful American supporter, Lewis H. Morgan in his *Ancient Society* (Chicago, 1877). The first societies, he agreed, were matriarchal: "When descent was changed from the female line to the male, it operated injuriously upon the position and rights of the wife and mother" (p. 481). Consider how the Greeks abused the Trojan women: "Men having no regard for the parental, marital or personal rights of their enemies, could not have attained to any high conception of their own" (p. 480). When in a society little use is made in the home of the female intellect, we may expect a wide collapse of public morals (p. 487). The "mature destruction" of ethnic life, of family, will cause a society, like Greece and Rome also, to collapse politically. This collapse will inevitably occur.

Professor Edward B. Tylor, Oxford University (1871) stressed and reinforced Morgan's dire predictions. We may expect "arrest and decline" in patriarchal societies, he said (p. 42). Are we not headed now towards the degradation of people, from civilization toward savagery? "Historical criticism, that is, judgment, is practiced not for the purpose of disbelieving but of believing." Thus, when we study accounts of the ancients, however bizarre it is to consider that the Romans believed oxen could speak, "our object is not to find fault with the author, but to ascertain how much of what he says may be reasonably taken as true" (p. 379).

In 1891 the American ethnographer Élie Reclus published in New York City his *Primitive Folk*, which is one of the most beautiful tributes to Matriarchs ever written. The book is prefaced by a photograph of an Apache-Navajo. American Indians, he said, used Hera's peacock to symbolize the sun, and Pasiphaë's hare to symbolize the moon. The "notorious idleness of . . . uncivilised males," he said (p. 57), threw "the heaviest labours" upon women, "their weaker companions." But "woman was the first architect," as she made a nest for her brood. She was the earliest guardian and preserver of fire, Prometheus notwithstanding. The woman alone looked with compassion upon the fawn left destitute by the male's slaughter of its mother. She tamed our domestic animals. "In fact, among all uncivilised men cultivation may be traced to the housewife" (p. 58).

> No doubt woman at the outset was but a human female, but this female nourished, reared, and protected those more feeble than herself, whilst her mate, a terrible savage, knew only how to pursue and kill.

In a primitive Matriarchy the mother "reigns and governs; she has her eldest daughter for prime minister . . ." (p. 165). The child's "maternal uncle is the real representative of the family" (p. 173). This proud and haughty warrior, "assisted by his uncle, and seconded by his eldest sister," hangs to the old branch, his mother, as long as possible (pp. 176–77).

Let us compare this honor with Greek savagery as described by Walter Copland Perry (1898), where women had no rights, and where they were bought, bartered, captured, stolen, or won as prizes at the Greek athletic games. Women slaves of royal and noble birth were captured and set to work manufacturing cloth, working looms, grinding grain at mills, drawing water, doing housework, nursing, carrying messages, washing guests, serving as concubines. Their mistress's life in marriage, because patriarchal, was no better than that of "great ladies in the age of medieval chivalry" when husbands often tied their pregnant wives to a horse and had them ridden or dragged to death (p. 73).

Yale Professor William Graham Sumner in 1906 analyzed what he termed Greek and Roman "pessimism." Whenever a people becomes conscious of their decline, they suffer a strange tendency to self-destruct, he argued (p. 104). The best of them commit suicide first.

Solon found no happy mortal in all Greece. By 300 B.C. their cities were empty and their lands uncultivated. There, as later in Rome, males had finally greatly exceeded the number of females, for such societies "used up women" (p. 107). "Sex vice, laziness, decline of energy and enterprise, cowardice, and contempt for labor were consequences of slavery, for the free. The population declined to such a point that it was more like group suicide" (pp. 106–7). Historians must be alert for such recurrence of decline in modern patriarchies.

Myths are precious to us in our determinations concerning ancient Matriarchies, also said Salomon Reinach, French philologist and archaeologist in *Orpheus* (Paris, 1909). Why? Because religion is by far anterior to literature, and only myths can explain it clearly. Thus, we find in large numbers statuettes of Mother Earth which date from 2500 B.C., and support our myths.

> Inside the States of Classical Greece we find priests and priestesses, . . . never grouped together in communities, . . . not prepared, as were the Druids in Gaul as teachers (p. 135).

Each priestess there learned only one rite, or one ritual, which was used in the service of a particular goddess. Each priestess, such as the Delphic Oracle, was chosen as a child. She usually served only until marriage. The priestess represented the goddess herself, took her name, and imitated her appearance. At Dodona they were called "doves," as at Ephesus, "bees."

Second in importance to Bachofen, comes in 1912 a book

called *The Advance of Woman* (London and Philadelphia) by a virtually unknown woman named Mrs. Jane Johnstone Christie. She was born in Ireland in 1860 and educated by her father, who was a vicar. She married and lived in Canada whence she removed to Chicago. She taught Bible studies there. First of all, one must impress upon the reader Christie's great scholarship. Secondly, one should hear some of her cogent arguments:

1. there was a first Matriarchy (if man had ever wielded power first, he never would have relinquished it);
2. females are pacific (women and animals too); old females governed once during a Matriarchy;
3. the Patriarchy initiated an age of strife, by "variable and fighting males" (p. 65) characterized by "self-gratification" and "general uselessness." Once they learned the economic value of women, they refused to liberate them. They continually increased their demands for services, power, and wealth;
4. civilization has allowed men permission to kill each other first, and then everybody else. Only muscle and force counted as women fell into abject slavery.
5. Thus, women were eventually demoted to "demons," and "causes of all evil"; they were burned in India, veiled in Iran, and shaved in Israel (and France in 1945).

She says that woman was certainly the dominant sex in the primitive hordes:

> Amazonism, matriarchy, and all forms of female gynaeocracy that are found among primitive peoples, instead of being anomalies or curiosities, are simple survivals of this early, and probably very long, stage in the history of man and society, of which no other evidence now exists, but which is the logical and inevitable conclusion, that must follow the admission of the animal origin of man (pp. 60–61).

In order to maintain his ascendancy, Christie continued, man has refused to accept or even to allow myths to be read as evidence of woman's prior supremacy (p. 85). Her conclusion also tars the twentieth century:

The human family now enters upon a period which is the blackest in its annals, a period marked by contention, strife, bloodshed, and unspeakable ferocity, a period which has by no means passed away, even among the most advanced nations (p. 94).

Christie agreed with Herbert Spencer that the suffering of women in our century will be not only unbelievable, but unspeakable. She says:

The student of history will have it constantly brought to his notice that the condition and position of the women in a nation is the unfailing index of the worth and eminence of its men (p. 128).[2]

In 1913 and 1920 two doctoral dissertations, from Columbia University and the University of Wisconsin, argued that literature in the Middle Ages *had retained abundant proof* of a prior matriarchal system in Europe, and that material proof was plainly exposed in medieval epic cycles of France and Germany. William Oliver Farnsworth at Columbia studied the survival of Matriarchy in the French *chansons de geste*, while Albert William Aron reported on maternal uncles, foster fathers, sister's sons, which kinships characterized German heroic literature as matriarchal. Aron concluded: "Likewise there can be little doubt that the matriarchal relation was much stronger in the centuries preceding Tacitus" (p. 69).

It is curiously observable that northern authors and northern peoples more readily accept and more easily discover evidence proving matriarchal survivals. Scotland, Ireland, Belgium, Germany, Norway, Finland, northern North America have continuously produced material concerning both priestesses and Matriarchy. What can the connection be between the ancient Hittite Empire and these peoples?

Robert Briffault in *The Mothers* (1927) wrote the longest, most eloquent, and most definitive volumes on women that have appeared anywhere thus far. He has offered multiple explanations for the exclusion of women from society and religion, the matriarchal phase and its decline, the magical faculties

---

[2] Dr. Sigmund Freud used to say the same. It is a ghastly and frightening thought, when one looks around.

natural to women, their tenure as priestesses of the moon and lunar calendars, the great numbers of priestesses especially in Gaul and Northern Europe as in so-called barbaric societies in Africa, America, and the Far North.

He also includes a most learned and masterful study of the wonderful Amazons themselves. The exclusion of women from the priesthood is recent, he decided (Vol. II, p. 514 ff.): "The ancient world was full of priestesses." Consider the priestly and prophetic women of Dodona and Delphi. Recall the supreme position in Rome of the Vestal Virgins and the magnitude of the absolute *insult* offered them for some trifling disobedience, if it was disobedience: a hideous death. Think of the organized and corporate colleges for priestesses in Babylonia, and in Assyria where they felt honored, and were honored by the title "Mothers": *ummati*. Recall how in Egypt only priestesses were permitted to serve the sea goddess Neith. And there also queens were High-priestesses. In Babylon only priestesses could enter the shrine of Bal-Marduk, where they accepted to be branded by hot irons if that allowed them to become priestesses.

In his Vol. III, Chapter VIII, Briffault gives exhaustive evidence for Matriarchies in Lycia, Minoan Crete, Anatolia, Sparta, and Etruria. He was surprised to discover that the change to Patriarchy took place "almost within the fringe of historical times, and at a relatively advanced stage of cultural development" (p. 430).

Briffault found a similar reversal in attitudes towards men and women at this change of societal structure. Despite the fall of woman, and the continued, long refusal of men to allow her the priesthood, it is a universal belief that women are gifted with magical powers. "The very people who exclude women," he concludes, "regard them as possessing to a remarkable degree" the powers and aptitudes precisely called for in the exercise of "priestly functions" (p. 561). By historical times the males had abrogated their prestige.

It is also a curious and rather frightening fact that the exclusion of women from the priesthood, he said, which is the present rule in civilized societies, is also found among some of the rudest, most uncultured, and most backward peoples on earth. Among such, women are routinely terrified by bull-roarers and phallic statues, still forced to strip naked and dance until exhausted before being allowed to dress. In some savage places, however, the women have formed secret societies aimed at punishing the men. And in Central America it was the Indian priestesses who resisted their Spanish conquerors the most fiercely. The Spaniards feared these women dreadfully.

Female warriors, who were priestesses among several tribes in Africa, as in Europe, and Asia, were admired and also feared by the ancients, says Briffault (Vol. III, p. 2 ff.). Among Nordic and Teutonic peoples of the tenth century they still went into battle beside the men. The Romans recorded their furious resistance and told how after the men had been slaughtered, they had to fight the women warriors, who had entrenched themselves. As the women saw defeat inevitable, they killed their children, and hanged themselves from trees rather than be taken into slavery, hard labor, and prostitution.

Briffault believed the word *Amazon* derived from the term for matrilinear descent: *emetchi*. He agreed with Diodorus Siculus that the Libyans under Medusa were the original Amazon warriors. His final argument was this: the ubiquity of Amazons proves they abounded, and not the contrary. George Thomson (London, 1949) largely agreed with and supported the findings and conclusions of Briffault.

Taking his cue from the pioneer studies on Matriarchy by Bachofen and Briffault, Kaarle Hirvonen published in Helsinki in 1968 this new argument and new scholarship from Finland, *Matriarchal Survivals and Certain Trends in Homer's Female Characters*. He defined Matriarchy more broadly as a society opposed to Patriarchy, where women's "interests and sentiments" play a more important part than in modern, civilized society, and where one would find:

1. cults of a Mother Goddess,
2. moral dominance by Mothers,
3. matrilineal and matrilocal weddings,
4. Matriarchs among older women; Amazonism among the younger women,

5. exceptions to sexuality, such as women working at men's jobs, priests wearing women's clothes.

Traces had survived from some ancient Matriarchy, which had lasted for "thousands, perhaps tens of thousands of years" (p. 15). The change occurred around the third millennium B.C., he thought, between 3000 B.C. and 2000 B.C.

Hirvonen points to pictorial evidence; for example, in the Mediterranean cults of the Mother Goddess, only priestesses are depicted and no males at all except those dressed in skirts. He points to the many representations of Amazons dressed in male costumes, and to the sophistication and aristocracy of court life in Minoan Crete. Certain non-physical survivals, such as myths, lays, legends and usages of language form another body of corroborative evidence. He then traces Homer's genealogies to a mother for his generally fatherless heroes. Thus, he found Homer's *Iliad* as shamanistic as the Finnish *Kalevala* where heroes have by and large a fatherless origin, where their mothers enjoy high prestige, where there are cases of brother-sister bonding, where the nephew is trained and fostered by his maternal uncle, the rights of inheritance come from the mother, and there still exist in the texts catalogues of outstanding women. The *Kalevala* also features a prophetess-priestess.

In her book on *Patriarchal Attitudes* (Manchester and New York, 1970) Eva Figes studies first the signs, even in the Old Testament, which indicate an earlier Matriarchy in prehistory, as evidenced by the story of Delilah, and the Sumerian paradise ruled by Siduri, Goddess of Wisdom, who was slain by the Sun god Shamash. But European history, she recognizes, was informed by historical attitudes attributing to men reason and spirituality, and to women, unreason, sensuality, and animal appetites. The Mosaic Law forbade any witch to be allowed to live, and the Papal Bull against women in the Renaissance condemned them all as lustful, weak-minded, impressionable, wicked, vicious, carnal, abominable, and secretly inimical—so far had the pendulum swung away from reason, tolerance, and justice. Figes concludes: "Now and in the future patriarchal attitudes will benefit no one, least of all men." Evidence from a study of priestesses might amend her conclusion to "least of all children."

Considering "matriarchy" in the world of Odysseus (New York, 1954), Moses I. Finley had found that vestiges of "mother-right," which was Bachofen's term for the privileges of Matriarchy, were merely bunk and/or *mere desperate solutions*. In no way did Penelope's story demonstrate any status as she wove and awaited the return of her philandering spouse. She had no status! Nor could Nausicaa's mother have interfered when the girl was offered by her father to Odysseus, for the mother was not even allowed into the dinner. Women such as Penelope and Nausicaa's mother were rather spoils of war, slaves regardless of rank, workers all, in laundry and home industry. The husbands spawned slave children and hanged their female slaves as they wished. "Not only was this a man's world, it was one in which the inferior status of women was neither concealed nor idealized, which knew neither chivalry (i.e., gallantry) nor romantic attachments" (p. 126). The only deep attachments felt by a Greek man *were to another man*. He called his spouse a "bed-fellow." He never said "husband." He also never said "love."

Finley refuses to compromise. He makes no mistake, he claims, when he reasserts his personal view, that this evaluation of Greek women, who were all inferior, was true "for the whole of antiquity" (p. 128). Because of their inferiority women were restricted to "the production of offspring and the performance of household duties."

How very far this bleak and condemnatory evaluation is from F.W.H. Myers, who seventy years earlier had marvelled at the genius of the prophetic priestesses at Delphi. Delphi is also inside the Greece Finley was describing. Myers had said: "Greek oracles reflect for a thousand years the spiritual need of a great people" (c. 700 B.C.–c. 300 A.D.). The Oracle, who was a woman, praised the Delphian Apollo as the conscience of Greece.

It was not so much Matriarchy which preoccupied the Greek mind as it was matricide. The theme of matricide, said Philip Elliot Slater in his *The Glory of Hera* (Boston, 1968), was one of their most constant preoccupations. The Greeks "lived amid sexual rancor" (p. 162). The battle between the sexes featured a "narcissistic petulance," a "resentful envy," and an "underlying queasy dread" (p. 163). The Greeks were terrified of passionate, statuesque women such as the priestess Medea, the murderess Clytemnestra, the old Queen of Troy Hecuba, Heracles's mother Alcmene, and the sister of Orestes, Electra. "The marital bond was the weakest point in the Greek family" (p. 164). Greek life centered around contest, not harmony. Not content to study Greece, as another person might have been, Slater applies what he has learned:

"I am arguing here that the one (American culture of today)[3] springs directly from the other (ancient Greek culture)—that the motivational basis of our own society is simply an advanced stage of the same disease that dominated Greek life" (p. 453).

When women are rejected and scorned, their home and the children in it are desolated. Any contempt for the mother reflects immediately upon the security necessary to children. The fear of the mother arises from the male's fear of women, a pathological condition.

Thus, madmen proliferated in Greek mythology, said Slater, and Heracles most notably, but also Dionysius who persecuted the women of Argos and who was driven insane expressly by the goddess Hera (or her priestess named "Hera"). When the Maenads went mad, they ate their own children raw. It was an insane world.

When scholars warn us to abandon the term Matriarchy as it applies to women in the ancient world, they are using a dictionary definition that may need amending. By Matriarchy they now mean a political system. But what of a religious organization? What of Ephesus, Samos, Delphi, even the Amazons?

Why may Matriarchy not be used to define a government by women of a temple precinct, like Ephesus, which comprised temple, buildings, lands, revenues, colonnaded ways, seaport, pilgrim's avenue, priests, priestesses, worshippers by the thousands every summer, tourists, philosophers, resident architects and sculptors (among the best on earth), students,

[3] My parenthesis.

maintenance staff, and working people? Ephesus, Samos, Knossus, Delphi flourished for centuries, even millennia in Ephesus's case. Were such not at least minor Matriarchies? Six thousand priestesses would require a capable and efficient administration similar to a 'College,' which has been Robert Graves's often repeated and constant understanding of ancient priestesses.

Professor Gerda Lerner and most classical scholars now working in England and the United States advise us to abandon Amazons also, but there again, one hesitates to oblige, and for several reasons. First, one must allow the warlike nature of both men and women when they are driven to defend native land and religion. Then, despite the overwhelming evidence which has caused sociologists today to look upon women *en masse* and to declare them victims of the Patriarchy, they have overlooked a large number of more adventurous females. Such less controllable, or "Amazonian" young women, particularly when urged on by some authority figure like a grandfather, two grandmothers, or a beloved teacher, manage to defy custom. They continually find ways to break taboos, defy opinion, survive the injury and wounds which follow, heal their hurt, and even withstand over decades the social and professional ostracism meted out to rebels and other nonconformists.

In the cases of Asian and earlier Libyan Amazons, the evidence is too convincing to be ignored, if one takes the time to hear it. Physical and nonphysical survivals persuade one more and more of their ancient presence. Pictorial material recounts their wars. Archaeology will probably find one of their funeral mounds reported to lie on the Plain of Troy. Then, too, we know the undiminished love of girl and woman for the horse, which is so easily gentled, and her delight in the freedom and joy of the equestrienne. Women, it is true, are very sensuous in that they love sports and gymnastics.

Another reason for believing in Amazons is the number and caliber of the French, British, and/or Oriental scholars who have proven their existence and admired their spirit and courage. A last reason comes from the brilliant Salomon Reinach, who in his day (1909) suffered considerable denigration. When he was told bluntly that Amazons never existed, he replied in the words of Voltaire: "But I believe, just between us, that you do not exist either."

Therefore, having studied priestesses, I personally wish to side with Bachofen, Christie, Briffault, Hirvonen, and the others who after long cogitation also concluded that women had once risen to great fame and renown in the ancient world where they became capable of governing by themselves, and fully supporting themselves, even in large numbers, and in varied activities and careers.

Statues and painting tend to prove it, as do the cult objects of ancient women, their pottery, jewelry, sites, grave goods, symbols, altars, and temple ruins. The nonphysical survivals that speak of them are even more impressive proof: myths, rituals, lays, rites, literature (epics, poems, tragedies), customs of marriage and inheritance, testimony from eyewitnesses, history, religions, memorials of athletic games, signs, and symbols. Most of all, the memory of their wars, contests, rapes, struggles, and their love and concern for others, warms the heart today, centuries after their demise.

Everybody, men and women both, worshipped at Artemis's temple in Ephesus. Everybody worshipped Atargatis and Niobe. Everybody adored the Mother Cybele and found comfort with her in Asia or Europe. The Queens of the Hittites, the matriarchal Ethiopian Queens of Egypt, and the fashionable Queens of Minoan Crete were venerated as they performed ritual ceremonies such as of marriage and fertility before their people.

The Mother Goddesses of Africa, still worshipped in Brazil today, are loved dearly as Medusa is admired, loved, and looked upon gratefully by all women who need to hold the image of her gallantry and her courage before their eyes, and her ex-oceanic blue beauty. Like Cybele and Niobe she was a Mother to whom everyone's daughters could look for guidance, health care, and support. And she symbolized female resistance to vilification, force, rape, cruel punishment, unjust sanctions, contempt, intolerable arrogance, and lonely ostracism.

Love for our own Mothers and Grandmothers urges us to reject certain other ancient women: Electra, who hated her mother; Praxithea, who allowed her own son to be sacrificed; Thetis, if she raised Achilles; and Andromache, who let the victorious Greeks dash her child to his death, and who survived her own abysmal lack of courage.

There are too many others to admire among priestesses, such as the superior Delphic Oracles and ancient Cumaean Sibyls; the priestesses serving Niobe, Artemis, and the temples of Cybele in Asia Minor; the fierce Medusas of Africa, Spain, and Etruria; the bold Heras at Argos and Samos; and the Druidesses of Iceland like Völva and of Gaul like Velleda, wild though they were. Therefore, Matriarchy or not, priestesses.

BIBLIOGRAPHY

(FOR PRIMARY SOURCES SEE THE
LOEB CLASSICAL LIBRARY)

Ad C. Herennium De Ratione Dicendi. Translated by H. Caplan. Cambridge, Mass., 1954.

Adcock, Frank E. *Caesar. As Man of Letters.* Cambridge, 1956.

Aeschylus, 2 vols. Translated by Herbert Weir Smyth. Cambridge, Mass., 1952. Includes: *Agamemnon, The Choephori, The Persians, The Suppliant Maidens.*

Aeschylus. *Eumenides.* Translated by Gilbert Murray. New York, 1925.

Aeschylus. *The "Oresteia" Trilogy and "Prometheus Bound."* Translated by Michael Townsend. Introduction by Lionel Casson. San Francisco, 1966.

Altmann, Alexander. *Studies in Religious Philosophy and Mysticism.* Ithaca, 1969.

Amandry, Pierre. *La Mantique apollinienne à Delphes.* Paris, 1950.

Ammianus Marcellinus, 3 vols. Translated by John C. Rolfe. Cambridge, Mass., 1952–56.

Anwyl, Sir Edward. *Celtic Religion in Pre-Christian Times.* London and Chicago, 1906.

Apollonius of Rhodes. *The Voyage of Argo,* edited by E. V. Rieu. London, 1959–72.

Aristophanes. Translated by Benjamin Bickley Rogers, 3 vols. Cambridge, Mass., 1950. Includes: *The Birds, Ecclesiazusae, The Frogs, Lysistrata, Plutus, Thesmophoriazusae.*

Aron, Abert William. *Traces of Matriarchy in Germanic Hero-Lore.* University of Wisconsin Studies in Language and Literature, Number 9. Madison, 1920.

Asimov, Isaac. "Historic Clues Found Written in Trees." *Los Angeles Times,* Part V (May 20, 1988): 3.

Bachofen, Johann J. *Myth, Religion and Motherright.* Bollingen Series. Princeton, 1973.

———. *Das Mütterrecht.* Stuttgart, 1861.

Baring-Gould, Rev. Sabine. *Curious Myths of the Middle Ages.* London, Oxford and Cambridge, 1873.

Barthell, Edward E., Jr. *Gods and Goddesses of Ancient Greece.* Coral Gables, 1971.

Becker, Ernest J. *Comparative Study of the Medieval Visions of Heaven and Hell*. Baltimore, 1899.

Beer, Sir Gavin de. *Alps and Elephants*. New York, 1956.

Bellamy, Hans Schindler. *The Atlantis Myth*. London, 1948.

———. *Moons, Myths and Man*. London, 1936.

Bennett, Florence Mary. *Religious Cults Associated with the Amazons*. New York, 1912; reprint, La Rochelle, 1987.

Bertrand, Alexandre. *La Religion des Gaulois. Les Druides et le Druidisme*. Lectures at the Ecole du Louvre, 1896. Paris, 1897.

Bittel, Kurt. *Hattusha, the Capitol of the Hittites*. Oxford, 1970.

Blackman, Edwin Cyril. *Marcion and His Influence*. London, 1948.

Bloch, Raymond. *Etruscan Art*. Greenwich, Conn. and Milan, 1959.

Blumenthal, A. von. *Hellicanea: de Atlantiade*. Halle, 1913.

Boèce, Hector. *Scotorum historiae a prima gentio origine*. Paris, 1526. Translated by John Bellenden. Edinburgh, 1536; reprint, 1821.

Bonwick, James. *Irish Druids and Old Irish Religions*. London, 1894.

Bornemann, E. *Das Patriarchat: Ursprung und Zukunft unseres Gesellschafts-systems*. Frankfurt, 1975.

Bothmer, Dietrich von. *Amazons in Greek Art*. Oxford, 1957.

Bowra, Cecil Maurice. *Heroic Poetry*. London, 1952.

Branston, Brian. *The Lost Gods of England*. London, 1957; reprint, 1984.

Breasted, James Henry. *Ancient Times: A History of the Early World*. Boston, 1916.

———. *The Dawn of Conscience*. New York and London, 1933.

———. *Development of Religion and Thought in Ancient Egypt*. New York, 1912; reprint, 1959.

Briffault, Robert. *The Mothers*, 3 vols. London and New York, 1927; reprint, Edinburgh, 1952.

Broch, Hermann. *Der Tod des Vergil*. [The death of Virgil]. Translated by Jean Starr Untermeyer. New York, 1945.

Budge, E. A. Wallis, ed. *Book of the Dead*. New York, 1960.

Burney, Charles Allen. *The Ancient Near East*. Ithaca. 1977.

———. *From Village to Empire*. Oxford, 1977.

Butler, Samuel. *The Authoress of the Odyssey*. London, 1897.

Cambridge Ancient History, ed. I. E. S. Edwards, C. J. Gadd, N. G. L. Hammond, E. Sollberger, Vol. II, Part II. "The Middle East and the Aegean Region, c. 1380 B.C.–1000 B.C." Cambridge, 1975.

Carcopino, Jérôme. *César*. Paris, 1936.

———. *Points de vue sur l'impérialisme romain*. Paris, 1934.

———. *Virgile et les origines d'Ostie*. Paris, 1919.

Carroll, Bernice A. *Liberating Women's History*. Urbana, 1976.

Cassirer, Ernst. *An Essay on Man*. Oxford, 1944.

Catullus, C. Valerius. "The Attis" of Caius Valerius Catullus. Translated with Dissertations, etc. by Grant Allen. Bibliothèque de Carabas. Vol. VI. London, 1892.

Chadwick, John. *The Decipherment of Linear B*. Cambridge, 1958.

———. *The Mycenaean World*. Cambridge and New York, 1976.

Chadwick, Nora K. *The Celts*.

———. *The Druids*. Cardiff, 1966.

Charles, Robert Henry. *The Apocrypha and Pseudepigrapha of the Old Testament*, Vol. II.

Chiera, Edward. *They Wrote on Clay*. Chicago, 1938.

Childe, V. Gordon. *The Most Ancient East. The Oriental Prelude to European Prehistory*. New York, 1929.

———. *What Happened in History*. London, 1976.

Christie, Jane Johnstone. *The Advance of Woman*. Philadelphia and London, 1912.

Chronicles of the Picts, Chronicles of the Scots, and Other Early Memorials of Scottish History, edited by William Forbes Skene. Edinburgh, 1867.

Chugerman, Samuel. *Lester F. Ward, the American Aristotle*. Durham, N.C., 1939.

Clarke, John Grahame and Stuart Piggott. *Prehistoric Societies*. London, 1963.

Clement of Alexandria. *Works*. Translated by W. Wilson. Edinburgh, 1876.

Clermont-Ganneau, Charles. *Journal Asiatique*. Series VII. Vol. XI (1878): 232–70; 444–544. Vol. XV (1880): 93–111.

Collins, William. "Odes," in *The Poetical Calendar*, edited by W. Woty. London, 1763.

Columba, G. M. *Ellanico. Studi di filologia e di storia*. Palermo, 1889.

Consoli-Fiego, Giuseppe. *Cumae and the Phlegraean Fields*. Translated by Alma Reed. Naples, 1927.

Cornford, Francis Macdonald. *From Religion to Philosophy*. London, 1913.

Costanzi, V. See "Ellanico," *Enciclopedia Italiana* (1932). Vol. VIII, p. 827.

———. "De Hellanici aetate definienda." *Rivista de filologia* XIX (1891): 489–95.

Cottrell, Leonard. *The Anvil of Civilization*. New York, 1957.

———. *Wonders of the World*. New York, 1959.

Coulborn, Rushton. *The Origin of Civilized Societies*. Princeton, 1959.

Cowell, Frank Richard. *Everyday Life in Ancient Rome*. London, 1968.

Coxe, A. D. H. *Haunted Britain*. London, 1973.

Crampton, Patrick. *Stonehenge of the Kings. A People Appear.* New York, 1968.

Crawford, Osbert Guy Stanhope. *The Eye Goddess.* New York, 1957.

Curtin, Jeremiah. *Myths and Folk Lore of Ireland.* London, 1890; reprint, 1975.

Darwin, Sir Charles Robert. *The Origin of Species.* London, 1859.

Davies, A. Powell. *The Dead Sea Scrolls.* New York, 1956.

Davies, Rev. Edward. *Mythology and Rites of the British Druids.* London, 1809.

Davis, Elizabeth Gould. *The First Sex.* New York and Toronto, 1971.

Dawkins, Richard McGillivray. *The Sanctuary of Artemis Orthia at Sparta.* London, 1929.

Decharme, Paul. *Euripide et l'esprit de son théâtre.* [Euripides and the spirit of his dramas]. Translated by James Loeb. Port Washington, N.Y., 1906; reprint, 1968.

Déchelette, Joseph. *Manuel d'archéologie préhistorique, celtique et gallo-romaine,* 2 vols. Paris, 1908–14.

Deffontaines, Pierre. *Géographie et religions.* Paris, 1948.

Delcourt, Marie. *Hermaphrodite. Mythes et Rites de la bisexualité dans l'antiquité classique.* Paris, 1958.

Dexter, Thomas Francis George. *The Sacred Stone.* Perranporth, Cornwall, 1929.

Dieterich, Albrecht. *Mütter Erde, ein versuch über Volksreligion.* Berlin, 1905.

Dillon, Myles and Nora Chadwick. *The Celtic Realms.* London, 1973.

Diner, Helen. [Berta Ekstein-Diner]. *Mothers and Amazons. The First Feminine History.* Translated and edited by John Philip Lundin. Introduction by Joseph Campbell. New York, 1965.

Dio Chrysostom, 5 vols. Translated by J. W. Cohoon. Cambridge, 1949–56.

Diodorus Siculus. The Library of History, 10 vols. Translated by C. H. Oldfather. Cambridge and London, 1935.

Dobrizhoffer, Martinus, S. J. *An Account of the Abipones, an Equestrian People of Paraguay.* Translated by Sara Coleridge. London, 1822.

Documents in Mycenaean Greek. ed. Michael Ventris and John Chadwick. Cambridge, 1956.

Dodds, E. R. *The Greeks and the Irrational.* Berkeley, 1951.

Donnelly, Ignatius. *Atlantis, The Antediluvian World.* Edited by Egerton Sykes. New York, 1949.

———. *Atlantis. The Antediluvian World.* (The Classic Illustrated Edition of 1882) Foreword by Donald Flanell Friedman. New York, 1985.

————. *Ragnarok: The Age of Fire and Gravel.* New York, 1883; reprint, 1899.

Dontenville, Henri. *Mythologie française.* Paris, 1973.

Dottin, Georges. *Manuel pour servir à l'Etude de l'Antiquité Celte.* Paris, 1906.

Douglas, Mary T. *Purity and Danger. An Analysis of Concepts of Pollution and Taboo.* London, New York, and Washington, 1966.

Drayton, Michael. "Englands Heroicall Epistles" (1598). In *The Works of Michael Drayton,* 4 vols., edited by J. W. Hebel. Oxford, 1933.

Duke, T. T. "Murder in the Bath." *Classical Journal* XLIX (1953–54): 325–30.

Dumézil, Georges. *Les Dieux des Indo-Européens.* Paris, 1952.

————. *Jupiter, Mars, Quirinus.* Paris, 1941.

————. *La Religion romaine archaïque.* [Archaic Roman religion]. Paris, 1966; reprint, London, 1971.

————. *Rituels Indo-Européens à Rome.* Paris, 1954.

Dunbabin, Thomas James. *The Greeks and their Eastern Neighbours.* London, 1957.

Durand, A. *La Cassandre de Lycophron.* Paris, 1953.

Durkheim, Emile. *Les Formes élémentaires de la vie religieuse.* Paris, 1912; reprint, 1968.

Duval, Paul-Marie. *Les Celtes.* Paris, 1977.

————. *Les Dieux de la Gaule.* Paris, 1957.

Easton, Stewart C. *Heritage of the Past.* New York, 1959.

Eddy, John A. "Medicine Wheels and Plains Indian Astronomy." *Technology Review* (December, 1977): 18–31.

Edwards, Iorwerth Eiddon Stephen. *The Pyramids of Egypt.* Baltimore, 1964.

Ehrenfels, Omar Rolf Freiherr von. *Mother-right in India.* Oxford, 1941.

Ehrenreich, Barbara and Deirdre English. *Witches, Midwives and Nurses: A History of Women Healers.* New York, 1973.

Ekstein. See Diner, Helen.

Elder Edda, The. See *Norse Mythology,* ed. Lawrence S. Thompson. Hamden, Conn., 1974.

Eliade, Mircéa. *Traité d'histoire des religions.* [Patterns in comparative religion]. Translated by Rosemary Sheed. London and New York, 1958.

Eliot, Alexander. "Ancient Ephesus. Echoes of Imperial Rome in Turkey's Great Classical Ruin." *Travel and Leisure* (March, 1987): 102–09.

Ellis, Havelock. *Man and Woman: A Study of Secondary Sexual Characters*. Cambridge, 1929.

Elworthy, Frederic Thomas. *The Evil Eye*. New York, 1958.

Euripides. 4 vols. Translated by Arthur S. Way. Cambridge, Mass., 1919, 1925, 1947. Includes the following: *Alcestis; The Bacchae; The Cyclops; Electra; Hecuba; Heracleidae; Heracles; Hippolytus; Ion; Iphigeneia in Aulis; Iphigeneia in Tauris; Medea; Orestes; Phoenissae; Suppliants.*

―――. *Iphigenia in Tauris*. Translated by Gilbert Murray. Oxford, 1915.

Evans, Sir Arthur. "The Mycenaean Tree and Pillar Cult." *Journal of Hellenic Studies*. Vol. XXI (1901): 99–204.

―――. *The Palace of Minos at Knossos*. 3 vols. London, 1921–30; reprint, New York, 1964.

Farnell, Lewis Richard. *The Higher Aspects of Greek Religion*. London, 1912.

Farnsworth, William Oliver. *Uncle and Nephew in the Old French Chansons de Geste. A Study in the Survival of Matriarchy*. New York, 1913; reprint, 1966.

Fell, Barry. *America B.C. Ancient Settlers in the New World*. New York, 1976.

Fell, Roland Arthur Lonsdale. *Etruria and Rome*. London, 1924.

Fellinger, Ferdinand. *Das Kind in der Altfranzösischen Literatur*. Göttingen, 1908.

Ferguson, James. *Rude Stone Monuments*. London, 1872.

Figes, Eva. *Patriarchal Attitudes*. New York, 1970.

Finlay, Ian. *Celtic Art. An Introduction*. Park Ridge, N.J., 1973.

Finley, Moses I. *The Ancient Greeks*. London, 1963.

―――. *The World of Odysseus*. Toronto, 1956; reprint, London, 1962.

Flower, Robin. *The Irish Tradition*. Oxford, 1947.

Forsdyke, Edgar John. *Greece Before Homer*. London, 1956.

Frankfort, Henri. *Kingship and the Gods*. Chicago and London, 1948.

Frazer, Sir James. *The Fear of the Dead in Primitive Religion*. New York, 1966.

―――. *The Golden Bough. A Study in Comparative Religion*. 12 vols. London, from 1911; abridged edition, 1922.

―――. *Les Origines de la famille et du clan*. Translated by Countess J. de Pange. Paris, 1922.

Freud, Sigmund. *Collected Papers*. 5 vols. London, 1924–50.

Frye, Northrop. *Fearful Symmetry*. Princeton, 1947.

Fustel de Coulanges, Numa Denis. *La Cité antique*. Paris, 1864.

Galanopoulos, A. G. and Edward Bacon. *Atlantis: The Truth Behind the Legend*. Indianapolis, Kansas City, and New York, 1969.

Gallichan, Catherine. *The Position of Woman in Primitive Society. A Study of the Matriarchy*. London, 1914.

Garstang, John. *The Hittite Empire*. New York, 1930.

Gaster, Theodore H. *Thespis*. Foreward by Gilbert Murray. New York, 1950, '61.

Gennori, Geneviève. *Le Dossier de la femme*. Paris, 1965.

Ghiano, Juan Carlos. "Las Mujeres en la *Iliada*." *Revista de Estudios Clásicos* II (1946): 179–94.

Gibbon, Edward. *The Decline and Fall of the Roman Empire*, 5 vols. New York, 1910.

Gingerich, Owen. "The Basic Astronomy of Stonehenge." *Technology Review* (December, 1977): 64–73.

Glueck, Nelson, *Rivers in the Desert*. New York, 1959.

Godwin, Joscelyn. *Mystery Religions in the Ancient World*. London, 1981.

Gökovali, Şadan. *EPHESUS*. Illustrated. Maps. Izmir, n.d., but ante 1971.

Gordon, Cyrus H. *Before the Bible. The Common Background of Greek and Hebrew Civilisations*. New York, 1962.

Gordon-Cummings, C. F. *In the Hebrides*. London, 1901.

Graf, Arturo. *Miti, leggende e superstizioni del Medio Evo*. Turino, 1925.

Graillot, Henri. *Le Culte de Cybèle*. Paris, 1912.

Grant, Michael. *The Ancient Historians*. New York, 1970.

———. *Roman Myths*. London, 1971, 1973.

Graves, Robert. *The White Goddess*. New York, 1961.

———. *The Greek Myths*. 2 vols. London, 1955.

Graves, Robert and Raphael Patai. *Hebrew Myths: The Book of Genesis*. London, 1964.

Gray, Louis Herbert. *Foundations of the Iranian Religions*. Bombay, 1925.

Gray, Louis Herbert, Editor. *The Mythology of All Races*, 7 vols. Boston, 1916. See *Greek and Roman*. Vol. I by William Sherwood Fox.

Grenier, Albert. *La Gaule Romaine* in *An Economic Survey of Ancient Rome*, edited by Tenney Frank. Baltimore, 1937.

———. *Les Gaulois*. Paris, 1945.

———. *Le Génie romain dans la religion, la pensée et l'art*. Paris, 1925.

Grimm, Herman Friedrich. *Homers Ilias*. Stuttgart, 1907 (Combined edition from 1890 and 1895 works).

Grimm, Jacob and Wilhelm. *Deutsche Mythologie*. Translated by J. S. Stalybrass. London, 1854.

Grote, George. *History of Greece*, 12 vols. New York, 1856–57.

Grupp, Georg. *Kultur der alten Kelten und Germanen, mit einer Rückblick auf die Urgeschichte.* München, 1905.

Güterbock, Hans G. *Mythologies of the Ancient World,* edited by Samuel Noah Kramer. Chicago, 1961. See "Hittite Mythology," pp. 139–79.

Halliday, William Reginald. *Indo-European Folk-tales and Greek Legend.* Cambridge, 1933.

Hamilton, Mary. *Greek Saints and Their Festivals.* London, 1910.

Hamilton, Sir William. "On the Philosophy of the Unconditioned" (1828). In *Discussions on Philosophy and Literature, Education, and University Reform.* Edinburgh and London, 1852.

Harris, John. *Patriarchy; or, The Family, its Constitution and Probation.* Boston, 1858.

Harrison, Jane Ellen. *Ancient Art and Ritual.* London, 1913.

———. *Themis.* Cambridge, 1927.

Hartland, Edwin Sidney. *Primitive Paternity. The Myth of Supernatural Birth in Relation to the History of the Family,* 2 vols. London, 1909.

Hathorn, Richmond Yancey. *Greek Mythology.* Beirut, 1977.

Hawkes, Charles Francis Christopher. *Prehistoric Foundations of Europe.* London, 1939.

Hawkes, Gerald S. and John B. White. *Stonehenge Decoded.* New York, 1965.

Hawkes, Jacquetta and Christopher. *Prehistoric Britain.* Cambridge, 1953.

Heath, Thomas Little. *Greek Astronomy.* London, 1932.

Herodotus, 4 vols. Translated by A. D. Godley. London and New York, 1920.

Herrmann, Luke. *Turner. Paintings, Watercolours, Prints and Drawings.* Boston, 1975. See Plate 77: "Dido Building Carthage" (oil on canvas, 1815).

Hesiod. *Hesiod and Theognis,* edited by E. V. Rieu. London, 1973.

Higden, Ranulf. *Polychronicon.* Translated by John de Trevisa. Westmestre, 1495.

Highet, Gilbert. *The Classical Tradition.* Oxford, 1949.

———. *Poets in a Landscape.* New York, 1957.

Hirvonen, Kaarle. *Matriarchal Survivals and Certain Trends in Homer's Female Characters.* Doctoral thesis, Finnish Academy of Science and Letters. Helsinki, 1968.

Hogarth, David George. *British Museum Excavations at Ephesus.* London, 1908.

Holter, Harriet, Editor. *Patriarchy in a Welfare Society.* Oslo, Bergen, Stavanger and Tromsø, 1984.

Homer. *The Iliad of Homer.* Translated by William Cullen Bryant. Boston, 1870.

Homeric Hymns. *Hesiod, The Homeric Hymns and Homerica.* Translated by H. G. Evelyn-White. Cambridge, 1959.

Hooke, Samuel Henry, Editor. *The Labyrinth,* illus. London, 1935. See the title essay by C. N. Deedes, pp. 1–42.

Horney, Karen. "The Dread of Women." *International Journal of Psychoanalysis,* Vol. 13 (London, 1932): 348–60.

Howell, James. *Dodona's Grove.* Cambridge, 1645.

Hutchinson, Richard Wyatt. *Prehistoric Crete.* London, 1962.

Huxley, George Leonard. *Early Sparta.* Cambridge, Mass., 1962.

Hyde, Douglas. *A Literary History of Ireland.* London, 1906.

Iamblichus. *Iamblichus on The Mysteries of the Egyptians, Chaldeans, and Assyrians.* Translated by Thoman Taylor. London, 1821, 1895, 1968.

Illich, I. *Gender.* New York, 1983.

Ivimy, John. *The Sphinx and the Megaliths.* London, 1974.

Jackson, Kenneth Hurlstone, Translator. *A Celtic Miscellany. Translations from the Celtic Literatures.* Cambridge, Mass., 1951.

Jamblichus of Chalcis. *On the Mysteries of the Egyptians, Chaldeans, and Assyrians.* Translated by Thomas Taylor. London, 1821; reprint, 1968.

James, Edwin Oliver. *The Ancient Gods.* New York, 1960.

———. *The Cult of the Mother Goddess.* London, 1959.

James, Montague Rhodes. *The Apocryphal New Testament.* Oxford, 1924.

Janeway, Elizabeth. *Man's World. Woman's Place.* London, 1971.

Jarvis, Stinson. *The Price of Peace.* Los Angeles, 1921.

Jones, Ernest. *On the Nightmare.* London, 1949.

Joyce, Patrick Weston, Translator. *Old Celtic Romances.* London, 1920.

———. *A Social History of Ancient Ireland.* 2 vols. London, 1907.

Jubainville, Henri d'Arbois de. *Le Cycle mythologique irlandais et la mythologie celtique.* Paris, 1884; reprint, 1969.

———. *Les Druides et les dieux celtiques à forme d'animaux.* Paris, 1906.

———. *La Famille celtique.* (Study in Comparative Law). Paris, 1905.

Judson, Henry Pratt. *Caesar's Army.* Boston, 1888.

Julian the Emperor. *The Works of the Emperor Julian,* 3 vols. Translated by Wilmer Cave Wright. London and New York, 1913.

Jullian, Camille Louis. *De la Gaule à la France. Nos origines historiques.* Paris, 1923.

———. *Gallia.* Paris, 1902.

———. *Histoire de la Gaule,* 3 vols. Paris, 1920.

Justinus, Marcus Junianus. *Epitome in Trogi Pompeii Historias,* edited by Marcus Antonius Sabellicus. Venice, n.d.

Kahle, Paul Ernst. *The Cairo Geniza.* New York, 1960.

Kendrick, Thomas Downing. *The Druids. A Study in Keltic Prehistory.* New York, 1927.

Kern, Otto. *Orphicorum Fragmenta.* Berlin, 1922.

King, Rev. James. *Recent Discoveries on the Temple Hill at Jerusalem.* St. Paul's Churchyard, 1885.

Kirk, G. S. *Myth, Its Meaning & Functions in Ancient and Other Cultures.* Sather Classical Lecture, Vol. 40. Cambridge, Berkeley, and Los Angeles, 1970.

Knox, Ronald A. *Enthusiasm. A Chapter in the History of Religion.* Oxford, 1950.

Kovalevsky, Maxime. *Modern Customs and Ancient Laws of Russia.* London, 1891.

Kramer, Samuel Noah. *The Sumerians.* Chicago, 1963.

Krappe, Alexander Haggerty. *Etudes de mythologie et de folklore germaniques.* Paris, 1928.

———. *La Genèse des mythes.* Paris, 1952.

———. *Mythologie universelle.* Paris, 1930.

Krige, E. J. and J. D. *The Realm of the Rain Queen.* London, 1943.

Kunze, Emil. *Temples and Sanctuaries of Ancient Greece.* Translated by F. Maxwell Brownjohn. London, 1973.

Kushner, Eva. *Le Mythe d'Orphée dans la littérature française contemporaine.* Paris, 1961.

Landor, Walter Savage. *The Poetical Works of Walter Savage Landor,* 3 vols. Edited by Stephen Wheeler. Oxford, 1937.

Lang, Andrew. *History of Scotland from the Roman Occupation,* 4 vols. New York, 1900.

———. *Myth, Ritual and Religion,* 2 vols. London, 1901.

Lea, Henry Charles. *A History of the Inquisition.*

LeBraz, Anatole. *La Légende de la mort chez les Bretons armoricains.* Paris, 1902; reprints, 1912 and 1945.

Lehmann, Andrée. *Le Rôle de la femme dans l'histoire de la Gaule.* Paris, 1944.

Leland, Charles Godfrey. *Etruscan Roman Remains in Popular Tradition.* London, 1892.

Leland, John. *The Itinerary of John Leland,* edited by L. T. Smith. London, 1907.

Leonardo da Vinci. *The Complete Paintings of Leonardo da Vinci,* edited by L. D. Ettlinger and Angela Ottino della Chiesa. New York, 1967. See *The Head of the Medusa* (#5, p.89), once thought to have been the work of Leonardo da Vinci.

Leonhard, Walther. *Hettiter und Amazonen.* Teubner, 1911.

Le Roux, Françoise. *Les Druides*. Paris, 1961.

LeRouzic, Zacharie. *Carnac. Les Monuments mégalithiques. Leur destination. Leur âge*. Vannes, n.d.

Lethaby, W. R. "The Earlier Temple of Artemis at Ephesus." *Journal of Hellenic Studies* Vol. 37 (1917): 1–16.

Lewis, I. M. *Ecstatic Religion*. London, 1971.

Libanius. *The Julianic Orations*. Vol. I, edited and translated by A. F. Norman. Cambridge and London, 1969.

Lloyd, Seton. *Early Anatolia*. London, 1961.

———. *Early Highlands People of Anatolia*. London, 1967.

Lockyer, J. Norman. *The Dawn of Astronomy*. Cambridge, Mass., 1964.

Logan, James. *The Scotish Gael, or Celtic Manners*. Hartford, Conn., undated, but c. 1830.

Loisy, Alfred Firmin. *Essai historique sur le sacrifice*. Paris, 1920.

Loomis, Laura Hibbard. *Adventures in the Middle Ages*. New York, 1962.

Lot, Ferdinand. *La Gaule*. Paris, 1945.

Luce, John Victor. *Homer and the Heroic Age*. London and New York, 1975.

Lucian. (Lucianus Samosatensis). *De Dea Syria*. Translated by Harold W. Attridge and Robert A. Oden. Missoula, Montana, 1976.

Lum, Peter. *The Stars in Our Heaven. Myths and Fables*. New York, 1948.

Macalister, Robert Alexander Stewart. *The Archaeology of Ireland*. London, 1928; reprints, New York, 1949 and 1972.

———. *Tara. A Pagan Sanctuary of Ancient Ireland*. New York and London, 1931.

MacCulloch, John Arnott. *The Mythology of All Races*. 13 vols. Boston, 1918.

———. *The Religion of the Ancient Celts*. Edinburgh, 1911.

MacQueen, James G. *The Hittites and their Contemporaries in Asia Minor*. London, 1975.

Maimonides, Moses. *Dalalāt al-Hairin*. [Guide for the perplexed]. Translated by M. Friedlander. London, 1881.

Maine, Sir Henry James Sumner. *Popular Government*. London, 1885.

Maiuri, Amedeo. *The Phlegraean Fields*. Translated by V. Priestley. Rome, 1947.

Mansuelli, Guido A. *Etruria and Early Rome*. London, 1966.

Marcuse, Herbert. *Eros and Civilization*. Boston, 1955.

Mariette-Bey, Auguste. *Itinéraire de la Haute Egypte*. Translated by Alphonse Mariette. Boston, 1890.

Markale, Jean. *L'Epopée celtique en Bretagne*. Paris, 1971.

Marlowe, Christopher. *The Tragedy of Dido, Queen of Carthage*. In

Marlowe's Plays, edited by Edward Thomas. London and New York, 1909, '10, '12.

Martin, Jean. *La Religion des Gaulois.* Paris, 1727.

Mason, Otis Tufton. *Woman's Share in Primitive Culture.* London, 1895.

Maspero, Gaston. *History of Egypt.* Vol. I. Translated by M. L. McClure. London, 1903.

———. *The Struggle of the Nations.* London, 1896.

Mavor, James W., Jr. *Voyage to Atlantis.* New York, 1969.

Mayer, Josephine. *Never to Die.* New York, 1938.

McKay, Alexander Gordon. *Naples and Campania. Texts and Illustrations.* Hamilton, Ontario, 1962.

———. *Vergil's Italy,* illus. New York and Bath, 1971.

McLennon, John Ferguson. *Primitive Marriage.* Chicago and London, 1865; reprint, 1970.

Mellaart, James. *Catal Huyuk.* New York, 1967.

Metropolitan Museum of Art Bulletin XXXII, #5 (1973–74). Ann Farkas and Boris Piotrovsky. *From the Land of the Scythians.* New York, 1975.

Michelet, Jules. *Satanism and Witchcraft. A Study in Medieval Superstition.* Translated by A. R. Alinson. New York, 1960.

Mies, Maria. *Patriarchy and Accumulation on a World Scale.* London, Atlantic Highlands, 1986.

Mills, Dorothy. *Books of the Ancient World.* New York, 1923.

Miltner, Franz. *Ephesos. Stadt der Artemis und des Johannes,* illus. Vienna, 1958.

Morgan, Lewis Henry. *Ancient Society.* Chicago, 1877.

———. *Systems of Consanguinity and Affinity of the Human Family.* Washington, 1878.

Morris, Sir Lewis. *The Epic of Hades,* 3 vols. London, 1881.

Mosk, Carl. *Patriarchy and Fertility: Japan and Sweden, 1880–1960.* New York, 1983.

Müller, Friedrich Max. *Comparative Mythology.* London, 1881.

———. *A History of Sanskrit Literature.* London, 1859.

Münsterberg, Hugo. *Symbolism in Ancient Chinese Art.* New York, 1986.

Murray, Margaret Alice. *The God of the Witches.* New York, 1931; reprints, 1952 and 1970.

———. *The Splendour That Was Egypt.* New York, 1949; reprint, 1961.

———. *The Witch-Cult in Western Europe.*

Myers, F. W. H. *Essays Classical.* London, 1883.

Myers, Philip Van Ness. *Remains of Lost Empires.* New York, 1875.

Nardi, Bruno. *Mantuanitas Vergiliana.* Rome, 1963.

Newcomer, Mabel. *A Century of Higher Education for American Women.* New York, 1959.

Nichols, Marianne. *Man, Myth and Monument.* New York, 1975.

Nickles, Elizabeth and Laura Ashcroft. *The Coming Matriarchy.* New York, 1981.

Niel, Fernand. *Dolmens et menhirs.* Paris, 1972.

Nilsson, Martin Persson. *Griechische Feste.* Leipzig, 1906.

———. *History of Greek Religion.* Oxford, 1925.

———. *Minoan-Mycenaean Religion.* Lund, 1927.

Norse Mythology. *The Elder Edda in Prose Translation,* edited by Lawrence S. Thompson. Hamden, Conn., 1974.

Nyberg, Bertel. *Kind und Erde.* Helsinki, 1931.

O'Curry, Eugene. *On the Manners of Customs of the Ancient Irish. A Series of Lectures,* 3 vols., edited by W. K. Sullivan. Dublin, Edinburgh and New York, 1873; reprint, New York, 1971. For lectures (1857) on Druids, Druidesses, Druidism see Vol. II, Chapters IX and X, pp. 179–228.

Ogilvie, Robert Maxwell. *The Romans and Their Gods in the Age of Augustus.* New York, 1969.

O'Leary, DeLacy Evans. *The Saints of Egypt.* London, 1938.

Olson, Carl, Editor. *The Book of the Goddess Past–Present* (17 essays, Preface, and Introduction). New York, 1983.

Ovid. *Fasti.* Translated by Sir James George Frazer. Loeb Library. Cambridge, Mass., 1951.

———. *Heroides and Amores.* Translated by Grant Showerman. Loeb Library. Cambridge, Mass., 1947.

———. *Metamorphoses.* Translated by Frank Justus Miller. Loeb Library. Cambridge, Mass., 1946.

———. *The Fasti, Tristia, Ibis,* and *Halieuticon.* Translated and notes by Henry T. Riley. London, 1872.

Owen, A. L. *The Famous Druids. A Survey of Three Centuries of English Literature on the Druids.* Oxford, 1962.

Palmer, Leonard Robert. *Mycenaeans and Minoans.* London, 1961.

Pannekoek, Antonie. *A History of Astronomy.* New York, 1961.

Parnell, Thomas. "Hesiod, or The Rise of Woman." In *The Poetical Works of Thomas Parnell.* London, 1832.

Pearson, Lionel. *Early Ionian Historians.* Oxford, 1939; reprint, Westport, Conn., 1975.

Pecorelli, Rosa Maria. "Iemanjá, a Deusa do Amor e da Maternidade." *Desfile* #185 (Feb., 1985): 203–05.

Pelloutier, Simon. *Histoire des Celtes.* Paris, 1770.

Pendlebury, J. D. S., Curator. *A Handbook to the Palace of Minos Knossos.* Foreward by Sir Arthur Evans. Introduction by Sir John Myres and Sir John Forsdyke. London, 1914.

Perret, Jacques. *Les Origines de la légende troyenne.* Paris, 1942.

Perry, Walter Copland. *The Women of Homer.* London, 1898.

Persson, Axel Waldemar. *The Religion of Greece in Prehistoric Times.* Los Angeles, 1942.

Pestalozza, U. "Hera Pelasga." *Studi Etruschi* XXV (1957): 161–82.

———. *The Pyramids of Egypt and Temples of Gizeh.* London, 1883.

Petrie, Sir W. M. F. *History of Egypt.* 6 vols. London, 1899.

Philostratus and Eunapius. The Lives of the Sophists. Translated by Wilmer Cave Wright. Cambridge, 1968.

Picard, Gilbert. *Le Monde de Carthage.* Paris, 1956.

Piganiol, A. *La Conquête romaine.* Paris, 1930.

Piggott, Stuart. *Ancient Europe.* Chicago, 1965.

Pliny the Elder. *Natural History,* 10 vols. Translated by H. Rackham. Cambridge, Mass. and London, 1945; reprint, 1952.

Plutarch. *De Iside et Osiride,* edited by J. Gwyn Griffiths. Cardiff, 1970.

Poincaré, Raymond. *Pour le suffrage des femmes.* Paris, 1922.

Pomeroy, Sarah B. *Goddesses, Whores, Wives, and Slaves. Women in Classical Antiquity.* New York, 1975.

Porphyre (Porphyry). *Vie de Pythagore. Lettre à Marcella.* Translated by Edouard des Places. Appendix by A.-Ph. Segonds. Paris, 1982.

———. *Porphyrii de Philosophia ex oraculis haurienda.* Librorum Reliquiae, edited by Gustavus Wolff. Hildesheim, 1962.

———. *On the Cave of the Nymphs.* New York, 1983.

Powell, Thomas G. E. *The Celts.* London, 1958.

Procopius (of Caesarea). Vol. VII "Buildings." Translated by H. B. Dewing and Glanville Downey. Cambridge and London, 1940; reprint, 1954.

Przyluski, Jean. *La Grande déesse.* Paris, 1950.

Rahner, Hugo. *Greek Myths and Christian Mystery.* Paris, 1954.

Rambaud, Michel. *L'Art de la déformation historique dans les "Commentaires" de César.* Paris, 1953.

Ramsay, Sir William Mitchell. *The Historical Geography of Asia Minor.* London, 1890.

———. "Sipylos and Cybele." *Journal of Hellenic Studies* Vol. III (1881): 33–68.

Randall, John Herman, Jr. *Hellenistic Ways of Deliverance and the Making of the Christian Synthesis.* New York and London, 1970.

Rawlinson, George. *The Five Great Monarchies of the Ancient Eastern World,* 4 vols. London, 1862–67.

————. *The Seven Great Monarchies of the Ancient Eastern World*, 3 vols. New York, 1871.

Reclus, Elie. *Primitive Folk. Studies in Comparative Ethnology.* New York, 1891.

Reinach, Adolphe. "L'Origine des Amazones." *Revue de l'histoire des religions* (1913): 277–307. Copy courtesy of the Library of Congress.

Reinach, Salomon. *Cultes, mythes et religions*, 5 vols. Paris, 1923.

————. *Orpheus. Histoire générale des religions.* Paris, 1909.

Renan, Ernst. "La poésie des races celtiques." In *Ernest Renan. Oeuvres complètes*, 10 vols. Paris, 1859; reprint, London, 1896.

Rhŷs, Sir John. *Celtic Folklore, Manx and Welsh.* Oxford, 1901.

————. *Studies in the Arthurian Legend.* London, 1891; reprint, 1966.

Richardson, Emmeline. *The Etruscans.* Chicago, 1964.

Rinehart, Mary Roberts. *The Album.* New York, 1933; reprint, 1988.

Rolleston, T. W. *Myths and Legends of the Celtic Race.* New York, undated.

Rossabi, Morris. *Khubilai Khan. His Life and Times.* Berkeley, 1988.

Rossetti, Dante Gabriel. *Poems,* edited by Oswald Doughty. London, 1957.

Rostagni, Augusto. *Da Livio a Virgilio.* Padua, 1942.

Rostovtzeff, Mikhail Ivanovich. *A History of the Ancient World*, 2 vols. Oxford, 1927.

Runeberg, Arne. *Witches, Demons and Fertility Magic.* Helsinki, 1947.

Sacheverell, Governor William. *An Account of the Isle of Man.* London, 1702.

Saint-Foix, Germain François Poullain de. *Essais historiques sur Paris.* Paris, 1766.

Saintyves, P. [Emile Dominique Nourry]. *Les Vierges mères et les naissances miraculeuses.* Paris, 1908.

Savramis, Demosthenes. *The Satanizing of Women.* Translated by Martin Ebon. New York, 1974.

Saxo Grammaticus. *The Nine Books of Danish History*, 2 vols., edited by Oliver Eaton. London, Copenhagen, Stockholm, Berlin, and New York, 1905.

Schele, Linda and Mary Ellen Miller. *The Blood of Kings. Dynasty and Ritual in Maya Art.* Photographs by Justin Kerr. Kimball Art Museum, Fort Worth, 1986.

Scherman, Katherine. *The Flowering of Ireland.* New York, 1981.

Schmidt, Hans. *Die Erzählung von Paradies und Sündefall.* Tübingen, 1931.

Schmidt, Karl. *Jus Primae Noctis.* Freiburg, 1881.

Schuré, Edouard. *The Ancient Mysteries of Delphi.* Paris, 1889.

———. *La Druidesse.* Paris, 1914.

———. *Les Grands initiés.* Paris, 1889; reprint, 1929.

Scott, Sir Walter. *Minstrelsy of the Scottish Broder,* 3 vols. Edinburgh, 1902–03.

Semple, Ellen Churchill. *Geography of the Mediterranean Region.* London, 1932.

Seneca. *Seneca's Tragedies,* 2 vols. London and New York, 1927.

Seznec, Jean. *The Survival of the Pagan Gods.* Translated by Barbara F. Sessions. New York, 1953.

Silius Italicus. *Punica,* 2 vols. Translated by J. D. Duff. London and Cambridge, 1949–50.

Slater, Philip E. *The Glory of Hera: Greek Mythology and the Greek Family.* Boston, 1968.

Smith, W. Robertson. *Kinship and Marriage in Early Arabia.* Cambridge, 1885.

Smyth, Alfred P. *Warlords and Holy Men.* London, 1984.

Sophocles. Translated by F. Storr. Loeb Library. Cambridge, Mass., 1951. Includes: *Ajax; Electra; Oedipus Tyrannus; The Trachiniae.*

Sophocles. *Four Plays by Sophocles.* Translated by Theodore Howard Banks. New York, 1966.

Sophocles. *Sophocles,* 2 vols. Translated by F. Storr. Cambridge, 1967.

Soumet, Alexandre. *Oeuvres complètes.* Paris 1845. Includes: *Clytemnestre* (1822); *Elisabeth de France* (1829); *Une Fête de Néron* (1830); *Jeanne d'Arc* (1825); *Saül* (1822); *La Divine épopée* (1840); *Cléopâtre* (1825).

Spence, Lewis. *Atlantis in America.* London and New York, 1925.

———. *History and Origins of Druidism.* London, 1947; reprint, Totowa, N.J., 1976.

———. *The Problem of Atlantis.* Great Britain, 1924; reprint, Second Edition, Brentano's, New York, n.d.

Spencer, Herbert. *First Principles.* London, 1862. See edition of New York, 1958.

Squire, Charles. *Celtic Myth and Legend.* London, 1903.

Statius, 2 vols. Translated by J. H. Mozley. London and New York, 1928. See "Silvae," #I, IV, 90, Vol. I, p. 54.

Stinson, Robert. *The Faces of Clio.* Chicago, 1987.

Stoessl, Franz. *Der Tod des Herakles. Arbeitsweise und Formen der antiken Sagendichtung.* Zürich, 1945.

Stone, Merlin. *When God Was a Woman.* Great Britain, 1976; reprint, New York, 1978.

Strabo. *Géographie*, 8 vols. Translated by Germaine Aujac. Introduction by Germaine Aujac and François Lasserre. Paris, 1969.

Strong, Herbert Augustus and John Garstang. *The Syrian Goddess*. English translation of Lucianus Samosatensis, *De Dea Syria*. London, 1913.

Stürz, Friedrich Wilhelm. *Hellanici Lesbii fragmenta e variis scriptoribus*. Leipzig, 1787. Emended edition, edited by William Canter, 1826.

Sumner, William Graham. *Folkways*. Introduction by William Lyon Phelps. Boston, New York, etc., 1906; reprints, 1934 and 1940.

Sykes, Egerton. *Medusa, the Polyp and the Kraken*. London, 1949.

Symons, Arthur. *The Symbolist Movement in Literature*. London, 1908.

Tacitus, Publius Cornelius. *Tactitus*, 5 vols., edited by E. H. Warmington. London and Cambridge, 1920; reprint, 1970. Includes: *The Histories* and *The Annals*. Translated by John Jackson; *Agricola*. Translated by M. Hutton. Revised by R. M. Ogilvie; *Germania*. Translated by M. Hutton. Revised by E. H. Warmington; *Dialogus*. Translated by Sir W. Peterson. Revised by M. Winterbottom.

Taillepied, Noël. *Histoire de l'estat et république des druides*. Paris, 1585.

Tatianus. *The Earliest Life of Christ. Tatian's Diatessaron*. Translated by J. Hamlyn Hill. Edinburgh, 1910.

Termier, Pierre. *La Dérivée des continents*. Paris, 1924.

Theocritus. *The Idylls of Theocritus with Bion and Moschus and the War Songs of Tyrtaeus*. Translated by Rev. J. Banks. London, 1911.

Thomas, Charles. *Christianity in Roman Britain to A.D. 500*. Berkeley, 1981.

Thompson, Stith. *Motif-Index of Folk Literature*, 6 vols. Helsinki, 1932.

Thomson, George D. *Studies in Ancient Greek Society: The Prehistoric Aegean*. New York, 1965.

Todd, J. H., Editor. *The Irish Version of the "Historia Britonum" of Nennius*. Dublin, 1848.

Toksöz, Dr. Cemil. *EPHESOS. The Glories of Ephesus Revealed in Drawing of Reconstructions* (sic). Translated by S. C. Murison Bowie. Illustrations by Dr. Mübin Beken. Istanbul, 1967.

Tompkins, Peter. *Secrets of the Great Pyramids*. New York, 1971.

Torrey, Charles Cutler. *Apocryphal Literature*. Oxford, 1945.

———. *Documents of the Primitive Church*. New York, 1941.

Toynbee, Arnold J. *A Study of History*, 6 vols. New York, 1947; reprint, 1963. And *Abridgment* by D. C. Somerwell, 2 vols. New York and London, 1946.

Tozer, Henry Fanshawe. *A History of Ancient Geography*. Cambridge, 1935.

Tylor, Sir Edward Burnett. *Anthropology.* New York, 1881; reprint, 1904.

———. *Primitive Culture,* 2 vols. London, 1871; reprints, 1920 and 1924.

Tyrell, William Blake. *Amazons. A Study in Athenian Mythmaking.* Baltimore and London, 1984.

Urfé, Honore d'. *L'Astrée.* Strasbourg, New York, 1920 (reprinted).

Urquhart, David. *The Pillars of Hercules; or, A Narrative of Travels in Spain and Morocco in 1848,* 2 vols. London, 1850.

Varro, Marcus Terentius. *De Lingua Latina, Re rustica,* 3 vol. Cambridge and London, 1951.

Verdaguer, Jacinto. *L'Atlantida* (1878). Barcelona, 1946.

Vermuele, Emily. *Greece in the Bronze Age.* Chicago, 1966.

Verne, Jules. *Vingt mille lieues sous les mers,* 2 vols. Paris, 1922. First published in 1870.

Vian, Francis. *La Guerre des géants.* Paris, 1952.

Villena, Enrique de. *Los Doze trabajos de Hércules,* edited by Margherita Morreale. Madrid, 1958.

VonMach, Edmund. *A Handbook of Greek and Roman Sculpture.* Boston, 1914.

Vries, Jan de. *Keltische Religion.* Stuttgart, 1961.

Wainwright, Gerald Averay. *The Sky-Religion in Egypt.* Cambridge, 1938.

Walby, Sylvia. *Patriarchy at Work.* Minneapolis, 1986.

Warenski, Marilyn. *Patriarchs and Politics. The Plight of the Mormon Woman.* New York, St. Louis, San Francisco, Mexico. Toronto, Dusseldorf, 1978.

Warmington, Eric Herbert. *Greek Geography.* London, 1934.

Warner, Marina. *Alone of All Her Sex. The Myth and the Cult of the Virgin Mary.* London and New York, 1976, 1983.

Weinhold, Karl. *Altnordisches Leben.* Berlin, 1856.

Westermarck, Edvard Alexander. *History of Human Marriage.* London, 1901.

Whitehead, Alfred North. *Religion in the Making.* The Lowell Lectures, New York, 1926.

Wilkin, Robert Louis. *The Christians as the Romans Saw Them.* New Haven, 1984.

Wilson, John C. *Lost Solar Systems of the Ancients.* London, 1856.

Wood, John Edwin. *Sun, Moon and Standing Stones.* Oxford, 1978.

Wood, John Turtle. *Discoveries at Ephesus including the Site, and Remains of the Greek Temple of Diana,* illus. London, 1877; reprint, Hildesheim and New York, 1975.

Wood-Martin, W. G. *Traces of the Elder Faiths of Ireland.* London, 1902.

Woolf, Virginia. *A Room of One's Own.* London, 1931.

Wormhoudt, Arthur. *The Muse at Length.* Boston, 1953.

Zafiropulo, Jean. *Histoire de la Grèce à l'âge de bronze.* Paris, 1964.

Zazius, W. *De gentium aliquot migrationibus.* Frankfort, 1600. See p. 130 for "Gerdrudis" = Druidess.

INDEX

ABOUT THE AUTHOR

Norma Lorre Goodrich is a professor emeritus at the Claremont Colleges and is the author of *Merlin, King Arthur,* and the forthcoming *Guinevere.* She lives with her husband near Los Angeles.